POLTE

C000007036

Are these Poltergeists? An artist's impression of mischievous little devils.
From an old coloured aquatint by Spooner. In the author's collection.

POLTERGEIST

TALES OF THE SUPERNATURAL

HARRY PRICE

SENATE

Poltergeist

First published as *Poltergeist Over England* in 1945
by Country Life, London

This edition published in 1994 by Senate, an imprint of
Studio Editions Ltd, Princess House, 50 Eastcastle Street,
London W1N 7AP, England

Copyright © 1994 The Harry Price Library,
University of London Library

All rights reserved. This publication may not be reproduced,
stored in a retrieval system or transmitted, in any form or by
any means, electronic, mechanical, photocopying or
otherwise, without the prior written permission
of the publishers.

ISBN 1 85958 066 1
Printed and bound in Guernsey by
The Guernsey Press Co. Ltd

Contents

Contents

List of Photographic Plates

Illustrations in Text

Foreword

It has long been at the back of my mind that I ought to write a history of Poltergeists, because they attract me so; and for some years I have been acquiring books, tracts, and other records of these mischievous 'entities' with a view to preparing a comprehensive work on the whole subject. But when I came to assemble my data, I found I had enough material for not one, but many books on Poltergeists, both British and foreign. I was thus faced with making a selection and a compromise. I decided I would publish in detail accounts of all the famous English cases, with some reference to outstanding foreign ones, when these merited inclusion. So, although this volume mentions some hundreds of Poltergeist hauntings, only the best English ones are given in the fullest detail—hence the title of this monograph. I have chosen the most interesting and varied cases, and have attempted some chronological order in their presentation. I will mention in passing that the world's most convincing Poltergeists are natives of these islands.

My selected cases have been extracted mostly from old and rare works on the subject, and I have been able to reproduce, *verbatim et literatim*, some ancient tracts, or portions of them, that today are almost unknown except to students of psychic phenomena. All these works are from my own collection, and are listed in the Bibliography.

A few cases to be found in the following pages have been taken from my published works; in some, I describe my own personal experiences, and in many more I relate the Poltergeist adventures of my friends and correspondents. Most of these examples are here published for the first time, and other cases included have not hitherto been given to the public in printed form. I take this opportunity of thanking my many friends for kindly supplying this new material, some of which is very convincing.

As I have intimated, the difficulty has been to select the best and most representative examples of Poltergeist infestation, and the task has not been an easy one. There are literally thousands of them. However, I have rigorously excluded all known fraudulent or negative cases, and not one of those I present to the reader has been explained. The Cock Lane affair is in the doubtful class, but this particular ghost is so famous and historical that I simply could not omit it from any collection of English Poltergeists.

In this volume I have, rather regretfully, abandoned the use of the correct German plural, *Poltergeister*, for the incorrect though Anglicised 'Poltergeists'. I thought it would appear less pedantic, especially as lay writers and the Press now favour the English rendering.

Owing to the activities of that super-destructive Poltergeist, the flying Hun, and the 'flying bomb', a portion of my library was dispersed, and I have put a number of persons to considerable trouble in retrieving for me some of my rarities. Especially, I would like to thank Mr. Reginald A. Rye and Miss M. S. Quinn, the Goldsmiths' Librarian and Sub-Librarian respectively of the University of London, for help in this matter and in other ways. And I am grateful to Bodley's Librarian, Dr. H. H. E. Craster, M.A., and to the Secretary of the Bodleian Library, Oxford, Mr. R. H. Hill, M.A., for assistance in the preparation of this work, and for giving me access to my rare books deposited in the Bodleian. And to the Acting Librarian—and his staff—of the Reform Club I am indebted in various ways, especially in obtaining for me, from other centres, old and rare books not in my collection or in their own magnificent library.

I am also indebted to Miss Eglantyne M. Jebb, M.A., Miss Florence M. Sharpe, the Rt. Hon. the Earl of Lytton, K.G., P.C., etc., Mr. H. Fetherstonhaugh-Frampton, J.P., Mr. A. J. B. Robertson, M.A., Mr. Percy Pigott, and Commander Rupert T. Gould, R.N., for original contributions or other help that have materially enhanced the value of this monograph.

To the Rev. J. P. Thompson, M.A., Rector of South Tidworth, my especial thanks are due, for his kindness in obtaining for me locally important information concerning the 'Poltergeist Drummer'.

I have, where possible, made suitable acknowledgment to every author whom I have cited, but I should like to say a special word of thanks for Andrew Lang's *Cock Lane and Common Sense*, a mine of ancient ghost-lore, and for the same author's other works; for Hereward Carrington's *Historic Poltergeists*, a list or census of Poltergeist cases that has been of great use to me; and for *The Books of Charles Fort*. Fort, almost unknown in this country, was an American genius —or madman!—who collected hundreds of thousands of cases of green rain, blue suns, red moons, and explosive hailstones; showers of fish, frogs, nails and coffins; chunks of other planets falling upon this earth; hordes of angels and strange appearances in the sky; inter-planetary communications and the doings of alleged extra-mundane visitors; signals from Mars and the fall of luminous objects from the same planet; spontaneous appearances and disappearances—and Poltergeist cases galore. All this, and much more, he published in four books, afterwards issued as an omnibus volume. His theories and 'arguments' for these 'unnatural' natural phenomena (accounts of which he took from such sedate journals as *The Times*, *Nature*, and other equally serious publications) are almost as outrageous as the wonders he recorded. Someone once said, 'To read Charles Fort is to ride on a comet'. I agree. His books fascinate me.

Finally, I have a request to make: If the reader has had a *first-hand*

Foreword

experience of Poltergeist disturbances, I should like to receive particulars. The account should be dated, detailed, and documented, with the real names of witnesses, though not necessarily for publication. Any information sent to me in the care of the publishers of this book will be gratefully acknowledged.

H. P.

The Reform Club,
Pall Mall, S.W. 1

xii

CHAPTER I

What is a Poltergeist?

A Poltergeist is an alleged ghost, elemental, entity, agency, secondary personality, 'intelligence', 'power', spirit, imp, or 'familiar', with certain unpleasant characteristics. Whereas the ordinary ghost of our story-books is a quiet, inoffensive, timid, noiseless, and rather benevolent spirit, with—usually—friendly feelings towards the incarnate occupants of any place where it has its abode, the Poltergeist is just the reverse. According to the many reports of its activities, in all lands and in all ages, the Poltergeist is mischievous, destructive, noisy, cruel, erratic, thievish, demonstrative, purposeless, cunning, unhelpful, malicious, audacious, teasing, ill-disposed, spiteful, ruthless, resourceful, and vampiric. A ghost *haunts*; a Poltergeist *infests*. A ghost likes solitude; a Poltergeist prefers company. A ghost seeks the half-light; a Poltergeist will 'perform' in sunlight.

A glance at the etymology of the word Poltergeist will tell us what sort of a character this nuisance has acquired. Turning to *Muret-Sanders' enzyklopädisches Wörterbuch* (Berlin, 1910), we find that the term is a compound of the German verb *polter*, 'to make a noise by knocking or tumbling things about, to knock or rattle, to scold or bluster,' and the noun *Geist*, a ghost. The noun *Polter* or *Polterer* is a 'blusterer, bully, hector, roisterer, or noisy person'.

Interesting derivatives are *Polterzimmer*, a room set aside for children, where they can make a noise, smash their toys, and work off their animal spirits; and *Polterabend*, the 'night before the wedding', on which occur noisy demonstrations by young people of both sexes, who smash things outside the bride's house. At least on two occasions I have witnessed this ceremony. I was walking along the Friedrichstrasse, Berlin, one summer evening when I saw a crowd of about forty persons hurling perfectly good china plates and empty bottles at the exterior walls of a flat over some shops. I inquired what the commotion was about and was informed there would be a wedding there on the following day and that the friends of the happy couple were just following the old custom. When they tired of breaking things outside the house, they would then go *inside*, break some more pots and pans, have several glasses of *Schnapps* and *Leibniz-Keks* and then the whole company would adjourn to the 'Esplanade' or 'Bristol' for supper and wine. (But not before all the litter outside the house had been cleared up—by law.) I was told that these *Polterabend* observances were symbolic of the breaking of the bride's home-ties, and other things.

1

The word Poltergeist can boast a long usage in Germany. **Martin Luther (1483-1546)** employed the term in his writings and he must have been one of the first to use it. Of course, all such phenomena were then ascribed to the devil. In the title of the pamphlet describing the Gerstmann-Dortmund case (1714), mentioned in the next chapter, occurs the term '*Gespentes und Polter-Geistes*', thus clearly differentiating between ordinary ghosts and Poltergeists. I could cite many more examples of the early use of the term Poltergeist, were I to look for them. But the two I have given will suffice. Very curiously, the word has now gone completely out of fashion in Germany, *Spuk* taking its place to describe every variety of ghost. In proof of this, I can mention a modern book, *Der Spuk von Talpa* (Munich, 1926), that gives an account of the decidedly Poltergeistic phenomena of the 'Poltergeist girl', Eleonore Zugun, who figures in the pages of the present volume.

The word Poltergeist was introduced into this country by Catherine Crowe in her *The Night-Side of Nature; or, Ghosts and Ghost-Seers* (London, 1848), a book of possible and impossible ghost stories. But the term did not at once become popular. We find the word (spelt *Polter giest*) in Adin Ballou's *An Exposition of Views Respecting the Modern Spirit Manifestations* (Boston, Mass., 1852, and Liverpool, England, 1853). In 1871, E. B. Tylor, the famous anthropologist, uses the term in his *Primitive Culture* (London, 1871) and notes the vampiric nature of the Poltergeist: 'Vampires appear in the character of the Poltergeist or knocker'.[1] Andrew Lang uses the German plural *Poltergeister* in an article in *Folk-Lore*,[2] in 1907.

There is no mention of Poltergeist in C. A. M. Fennell's *Stanford Dictionary of Anglicised Words* (Cambridge, 1892), and we look for it in vain in the 1902 edition of the *Standard Dictionary*. However, in the *Oxford English Dictionary* (fasciculus of 1910) the word makes its bow, so to speak, and is officially incorporated into the English language. It is here described as 'a spirit that makes its presence known by noises'. From now onwards the word appears frequently in the terminology of psychical research and in spiritualistic literature. But it was not until I brought Eleonore Zugun to London in 1926 that the word Poltergeist became common in the British Press.

We had no occasion to go to Germany for the word Poltergeist. We could have employed the term *polterghost*, which would have been thoroughly British. *Polt* and *polter* are common, though obsolete, English words that have been used in the provinces for centuries and they can be found in many of our dialects. The *Oxford English Dictionary* (1910) gives the verb *polt*, 'to knock, thrash, beat, and bang'. The *Standard Dictionary* (1902) gives the noun *polt*, 'a striking, stroke, blow'. And if the Germans can boast of some compound words

---

[1] Vol. II, p. 176. Cited by the O.E.D.

[2] Article, ' "Death-Deeds"—a Bi-Located Story'. Vol. XVIII, 1907, pp. 376–390.

embodying the term, so can we. J. O. Halliwell cites[1] several of them: A *polt-trap*, a rat-trap that *falls* down (Kent); *polting-lug*, a long thin rod used for *beating* apples off trees (Gloucester).

I think that most civilised countries employ the word Poltergeist in describing the 'racketing spirit'; but the Maltese have a word *hares* (pronounced *har-es*), and the Russians have a ghost named *domovoy*.

By permission of *Punch*.

"Poltergeists, I believe they're called.'

These entities have correspondences with the Poltergeist conception, but, like the 'brownies' or *Lares domestici*, they are beneficent. In the night, while the maids sleep, they churn the butter, clean the kitchen, polish the silver, scour the dishes, etc. Poltergeists don't do *that*!

[1] *Dictionary of Archaic and Provincial Words*, London, 1901, 5th Edition, Vol. II, p. 636.

I have called the Poltergeist an alleged spirit, but it is not a spirit in the spiritualistic sense. I believe I am right in stating that the spiritualists do not accept the Poltergeist as a discarnate entity, 'the ghost that once was man', as Tennyson wrote, but rather as an 'elemental' or Nature-spirit; a being evolved from, or constituting the lower elemental nature of man. Franz Hartmann[1] puts it rather neatly; 'The elementals are the beings which may produce so-called "physical manifestations", cause the appearance and disappearance of objects, throw stones, etc. . . . yet the elementals are not spirits, because they are flesh, blood, and bones.' Hartmann was not writing of Poltergeists, but he described exactly what Poltergeists do—or are alleged to do.

If the spiritualists do not accept Poltergeists as spirits of men who once walked this earth, it can hardly be doubted that Poltergeists—or their phenomena—were the precursors of the modern cult of spiritualism. And it can be said, too, that Poltergeists themselves are a legacy from the old witchcraft days. The 'Drummer of Tedworth', a classic Poltergeist, was thought by Mompesson, Glanvill, and their contemporaries to have produced his noisy phenomena by means of witchcraft, and was arraigned as a warlock. And in other stories from Glanvill's collection (included in this monograph), the reader will note that, in an effort to put an end to the disturbances, some old woman or 'witch' was sought for. The Wesleys were convinced that the trouble at Epworth Parsonage was the result of witchcraft.

Modern spiritualism, as a cult, dates no farther back than 1848, when the two young girls, Margaret and Katie Fox, were the centre of typical Poltergeist disturbances in their little cottage at Hydesville, near Rochester, New York. This was on the evening of March 31, 1848—the day on which modern spiritualism was born. Why it was not born nearly a hundred years earlier, has always puzzled me because another young girl, Elizabeth Parsons, was the prime-mover, *nexus*, or *point d'appui* of the Cock Lane Poltergeist—a case on all fours with the Hydesville haunt. Perhaps the time was not then ripe for the new religion.

Hartmann[2] says that 'elementals' are not spirits, but are made of flesh, blood, and bones. If Poltergeists are elementals, has one ever been seen? Personally, I think not. Yet the Wesley family claimed to have seen *their* Poltergeist on several occasions. Hetty saw 'something like a man, in a loose night gown trailing after him'. Mrs. Wesley (as we are informed by Emily in a letter to her brother Samuel) saw the Poltergeist 'like a badger'. Their serving-man saw a similar creature sitting by the dining-room fire. He again met it 'like a white rabbit', in the kitchen. 'I believe it to be witchcraft', says Emily.

In the Willington Mill case, little Joseph Procter, aged eight, saw a monkey 'and that it had pulled his leg by his shoe-strap'. Just previously,

[1] *Paracelsus*, London, 1878, pp. 72, 79.   [2] *Op. cit.*

4

Edmund, his young brother, had seen a 'funny cat'. Mr. Mompesson, noticing some wood moving in a chimney, fired his pistol at it, hoping to hit the 'Drummer'. Investigation proved that he hit something, because 'they found several drops of blood on the Harth, and in divers places of the Stairs'. The Soper Lane case is remarkable for the 'ungrateful skippings' of an animal that crept into a bed occupied by two young girls, and nearly frightened them to death. 'It seemed cold and very smooth', they recorded. I could quote from many similar records of Poltergeist infestations but they all have a family likeness. And I very much doubt this sort of evidence—so very reminiscent of the witchcraft days when the unholy doings of such imps and 'familiars' as Pyewacket, Ilemauzar, Pecke-in-the-Crown, Grizzell Greedi-Guts, Sacke and Sugar, Vinegar Tom, and the rest of the animal brood, filled the pages of the court reports of those terrible times.

I believe that Poltergeists are invisible, intangible, and inarticulate. But as we have not the faintest idea *what* they are, or what they look like, I may be wrong. Anyway, the evidence for visible Poltergeists is very unsatisfactory. For all I know, the strange creature that walked (or hopped) nearly a hundred miles in the snow, *in one night* (February 8, 1855), might have been a Poltergeist. It certainly was not human, and its single-track hoof-marks, each spaced exactly eight-and-a-half inches apart, and exactly in advance of each other, were never identified as those belonging to any animal. If they did, then the animal had only one leg and must have *hopped* in the snow right through Topsham, Totnes, Exmouth, Teignmouth, Dawlish, and scores of other places in Devonshire; over roof-tops, through gardens enclosed by high walls, across fields, wide rivers, streets, etc., and on both sides of the estuary of the River Exe. The creature made a bee-line to where it wanted to get to, and if a house got in its way, then it walked over the house, leaving hoof-marks on the roof. We should never have known a word about this except for the fact that it was snowing that night and the creature's tracks were left for thousands of persons to see. And no Poltergeist case is better documented or authenticated.[1] The mystery was never solved, and the 'animal' was never found. Similar strange foot-tracks were found in the snow during Captain Gregson's occupation of Borley Rectory.[2]

I have stated that Poltergeists are inarticulate, but there are exceptions, a brilliant one being that of the 'Saragossa ghost', mentioned in another chapter. It did *nothing* but talk!

Can a Poltergeist appear in the guise of a man? A writer in the *Guardian*[3] thinks so. Speaking of Germany, he says that there are 'extraordinarily significant points of resemblance between the records of

[1] *The Times*, Feb. 16, Mar. 6, 1855. See also the *Illustrated London News*, Feb. 24—March 17, 1855, for full account and sketches of foot-tracks.
[2] See Chapter XXV.   [3] For July 25, 1941.

Poltergeist hauntings and the Nazi movement. Both are manifested in a subconscious uprush of desire for power . . . both suck, like vampires, the energies of adolescents; both issue in noise, destruction, fire and terror. . . . Hitler speaks best in a state of semi-trance. . . . Whether the uprush of unconscious energy generated through him and sucking into itself the psycho-physical forces of German youth is merely the outcome of an unformulated group-desire for power, or whether, like some of the Poltergeist hauntings, it would seem to have another source, is an open question'. Mr. Sacheverell Sitwell says something similar: 'Adolf Hitler, the perfect type of a medium, if ever there was one. . . . We could readily believe that this remarkable person, did he feel so inclined, could displace objects and move them about in oblique or curving flight; could rap out equivocal answers; or cause lighted matches to drop down from the ceiling'.[1]

To sum up, then, if we are to accept Poltergeists, my own view is that they are invisible, intangible, malicious and noisy entities. Unlike the ghost of fiction—or even of fact—they are never seen and seldom speak. ('Ordinary' ghosts are always seen, and frequently speak.) Poltergeists are able, by laws as yet unknown to our physicists, to extract energy from living persons, often from the young, and usually from girl adolescents, especially if they suffer from some mental disorder. They are able, by some means, and by using these young people as a fulcrum, lever, or support, to increase and nourish this energy, and to direct intelligently this stolen power. They are able to use this power tele-kinetically for the violent propulsion or displacement of objects, for purposes of destruction, and especially for the production of every variety of noise—from the 'swish' of a silk skirt to an 'explosion' that makes the windows rattle. And they can do many other strange things, as the reader will discover if he peruses the pages that follow.

---

[1] *Poltergeists*, London, 1940, p. 54.

CHAPTER II

Historical Background

In the last chapter I endeavoured to show that the term 'Poltergeist', as descriptive of a certain class of paranormal manifestations, is of fairly recent origin—at least in this country. And this fact has, I think, given rise to the assumption, among many people, that the disturbances themselves are 'new', or have only recently been observed. Nothing could be farther from the truth; and in this chapter I will lightly sketch the background against which modern science is endeavouring to elucidate the mystery of contemporary Poltergeist phenomena.

If Poltergeists are a fact in Nature, then, it is logical to assume, they must have manifested themselves since the world began. But I am afraid that prehistoric archæology has not yet directed its attention to these matters, and pre-documentary history can tell us nothing about Poltergeists or the phenomena associated with them. Yet I am convinced that such phenomena have always occurred, and I can visualise the consternation that must have ensued when, say, a shower of reindeer horns suddenly dropped 'from nowhere' among some Palæolithic family, as they were peacefully sucking their marrow-bones in a rock-shelter or limestone cave—perhaps half a million years ago.

A number of students have diligently searched for accounts of ancient Poltergeists: the names of Andrew Lang, Frank Podmore, the Rev. Fr. Herbert Thurston, S.J., and Hereward Carrington occur to me in this connection. Andrew Lang's *Cock Lane and Common-Sense* (London, 1894) is a veritable mine of information[1] concerning classical, ancient, and savage spiritualism. And Carrington compiled a most useful chronological summary, *Historic Poltergeists*, (London [1935]),[2] all too brief, of the 'march of the Poltergeist'. I am indebted to these writers for some of the early cases included in this chapter.

We have evidence from papyri and other remains, covering a period of 4,000 years, that the ancient Egyptians believed in, and were afraid of ghosts. In my own collection is a fragment of papyrus (*c.* 500 A.D.) giving instructions how to raise the dead. G. C. C. Maspero, in his *Études de Mythologie . . . . Égyptiennes* (Paris, 1893, etc.), mentions another fragment which is a letter written by an ancient scribe, 'To the Instructed Khou of the Dame Onkhari', his own dead wife, the *Khou* being her spirit. He complains to his wife that her spirit is assailing him and that 'disturbances' have occurred in his home: clearly a Poltergeist case. He tells her to stop it!

[1] Marred by the absence of any index.
[2] *Bulletin I*, International Institute for Psychical Research.

Poltergeist Over England

There are many references to ghosts, Poltergeists, phenomena, and the occult generally in the works of classical writers. Poets, dramatists, and philosophers have alluded to them, and taking them in chronological order, I can cite the following names: Homer, Plautus, Horace, Livy, Pliny, Plutarch, Suetonius, Lucian, Porphyry, and Iamblicus—names covering a period of some 1,200 years. There is a famous letter from the Neoplatonist philosopher, Porphyry, to Anebo, in which the former discusses all the phenomena which are now included in psychical research: prophecy, fire-walking, levitation of mediums, ghosts, and what we should now term Poltergeist phenomena.[1] And this was more than 1,600 years ago! Plautus, the comic dramatist, introduced the subject into his play *Mostellaria* more than 2,000 years ago! And Lucian (A.D. 120–180) tells us—humorously, of course—of a sort of 'ghost club' whose members met in order to discuss apparitions and other psychic phenomena. One man complains that his dead wife had visited him! Some of these classical writers even had theories to account for the phenomena. For example, Lucretius, the Latin didactic poet (*c*. 98–55 B.C.), thought a ghost was a sort of film or shell diffused from the living body and persisting in the atmosphere—just as spiritualists now speak of 'astrals' and astral bodies leaving the human frame under certain conditions of trance or sleep. St. Augustine (A.D. 354–430) also wrote about 'psychical research', and was sceptical.

Jacob Grimm, the mythologist, in his *Deutsche Mythologie*[2] (Göttingen, 1835), mentions several Poltergeist cases, including two at Bingen-am-Rhein, in 355 and 856 respectively. Stones were thrown; people were pulled out of bed; raps and then terrific blows were heard. A voice accused various people of terrible crimes and one of the alleged offenders had his property destroyed by fire. Another case concerned Rudolph of Fulda, (858), who 'communicated' with a rapping spirit in the modern way. Grimm calls these Poltergeists 'House Sprites'.

In that vast work, the *Monumenta Germaniæ Historica*, edited by G. H. Pertz, the first volume of which was published in 1826, is an account (Vol. III, p. 473) of a Poltergeist that infested the home of Helpidius of Ravenna, physician to King Theodoric (*c*. 454–526). Showers of stones and other disturbances were noted. Georgius, a disciple of Theodorus (759–826), the Greek theological writer, mentions a house in which paranormal stone-throwing was a major nuisance.[3] Alcuin, the famous ecclesiastic, who was born at York in 735, tells us in his biography of his kinsman, Willibrord (first bishop of Utrecht) how, about the year 700, Poltergeist phenomena occurred, in which food and clothing were snatched away, fires lighted, the baby thrown into a lighted fire, and the house finally destroyed.

[1] See also *Porphyry, the Philosopher, to his wife, Marcella*, London, 1896.
[2] First English Edition, *Teutonic Mythology*, London, 1879–88.
[3] Cited by Lang.

8

The late Fr. Herbert Thurston, S.J., in one of his many articles on Poltergeists and allied subjects, mentions the 'thorybistic[1] phenomena' in the lives of the saints, and which were usually attributed to the work of the devil. He cites the incident in the life of St. Godric, the twelfth-century poet (*d.* 1170): 'His hermitage was bombarded with showers of stones, and the "Poltergeist" threw at him the box in which he kept his altar-breads; took the horn which contained the wine he needed for Mass and poured it over his head; and ended by pelting him with almost every movable object that his poor cell contained'. A much later case was that of the Curé d'Ars[2] (Jean Baptiste Vianney, 1786–1859), who was plagued by a Poltergeist, but which he called the devil. The trouble lasted for thirty-five years. Loud knocks on his gate, a storm of blows on his furniture, sounds as of a horse galloping in the hall below his room, and similar disturbances were frequent. Once, he declared, as he lay in bed, the devil pushed him about the room all night! Lang states[3] that the Church has special prayers for protection against the *spiritus percutiens*, or 'spirit that produces percussive noises'.

In the Icelandic *Eyrbyggia* saga (890–1031) is told the story of Polter-geist manifestations: of how fish were audibly torn apart by unseen hands, etc. This was in the year 1000. The medieval historian, Giraldus Cambrensis (1146?–1220), in his *Itinerarium Cambrense* relates some Poltergeist 'miracles'. At South Malling, in 1170, a table suddenly turned and threw off the arms of Thomas Becket's murderers. In Pem-broke, about 1190, in the house of Stephen Wiriet and, later, in the home of William Not, there were typical Poltergeist phenomena. In both places 'dirt and other things were thrown'. They 'seemed to be teasing rather than injuring'. In William's house, 'not without frequent damage to both host and guests', rips and tears were made in both woollen and linen garments. And, continues Giraldus, locks did not prevent the damage. In Stephen's house a 'voice' used to talk with people and tell them of their past misdeeds.

Also about 1190, another 'voice', like the Pembroke one, revealed the dark deeds of the hearers, much to their chagrin. There were also the usual disturbances in the house, the throwing of objects, etc. The infestation occurred at Dagworth, in Suffolk, in the home of Sir Osborne of Bradaewelle, during the reign of Richard I. The story is related by Ralph of Coggeshall in the *Chronicon Anglicanum*, an existing work that he continued, his own share beginning at 1187—three years before the above disturbances took place. In the *Chronicon* Ralph refers to a book of visions and miracles that he had compiled, but which, alas, is not now extant. Ralph died some time after 1227.

---

[1] From the Greek *thorubis*, a confused noise.

[2] A relic of the Curé d'Ars was used at Borley by Mr. Foyster, who 'magically' opened locked doors by its means.

[3] *Cock Lane*, p. 30.

9

In a masterly review of Carrington's *Historic Poltergeists*, a writer in the *Times Literary Supplement*[1] mentions a Poltergeist, 'the greislie Gaist of Gye', that was heard, but not seen, at Alais, near Avignon, in 1324. The case became famous all over Europe, and it formed the subject of a papal inquiry. It was known to the English poet, John Skelton (*c.* 1460–1529) and Sir David Lindsay. Details were published for the first time by Charles Langlois, the French Academician, a few years ago.

A case recorded by Jean Bodin in his *Démonomanie des sorciers* (Paris, 1580) concerns a Poltergeist that threw stones in 1447. And the rest of the sixteenth-century authors (Jean Wier, Reginald Scot, F. Pierre Nodé, Guido de Suza, John Baptista Porta, Pierre Massé, Pierre le Loyer, King James I, Angeli de Gambilionibus, Christophe de Cattan, Lewes [Ludwig] Lavater, and many others) who have written books on witchcraft and magic tell similar stories.

A famous sixteenth-century case is cited by Andrew Lang[2] and concerns a Poltergeist in the nunnery of St. Pierre de Lyon. The account is by Adrien de Montalembert,[3] almoner to Francis I, who says that on March 21, 1528, 'the spirit of Sister Alix de Telieux struck thirty-three great strokes on the refectory of her convent'. A bright light, scarcely endurable, then appeared and lasted for eight minutes. The Poltergeist was supposed to be the spirit of Alix de Telieux, a Sister who had fled the convent, broken her vows, and had died miserably in 1524. Many raps were heard, and by this means intelligent answers were given to questions. One of the Sisters was 'levitated'. A feature of this story is that the phenomena were centred upon the usual 'young girl', a Sister, Anthoinette de Grolée, aged eighteen. As Lang points out, this must be one of the very first cases in which rappings and a medium are recorded. Lang also mentions[4] a case analogous to the Cock Lane Ghost. In 1533, some Franciscan monks investigated a story of how raps and scratchings were heard coming from the bed in which a young child lay. As in the Cock Lane affair, the cause was never discovered. Also, as in the case of Elizabeth Parsons, there was a judicial inquiry, but nothing came of it. The only thing that happened was that the Franciscans were severely punished for allowing themselves to be hoaxed! Lang cites[5] another case in which Cieza de Leon (1549) relates how the cacique of Pirza, in Popyan, during his conversion to Christianity, was troubled by showers of stones mysteriously falling through the air, 'from nowhere', while Christians saw at his table a glass of liquor raised in the air, by no visible hand, put down again empty, and then replenished!

[1] 'Census of Poltergeists. In Quest of the Racketing Spirit', Feb. 29, 1936.
[2] *Op. cit.*, pp. 110-113.   [3] In a quarto Black Letter tract, Paris, 1528.
[4] *Op. cit.*, p. 168.
[5] Article 'Poltergeist', in the *Encyclo. Brit.*, Eleventh Edition, Cambridge, 1911, Vol. 22, p. 14.

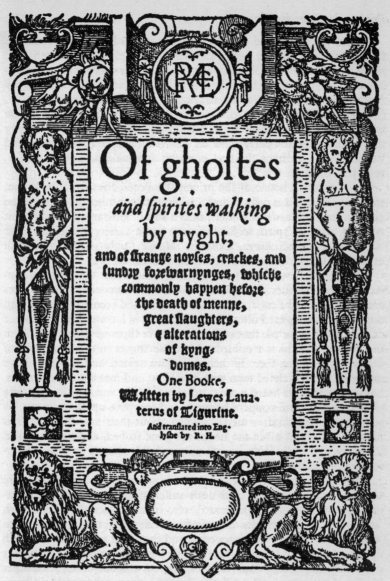

Of ghostes and spirites walking by nyght, and of strange noyses, crackes, and sundry forewarnynges, whiche commonly happen before the death of menne, great slaughters, & alterations of kyngdomes. One Booke, Written by Lewes Lauaterus of Tigurine. And translated into Englyshe by R. H.

Printed at London by Henry Benneyman. for Richard VVatkyns. 1572.

Title-page of the first English edition of 'Of Ghostes and Spirites Walking by Nyght,' by Ludwig Lavater, London, 1572. Probably the first book in the English language to describe Poltergeist phenomena. From the author's collection.

11

One of the rarest and most fascinating books that touch upon the subject of Poltergeists is Lewes Lavater's (1527–1586) *De Spectris . . .*, printed in Geneva in 1570. An edition, now extremely rare, was published in English under the title of *Of Ghostes and Spirites Walking by Nyght, and of Strange Noyses, Crackes, and Sundry Forewarnynges . . .* (London, 1572).[1] Another edition was published in Amsterdam. I have a copy of every known edition in my library, and I never tire of reading this illuminating and early work on 'survival', ghosts, phenomena, and 'spiritualism'—perhaps the first book on spiritualism, as we know it, to be published.

Lavater's work is one of the principal source-books for Elizabethan spiritualism, and it is certain that Shakespeare consulted it—witness the ghost-scenes in *Hamlet*. Lavater prints a sort of glossary of the different types of ghost or spirit, so Shakespeare had a variety to choose from: 'Domesticall gods', *Lares, Lemures, Maniæ* ('ugly shapes, wherwith nursses make children afrayd'), *Striges*, and the rest of them.

However, it is with the Poltergeist references that we are here concerned, and Lavater lists several of the phenomena: 'Many tymes candles and small fiers appeare in the night, and seeme to run up and downe'. So there were Poltergeist incendiaries in Lavater's day. Another extract: 'It is reported, that some spirits have throwne the dore of from the hookes, and have troubled and set all things in the house out of order, never setting them in their due place againe, and that they have marvellously disquieted men with rumbling and making a great noise. Sometimes there is heard a great noise in Abbeis, and in other solitarie places, as if it were coupers hooping and stopping up wine vessels, or some other handicraftes men occupied about their labour, when it is most certayn, that all in the house are gone to bed, and have betaken themselves to rest'. How *very* familiar all this sounds to a twentieth-century investigator!

There are chapters telling the reader how to behave 'when we heare straunge crackes'; 'why God doth suffer straunge noyses, or extraordinarie rumblings to be heard', etc. In a chapter that deals with 'sodeyn noises and cracks and suchlike', Lavater speaks of those who 'heare the dores and windowes open and shut, that some thing runneth up the staires, or walketh up and downe the house or doth some one or other such like thing'. And 'Gunnes, launces and halberdes, with other kindes of weapons, and artillerie, do often times move of their owne accord as they lye in the armories'.

It is a great temptation to cite further examples of Poltergeist phenomena from Lavater's work, but I will resist it. And it must not be thought that our author was credulous. He was far less credulous than most of the writers of his time and throughout his book he urges the reader to be on his guard against accepting natural occurrences for paranormal

---

[1] A line-for-line reprint was issued at Oxford, 1929.

ones. For example, he says: 'Melancholike persons, and madde men, imagin many things which in verie deede are not'. He warns us, 'That many naturall things are taken to be ghosts, as for example, when they heare the crying of rats, cats, weasles, martins, or any other beast, or when they heare a horse beate his feete on the plankes in the stable at midnight, by and by they sweate for feare, supposing some buggs[1] to walke in the dead of the night. . . . If a worme which fretteth wood, or that breadeth in trees chaunce to gnawe a wall or wainscot, or other tymber, many will judge they heare one softly knocking upon an andvill with a sledge'. Some modern investigators might well take Lavater's words to heart. It seems incredible that Lavater's book was published nearly 400 years ago.

One cannot mention Lavater without referring to his contemporary, Reginald Scot (*c.* 1538–1590), whose *Discoverie of Witchcraft* (London, 1584), is another source-book for Elizabethan spiritualism. The subject matter of the *Discoverie* is recognisable in several of Shakespeare's plays. It is really an 'anti-witchcraft' book and is a defence of the poor wretches who were tortured into confessing to magical practices. Scot covers every phase of the occult and discusses the 'idols of the gentiles', spirits of all shades, apparitions, tricks of the clairvoyants, astrologers' miracles, charms, incantations, and Poltergeist phenomena. Incidentally, the *Discoverie* is the first book in the English language to describe and illustrate conjuring tricks as we know them today. The first edition of the *Discoverie* is excessively rare, and so are most of the other editions. I have a copy of every known edition in my library. James I was so infuriated at Scot's defence of the witches that he caused every copy that could be found (the 1584 edition) to be burned on Tower Hill by the common hangman. Hence its rarity. He also wrote a scurrilous reply (*Dæmonologie*, Edinburgh, 1597) to it.

A few years after the appearance of Scot's *Discoverie*, Petrus Thyraeus, S.J. (1546–1601), published his '*Loca Infesta* [That is, concerning Places Haunted by Mischievous Spirits of Demons and of the Dead. Thereto is added a Tract on Nocturnal Disturbances. . . .]' Cologne, 1598. This important work, cited by Lang, contains many stories of ghosts, Poltergeists, and haunted houses. There is mention of a house haunted by stone-throwing Poltergeists. There is also an account of how 'the dormitory of some nuns was haunted by a spectre who moaned, tramped noisily around, dragged the Sisters out of bed by their feet, and even tickled them nearly to death!' This annoyance lasted for three years. Thyraeus, like Lavater, differentiates between the various orders of ghosts. 'Some are *mites*'—I am quoting Lang—'mild and sportive; some are *truculenti*, ferocious'. Some (the *Lares domestici*) throw stones, lift beds, and make a hubbub and crash with the furniture.

[1] Not insects. From the Middle English *bugge*, from *bwg*, a spectre. *Cf.* bugaboo, boggart, bugbear, bogie, bogle, and the West Country bugan (the Devil).—H.P.

The discouerie
of witchcraft,

Wherein the lewde dealing of witches
and witchmongers is notablie detected, the
knauerie of coniurors, the impietie of inchar-
tors, the follie of soothsaiers, the impudent fals-
hood of cousenors, the infidelitie of atheists,
the pestilent practises of Pythonists, the
curiositie of figurecasters, the va-
nitie of dreamers, the begger-
lie art of Alcu-
mystrie,

The abhomination of idolatrie, the hor-
rible art of poisoning, the vertue and power of
naturall magike, and all the conueiances
of Legierdemaine and iuggling are deciphered :
and many other things opened, which
haue long lien hidden, howbeit
verie necessarie to
be knowne.

Heerevnto is added a treatise vpon the
nature and substance of spirits and diuels,
&c : all latelie written
by Reginald Scot,
Esquire.

1. Iohn. 4, 1.

Beleeue not euerie spirit, but trie the spirits, whether they are
of God ; for manie false prophets are gone
out into the world, &c.

1584

Title-page of the First Edition of 'The Discoverie of Witchcraft',
by Reginald Scot, London, 1584. Describes Poltergeist pheno-
mena. From the author's collection.

14

Some push people.[1] Lang concludes: 'And the strange thing is that, in an age of science, people are still discussing his problems, and, stranger still, that the reported phenomena remain the same'.[2]

Another case, mentioned by Lang[3], is taken from Richard Bovet's *Pandæmonium or the Devil's Cloyster* [London, 1684], and was known as the 'Demon of Spraiton' (or Spreyton), a village near Okehampton, Devon. As an exception to the usual 'young girl', this affair concerned a young man named Francis Fey, employed as servant in the household of Sir Philip Furze. This youth was subject to fits and trances, when ghosts were seen and physical disturbances occurred. There were many witnesses, including the Rector of Barnstaple. One of the most extraordinary phenomena concerned a shoe-lace: 'One of his shoe-strings was observed (without the assistance of any hand) to come of its own accord out of his shoe and fling itself to the other side of the room; the other was crawling after it, but a maid espying that, with her hand drew it out, and it clasp'd and curl'd about her hand like a living eel or serpent. A barrel of salt of considerable quantity hath been observed to march from room to room without any assistance'. Truly, Poltergeist phenomena!

We are now well into the period of the witchcraft mania, and a volume could be written on the Poltergeist phenomena that were recorded in the courts dealing with the poor 'witches' on trial. Just as true Poltergeist cases almost invariably centre upon some young girl or adolescent, so in many witchcraft trials it transpired that young girls received the 'diabolic' attentions of something that acted remarkably like a Poltergeist. I will quote one or two cases.

In Britain the trials for witchcraft were most numerous in the seventeenth century, and Joseph Glanvill has recorded the verbatim court records of several of them. One, the 'witch of Youghal', particularly interests us. Youghal is in the county of Cork, and on March 24, 1661, Florence Newton was committed to the Cork Assizes for bewitching a young maidservant named Mary Longdon. Glanvill[4] records the case very fully. Mary, in evidence, tells the familiar story of refusing to give Florence Newton 'a piece of beef out of her master's powdering tub', at which Florence was very angry. About a week later the girl met the witch, who violently kissed her. From then, onwards, the strangest things began to happen. Mary saw grotesque figures about the house. Then she 'fell very ill of Fits or Trances'. These fits were so violent that 'three or four men could not hold her'. Then—as most accounts allege of these bewitched girls—she began to 'Vomit up Needles, Pins, Horsenails, Stubbs, Wooll and Straw, and that very often'. Then—and this is

---

[1] The Rev. Samuel Wesley complained that he was pushed three times by the Epworth Poltergeist. (See page 95.)

[2] *Cock Lane*, p. 135.   [3] *Op. cit.*, p. 122.

[4] *Saducismus Triumphatus*, London, 1681, Part II, pp. 168–190.

where the Poltergeist enters into the story—'Several (and very many) small stones would fall upon her as she went up and down, and would follow her from place to place, and from one room to another, and would hit her on the head, shoulders, and arms, and fall to the ground and vanish away'. Then she was 'transported': 'That sometimes she should be removed out of her bed into another room, sometimes she should be carried to the top of the house, laid on a board betwixt two Sollar[1] Beams, sometimes put into a Chest, sometimes betwixt two Feather-beds on which she used to lie, and sometimes betwixt the Bed and the Mat in her Master's Chamber in the day time'.

The showers of stones were witnessed by Mary's master, John Pyne, whose evidence was taken in court. He had seen 'very great quantities of them', and all vanished as they hit the ground. On one occasion, said Pyne, Mary was sitting reading the Bible when suddenly he saw the book struck out of her hand and fly into the middle of the room. And that once, when two Bibles were laid on her breast, they instantly disappeared and were found in Mary's bed. There is much more of the same sort of thing in the report of this trial of Florence Newton who was, apparently, put in prison and not sentenced to death. She was lucky!

Graham Dalyell, in his *Darker Superstitions of Scotland* (Glasgow, 1834, p. 593), cited by Lang, gives two examples of Poltergeist-witches. In the first, during the trial (1629) of Isobell Young, is an account of 'the firlote[2] rynning about with the stuff popling' on the barn floor. In the second case, during the trial of Jonet Thompson, February 7, 1643, 'the sive and the wecht[3] dancit throw the hous'.

I have in my collection a number of contemporary works[4] dealing with the famous case (1697) of Christian Shaw, the daughter of the laird of Bargarran, Renfrewshire—a case conspicuous in the judicial annals of witchcraft. Christian, aged about eleven years, was thrice formally cursed by a 'witch' with the words, 'The De'il harle ye throw Hell!' This had its effect upon Christian, and soon after, typical Poltergeist phenomena occurred, including the alleged levitation of the girl, who was said to have floated through a room full of ministers of the Gospel. Bewitched, or 'only pretending', Christian's evidence caused no fewer than twenty persons to be condemned, of whom five were executed, besides one John Reed, who was found strangled in prison. During my researches into this case, I made the interesting discovery[5] that twenty-three years later, this same Christian Shaw introduced (1720) the manu-

---

[1] i.e., garret.—H.P. [2] A four-peck (dry) measure.—H.P.
[3] A scoop for lifting corn.—H.P.
[4] *A Relation of the Diabolical Practices of above Twenty Wizards and Witches. . . .* London, 1697. And *A True Narrative of the Sufferings and Relief of a Young Girl. . . .* Paisley, 1698.
[5] *Ency. Brit.*, Cambridge, 1911, Eleventh Edn., Vol. 20, p. 520 (article 'Paisley').

facture of linen thread into Paisley. I could cite many more cases of Poltergeist-witch phenomena.

Mention of Scotland reminds me that no collection of British Poltergeists is complete without a brief account of the classic disturbances that occurred at Abbotsford, the home of Sir Walter Scott. He records the experience in a letter to 'D. Terry, Esq., London', published in J. G. Lockhart's *Memoirs of the Life of Sir Walter Scott, Bart.* (Edinburgh and London, 1837, Vol. iv, pp. 138–43). Scott's agent, George Bullock, had been responsible for some alterations to Abbotsford, and during the progress of the work Sir Walter wrote:

> *Selkirk,*
> *April* 30, 1818.

'The exposed state of my house has led to a very serious disturbance. The night before last we were awaked by a violent noise, like drawing heavy boards along the new part of the house. I fancied something had fallen, and thought no more about it. This was about *two* in the morning. Last night, at the same witching hour, the very same noise occurred. Mrs. S., as you know, is rather *timbersome*,[1] so up got I, with Beardie's broadsword under my arm,

> "So bolt upright,
> And ready to fight."

But nothing was out of order, neither can I discover what occasioned the disturbance'.

On the night of the disturbance, at the very hour when the noises awakened Sir Walter and Lady Scott, and the former sallied forth with old Beardie's Killiecrankie claymore—George Bullock died suddenly. Scott records this fact in a further letter to Terry:

> *Edinburgh,*
> *May* 16, 1818.

'Were you not struck with the fantastical coincidence of our nocturnal disturbances at Abbotsford with the melancholy event that followed? I protest to you the noise resembled half-a-dozen men hard at work putting up boards and furniture, and nothing can be more certain than that there was nobody on the premises at the time. With a few additional touches, the story would figure in Glanvill or Aubrey's *Collection*[2]. In the mean time, you may set it down with poor Dubisson's warnings, as a remarkable coincidence coming under your own observation.'

The reference to Dubisson is interesting. Scott, in a letter (published by Lockhart, *op. cit.*, Vol. ii, p. 344) to a Mr. Morritt, mentions the fact that both the judge, Lord President Blair, and Lord Melville, died suddenly. The letter is headed Edinburgh, and is dated July 1, 1811:

[1] i.e., timorous.—H.P.
[2] i.e., John Aubrey's *Miscellanies*, London, 1696.—H.P.

'There is a very odd coincidence between the deaths of these eminent characters, and that of a very inferior person, a dentist of this city, named Dubisson. He met the President the day before his death, who used a particular expression in speaking to him; the day before Lord Melville died, he also met Dubisson nearly on the same spot, and to the man's surprise used the President's very words in saluting him. On this second death, he expressed (jocularly, however) an apprehension that he himself would be the third—was taken ill and died in an hour's space. Was not this remarkable?'

I will conclude this brief historical survey of the march of the Poltergeist with an account of a very important case that was quite unknown to me until the erudite writer of the review[1] in the *Times Literary Supplement* brought it to my notice. It concerns disturbances at Dortmund in the house and laboratory of Berthold F. Gerstmann and his son. A diary was kept, and the most extraordinary things happened. The trouble started when stones began to be thrown at the Gerstmanns' house on May 5, 1713. Then glass articles broke in their laboratory. The stones were not seen in flight, but were seen to fall. The visitation lasted twenty-five days, during which a sword was broken and a number of objects thrown. These included slates, old iron, potsherds, etc. Voices were heard. Gerstmann's youngest son had his clothes slashed to pieces on the last day of the infestation. The account of the manifestations was written by F. B. Gerstmann under the title of *Vorstellung des Gespenstes und Polter-Geistes welches in der Stadt Dortmundt und zwar in dessen Vatters Hause* (Dortmund, 1714). A copy is in the British Museum.

Such classical and early British cases as the Drummer of Tedworth (1662); the Ringcroft disturbances (1695); the Wesley Poltergeist (1716); the Cambridge Castle case (1718); the Cock Lane Ghost (1762); the Hinton Ampner affair (1771); the Stockwell Poltergeist (1772); the Willington Mill case (1835); and the Great Bealings bell-ringing nuisance (1841), have been dealt with in detail in this monograph, and need no further reference here. In conclusion, I will state that, in my opinion, cases of alleged Poltergeist disturbances appear to be becoming more frequent and, I think, more interesting.

[1] *Op. cit.*

CHAPTER III

What Poltergeists Do

The reader will have gathered from the last chapter that Poltergeists smash, crash, burn, spoil, and destroy. Especially, they throw things, or cause things to be thrown, sometimes slowly. But they throw things in a peculiar manner. The strange flight of their projected objects is one of the most interesting puzzles connected with the Poltergeist. Things are not often thrown *up*, but usually *down*.

Objects are seldom *seen* to rise, or to *leave* their normal stationary positions. In the most interesting Swanland case,[1] a number of workmen in a carpenter's shop at Swanland (a village in the East Riding of Yorkshire) were pelted with bits and pieces of wood. Some of the pieces travelled in a straight line, some 'as though borne along on gently heaving waves'. Some of the bits struck a door 'as noiselessly as a feather'. However, my point in citing this case is, that though the phenomena lasted six weeks, not one of the workmen ever saw a piece in the act of rising. But there are rare exceptions to this general rule. At Vienna, on May 1, 1926, during my investigation of Eleonore Zugun,[2] I saw a cushion on a chair *begin* to move, then it appeared to hesitate, and then it slipped quietly to the floor. It was just as though the cushion knew I was looking at it and decided not to make a real flight (as so many things did that afternoon)—as I hoped it would. It was caught in the act, as it were. During that same period, we tried to pit our wits against the *Geist*. In the room was a bookcase with open shelves filled with books. Time after time these books were placed by us in perfect alignment—the back of every volume flush with its neighbours on either side. Then, when we were not looking, some of the books would be pushed back or brought forward, as we were standing by them. Then they would be aligned again and we would stare at them for ten minutes, hoping to see them move. But we were always disappointed. But the moment we took our eyes off them, the books were again disarranged.

Poltergeist-projected missiles behave very strangely. They seem to be under perfect control during their flight—almost as if they were *carried*, or could control their own movements, or as if they were living things imbued with intelligence. Sometimes they move very slowly and deliberately, with low velocity; sometimes very quickly and with an impetus that suggests some sort of propellant behind them. Occasionally, their flight appears truly directional, but usually the things are thrown apparently haphazard.

[1] *Proc.*, S.P.R., Vol. VII, 1891–92.   [2] See p. 259.

Poltergeist Over England

Poltergeist projectiles do not always travel in straight lines. They turn corners, twist about, move slowly,[1] wobble up and down, zigzag, or take a curved path, with an unnatural trajectory. This question of curvilinear flight and curvilinear motion is as interesting as it is puzzling. Sometimes the objects themselves appear to hover, hesitate, and, during their flight, remain suspended in the air for an appreciable amount of time. Dom Richard Whitehouse, O.S.B., in the account of his experiences at Borley Rectory, describes some remarkable bottle-hurling feats on the part of the Poltergeists. He says: 'Shortly after this, all three of us witnessed another extraordinary incident. We were standing in a row with our backs to the fire, talking and looking out towards the window. Suddenly, before our eyes, a bottle poised itself in mid-air within a foot or so of the kitchen ceiling. *It remained there for a second or two* and then fell with a crash on the floor before us.'[2]

It was at Borley, too, that we saw the red glass candlestick hurtle down the well of the Rectory stairs, it having been projected from its usual position on the mantelpiece of the Blue Room. This ornament *must* have turned at least two corners in its flight from the Blue Room to the hall.[3] In the Battersea case, the bronze cherub ornament that 'followed' us from the front room to the kitchen, *must* have made two right-angled turns.

Sometimes objects, when in flight, appear to change their mind: they start off in a straight line, alter their course, and finish up in quite another direction. Occasionally people are pelted with things, the entity using intelligence in this matter. And, though it is true that people are seldom physically injured in this way, there are exeptions. Mrs. Foyster at Borley received at least one black eye and other injuries, and was thrown out of bed three times. A boy named Randall was pulled out of bed in the Enniscorthy case.[4] Petrus Thyraeus mentions the case of the nuns being dragged out of bed by their feet. Eleonore Zugun had pins and needles stuck into her. I could cite other cases of physical hurt being caused by Poltergeists. Nearly every Poltergeist causes *mental* injury or vexation—witness the Procters at Willington Mill, and Mrs. Ricketts at Hinton Ampner.

Projected objects, when picked up, sometimes appear warm or even hot. In the Cideville case a nail in a floor became red hot and the wood round it smoked and charred. And, of course, Poltergeists cause fires, though seldom at night. There is no control of Poltergeist phenomena. Sometimes objects fall on places to which no person present could possibly have thrown them. They fall in locked and empty rooms, passing through solid obstacles—thus demonstrating the theory of the

[1] Charles Fort, in his books, records many instances of 'slow-moving' objects, stones, hailstones, etc. that fall from the sky.

[2] *Most Haunted House in England*, by Harry Price, London, 1940, p. 98.

[3] *Op. cit.*, p. 39.   [4] See *Proc.* of the S.P.R., 1910, Vol. XXV, pp. 380–90.

Poltergeist projectiles do not always travel in straight lines. They turn corners, twist about, move slowly, wobble up and down, zigzag, or take a curved path, with an unnatural trajectory.

21

fourth dimension. Articles also *disappear* out of locked rooms, as happened to the Foysters at Borley. Objects, never seen before, suddenly appear from nowhere, and as suddenly disappear, leaving no trace. The Rev. L. A. Foyster, in his diary of the Borley phenomena, records a number of objects that spontaneously appeared. A lavender bag, hymn books, a gold wedding-ring, a paint pot, a tin trunk, etc., that no one knew anything about, were found lying in various places— and all as mysteriously and as suddenly disappeared. The wedding-ring —or another very much like it—suddenly appeared in the Blue Room on the last day of my tenancy of Borley Rectory. It now reposes—I hope!—in the inner recesses of my cash-box. These articles, like so many of the objects that are thrown, 'appear' and disappear when no one is looking. It is almost as if *visible* entities transport these things and are afraid of being seen. In a few cases (especially Poltergeist-witch cases), the objects disappear as they hit the ground. I do not remember ever having seen a genuine photograph of a Poltergeist-propelled object in flight.

A curious fact about the missiles projected by Poltergeists is that when these are picked up and thrown out-of-doors, they sometimes *return*. When the reader comes to the chapter on the childhood of Eleonore Zugun, he will learn how a pebble was thrown into the girl's cottage, and after being marked by a priest and pitched in the river—it at once *returned* to the cottage. There are many similar instances on record.

Poltergeists are fond of throwing stones. Well, they are plentiful, handy, easily transportable, light in weight, and small. The reader will find many examples of stone-throwing in this volume. Camille Flammarion, in his *Haunted Houses* (London, 1924) relates a remarkable case of stone-throwing that occurred at Marcinelle, in Belgium, in 1913. The usual 'young girl', a maidservant, was present. Showers of stones and pebbles were hurled at the window of the house, the panes of glass being perforated as if by rifle bullets. A feature of the case was that some pebbles would pass through the holes already made by stones thrown previously. One witness declared that one stone got jammed in the glass, and was knocked through by another pebble that came immediately after!

An extraordinary case of paranormal stone-dropping was recorded in *The Times* for January 13, 1843. Two young girls were picking up leaves in the commune of Livet, France. Suddenly, stones, of different colours, began falling on them, though without injuring them in the slightest degree. They fetched their parents and again they attracted a shower of stones. The parents, 'in the sphere of attraction', also had stones poured on them. Many other persons, including the clergy and medical men, saw the phenomenon, which continued for several days, but only when these particular girls were on a certain spot.

I have remarked that sometimes heavy objects fall 'as lightly as feathers'.[1] Professor Charles Richet, in his *Thirty Years of Psychical Research* (London, 1923), records a remarkable example of this phenomenon. In an unoccupied house at L'Absie, France, in 1867, the usual Poltergeist demonstrations were occurring. Stone-throwing and furniture-moving were amongst the witnessed manifestations. Gendarme Mousset testified that the stones fell and did no harm; that a glass lamp was knocked from the table to the floor by a large stone without being broken; that the stones were seen only when they struck the ground; and that they entered the room without, apparently, leaving any holes or apertures in walls or windows. Stones still fell when an observer was in the room and standing on guard by the chimney aperture.

If objects fall lightly when they should fall heavily, the converse is sometimes the case. In the Phelps affair, to be referred to later, a matchbox was (unusually) seen to fall from the mantelpiece, 'landing with a noise like a bar of iron'. At Borley Rectory (see page 287), a tablet of soap fell from off the washstand and was deeply indented as if it had been *propelled* by something.

Though lighted matches have been seen to fall from ceilings, I cannot recollect a case where such articles have *risen* to ceilings. Other things that fall from ceilings are (according to evidence) water, paraffin, oil, etc.

Poltergeists can *push* and *pull*. The Rev. Samuel Wesley was pushed three times by the Epworth Poltergeist. And people have been both pushed and pulled out of bed, as I have recorded. Poltergeists can easily displace heavy pieces of furniture and other weighty objects that would normally take several men to move. For examples, see the disturbances in the Scotch 'Poltergeist Manor' and in the old home of Mrs. Mara Mack, both detailed in this volume. And some of these objects move and wander about the room of their own accord: At Battersea, 'a row of chairs marched down the hall'. Sometimes tables, etc., spin round on their own axes—often 'widdershins' or anti-clockwise.

Poltergeists cause fires and set light to various places, objects—and people, as the account of the Poltergeist incendiaries (Chapter XXVII) shows. And some of the victims appear not to feel the flames, as a sort of anæsthesia is produced. They drop lighted papers about the place. They burn clothes and furniture, and the fire even penetrates closed drawers and boxes. Sometimes, as at Borley, a column of smoke is seen, *but no fire is to be found*. Cold water boils in kettles, etc., when no normal heat is applied, and lighted matches are discovered on floors during an infestation. Sparks are often seen.

Poltergeists produce noises of every description: voices, whisperings,

---

[1] Charles Fort points out in one of his books (*Lo!*) that during the strange showers of frogs, fish, and other living things that fall from the sky, the animals are very seldom injured.

squeaks, moans, sobs, the rustle of clothing, cannon fire, or a clap of thunder. Sometimes the voices say sentences that are coherent, as at Borley or in the 'Great Amherst Mystery'. And in the Saragossa case, the *only* phenomenon was a voice—a voice *without* a speaker, or an invisible ghost *with* a larynx. This was in the late autumn of 1934.

The Saragossa case caused a stir not only in Spain, but in most other countries, too. The 'voice' was heard speaking down a stove-pipe in a flat in a detached house inhabited by a family named Palazon, in the Calle Gascon de Gotor, Saragossa. Of *course*, they had a young maid-servant, named Maria Pascuela, aged 16 years. Suddenly, in the house, a voice 'appeared'. It was heard by scores of people, including the police and medical men. It was the voice of an intelligent entity, which spoke for hours on end, answered questions, and even asked them! 'All yesterday afternoon', said the London *Times* (November 26, 1934), 'the ghost talked almost incessantly'. The police evicted the tenants of the flat, sat up all night, and waited for something to happen. Nothing did happen. The 'voice' had disappeared with the Palazons—and Maria.

When Maria returned, so did the 'Duenda de Zaragoza', as the ghost was called. The police then examined the fluepipe and its connections, the other flats in the building, and put a guard against every outlet from the flue that could possibly be used as a sort of speaking tube. A local magistrate conducted this last inquiry, for last it was, because on this night of December 3, 1934, the ghost said its final piece—and vanished, perhaps for ever. The mystery was never solved. The authorities thought that Maria might have been an 'unconscious ventriloquist' (whatever that is) without knowing it—a 'gift' that would have been worth a fortune to her. But Authority had to give *some* sort of explanation. And so the 'voice' faded away and died. And on the grave of this Talking Poltergeist, we can place, as epitaph (as Mr. R. S. Lambert and I placed on the tomb of the Talking Mongoose),[1] the words:[2]

Vox et Præterea Nihil

Sometimes, Poltergeists place objects in people's pockets, as recorded by Dr. R. J. Tillyard and the Rev. L. A. Foyster. They can also see *inside* pockets or, alternatively, read one's thoughts. In the Derry-gonnelly case (in 1877) Sir William Barrett, F.R.S. *mentally* asked a Poltergeist to tell him, by means of raps, how many fingers he had open while his hands were hidden in the side pockets of his overcoat. Sir William changed the number of his 'open' fingers four times, and the

[1] See *The Haunting of Cashen's Gap*, by Harry Price and R. S. Lambert, London, 1936.

[2] For a full, illustrated account of this case, see *The Times*, London, from November 24, to December 5, 1934. *The Manchester Guardian* and other national journals can also be consulted. For a summary of the case, with comments, see article by Nandor Fodor in *Bulletin I*, International Institute for Psychical Research, London [1935].

Poltergeist was correct each time, though no word was spoken during the experiment. For further details of this Irish case, see the *Dublin University Magazine* for December, 1877.

Poltergeists are fond of beds *and* the sleepers (usually young girls) in them. They were not so fond of Mrs. Foyster when they repeatedly pushed her out of bed—but this was exceptional. The 'two little modest girls' in the Tedworth case; Hetty Wesley at Epworth; Elizabeth Parsons in Cock Lane; the 'young maiden gentlewoman' in Soper Lane, and other beds and their occupants (as the reader will find in the various cases detailed in this volume)—all played major parts, or were the victims of Poltergeists' pranks. Stella C., a 'Poltergeist medium', first had her attention drawn to her curious faculty by raps *on her bed*, and flashes in her bedroom. In the Sunderland case, Olive's bed had special attractions for the Poltergeist. Sometimes, for a change, beds are soaked with water. Mr. Foyster and his wife were frequently disturbed after they had retired to rest. Once, Mr. Foyster was awakened by being banged on the head with his own hairbrush.

Poltergeists also disturb people at their devotions, though seldom on Sundays or Holy Days. The Rev. Samuel Wesley has recorded instances where the Epworth Poltergeist interrupted the family prayers. At Borley something similar happened. In the Ringcroft disturbances, the *Geist* seemed extra violent during prayers. Occasionally, prayers seem to have a quietening effect on the entities—who make up for it later by being unusually violent.

From prayers to exorcisms is but a short step, and Poltergeists dislike being exorcised—or the rites have no effect upon them. Father Hayden, at Ballechin, recited the *Visita quæsumus*—but all to no purpose. Mr. Foyster, at Borley, had some good results after he had 'exorcised' the ghosts with burning creosote, but the relief was only temporary. My opinion is that Poltergeists *cannot* be exorcised—with exceptions.

I have enumerated many of the things that Poltergeists do. But they also untether horses and cattle and tie their tails in knots; scribble on walls and pieces of paper—but unfortunately, they never tell you anything about themselves; play musical instruments; lock people in rooms (as at Borley and Wimbledon); 'transport' or levitate people (as St. Joseph of Copertino [1603–1663] is supposed to have 'flown' at least seventy times); pinch and bite and scratch, and pull your hair and tweak your nose; drag people about; ring bells and make the china dance upon the table; hallucinate their victims into thinking they see imps, animals, 'black hands' (as at Borley) and phantasms—or really *do* produce these effects; simulate rushing winds and gales, especially after a phenomenon, with sometimes a drop in temperature, etc. etc. And they drive people out of their homes. (As at Borley, Willington, Hinton Ampner and Battersea.)

A curious effect produced or caused by Poltergeists is that of 'whirring' noises. In my *Confessions of a Ghost-Hunter* (London, 1936, pp. 39–42), I have described in detail a very curious experience I had in an old, empty house (now a girls' school) near Minehead, Somersetshire. Almost the only phenomenon we experienced was a loud whirring noise in *one room only*. I compared the noise with that made by a large bird flying, or a circular saw in motion, or a strong wind rushing through a gully or narrow passage. We never discovered what caused the noise, which was incessant. When we opened the window, however, it disappeared.

In the same book (pp. 82–84) I have given an account of my only real personal experience with a Poltergeist; I mean the only Poltergeist that has ever invaded my home. One January night I was instantly awakened by hearing pattering footsteps in my bedroom. I could hear the soft patter of naked feet round my room as if a little child were running round the bed. Sometimes the pattering came from *under* the bed, proving that the 'intruder' was of very small stature. I listened to that 'pattering' for ten minutes, turning over in my mind what could be making the noise. My bedroom door was closed and fastened and one of the windows was open a very few inches. No animal could have entered my room. When I judged the 'footsteps' were nearest to me, I switched on a powerful electric lantern that I kept by the side of the bed (there was no electric light in my village). The noise ceased instantly; I jumped out of bed and searched every nook and corner in the room. I even removed some of the furniture, but found nothing. As it was then nearly 5 a.m. I got up and dressed. I never solved the mystery.

The mention of my *Lar domesticus* reminds me that I once investigated a Poltergeist near Horley, Surrey, the peculiarities of this case being that footsteps (only) were heard *outside* (only) a detached cottage. The footsteps could be heard crunching the gravel as they perambulated the path that encircled the cottage—punctually at 8.30 on most mornings, but *never* on a Sunday. I set traps (shallow trenches filled with sand and flour, cut across the path at intervals) in order to get impressions of the 'feet' (or hooves!) but was unsuccessful.

As for the best conditions under which Poltergeists 'perform', it is obvious that they prefer company—a nice, quiet family (which should include at least one young girl, though exceptionally, as at Borley, Willington Mill, etc., there is no apparent *nexus* between persons and phenomena) in a quiet neighbourhood. But the 'home of the Poltergeist' can be almost anywhere, as we shall see later. If the conditions are good, or suitable, then the Poltergeist will manifest itself in daylight or under the electric arc. I think that phenomena are more varied and more violent when many people are present. And Poltergeists will infest a place for years—or hours. No one knows why they so suddenly appear, or disappear. It is strange that we know so little of the ways of these entities, considering that nearly half of all reported cases of hauntings exhibit Poltergeist characteristics. And once a Poltergeist has departed from the scene of its 'triumphs', it *very seldom* returns. But, as at Borley, it sometimes quits a place very reluctantly.

If sex has some bearing upon Poltergeist subjects, as I am certain it has, it does *not* enter into the manifestations themselves—very unlike the later phases of the witchcraft mania, with its *incubi* and *succubi* and their unholy sex relations; the teat-sucking imps, and the witches' carnal intercourse with the devil.

Poltergeists appear to have a morbid liking for homes where people are dying or are very ill. The reader will meet such instances in this volume, notably in the Battersea case, where the head of the house, Mr. Henry Robinson, actually died during my investigation.

Well, I have given a list of some of the usual things that Poltergeists do. I will now cite a few examples of the *unusual,* and will take as my first, the extraordinary affair known as the Phelps Case.

On April 19, 1850, there appeared in the *New Haven Journal and Courier,* Conn., an interview with the Rev. Dr. E. Eliakim Phelps, who was a Presbyterian minister in the village of Stratford, Conn. He stated that, with a friend, Dr. Webster, he had tried some spirit-rapping experiments—with success: 'A few days later, on Sunday, March 10, 1850, when the Phelps family returned from church, they found the furniture strewn about the rooms, and curious figures, constructed of clothing, arranged in one of them, constituting a sort of *tableau*—depicting a scene of worship. There were eleven figures, arranged in life-like attitudes. All but one were female figures; all were in postures of extreme devotion, some with their foreheads nearly touching the floor; others kneeling about the room with open Bibles before them, which indicated different passages sanctioning the phenomena then going on. In the centre of the group there was a figure suspended as though flying through the air'.

The above most amazing Poltergeist prank is almost unique, but not quite. In the Ringcroft disturbances, when the family (all of whom had been away) returned to their home, they saw a blanket, formed to look like a figure, sitting by the fire. The youngest boy, recognising his property, cried out: the figure suddenly collapsed and left the blanket on the four-legged stool, which curiously was found upside down.

There were, of course, two young girls in the Phelps household. They were aged sixteen and six respectively, and there were two younger boys. Dr. Webster, writing in the *New Haven Journal,* said: 'From this time on, the rooms were closely watched and figures appeared when no human being could have entered the room. They were constructed and arranged, I am convinced, by no visible power, with a *tout ensemble* most beautiful and picturesque. The clothing of which the figures were constructed was somehow gathered from all parts of the house, in spite of the strict watch which was kept to see that nothing of the sort could

27

possibly happen. Some of the figures were so life-like that, a small child being shown the room, thought his mother was kneeling in prayer'.

The phenomena were witnessed from March 10, 1850, to October 1, 1851. As in the 'Mill on the Eden',[1] many of the manifestations took place when the family were having their meals. And these manifestations included the pinching of the children; flaming paper found in a bedroom; raps; the flight of keys, nails, spoons and forks (and these were bent double in mid-air!); the levitation and upsetting of a supper table when no people were in the room; the slashing to pieces of a boy's clothes (as at Dortmund); and the transportation of the elder boy, who was carried across the room by invisible hands, and deposited gently on the floor. There is a good deal more of this sort of stuff, all fully documented and authenticated. Accounts of the phenomena have appeared in many books, and I have extracted my citation from the excellent summary of the case that Hereward Carrington wrote for his *Historic Poltergeists*.[2]

A very amusing Poltergeist case was reported in the *Daily Mail* for May 1, 1907. An elderly woman, Mme Blerotti, called on the magistrate of the Sainte Marguerite district of Paris and complained that 'something' in her flat in the Rue de Montreuil compelled her to enter her home on her hands, with her legs in the air. She simply could *not* resist employing this peculiar mode of locomotion. The magistrate detained her (thinking she was mad) and sent a *sergent de ville* to the address given. He returned with the woman's son, a bank clerk, aged twenty-seven, who said: 'What my mother has told you is true. I do not pretend to explain it. I only know that when my mother, my uncle, and myself enter the flat, we are immediately impelled to walk on our hands'. Then the uncle, Paul Reiss, who lived with them, was sent for and he told the same story. He, too, when he entered the flat, could not walk the right way up. Finally, the concierge of the building was brought before the magistrate. 'All that you have heard is true' said he. 'I thought that my tenants had gone mad, but as soon as I entered the rooms occupied by them, I found myself on all fours, endeavouring to throw my feet in the air'. The magistrate ordered the rooms to be disinfected!!

Another unusual phenomenon produced by (or through) a Poltergeist, was observed in the 'Great Amherst Mystery'. The medium or *point d'appui* in this case was Esther Cox, about nineteen years old, the same age as Hetty Wesley was during the Epworth disturbances. Amherst is in Nova Scotia and the infestation persisted from August 1878 to August 1879.

Esther slept with her sister Jennie, a few years her senior. One night they had retired to rest when Esther suddenly jumped out of bed with a scream, declaring that there was a mouse under the bedclothes—which is reminiscent of the 'ungrateful skippings' of the 'animal' that invaded the bed of the 'young maiden gentlewoman' in Soper Lane, as described in Chapter VI. And, as I have remarked, *how* Poltergeists love beds!

The sisters stripped the bed in an effort to find the mouse, which was not caught. But they could still see the effects of the animal, which had run into the mattress and was moving the straw about. They got into bed again and went to sleep.

On the next night, they heard the mouse again, moving about under the bed. They looked, and saw a 'green pasteboard box, filled with patchwork' jumping up and down under the bed. Their screams brought help, and the jumpings ceased. The next evening, the girls retired as usual, but at about 10.15, Esther 'jumped with a sudden bound into the centre of the room, taking all the bedclothes with her, exclaiming: "My God! what is the matter with me? I'm dying!" '

Now this is where the unique phenomenon comes in: Esther's hair was standing on end; her face was blood-red; her eyes were starting from their sockets; and in her agony her finger-nails crushed the wood of the chair she was clutching. Jennie screamed, and assistance arrived. Then it was found that *Esther was swelling visibly*! Arms, legs, trunk, hands—all were inflated. Suddenly, there was a loud report like a clap of thunder. Then three more terrific reports shook the room in which the group was standing—and Esther instantly 'deflated', and 'sank into a state of calm repose'. We are told that 'next morning Esther's appetite was not as good as usual. All she could eat was a small piece of bread and butter, a large green pickle, washed down with a cup of strong black tea!'

For the rest of this diverting story, one must read Walter Hubbell's *The Haunted House: A True Ghost Story. Being an Account of the Mysterious Manifestations that have taken place in the Presence of Esther Cox. . . . The Great Amherst Mystery.* (Saint John, N.B., 1879.) I have a copy of this first edition and in it the student will find the whole gamut of Poltergeist phenomena: more swellings, thunder-claps, and sudden 'deflations'; bedclothes floating all over the room; tug-of-war with a pillow, the invisible *Geist* proving the more powerful; writings on the wall, one of the messages being, 'Esther Cox, you are mine to kill'; plaster falling off the walls; showers of potatoes; sledgehammer blows on the roof; lighted matches falling on the bed, after the *Geist* had threatened to burn the house down (as at Borley); the spontaneous bursting into flames of a dress, that the Poltergeist removed from a nail and had thrown under the bed; the igniting of shavings in the cellar; and so on and so on.

In spite of the apparent impossibilities and absurdities of the 'Great Amherst Mystery', the story is well authenticated and the phenomena were witnessed by a number of reputable people, including medical men. In 1907, Mr. Hereward Carrington[1] was able to interview a number of surviving witnesses, including Esther herself, who testified to the fact that Hubbell's account is substantially true, if exaggerated. It is significant that the disturbances began shortly after a nervous shock caused by an attempted assault on Esther in the woods near her home.

Another 'unusual' case was reported in the *Daily Mail* for May 28, 1906. At Furnace Mill, Lamberhurst, Kent, lived Mr. J. C. Playfair. One morning during this month of May he went to his stables and found all the horses had been turned the reverse way round in their stalls. Their tails were in the mangers and their heads were where their tails should have been. One of the horses was missing. Mr. Playfair hunted high and low and, happening to look into the hay-room, nearby, discovered the horse. How it got there is still a mystery, because *a partition had to be knocked down to get it out*. The doorway of the hay-room was barely wide enough for a man to enter. Other phenomena included the removal of some heavy barrels of lime which were hurled down the wooden stairs; a large water-butt, 'too heavy for any human being to move', was overthrown; and locked and bolted doors were found open. No one could approach the mill unseen, and two watch-dogs were on guard. There was no 'young girl' in this case, but we read of a 'young son'.

Among the many 'electric girls' I could name, a few appear to have been Poltergeist mediums in their young days. Lulu Hurst (i.e., Mrs. Paul Atkinson), the 'Georgia Wonder', at the age of 15, could cause pebbles to move towards her, and china was spontaneously smashed by unseen hands at a distance of many feet from her. Raps, as in the case of Stella C., were heard on her bedstead.[2] Mrs. Annie Abbot, the 'Little Georgia Magnet', another vaudeville 'medium', could resist the exertions of several strong men.[3] Mary Richardson was another 'strength-resister'. But the most interesting of all these 'electric girls' was Angélique Cottin, of La Perrière, France, when she was fourteen years old. The first manifestation occurred on January 15, 1846, when the glove-making frame at which she was working began to jump about. Later, it was found that the mere approach of the girl towards an object, or the slightest touch of her hand on a piece of heavy furniture, sent it spinning. A heavy table was displaced when her petticoat touched it. Balls of pith or of feathers hung on silk threads would be attracted or repelled by the force emanating from her, which reminds one of the pendulum-swinging feats of Anna Rasmussen, mentioned in another chapter. The manifestations continued for ten weeks, during which a number of scientists, including François Arago, the famous French

---

[1] See his *Personal Experiences in Spiritualism*, London [1913], pp. 95–124.
[2] *Lulu Hurst Writes her Autobiography*, Rome, Georgia [1897].
[3] *The Little Georgia Magnet*, London, n.d.

physicist (who received the Copley medal of the Royal Society in 1825), were absolutely convinced that the girl exhibited a 'new power', probably of an electrical nature.[1]

Another 'Poltergeist girl' was Mary Jobson, of Bishop Wearmouth, Durham, who, in November, 1839, when she was about thirteen years old, experienced some most unusual physiological changes: swelling of the abdomen (not like the spontaneous 'inflations' of Esther Cox), convulsions, and areas on the body insensitive to pain, as if she had been given a local anæsthetic. The phenomena that accompanied these changes were the usual displacement of objects, raps, knocks, scratchings, water 'from nowhere' falling on the floor, and 'astronomical designs that appeared on the ceiling'.[2] But the reason I am including Mary's phenomena in my collection of 'unusual' manifestations is because 'exquisite music' was heard by many witnesses, and a voice, of 'angelic sweetness', declaimed passages from the Scriptures. Dr. W. Reid Clanny, F.R.S., has fully recorded[3] this case.

I could cite many more queer pranks of the Poltergeist, had I the space. Lord Portman's gamekeeper, at Durmeston, in December, 1894, had his hat knocked off by a boot that leapt up at him. A young child was in the family. Dr. J. J. Williams in his *Psychic Phenomena of Jamaica* (pp. 9–11) speaks of swinging doors that swung for forty-five minutes on end without being touched, in the presence of observers. There was no child connected with this case. The swinging door reminds me of the 'swinging pendant', a gold bracelet set with diamonds, that rests on the arm of a Madonna in the Church of the Immacolata, Naples. It swings night and day and the cause of the swinging is alleged to be a paranormal one.

The Rev. Caleb Colton, in his *Sampford Ghost* (Tiverton [1810]), relates how, in the home of Mr. John Chave in the village of Sampford Peverell, near Tiverton, Devon, a Poltergeist beat the women of the house black and blue. And yet they say that these entities never harm anyone! And some equally hefty Poltergeists were busy in the home of Mr. Scrimshaw, of Gorefield, near Wisbech. In addition to the usual crockery-smashing orgies, in the best 'Stockwell' manner, a piano, weighing 400 pounds, was dragged from place to place. The total damage was £140. For details, see the *Wisbech Advertiser* for February 27, 1923. Another strong *Geist* that I encountered—not in person!—infested a house in the Stifts-Platz, Hall, near Innsbruck, in June, 1925. There were the usual disturbances: furniture wandering from room to room,

[1] See Arago's account in the *Journal des Débats*, Paris, February, 1846; and Dr. Tanchou's *Enquête sur l'Authenticité des Phénomènes Électriques d'Angélique Cottin*, Paris, 1846.

[2] In 1872, in a house at Baden-Baden, strange pictures were found etched on the windows.

[3] *A Faithful Record of the Miraculous Case of Mary Jobson*, Monkwearmouth, 1841.

31

pictures falling from the walls, etc. and there was also the usual 'young girl' *nexus*. But the peculiarity about this particular Poltergeist was that, at night, *it pitched the investigators into the street*! Unfortunately—or perhaps fortunately!—I was there in the afternoon, as I was on my way to Vienna to keep a lecture engagement. But I may still be able to enjoy the sensation of being thrown out by a Poltergeist as the one that infests a house in the Utengasse, Basle (that I have been invited to visit) employs similar means to rid itself of unwelcome 'researchers'.

CHAPTER IV

The Home of the Poltergeist

The home of the Poltergeist is everywhere—except, apparently, in ships, shops, boarding-houses, hotels, and in the abode of criminals. There are exceptions as regards shops; ships *may* have been infested—or sunk—by Poltergeists; but I have yet to hear of one of these entities infesting the home of a habitual criminal. Perhaps they think that one rascal in a house is enough! I do not pretend to understand why criminals should enjoy this immunity, except on the principle that 'dog doesn't eat dog'.

There have been reports of Poltergeists infesting aircraft; and there is the silly myth about 'Gremlins' (the air-borne equivalent of Puck and pigwidgeon) that make aviators' lives a misery—a fable that must have been killed stone dead by W. E. Woosnam Jones's amusing article in the *Spectator*.[1] The fiction of the Gremlins arose, of course, through the strange anti-gravitational phenomena witnessed when an aircraft takes sudden and violent 'evasive action'. When a machine makes a sharp plunge downwards, anything loose in the cabin is displaced and temporarily suspended in mid-air. For example, I read[2] how a wireless operator was 'amazed to see two milk bottles floating about the cabin of a Hudson as if suspended on invisible wires. He reached up to catch one—and found himself hanging on to it with his feet clear of the floor.' The reader can reproduce this effect for himself. Let him take a thin board or metal tray and on it place an empty matchbox or other light object. Then hold the board at arm's-length, at right angles to his body. Then lower the board (supporting matchbox) *very suddenly*. He will find that the box, being the lighter of the two, will part company from the board, and remain 'suspended' for an appreciable amount of time. If the downward motion of the arm could be continued indefinitely, the box would never touch the board.

It is curious that we seldom hear of Poltergeists on board ships. (Perhaps they are bad sailors!) And yet many vessels have been 'lost without trace', and the disasters were never explained. Sometimes ships are discovered abandoned with not the slightest sign of life aboard. The *Mary Celeste* (1872) is a famous case. This American brigantine was discovered by the British ship *Dei Gratia*, floating peacefully on a calm sea, with sails set, between Lisbon and the Azores. But she was

[1] For Jan. 1, 1943 (article 'Gremlins').
[2] *New York Herald Tribune*, Nov. 18, 1942.

sailing erratically—so much so, that the British crew boarded her to investigate. There was no sign of life on board. There were half-eaten meals; the captain's wife had left a piece of material in her sewing-machine; the crew had left even their pipes and tobacco; there were no signs of mutiny or fire; there had been a spell of fine weather and the ship, which must have been abandoned at a moment's notice, was in first-class condition. The last entry in the log book was dated November 25, 1872. So when the British found her on December 5, she had been abandoned for, probably, ten days. From that day to this, not a trace of the crew or the captain or his wife and child has been found and the mystery was never solved. There have been theories galore—but no facts. I do not remember ever having heard the suggestion that Poltergeists might have been the cause of the precipitate and unpremeditated flight. But that is a possibility. If Poltergeists can cause people to abandon their homes (as at Willington Mill, Borley, Battersea, Hinton Ampner, Calvados Castle, etc.), they can make life equally unbearable aboard ship.[1] A large French vessel, the *Rosalie*, was found abandoned in 1840: all sails set, perfect condition, calm weather, and a valuable cargo. Every living soul (except a canary) had disappeared without trace.[2] The mystery was never solved. Another ship, the *Carol Deering*, went ashore off the coast of North Carolina. There was not a soul on board. All had disappeared about the time that a meal was about to be served, and the craft was in first-class order. The mystery remains a mystery.

A still greater mystery was that recorded by *The Times* (September 24, 1875). A small fleet of 'fore and aft' fishing vessels was becalmed off Chance Cove, Newfoundland. Suddenly one of them, the *Mary*, was struck by something 'coming directly from the heavens; was lifted out of the water, and without a moment's warning, went to the bottom in sixteen fathoms of water'. The crew were saved, with difficulty, by men from the other vessels, who rowed out to them. An equally mysterious affair occurred quite recently. At a Ministry of War Transport inquiry, held on May 3, 1944, it was revealed that the 200-ton coasting steamer *Speke* completely disappeared in September, 1943, on a forty-mile trip from Liverpool to Preston, with a load of woodpulp and a crew of nine. She was neither seen nor heard of again, though her two lifeboats were washed ashore. The Ministry stated that there was nothing wrong with the ship, which was equipped with radio. (See the London dailies for May 4, 1944.)

If Poltergeists can cause the disappearance of the crews, then they can cause the disappearance of the ships. During the year 1921 about twelve vessels completely vanished without trace—almost simultaneously. The White Star steamship *Naronic* disappeared in February, 1893—without trace. There were seventy-five men on board. Not one

[1] For account of the finding of the *Mary Celeste*, see *The Times*, Feb. 14, 1873.
[2] See *The Times*, Nov. 6, 1840.

was ever heard of again, though there were lifebelts for all and many lifeboats. The Danish training ship *København* vanished at the end of 1928, and a British training ship, the *Atalanta*, disappeared in the early part of the year 1880. There are records of other large vessels, all disappearing mysteriously. Are we wrong then, in assuming that Poltergeists do not infest ships?[1] Perhaps. I have yet to hear of a Poltergeist in a submarine.

There are few records of Poltergeists infesting shops, but one at South Kensington in 1907 attracted some attention. This was the stationery shop of Arthur George. Books jumped from shelves, bottles of ink were

'*Books jumped from shelves, bottles of ink were flung all over the place . . .*'

flung all over the place, and a lamp fell over.[2] In the press room and printing shop of the *Charleston News and Courier*,[3] South Carolina, on August 31, 1886, showers of hot stones fell over an area of seventy-five square feet. More than a gallon of them was picked up. One does not read of the *Geist* making 'pie' of the type—but what an opportunity!

When is a shop not a shop? The Poltergeist answer is 'when it's a British Restaurant'. According to the *Caterer and Hotel Keeper* (December 25, 1942), and the *Evening News* of December 21, 1942, a Polter-

---

[1] See *A True and Perfect Account of a Strange and Dreadful Apparition which lately Infested and Sunk a Ship bound for New-Castle* [by John Pye], London, 1672.

[2] *Weekly Dispatch*, August 18, 1907.   [3] See this journal for Sept. 6, 1886.

geist interfered with the conversion of 'Fairseat', a 400-year-old mansion on Highgate Hill, into a British Restaurant. Workmen complained that their tools were moved to distant parts of the house, bells were rung, materials disappeared, and 'the most weird noises are heard'. A policeman heard a bell ringing in the middle of the night. He had the house surrounded, and investigated, but the bell-ringer was never discovered.

Poltergeists do not often interfere with those running hotels, hostels or catering establishments. But only this summer there was a great commotion in the hostel of the Women's Land Army, at Gill House, Aspatria, Cumberland. There were strange noises, 'ghastly smells', etc., all of which disappeared with daylight. 'Several girls vowed they had seen a phantom shape walking through doors.' (There was plenty of 'girl' material here to work on.) One girl was awakened 'with the feeling that she was being strangled and pulled through the bed'. A local clergyman was asked to exorcise the place. He and his wife slept there and though nothing exciting happened, 'they felt there was something unearthly about the place.' Then two W.L.A. chiefs decided to spend a night in the 'haunted dormitory'. But before dawn, 'they left the dormitory pale and haggard'. All this was early in August, 1943, and I take my account from the *South Wales Echo* (August 2, 1943). The *Daily Mail* (August 3, 1943) followed up the story, and said that the room was to be closed and locked. The vicar, in an interview with the *Daily Mail*, is reported to have said: 'I heard rappings travelling to and fro along one of the walls and a sound which suggested an alarm clock being wound up. . . . In my opinion they were caused by a Poltergeist'. I wonder whether the vicar had ever read John Wesley's account of the Epworth Poltergeist that made a noise 'like the winding-up of a jack'.

Poltergeists are domestically-inclined, and their chief haunts are private houses, comfortable homes, family circles (especially if a young girl is present), small houses in preference to large ones, and they prefer the country and quiet places to the town and noise. They are fond of farms, and can hardly keep away from rectories! And they love the homes of holy men. Poltergeists infest new houses as well as old, cottages have attractions for them, but they shun hotels and boarding-houses like the plague! Poltergeists like company—young company for preference. And they like girls better than boys, and if they are infesting a place one can be sure that the focus of the disturbances is in or near a girl's bed. The reader will find some striking examples of this in the present volume. For every interference with a boy's bed, there are a hundred girls' beds disturbed. I think they are afraid of schools, even girls' schools. Tombs and crypts have an occasional—and morbid— interest for Poltergeists, with a famous example in the haunted vault at Barbados.

Though most Poltergeists prefer to have a roof over their heads when 'performing', a few roam the fields and make a nuisance of themselves.

The *New York Sun* for June 22, 1884, reported the bombarding by stones of two young men, George and Albert Sanford. Stones, from the sky, fell on them, and the showers lasted two days. They were witnessed by fifty people. Two years later, showers of leaden shot fell from the sky on two men working in a field near Waterboro, S.C., according to the *Charleston News and Courier* (November 12, 1886). And the *Hindu Magazine* for March, 1906, reported showers of stones falling outside the house of Gonori Deoghur. In the fields, 'clods of earth danced all round the spectators, rising five or six feet into the air, in broad daylight'. A stone, weighing 100 pounds, was 'levitated' out of a well and flung into the yard.

I was once asked to investigate a 'fresh-air' Poltergeist that was alleged to infest the Great North Road at the cross-roads (last resting-place of suicides and criminals) at Potter's Bar, Middlesex. If one stood at these cross-roads, I was informed, sounds of galloping hoofs could be heard every night between 10 and 11. I stood there on three evenings and heard the 'galloping' on each occasion. But I also made the discovery that the sounds always preceded the Edinburgh express that dashed through Potter's Bar station, a few hundred yards away. The phenomenon was probably an auditory illusion.

While I am on the subject of my own investigations, I may mention that, after a lecture I gave at the Institut Métapsychique, Paris, a few years ago, a member of the audience asked me whether I would 'lay' the ghost that was frightening the attendants in charge of the kiosks at— of all places!—the top of the Eiffel Tower. In these kiosks were sold souvenirs of the Tower—models of the erection made of soap, marzipan, etc. and cheap jewellery. At night, these articles were locked in flat glass-topped trays or cases, screened by roller-blind shutters which, when locked, protected the kiosk and its contents from ordinary human interference. Anyway, it was difficult to get to the summit of the Tower after the lifts had stopped working for the day. And yet, night after night, the glass cases were disturbed, though they were never found unlocked. But the souvenirs inside them were discovered broken, out of alignment, and many of them disappeared. I visited the kiosk and inspected the locks and saw the damaged goods. I then asked the management whether I could spend a night on the top stage of the Tower, but I was refused permission. So my projected investigation fell through.

Another 'high' Poltergeist that I was asked to investigate was making life unbearable in the Concordia Hütte—that haven of refuge[1] for climbers lost or stranded on the Great Aletsch Glacier near the Jungfraujoch, 9,415 feet above sea level. I heard about the disturbances there from a party of Alpinists who arrived at the Schweizerhof Hotel,

[1] Compare the 'Haunted Rest-House', Chap. V, *Ju-Ju and Justice in Nigeria*, by Frank Hives, London, 1930.

Interlaken, during one of my visits to this famous Swiss resort. The climbers had spent the previous night in the hut and—allowing for exaggeration—there certainly appeared to have been pandemonium amongst their belongings. Their clothes, their food, the blankets and lanterns supplied by the Swiss Alpine Club, their own ice-axes and alpenstocks—all became displaced during the night, or 'wandered about', or lost themselves. Sleep became impossible. They also told me a story of how a man had perished in the Hut, after dragging himself there out of a terrific snow blizzard. They asked me whether I would visit the Hut and 'investigate'. I said I would—if they would guarantee the phenomena happening while I was there. Unfortunately, Poltergeists, like some humans, cannot be relied upon. As the poet once wrote:

> *That when the glum researchers come,*
> *Those brutes of bogeys go . . .*

And it is a tiring and expensive journey from Interlaken to the Jungfraujoch, the terminus of the Jungfrau Railway. And the Concordia Hut is a long way from the terminus. So I declined, especially as I had been to the *Joch* only a few days previously.

It is not often that Poltergeist disturbances are directly connected with a murder, suicide or, in fact, a death of any sort. But in the Orient Express I once had a strange experience that one could link up with a suicide. In May, 1926, I was travelling from Vienna to Ostend. During the night I was awakened suddenly as if a pistol had been fired. It was then nearly 2 a.m., and we were approaching Frankfort-am-Main. I went to sleep again. At about 5 a.m. I was again startled out of a sound sleep, as we were nearing Cologne. When we arrived at Ostend, the attendant in charge of my compartment in the *Schlafwagen* admitted, after some coaxing, that a representative of an Amsterdam diamond firm had blown out his brains in the very carriage I had occupied. The tragedy occurred just outside Würzburg, and it was near this town that I was first awakened. The body was put out at Frankfort. The attendant told me that he had had other complaints of noises, 'pistol shots', etc., including the horrible auditory illusion (as it must be) of the train leaving the metals.[1]

Places of entertainment are seldom 'infested', but in March, 1928, June, the actress, complained that when resting in her dressing-room at the Adelphi Theatre, the couch on which she was lying received a number of blows from an unseen hand. Also, she declared, her arm had been gripped by something that had raised four weals. And taps could be heard coming from behind a mirror. I was asked to hold a séance in June's dressing room. This I did on March 14, 1928, and Miss Cicely Courtneidge was among the sitters. Nothing happened. I similarly in-

[1] I have told of this experience in greater detail in my *Confessions of a Ghost-Hunter*, London, 1936, pp. 71–74.

vestigated reports of 'happenings' at Drury Lane Theatre and at St. George's Hall, but the Poltergeists had fled by the time I arrived.

In the last chapter I recorded an occurrence at Lamberhurst in which a horse was spirited out of a stable into a hay-room, the door of which was too small to admit even a man, except with difficulty. Similar 'stable miracles' were actually *witnessed* at Gross-Erlach, in Württemberg. In addition to the usual disturbances inside the house, the stables were the focal-point for many of the phenomena. These included the untethering of the cattle which, when re-tied, were again untied in the presence of witnesses. The annoyance became unbearable and the place was vacated.[1]

If Poltergeists infest cottages, they also haunt castles. I was once asked to investigate alleged disturbances at Arthog Castle, Merionethshire. There was the usual bell-ringing nuisance, knockings and other noises. I wrote for further particulars, and receiving none, concluded the *Geist* had disappeared. The castle is some 750 years old.

The classic castle-Poltergeist is that which infested the Château de T., in Calvados, Normandy. The case is fully recorded in *Haunted Houses* by Camille Flammarion (London, 1924),[2] and should be read in detail. Briefly, the castle had a 'reputation'. As far back as 1867, when Monsieur de X. inherited it, there were heard typical Poltergeistic thumps and bumps. Then things were quiet for some years. In the autumn of 1875, X. engaged the young abbé Y. as tutor for his little son. That restarted the trouble. Whether the abbé or the boy was the medium is doubtful, but most of the phenomena centred in or about the abbé and his room and the manifestations (which persisted with hardly a pause from October 12, 1875 to January 30, 1876) were of the most amazing description, and were as diverse as they were amazing. In an attempt to put an end to the disturbances, the castle was exorcised on January 14, 1876. This did stop the nuisance for a time, but the trouble broke out again in August and September of 1876, and, I believe, continued intermittently for many years. A Novena[3] was said at Lourdes (just as one was said at Borley nearly seventy years later) for the peace of the castle, and, we read, 'everything has stopped'. But, as I have stated, the exorcism did not have a very lasting effect. I reiterate that Poltergeists *cannot* be exorcised. Prayers may make them quiet, but they won't make them quit. But the Poltergeists at 'Beth-oni', Tackley, Oxon., were successfully exorcised.

As at Borley, Willington, the 'Mill on the Eden', Mrs. Mara Mack's home, and some other places, the dates and times of the phenomena were entered in a diary. I cannot reproduce even a tenth of the entries, but will mention some of the striking incidents, which included: the

[1] See *Der Spuk von Gross-Erlach*, by Johann Illig, Leipzig, 1916.

[2] T. Fisher Unwin.

[3] A devotion consisting of a prayer said on nine successive days, asking for some special blessing.

usual nocturnal thumps, knocks and hammer-blows; noise like the 'winding of a big clock'[1] heard by the abbé; the movement and piling up of furniture; conversation mimicked and persons followed by footsteps (that recalls Mr. Hayes' adventure at Borley); sounds 'like a big log being thrown against the wall' and 'a heavy elastic body rolling down the stairs'; 'tripping noises' like the steps of animals; a 'rushing gallop in the hall'; 'a long-drawn trumpet call'; 'the sobs and cries of a woman in horrible suffering'; spontaneous opening and closing of doors and windows; toilet articles on a dressing table upset (as in the Scottish 'Poltergeist Manor'); horrible 'cries of demons or the damned'; chairs piled on table in the Blue Room (why do so many haunted houses possess Blue Rooms?); beds and bedding disturbed (of course!); all the books (about 100), 'except three on Holy Scriptures', thrown out of a bookcase on to the floor; in the Blue Room a coverlet thrown into the middle of the room, and a night-table found resting on a pillow; the disappearance of a collection of Roman Catholic medals and crosses that had been attached to doors, and their sudden reappearance in a room three days later (Roman Catholic medallions[2] also came tumbling down the stairs at Borley); a 'noise like that of an animal with boards under its feet' and another 'like a stick jumping on one of its ends'; 'loud cries like bellowings'; on January 25, 1876, two beds turned over 'in an absolutely identical manner'; the music played on a harmonium was 'repeated for a considerable time' in the opposite corner of the room, when player had ceased; the levitation of a cupboard heavily laden with books and linen, 'which rose 20 inches from the ground', 'remained up for some time', and resisted the efforts of the abbé to push it down again; the continued movement of some bedclothes which continued to be disturbed after a pistol had been fired at them; and the playing of a locked organ, when the key was in its owner's pocket many miles away.

Well, the reader now knows of a *very few* of the things that occurred— and may be still occurring—in this strange castle in Calvados. And if ever a case was authenticated and documented, this one is. The owner, his wife, his servants, priests and visitors, all testify to having witnessed the phenomena—many of them in daylight. I repeat, the case should be read in full in Flammarion's *Haunted Houses* in order that justice may be done to it.

Many British castles and family seats can boast of ghosts or stories about them. One of the most picturesque is the tradition, that has persisted for centuries, connected with Knebworth House, the ancestral home of the Lyttons. In the East wing of the mansion was (the wing was demolished in 1811) a haunted chamber known as 'Spinning Jenny's

---

[1] At Epworth, a noise was 'like the winding up of a jack'; at Aspatria, the sound was as if an alarm clock was being wound. And all were heard by parsons.

[2] These, too, were French—a strange and interesting coincidence.

room'. In this room was incarcerated a young girl who was forced to spin, and spin, and spin, with little food and less leisure. Semi-starvation, plus incessant toil, plus the treatment meted out to her, drove Jenny out of her mind—and she died. Variants of the story say she was starved to death or committed suicide. Then came the Poltergeist phenomena. From the day of her demise could be heard the rhythmic whir of Jenny's spinning-wheel and the movements of the young girl as she toiled at her work. 'Whirring noises' are not very common in Poltergeist haunts, and several correspondents have told me about this phenomenon connected with the Knebworth ghost.

The story of 'Spinning Jenny' was published as a tract (*The History of Jenny Spinner, the Ghost of Knebworth House. [Written by Herself]* London, 1800), and through the kindness of Miss Eglantyne M. Jebb, M.A., Principal of the Froebel Educational Institute (temporarily evacuated to Knebworth House), and the Rt. Hon. the Earl of Lytton, K.G., P.C., etc., I have been enabled to study a reprint. This was included in the privately-printed *A History of Knebworth House and its Owners* (Letchworth, 1915). How the tract came to be written is interesting. It appears that at a jolly Christmas party at Knebworth House in 1800, the châtelaine of the mansion challenged her guests to write the complete story of 'Spinning Jenny'. The only one who responded was a Miss E. M. James, then aged twenty-five, who, in three days, composed the fictional autobiography of Jenny that I have mentioned. The tract (which was afterwards privately printed) is cleverly written and is reminiscent of one of Ann Radcliffe's[1] horrific novels. In Miss James's narrative, all ends well—as it should do at a Christmas party. Jenny is rescued by her boy friend, whom she marries; the villain of the piece (whose intentions were strictly dishonourable) is foiled and unmasked, and all—except the villain, of course—live happily ever after. The real story is, as I have stated, very ancient, and Lord Lytton tells me that 'Spinning Jenny's room' is mentioned in some of the old documents connected with the house.

From *châteaux* to telegraph offices is rather a jump, but this chapter is intended to show how varied is the 'home of the Poltergeist'. And this is why I am including a brief account (published originally in the *Occult Review* for May, 1911)[2] of the Dale Tower case. The 'tower' was a two-storied telegraph office on the main line of the Atlantic Coast Railroad, at Dale, Georgia. It was opened only for three months of the year during the tourist traffic. The upper storey was a living room occupied by three young operators, and the lower apartment was the instrument room. Stairs, closed by a trap, gave access to the upper apartment

[1] In 1800 Mrs. Radcliffe (1764-1823) was at the zenith of her fame. Her novel, *The Italian*, appeared in 1797—the last work to be published during her lifetime.

[2] Reproduced, with other cases, by Sacheverell Sitwell in his *Poltergeists*, London, 1940.

from the lower one. There was no house of·any description within a quarter of a mile.

On January 4, 1911, the 'tower' was opened for the season. The first untoward incident was the spontaneous opening of the trap-door, which would not remain closed. Even nailing and an iron bar would not keep it down. Then strange footsteps were heard, and things began to float about the room, rather like the anti-gravitational phenomena mentioned a few pages back. A cooking dish rolled down the stairs, through the lower apartment, and landed *under* the structure. 'An ordinary can-opener flew wildly about the room and fastened itself on the centre of the ceiling'. Then bolts and nuts were hurled through the window *from outside*. The young men beat a hasty retreat and left the tower. Immediately, a chair was hurled at them out of the window by—what? Apparently, the manifestations then ceased. This is a typical Poltergeist story, in a new setting. Trickery appears to have been impossible, though collusion on the part of the young men might be the explanation.

I could cite many more queer tricks of the Poltergeists—queer tricks in queerer places. But I have said enough, I think, to illustrate the versatility of the entities as regards both pranks and places. I have not touched upon those Poltergeists that molest savage men and infest savage homes. In every land, literally 'from China to Peru', the Poltergeist is found doing the same old tricks in the same old way. I hope to cite a few of these cases when I come to discuss the 'evidence for the Poltergeist'. But the only thing new about them will be their settings.

In this and the three preceding chapters, I have briefly summarised nearly a hundred Poltergeist cases, ancient and modern, in order to give the reader a clear and general picture of what these entities are, what they do, and where and how they do them. But the evidence I have found room for has been scanty and sometimes unconvincing, though fully documented. We will now examine in detail (sometimes in great detail) a few of the classical cases (mostly English) of Poltergeist-infestation, beginning with the famous Drummer of Tedworth, who made such a noise in the world in 1661[1].

[1] But see Appendix A.

CHAPTER V

The Drummer Poltergeist

It would be interesting to know when groups of people first met in order to relate ghost stories, or to tell of exciting personal experiences in the realm of the occult. I should imagine it was a very long time ago! Lucian the Satirist (*c.* A.D. 120–180), that amusing sceptic whose works are full of exposures of frauds, humbug, superstitions, myths, miracles and miracle-mongers (did he not unmask Alexander the Paphlagonian, the 'false prophet' and 'medium'?) tells us in one of his books (*Philopseudes*) of a sort of Ghost Club, whose members met to discuss apparitions, phenomena, and what we should now call psychical research. So nearly 2,000 years ago people took an interest in these things, and there were not only believers, but also scoffers and sceptics, of whom the Syrian satirist was one of the most critical.

There must have been many societies formed for the study of the occult since the time of Lucian, and one of the most important, and one whose records are available today, was the sort of 'society for psychical research' that met at Lady Conway's residence at Ragley, Warwickshire, in the early months of 1665. Ragley Castle, or Ragley Hall, as it is now called, is one and a half miles south-west of Alcester. It is the seat of the present eighth Marquess of Hertford, who is also Baron Conway of Ragley.

There were some distinguished members of this society. Dr. Henry More, the Rev. Joseph Glanvill, Lady Roydon, and Robert Boyle were frequent visitors to Ragley Castle. It is chiefly through Glanvill that we know anything about Lady Conway's circle, though Ferris Greenslet, in his biography[1] of the philosopher, has gathered further interesting details of its proceedings.[2] Glanvill was born in 1636.

Apparently, the members of the 'Ragley S.P.R.' met in order to relate personal psychic experiences, read reports on current or contemporary haunted houses, ghosts, apparitions, Poltergeists and 'miracles'—just as we do today. They also—and this is very interesting—investigated and tested mediums, as we, too, do today. One of these mediums was Valentine Greatrakes, the well-known healer, whom Lady Conway imported from Ireland to be tested at a cost of about £155—a lot of money in the middle of the seventeenth century. Lady Conway suffered from chronic headaches, and it was decided that Greatrakes should

[1] *Joseph Glanvill*, Columbia University Press, N.Y., 1900.
[2] J. H. Shorthouse, in *John Inglesant* (1880: Chap. XV), tells us something of Ragley and its psychic 'marvels'.

demonstrate his alleged healing powers on her ladyship, and before the assembled 'psychic' house-party. This was in February, 1665. Greatrakes completely failed to cure Lady Conway's headaches, though he appears to have had some success locally among the Warwickshire rustics. Greatrakes, known as the 'Irish Stroker', used methods comparable with the technique employed by the 'magnetisers' and faith-healers of a later date.

So the Ragley party having failed to be convinced by Greatrakes, contented themselves with recounting personal experiences of ghosts and haunted houses, mostly of a recent date. Among the speakers was Joseph Glanvill and he related the story of what he called the 'Dæmon of Tedworth', now better known as the 'Drummer of Tedworth', and it has become a classic—if not *the* classic—amongst Poltergeist cases. Many years later the story inspired Joseph Addison with the idea of writing it up in the form of a play. This appeared (1716) as a comedy, *The Drummer, or The Haunted House.* It was not a success, and ran for three nights only. Miss Edith Sitwell has also written a poem, *The Drum* (*Selected Poems*, London, 1936), based on Glanvill's exciting narrative.

The Rev. Joseph Glanvill was a very distinguished divine and philosopher. He was a chaplain to Charles II, a Fellow of the Royal Society, an author of great repute—and somewhat of a sceptic. He was also a collector of ghost stories, and did a little investigating himself. His account of the Drummer of Tedworth (a man named William Drury) was, therefore, well received by not only the 'Ragley S.P.R.', but by the public at large when the story came to be published.

The first printed account, in book form, of the Drummer of Tedworth[1], appeared the year following (1666) the Ragley meeting. Glanvill published it in his *Philosophical Considerations concerning the existence of Sorcerers and Sorcery.* The story[2] was reprinted in subsequent books written by Glanvill, who left an enlarged account of the case amongst his papers that were published after his death, which occurred at Bath in 1680. This posthumous work was issued in 1681, under the title of *Saducismus Triumphatus: or, Full and Plain Evidence Concerning Witches and Apparitions. In Two Parts. The First, Treating of Their Possibility, the Second of Their Real Existence.* . . . London, J. Collins, 1681. The second part of the book contains twenty-six 'cases' or 'Relations', similar to that of the Drummer, which were collected by Glanvill from

---

[1] More correctly, North Tidworth, on the Wiltshire-Hampshire border, two miles south-west of Ludgershall. It is in Wilts. South Tidworth, nearby, is in Hants. The Rev. J. P. Thompson, M.A., Rector of South Tidworth, tells me that the change from 'Tedworth' to 'Tidworth' was due to a War Office misprint.

[2] Actually, the first official reference to the case appeared in the *Mercurius Publicus* for April, 1663. This contains an abstract of the sworn deposition of Mr. Mompesson. There is also a printed ballad about the case that appeared in 1662 (Anthony Wood's collection in the Bodleian Library). Pepys mentions 'books' about the affair in his *Diary* for June, 1663. For Mompesson's deposition and a reprint of the ballad, see Appendix A.

44

various sources. The first edition of this work is very rare. I have two copies, and it is from one of them that I will now give, in Glanvill's rather quaint idiom, the story of the Tedworth Poltergeist:

Mr. John Mompesson [a magistrate] of Tedworth, in the County of Wilts, being about the middle of March, in the year 1661[1] at a Neighbouring Town called Ludgarshal, and hearing a Drum beat there, he inquired of the Bailiff of the Town, at whose House he then was, what

An itinerant drummer of the seventeenth century. (From 'Tarlton's Jests', 1638.)

it meant. The Bailiff told him that they had for some days been troubled with an idle Drummer, who demanded money of the Constable by vertue of a pretended Pass, which he thought was counterfeit. Upon this, Mr. Mompesson sent for the Fellow, and askt him by what authority

[1] Andrew Lang ('Poltergeist', *Encyclo. Britann.*, Cambridge, 1911, Eleventh Edn., Vol. 22, p. 17) says that Glanvill is mistaken in his dates, and that the disturbances occurred between Mar. 1662 and April 1663. See Appendix A.—H.P.

he went up and down the Country in that manner with his Drum. The Drummer answered, he had good authority, and produced his Pass, with a Warrant, under the Hands of Sir William Cawly, and Colonel Ayliff of Gretenham. Mr. Mompesson, knowing these Gentlemens Hands, discovered that the Pass and Warrant were counterfeit and thereupon commanded the Vagrant to put off his Drum, and charged the Constable to carry him before the next Justice of the Peace, to be further examined and punisht. The Fellow then confessed the cheat, and begged earnestly to have his Drum. Mr. Mompesson told him, that if he understood from Colonel Ayliff, whose Drummer he said he was, that he had been an honest Man, he should have it again, but in the meantime he would secure it. So he left the Drum with the Bailiff, and the Drummer in the Constables hands, who it seems was prevailed on by the Fellows intreaties to let him go.

About the midst of April following, when Mr. Mompesson was preparing for a Journey to London, the Bailiff sent the Drum to his House.[1] When he was returned from that Journey, his Wife told him, that they had been much affrighted in the Night by Thieves, and that the House had been like to have been broken up. And he had not been at home above three Nights, when the same noise was heard that had disturbed his Family in his absence. It was a very great knocking at his Doors, and the Outsides of his House. Hereupon, he got up and went about the House with a brace of Pistols in his Hands. He opened the door where the great knocking was, and then he heard the noise at another Door. He opened that also, and went out round his House, but could discover nothing, only he still heard a strange noise and hollow sound. When he got back to bed, the noise was a Thumping and Drumming on the top of his House, which continued a good space, and then by degrees went off into the Air.

After this, the noise of Thumping and Drumming was very frequent, usually five nights together, and then it would intermit three. It was on the Outsides of the House, which is most of it Board. It constantly came as they were going to sleep, whether early or late. After a months disturbance without, it came into the Room, where the Drum lay, four or five nights in seven, within half an hour after they were in bed, continuing almost two. The sign of it just before it came was, they still heard an hurling in the Air over the House and at its going off, the beating of a Drum like that at the breaking up of a Guard. It continued in this Room for the space of two Months, which time Mr. Mompesson himself lay there to observe it. In the fore part of the night, it used to be very troublesome, but after two hours all would be quiet.

---

[1] According to the *Beauties of England and Wales* (London, 1814, Vol. XV, pp. 396–7), Mompesson lived at the Manor House, North Tedworth, which is still standing. In Mompesson's time it was 'surrounded with a large park'. Monuments to the Mompesson family can still be seen in the churchyard of Holy Trinity.—H.P.

Zouche Manor, North Tidworth, Wiltshire (photographed in November, 1944), the Poltergeist home of Mr. John Mompesson. It was in this house, in 1662-3, that the 'Drummer of Tedworth' made so much noise. The place has since been altered, because Mompesson speaks of 'cock lofts' (i.e. attics). According to The Beauties of England and Wales (London, 1814, Vol. 15, pp. 396-97), the Manor 'was formerly surrounded with a large park'.

Mrs. Mompesson being brought to bed, there was but little noise the night she was in Travail, nor any for three weeks after, till she had recovered strength. But after this civil cessation, it returned in a ruder manner than before, and followed and vext the youngest Children, beating their Bedsteds with that violence, that all present expected when they would fall in pieces. In laying Hands on them, one should feel no blows, but might perceive them to shake exceedingly. For an

One compartment of the engraved Frontispiece, by W. Faithorne, to Part 2 of Joseph Glanvill's 'Saducismus Triumphatus', London, 1681. This is the artist's impression of the Drummer of Tedworth producing his Poltergeist effects over the house of Mr. Mompesson. From the author's collection.

hour together it would beat, Round-heads and Cuckolds, the Tat-too, and several other points of War, as well as any Drummer. After this, they should hear a scratching under the Childrens Bed, as if by something that had Iron Tallons. It would lift the Children up in their Beds,

47

follow them from one Room to another, and for a while haunted none particularly but them.

There was a Cock-loft[1] in the House which had not been observed to be troubled, thither they removed the Children, putting them to Bed while it was fair day, where they were no sooner laid, but their troubler was with them as before.

On the Fifth of Novemb. 1662, it kept a mighty noise, and a servant observing two Boards in the Childrens Room seeming to move, he bid it give him one of them. Upon which the Board came (nothing moving it that he saw) within a yard of him. The Man added, Nay let me have it in my Hand; upon which it was shov'd quite home to him. He thrust it back, and it was driven to him again, and so up and down, to and fro, at least twenty times together, till Mr. Mompesson forbad his Servant such familiarities. This was in the day-time, and seen by a whole Room full of People. That morning it left a sulphurous smell behind it, which was very offensive. At night the Minister one Mr. Cragg, and divers of the Neighbours came to the House on a visit. The Minister went to Prayers with them, Kneeling at the Childrens Bed-side, where it was then very troublesome and loud. During Prayer-time it withdrew into the Cock-loft, but returned as soon as Prayers were done, and then in sight of the Company, the Chairs walkt about the Room of themselves, the Childrens shooes were hurled over their Heads and every loose thing moved about the Chamber. At the same time a Bedstaff was thrown at the Minister, which hit him on the Leg, but so favourably that a Lock of Wool could not have fallen more softly, and it was observed, that it stopt just where it lighted without rolling or moving from the place.

Mr. Mompesson perceiving, that it so much persecuted the little Children, he lodged them out at a Neighbours House, taking his Eldest Daughter, who was about ten years of age into his own Chamber, where it had not been a Moneth before. As soon as she was in Bed, the disturbance begun there again, continuing three Weeks Drumming, and making other noises, and it was observed, that it would exactly answer in Drumming any thing that was beaten or called for. After this, the House where the Children were Lodged out, happening to be full of strangers, they were taken home, and no disturbance having been known in the Parlour, they were lodged there, where also their persecutour found them, but then only pluckt them by the Hair and Night-cloaths without any other disturbance.

It was noted, that when the noise was loudest, and came with the most sudden and surprising violence, no Dog about the House would move, though the knocking was oft so boisterous and rude, that it hath been heard at a considerable distance in the Fields, and awakened the Neighbours in the Village, none of which live very near this House.

[1] i.e., an attic.—H.P.

'*The Chairs walkt about the Room of themselves, the Childrens shooes were hurled over their Heads and every loose thing moved about the Chamber.*'

The servants sometimes were lift up with their Beds, and then let gently down again without hurt, at other times it would lye like a great weight upon their Feet.

About the latter end of Decemb. 1662, the Drummings were less frequent, and then they heard a noise like the gingling of Money,[1] occasioned, as it was thought, by somewhat Mr. Mompesson's Mother had spoken the day before to a Neighbour, who talkt of Fayries leaving Money, *viz*. That she should like it well, if it would leave them some to make amends for their trouble. The night after the speaking of which, there was a great chinking of Money over all the House.

After this, it desisted from the ruder noises, and employed it self in little Apish and less troublesome Tricks. On Christmas Eve a little before day, one of the little Boys arising out of his bed, was hit on a sore place upon his Heel, with the Latch of the Door, the Pin that it was fastened with, was so small that it was a difficult matter to pick it out. The night after Christmas day, it threw the old Gentlewomans cloaths about the Room, and hid her Bible in the Ashes. In such silly Tricks it was frequent.

After this, it was very troublesome to a Servant of Mr. Mompesson's, who was a stout Fellow, and of sober Conversation. This Man lay within, during the greatest disturbance, and for several nights something would endeavour to pluck his cloaths off the Bed, so that he was fain to tug hard to keep them on, and sometimes they would be pluckt from him by main force, and his shooes thrown at his head. And now and then he should find himself forcibly held, as it were bound Hand and Foot, but he found that whenever he could make use of his Sword, and struck with it, the Spirit quitted its hold.

A little after these contests, a Son of Sir Thomas Bennet, whose Workman the Drummer had sometimes been, came to the House, and told Mr. Mompesson some words that he had spoken, which it seems was not well taken. For as soon as they were in Bed, the Drum was beat up very violently and loudly, the Gentleman arose and called his Man to him, who lay with Mr. Mompesson's Servant just now spoken of, whose name was John. As soon as Mr. Bennet's Man was gone, John heard a rusling noise in his Chamber, and something came to his Bed-side, as if it had been one in silk. The Man presently reacheth after his Sword, which he found held from him, and 'twas with difficulty and much tugging that he got it into his power, which as soon as he had done, the Spectre left him, and it was always observed that it still avoided a Sword.

About the beginning of January 1662,[2] they were wont to hear a Singing in the Chimney before it came down. And one Night about this time, lights were seen in the House. One of them came into Mr. Mom-

---

[1] Compare a similar auditory impression in the Wesley and Willington cases.—H.P.
[2] i.e. January, 1663. (See Appendix A.)—H.P.

pesson's Chamber which seemed blue and glimmering, and caused great stiffness in the Eyes of those that saw it. After the light something was heard coming up the Stairs, as if it had been one without shooes. The light was seen also four or five times in the Childrens Chamber; and the Maids confidently affirm that the Doors were at least ten times opened and shut in their sight, and when they were opened they heard a noise as if half a dozen had enterd together. After which some were heard to walk about the Room, and one rusled as if it had been in silk. The like Mr. Mompesson himself once heard.

During the time of the knocking, when many were present, a Gentleman of the Company said, Satan, if the Drummer set thee to work, give three knocks and no more, which it did very distinctly and stopt. Then the Gentleman knockt, to see if it would answer him as it was wont, but it did not. For further trial, he bid it for confirmation, if it were the Drummer, to give five knocks and no more that night, which it did, and left the House quiet all the night after. This was done in the presence of Sir Thomas Chamberlain of Oxfordshire, and divers others.

On Saturday Morning, an hour before day, Jan. 10, a Drum was heard beat up on the out-sides of Mr. Mompesson's Chamber, from whence it went to the other end of the House, where some Gentlemen strangers lay, playing at their door and without, four or five several Tunes, and so went off into the air.

The next night, a Smith in the Village lying with John the Man, they heard a noise in the room, as if one had been shoeing of an Horse, and somewhat came, as it were with a pair of Pincers, snipping at the Smiths Nose most part of the night.

One morning Mr. Mompesson rising early to go a journey, heard a great noise below, where the Children lay, and running down with a Pistol in his Hand, he heard a voice crying a witch, a witch, as they had also heard it once before. Upon his entrance all was quiet.

Having one Night played some little tricks at Mr. Mompesson's Beds feet, it went into another Bed, where one of his Daughters lay; There it passed from side to side, lifting her up as it passed under. At that time there were three kinds of noises in the Bed. They endeavoured to thrust at it with a Sword, but it still shifted and carefully avoided the thrust, still getting under the Child when they offered at it. The Night after it came panting like a Dog out of breath. Upon which one took a Bedstaff[1] to knock, which was caught out of her hand, and thrown away, and company coming up, the room was presently filled with a bloomy noisome smell, and was very hot, though without fire, in a very sharp and severe Winter. It continued in the Bed panting and scratching an hour and half, and then went into the next Chamber, where it knockt a

---

[1] A stick or staff used to smooth a feather bed or to spread the coverlet; also a bar at the side to keep the bedclothes in place.—H.P.

little, and seemed to rattle a Chain; thus it did for two or three nights together.

After this, the old Gentlewomans[1] Bible was found in the Ashes, the Paper side being downwards. Mr. Mompesson took it up, and observed that it lay open at the Third Chapter of St. Mark, where there is mention of the unclean Spirits falling down before our Saviour, and of his giving power to the Twelve to cast out Devils, and of the Scribes Opinion, that he cast them out through Beelzebub. The next night they strewed Ashes[2] over the Chamber, to see what impressions it would leave. In the morning they found in one place, the resemblance of a great Claw, in another of a lesser, some Letters in another, which they could make nothing of, besides many Circles and Scratches in the Ashes.

About this time I went to the House, on purpose to inquire the truth of those passages, of which there was so loud a report. It had ceased from its Drumming and ruder noises before I came thither, but most of the more remarkable circumstances before related, were confirmed to me there, by several of the neighbours together, who had been present at them. At this time it used to haunt the Children, and that as soon as they were laid. They went to Bed that night I was there, about Eight of the Clock, when a Maidservant coming down from them, told us it was come. The neighbours that were there, and two Ministers who had seen and heard divers times went away, but Mr. Mompesson and I, and a Gentleman that came with me went up. I heard a strange scratching as I went up the Stairs, and when we came into the Room, I perceived it was just behind the Bolster of the Childrens Bed, and seemed to be against the Tick. It was as loud a scratching, as one with long Nails could make upon a Bolster. There were two little modest Girls in the Bed, between seven and eleven years old as I guest. I saw their hands out over the Cloaths, and they could not contribute to the noise that was behind their heads. They had been used to it, and had still some body or other in the Chamber with them, and therefore seemed not to be much affrighted. I standing at the Beds-head, thrust my hand behind the Bolster, directing it to the place whence the noise seemed to come. Whereupon the noise ceased there, and was heard in another part of the Bed. But when I had taken out my Hand it returned, and was heard in the same place as before. I had been told that it would imitate noises, and made trial by scratching several times upon the Sheet, as 5, and 7, and 10, which it followed, and still stopt at my number. I searcht under and behind the Bed, turning up the cloaths to the Bed-cords, graspt the Bolster, sounded the Wall behind, and made all the search that possible I could to find if there were any trick, contrivance, or common cause of it; the like did my friend, but we could discover nothing. So that I was then verily perswaded, and am so still, that the noise was made by some Dæmon or Spirit. After it had scratcht about half an hour or more, it

---

[1] i.e. Mompesson's mother.—H.P.   [2] This is a test often made today.—H.P.

. . . sitt sitting at the stairhead and working them every stroke. they seemed: they myself . . . when they were up, and made fire come, perfectly.

Tuesday night all was quiet, but i gave warn to Sarum hifie my chilg . . . Being on i heard a great noise below where my children lay, and so ran down with a pistol in my hand into the room, where there was a voice owning a witch, a witch, as once before, and the chairs jumping togither and presently vanished.

Wednesday night there was no noise not us in my crib loft.

Thursday night . . . now if my high and i were into my bed, the chairs at my beds feet tumbled over hard up and downe, and it knocked very hard upon the . . . boards, and then and sighted a candle and it went away.

Friday night it came into my chamber being of a noise about i before i went to bed, and went into the bed to be where my daughter lay, and ran from one side of the bed to the other and heard her an i retrived two hearts, many living in the room. There were at one time twice turned round in the . . . bed, and was very seeming to blow and said like a dee out of breath and continued not with standing two lights were held to the bed and . . . words but i was so loud that we could not hear it without endangering it, for it would run under her head and and at the foot and you as soon as we were ready to throw at it, it would run under her bed and me was with her they . . .

Saturday night the like passing was in her bed and she was with her, they

Extracts, dated Tuesday, January 13 to Friday, January 16 1662-3, from John Mompesson's journal, hitherto unpublished. A strange voice, dancing chairs, disturbances in his daughters' bed, and other phenomena, are recorded. Reproduced from the Corpus Christi College MSS. (No. 318) in the Bodleian Library, Oxford. (By courtesy of the Bodleian Library.)

went into the midst of the Bed under the Children, and there seemed to pant like a Dog out of Breath very loudly. I put my hand upon the place, and felt the Bed bearing up against it, as if something within had thrust it up. I graspt the Feathers to feel if any living thing were in it. I looked under and every where about, to see if there were any Dog or Cat, or any such Creature in the Room, and so we all did, but found nothing. The motion it caused by this panting was so strong, that it shook the Room and Windows very sensibly. It continued thus, more than half an hour, while my friend and I stay'd in the Room, and as long after, as we were told. During the panting, I chanced to see as it had been something (which I thought was a Rat or Mouse) moving in a Linnen Bag, that hung up against another Bed that was in the Room. I stept and caught it by the upper end with one Hand, with which I held it, and drew it through the other, but found nothing at all in it. There was no body near to shake the Bag, or if there had, no one could have made such a motion, which seemed to be from within, as if a Living Creature had moved in it. This passage I mention not in the former Editions, because it depended upon my single Testimony, and might be subject to more Evasions than the other I related; but having told it to divers Learned and Inquisitive Men, who thought it not altogether inconsiderable, I have now added it here. It will I know be said by some, that my friend and I were under some affright, and so fancied noises and sights that were not. This is the Eternal Evasion. But if it be possible to know how a Man is affected, when in fear, and when unconcerned, I certainly know for mine own part, that during the whole time of my being in the Room, and in the House, I was under no more affrightment than I am, while I write this Relation. And if I know that I am now awake, and that I see the Objects that are before me, I know that I heard and saw the particulars I have told. There is, I am sensible, no great matter for story in them, but there is so much as convinceth me, that there was somewhat extraordinary, and what we usually call preternatural in the business. There were other passages at my being at Tedworth, which I published not, because they are not such plain and unexceptionable Proofs. I shall now briefly mention them, *valeant quantum valere possunt.* My friend and I lay in the Chamber, where the first and chief disturbance had been. We slept well all Night, but early before day in the Morning, I was awakened (and I awakened my Bed-fellow) by a great knocking just without our Chamber door. I askt who was there several times, but the knocking still continued without answer. At last I said, 'In the Name of God, who is it, and what would you have?' to which a voice answered, 'Nothing with you'. We thinking it had been some Servant of the House, went to sleep again. But speaking of it to Mr. Mompesson when we came down, he assured us, that no one of the House lay that way, or had business thereabout, and that his Servants were not up till he called them, which was after it was day.

Which they confirmed and protested that the noise was not made by them.

Mr. Mompesson had told us before, that it would be gone in the middle of the Night, and come again divers times early in the Morning about Four a Clock, and this I suppose was about that time.

Another passage was this, my Man coming up to me in the Morning, told me that one of my Horses (that on which I rode) was all in a sweat, and lookt as if he had been rid all Night. My friend and I went down, and found him so. I enquired how he had been used, and was assured that he had been well fed, and ordered as he used to be, and my Servant was one that was wont to be very careful about my Horses. The Horse I had had a good time, and never knew but that he was very sound. But after I had rid him a Mile or two, very gently over a plain Down from Mr. Mompesson's house, he fell lame, and having made a hard shift to bring me home, dyed in two or three days, no one being able to imagine what he ailed. This I confess might be accident or some unusual distemper, but all things being put together, it seems very probable that it was somewhat else.

But I go on with Mr. Mompesson's own particulars. There came one Morning a light into the Childrens Chamber, and a voice crying, 'A Witch, a Witch', for at least an hundred times together.

Mr. Mompesson at another time (being in the day) seeing some wood move that was in the Chimney of a Room, where he was, as of it self, discharged a Pistol into it, after which they found several drops of Blood on the Harth, and in divers places of the Stairs.

For two or three nights after the discharge of the Pistol, there was a calm in the House, but then it came again, applying it self to a little Child newly taken from Nurse. Which it so persecuted, that it would not let the poor Infant rest for two nights together, nor suffer a Candle in the Room, but carry them away lighted up the Chimney, or throw them under the Bed. It so scared this Child by leaping upon it, that for some hours it could not be recovered out of the fright. So that they were forced again to remove the Children out of the house. The next night after which something about Mid-night came up the Stairs, and knockt at Mr. Mompesson's door, but he lying still, it went up another pair of Stairs, to his Mans Chamber, to whom it appeared standing at his Beds foot. The exact shape and proportion he could not discover, but he saith he saw a great Body with two red and glaring Eyes, which for some time were fixed steadily upon him, and at length disappeared.

Another night strangers being present, it purr'd in the Childrens Bed like a Cat, at which time also the Cloaths and Children were lift up from the Bed, and six Men could not keep them down. Hereupon they removed the Children, intending to have ript up the Bed. But they were no sooner laid in another, but the second Bed was more troubled than the first. It continued thus four hours, and so beat the Childrens

Leggs against the Bed-posts, that they were forced to arise, and sit up all night. After this, it would empty Chamberpots into their Beds, and strew them with Ashes, though they were never so carefully watcht. It put a long piked Iron into Mr. Mompesson's Bed, and into his Mothers a naked Knife upright. It would fill Porrengers with Ashes, throw every thing about and keep a noise all day.

About the beginning of April, 1663, a Gentleman that lay in the house, had all his money turned black in his Pockets; and Mr. Mompesson coming one Morning into his Stable, found the Horse he was

'*Mr. Mompesson ... found the Horse he was wont to Ride, on the Ground, having one of his hinder Leggs in his Mouth.*'

wont to Ride, on the Ground, having one of his hinder Leggs in his Mouth, and so fastened there, that it was difficult for several Men to get it out with a Leaver. After this, there were some other remarkable things, but my account goes no further. Only Mr. Mompesson writ me word, that afterwards the House was several nights beset with seven or eight in the shape of Men, who, as soon as a. Gun was discharged, would shuffle away together into an Arbour.

The Drummer was tryed at the Assizes at Salisbury upon this occasion. He was committed first to Gloucester Gaol for stealing, and a

Wiltshire Man coming to see him, he askt what news in Wiltshire. The Visitant said, he knew of none. 'No,' saith the Drummer! 'do not you hear of the Drumming at a Gentlemans house at Tedworth?' 'That I do enough', said the other. 'I,' quoth the Drummer, 'I have plagued him (or to that purpose) and he shall never be at quiet, till he hath made me satisfaction for taking away my Drum.' Upon Information of this, the fellow was tryed for a Witch at Sarum, and all the main circumstances I have related, were sworn at the Assizes by the Minister of the Parish, and divers others of the most intelligent and substantial Inhabitants, who had been Eye and Ear witnesses of them, time after time for divers years together.

The fellow was condemned to Transportation, and accordingly sent away; but I know not how ('tis said by raising storms and affrighting the Seamen) he made a shift to come back again. And 'tis observable, that during all the time of his restraint and absence the house was quiet, but as soon as ever he came back at liberty, the disturbance returned.

He had been a Souldier under Cromwel, and used to talk much of Gallant Books he had of an odd fellow, who was counted a Wizzard. Upon this occasion, I shall here add a passage, which I had not from Mr. Mompesson, but yet relates to the main purpose.

The Gentleman, who was with me at the House, Mr. Hill, being in company with one Compton of Summersetshire, who practiseth Physick, and pretends to strange matters, related to him this story of Mr. Mompesson's disturbance. The Physician told him, he was sure it was nothing but a Rendezvous of Witches, and that for an hundred pounds, he would undertake to rid the House of all disturbance. In pursuit of this discourse, he talkt of many high things, and having drawn my friend into another Room apart from the rest of the company, said he would make him sensible he could do something more than ordinary, and askt him who he desired to see. Mr. Hill had no great confidence in his talk, but yet being earnestly prest to name some one, He said, he desired to see no one so much as his Wife, who was then many miles distant from them at her home. Upon this, Compton took up a Looking-glass that was in the Room, and setting it down again, bid my friend look in it; which he did, and there, as he most solemnly and seriously professeth, he saw the exact Image of his Wife in that habit which she then wore, and working at her Needle in such a part of the Room (there represented also) in which and about which time she really was as he found upon inquiry when he came home. The Gentleman himself averred this to me, and he is a very sober, intelligent, and credible person. Compton had no knowledge of him before, and was an utter stranger to the person of his Wife. The same Man we shall meet again in the story of the Witchcrafts of Elizabeth Style, whom he discovered to be a Witch by foretelling her coming into an house, and going out again without speaking, as is set down in the third Relation. He was by all counted a very odd person.

Thus, I have written the summ of Mr. Mompesson's disturbance, which I had partly from his own mouth related before divers, who had been witnesses of all, and confirmed his relation, and partly from his own Letters, from which the order and series of things is taken. The same particulars he writ also to Dr. Creed, then Doctor of the Chair in Oxford.[1]

Mr. Mompesson is a Gentleman, of whose truth in this account, I have not the least ground of suspicion, he being neither vain nor credulous, but a discreet, sagacious and manly person. Now the credit of matters of Fact depends much upon the Relatours, who, if they cannot be deceived themselves nor supposed any ways interested to impose upon others, ought to be credited. For upon these circumstances, all humane Faith is grounded, and matter of Fact is not capable of any proof besides, but that of immediate sensible evidence. Now this Gentleman cannot be thought ignorant, whether that he relates be true or no, the Scene of all being his own house, himself a witness and that not of a circumstance of two, but of an hundred, nor for once or twice only, but for the space of some years, during which he was a concerned, and inquisitive Observer. So that it cannot with any shew of reason be supposed that any of his Servants abused him, since in all that time he must needs have detected the deceit. And what interest could any of his family have had (if it had been possible to have managed it without discovery) to continue so long so troublesome, and so injurious an Imposture? Nor can it with any whit of more probability be imagined, that his own melancholy deluded him, since (besides that he is no crazy nor imaginative person) that humour could not have been so lasting and pertinacious. Or if it were so in him, can we think he infected his whole Family, and those multitudes of neighbours and others, who had so often been witnesses of those passages? Such supposals are wild, and not like to tempt any, but those whose Wills are their Reasons. So that upon the whole, the principal Relatour Mr. Mompesson himself knew, whether what he reports was true or not, whether those things acted in his house were contrived Cheats, or extraordinary Realities. And if so, what interest could he serve in carrying on, or conniving at a juggling Design and Imposture?

He suffered by it in his Name, in his Estate, in all his Affairs, and in the general peace of his Family. The Unbelievers in the matter of Spirits and Witches took him for an Impostour. Many others judged the permission of such an extraordinary evil to be the judgment of God upon him, for some notorious wickedness or impiety. Thus his name

---

[1] This letter, dated Decr. 6, 1663, addressed to the Rev. Dr. William Creed, Regius Professor of Divinity at Oxford, is published for the first time in the present volume. (See Appendix A.).—H.P.

was continually exposed to censure, and his estate suffered, by the concourse of people from all parts to his house, by the diversion it gave him from his affairs, by the discouragement of Servants, by reason of which he could hardly get any to live with him. To which if I add the continual hurry that his Family was in, the affrights, vexations and tossings up and down of his Children, and the watchings and disturbance of his whole house (in all which, himself must needs be the most concerned person) I say, if these things are considered, there will be little reason to think he could have any interest to put a cheat upon the World, in which he would most of all have injured and abused himself. Or if he should have designed and managed so incredible, so unprofitable a Delusion, 'tis strange that he should have troubled himself so long in such a business, only to deceive, and to be talkt of. And it is yet more so, that none of those many inquisitive persons that came thither purposely to criticize and examine the truth of those matters, could make any discoveries of the Juggling, especially since many came prejudiced against the belief of such things in general and others resolved before-hand against the belief of this, and all were permitted the utmost freedom of search and inquiry. And after things were weighed and examined, some that were before greatly prejudiced, went away fully convinced. To all which I add, that there are divers particulars in the story, in which no abuse or deceit could have been practised, as the motion of Boards and Chairs of themselves, the beating of a Drum in the midst of a Room, and in the Air, when nothing was to be seen; the great heat in a Chamber that had no Fire in excessive cold weather, the scratching and panting, the violent beating and shaking of the Bedsteads, of which there was no perceivable cause or occasion: In these and such like instances, it is not to be conceived how tricks could have been put upon so many, so jealous, and so inquisitive persons as were witnesses of them.

'Tis true that when the Gentlemen[1] the King sent were there, the House was quiet and nothing seen nor heard that night, which was confidently and with triumph urged by many, as a confutation of the story. But 'twas bad Logick to conclude in matters of Fact from a single Negative and such a one against numerous Affirmatives, and so affirm that a thing was never done, because not at such a particular time, and that no body ever saw what this Man or that did not. By the same way of reasoning, I may inferr that there were never any Robberies done on Salisbury Plain, Hounslow Heath, or the other noted places, because I have often Travelled all those ways, and yet was never Robbed; and the Spaniard inferred well that said, 'There was no Sun in England', because he had been six Weeks here and never saw it. This is the common argument of those that deny the Being of Apparitions, they have Travelled all hours of the night, and never saw any thing worse than

[1] Lord Falmouth and Lord Chesterfield.—H.P.

themselves (which may well be) and thence they conclude, that all pretended Apparitions are Fancies or Impostures. But why do not such arguers conclude, that there was never a Cut-purse in London, because they have lived there many years without being met with by any of those Practisers? Certainly he that denies Apparitions upon the confidence of this Negative against the vast heap of Positive assurances, is credulous in believing there was ever any Highway-man in the World, if he himself was never Robb'd. And the Trials of Assizes and Attestations of those that have (if he will be just) ought to move his Assent no more in this case, than in that of Witches and Apparitions, which have the very same evidence.

But as to the quiet of Mr. Mompesson's house when the Courtiers were there, it may be remembered and considered, that the disturbance was not constant, but intermitted sometimes several days, sometimes Weeks. So that the intermission at that time might be accidental, or perhaps the Dæmon was not willing to give so publick a Testimony of those Transactions, which possibly might convince those, who he had rather should continue in the unbelief of his existence. But however it were, this circumstance will afford but a very slender inference against the credit of the story, except among those who are willing to take any thing for an Argument against things which they have an interest not to acknowledge.

I have thus related the sum of the story, and noted some circumstances that assure the truth of it. I confess the passages recited are not so dreadful, Tragical and amazing, as there are some in story of this kind, yet are they never the less probable or true, for their being not so prodigious and astonishing. And they are strange enough to prove themselves effects of some invisible extraordinary Agent, and so demonstrate that there are Spirits, who sometimes sensibly intermeddle in our affairs. And I think they do it with clearness of evidence. For these things were not done long ago, or at far distance, in an ignorant age, or among a barbarous people, they were not seen by two or three only of the Melancholick and superstitious, and reported by those that made them serve the advantage and interest of a party.[1] They were not the passages of a Day or Night, nor the vanishing glances of an Apparition; but these transactions were near and late, publick, frequent, and of divers years continuance, witnessed by multitudes of competent and unbyassed Attestors, and acted in a searching incredulous Age: Arguments enough one would think to convince any modest and capable reason.

* * * *

The affair of the Drummer of Tedworth is of great importance to psychical researchers for a number of reasons: It has become a classic, and the story prompted investigators to take a keener interest in, and

[1] Was Glanvill thinking of the merry meetings at Ragley?—H.P.

to search ancient literature for, similar cases of Poltergeist activity. To use a colloquialism, it put Poltergeists on the map—though the word itself was not current in this country until many years later.

Another interesting feature is that the 'prime mover' or person alleged to be causing the trouble was not only known, but was actually arrested and charged with what amounts to witchcraft. Though perhaps the little 'modest girls' were the *point d'appui* on which the 'drummer' relied if, indeed, he had anything to do with it. Mr. Mompesson, in a letter to Collins, the publisher of *Saducismus Triumphatus*, says (August 8, 1674): 'When the Drummer was escaped from his Exile, which he was sentenced to at Gloucester for a Felony, I took him up, and procured his Committment to Salisbury Gaol, where I Indicted[1] him as a Felon, for this supposed Witchcraft about my House. The Assizes came on, where I Indicted him on the *Statute Primo Jacobi cap. 12*, Where you may find that to feed, imploy, or reward any evil spirit is Felony. And the Indictment against him was, that he did *quendam malum Spiritum negotiare*. The grand Jury found the Bill upon the Evidence, but the Petty Jury acquitted him, but not without some difficulty.'

Though acquitted of witchcraft, the Drummer was sentenced to transportation (probably as a rogue and a vagabond). He escaped (by means of magic?). The Elizabethan Act[2] (*An Acte for the Punishment of Rogues, Vagabonds, and Sturdie Beggars*) of 1597 increased the punishment for what we should now call mediumship, and the penalty was transportation on conviction. If the offender returned to this country, the penalty was death. Cromwell's Parliament of 1656 found that the Elizabethan fortune-telling Act was rarely administered, so a further Act was introduced by the Lord Protector to strengthen the statute made in the thirty-ninth year of Elizabeth. I presume that it was under this latter enactment that the Drummer was convicted.

The Drummer case created a great sensation and there were sceptics —as there are today! Mompesson himself was accused of all sorts of things, and felt constrained to send Glanvill a letter, for publication, denying that he had 'confessed' that a simple explanation of the disturbances had been discovered. I will conclude this chapter by reproducing Mr. Mompesson's disclaimer. The letter is dated November 8, 1672:

Worthy Sir,
Meeting with Dr. Pierce accidentally at Sir Robert Button's he acquainted me of something that passed between my Lord of R——— and your self about my troubles etc. To which (having but little leisure) I do give you this account, that I have been very often of late asked the

---

[1] For Mompesson's sworn deposition, see Appendix A.—H.P.

[2] I have one of the two known original copies of this Elizabethan Act. A full account of it and of the laws—ancient and modern—as applied to mediums can be found in my *Fifty Years of Psychical Research* (1939), pp. 213–34, and Appendix C.

question, whether I have not confessed to his Majesty or any other, a cheat discovered about that affair. To which I gave, and shall to my Dying day give the same answer, That I must bely my self, and perjure my self also to acknowledge a cheat in a thing where I am sure there was nor could be any, as I, the Minister of the Place, and two other Honest Gentlemen deposed at the Assizes, upon my Impleading the Drummer. If the world will not believe it, it shall be indifferent to me, praying God to keep me from the same, or the like affliction. And although I am sure this most damnable lye does pass for current amongst one sort of people in the World, invented only, I think, to suppress the Belief of the Being either of God or Devil; yet I question not but the Thing obtains credit enough amongst those, whom I principally desire should retain a more charitable Opinion of me, than to be any way a deviser of it, only to be talk't of in the World, to my own disadvantage and reproach; of which sort I reckon you one, and rest in hast,

Sir,

Your Obliged Servant,

JO. MOMPESSON.

Such is the diverting tale of the Drummer Poltergeist.[1] There can be little doubt that the story as related by Glanvill at the Ragley party was highly exaggerated. That there was a good deal of truth in it is, I think, certain, as Mompesson himself confirms many of the extraordinary incidents. (See Appendix A.) Further Poltergeist stories from Ragley will form the subject of our next chapter.

---

[1] The subsequent history of William Drury is not known. As an itinerant drummer and ne'er-do-well, he roamed the country and doubtless seldom visited his home at Uffcott, near Broad Hinton, N. Wilts. It is pretty certain that he again fell into the hands of the police and possibly a second attempt to transport him was successful.

CHAPTER VI

More Tales from Ragley

It is a fact that most psychic and spiritualist societies are run by women. Whether the gentler sex have a flair for this sort of work, or find it peculiarly congenial—spiritually or socially—I don't know. But the fact remains. And probably my remarks could be applied to those groups or 'societies' of past centuries if we had the data or records upon which to base an opinion. In the case of the Ragley group, we *can* form an opinion, and that is, that Lady Conway was the soul of the party, organiser, and prime-mover all rolled into one.

Lady Conway (we hear little of his lordship) was a very accomplished, attractive and unusual woman with a dominant personality. She was steeped in occultism, was rather credulous, deeply religious—and she finally joined the Quakers. She was a daughter of Sir Heneage Finch, Recorder of London, and her brother was Lord Finch, afterwards Earl of Nottingham. She was a pupil of Dr. Henry More, the Cambridge Platonist. She became his ardent admirer, and she and her husband were firm friends of the philosopher till his death in 1687. More spent a great deal of his time at Ragley, and amidst the woods of this lovely retreat, he wrote several of his books.

Lady Conway suffered horribly from migraine, which afflicted her to the end of her days. She kept open house for those distinguished people who were interested in the occult and she collected ghost stories.

I have already remarked that we can learn a great deal of Lady Conway and her 'psychic *salon*' from Dr. Joseph Glanvill's *Saducismus Triumphatus*. And from his own correspondence, and that of Henry More and Robert Boyle, we get a further insight into what happened at Ragley Castle in the middle of the seventeenth century. In the 'Demon of Tedworth' is told the story of the classic Wiltshire Poltergeist, related, I am sure, with much gusto by Glanvill at one of Lady Conway's house-parties. But many of the Poltergeist cases that entertained those jolly meetings were not published until Glanvill wrote them up in his various books and tracts. They are mostly contemporary. I now propose to select the best of them—especially the best-authenticated—from those that Glanvill recorded in his *Saducismus Triumphatus* (1681). Not all these 'Relations', as the philosopher terms them, were first heard at Ragley; but many of them were, and Lady Conway added others to the collection that was being formed by Glanvill who, it must be stated, usually insisted on first-hand accounts often signed by eye- and ear-witnesses. In fact, Glanvill can be regarded as the Father of Psychical

Research. In reproducing the stories, I have paraphrased Glanvill's reports and rather quaint idiom into a more modern mode of expression. I have done this in case the reader has had a surfeit of the original narrator's robust style in the adventures of the Drummer, which are so graphically described in the last chapter. Here, then, are some more tales from Ragley:

An account of a London Poltergeist was sent to Glanvill by Dr. Henry More, who received the story from the Rev. Dr. Gibbs, a Prebendary of Westminster, who had inquired into the case. The house concerned was at Bow, near Plaistow, now a London suburb, but in Glanvill's time a rural village.

An Essex gentleman riding to London had occasion to call at the house of Paul Fox, a weaver. He was told of some extraordinary happenings that were taking place. In particular, a young girl had been 'plucked by the thigh by a cold hand' as she lay in her bed, and had died shortly afterwards.

Some weeks later, on his return home, he again called at the house and was given an account of what had happened since his last visit. After the death of the girl, the disturbances in the upper portion of the house became so bad that the family were compelled to keep to the lower rooms. The phenomena consisted of 'such flinging of things up and down, of stones and bricks through the windows', all familiar Poltergeist stuff, and running true to type. The visitor was sceptical and suggested it might be the work of practical jokers. He was invited to remain and witness the wonders for himself.

Even as the traveller and the woman of the house were conversing at the front door, an upper window was flung open and a piece of an old wheel was thrown out. Then the window closed again. A moment later it was again opened and half a brick was dropped very near the sceptic in the street. However, this incident merely 'inflamed the gentleman with a more eager desire to see what the matter was, and to discover the knavery'. So, alone, he went upstairs to investigate. He found no one in the upper storey, but in the 'haunted bedroom' was a scene of indescribable disorder. Bedding, chairs, stools, candlesticks, and other odds and ends were scattered about the floor—but no one was in the room. As he was gazing at the objects around him, a 'bed-staff began to move, and turned itself round a good while together upon its toe', and then fell to the floor. The investigator at once put his foot on it, supposing that some thread or hair was attached to it. But he found nothing, nor could he find any hole or projection on the walls or ceiling that could accommodate a wire or spring by which the bed-staff was made to dance.

Suddenly another bed-staff rose from the floor of its own volition and flew at him. His scepticism now giving way to fright, he hurriedly left the room, closing the door after him. It was immediately opened by

63

something in the room, and, with a terrific clatter, the chairs, bedstaves, candlesticks, stools and whatnot chased him down the stairs, 'as if they intended to have maimed him'. But, and this is very true to Poltergeist technique, 'their motion was so moderated, that he received no harm'.

While discussing the disturbances with the family below stairs, a tobacco pipe (probably a long clay one, like a churchwarden) rose from a side table, when no one was near it, flew across the room and smashed itself against a wall.

At the time Glanvill received this report, witches and witchcraft were much in men's minds. So the Bow family roasted a bedstaff in

'In the "haunted bedroom" was a scene of incredible disorder . . .'

order, according to one of the popular tests then current, to discover the person who was 'overlooking' them. Sure enough, an old woman, a 'suspected witch', came to the house shortly afterwards. She was promptly arrested, but, says Glanvill (rather regretfully, I think) 'escaped the law'. Anyway, the disturbances increased, the trouble spreading to every room in the house. This drove the family out of the place, 'which stood empty for a long time after'.

This Bow Poltergeist case has some striking correspondences with the one at Battersea that I investigated, an account of which is included in this volume. In each case a death occurred during the disturbances; at both places the trouble started in the upper rooms, with furniture 'marching about' the house; and at both Bow and Battersea the inmates left their homes as life became intolerable within them.

The next 'Relation' that Glanvill treats us to concerns a house occupied by the sister-in-law of a Mr. Jermin, who was Rector of Bignor, Sussex. His wife's relative and her husband occupied a large house in the country and the Rector was invited to visit them. On the night of his arrival, he found the young woman distraught and miserable. Upon inquiring the cause of the trouble, he was informed that 'he would know in the morning'. *Two* maids showed him up to his room—which he thought unusual. He afterwards discovered that no servant would go into a room alone.

The Rector had an exciting night. As he lay in bed, he heard the tramping of many feet upon the leads over his head. Then he heard a sound as if a gun had been fired—'upon which followed a great silence'. Then 'they' suddenly invaded his bedroom, 'where they fell a-wrestling and tumbling each other down, and so continued a great while'. After a lull in the disturbances, there was a great buzzing noise and sounds of whispering, though he could not understand what was being said. Then a voice came from the doorway: 'Day is broke, come away!' Then the parson heard a scampering of feet up the stairs and the manifestations ceased.

In the morning his wife's relatives visited him and asked him how he had slept. 'The worst night in my life!' he replied. His sister-in-law then remarked that it was not surprising that she was miserable. She complained that her husband would not move out of the place, to which this gentleman answered that, apart from the noise, the Poltergeists never harmed them. No one was ever hit or hurt. However, Mr. Jermin appears to have been thoroughly scared because, as Glanvill informs us, 'he fell into a fever with the disturbance he experienced that endangered his life'.

The next 'Relation' that Glanvill prints concerns a haunted house at Welton, near Daventry. The story was sent to him on May 22, 1658, by a Mr. G. Clark of Loddington, Northamptonshire.

The house was occupied by a Mrs. Cowley, the grandmother; her widowed daughter, Mrs. Stiff; and the latter's two young daughters. The reader will note the recurrent 'young girls' in these Poltergeist cases.

After a good deal of witchcraft nonsense about the younger girl vomiting stones and coals ('they came to five hundred, some weighed a quarter of a pound'!) Clark heard the story from eyewitnesses of the Poltergeist activities. As so often happens in many such cases, the 'manifestations' began in the (girls'?) bedroom. Clark interviewed the family and other witnesses, and was told that the bedclothes were thrown off the bed when no one was near, and though replaced several times, they were as often removed by unseen hands—when no person was in the room.

Then a 'strike[1] of wheat' that was standing by the bed was thrown down time after time, though always replaced in a different way. Then the furniture in the room began to move of its own volition, articles being transposed 'as they could scarce stir about the room'. An eye-witness told Clark that once he laid a Bible upon the bed in order, apparently, to exorcise the entities that were causing the trouble. However, the bedclothes were again thrown off and the Bible was found hidden in another bed. When all the inmates were in the parlour, furniture from the bedroom would be transported to the hall, and their spinning wheel taken to pieces, which were thrown about. In the dairy (favourite playgrounds for Poltergeists) pans filled with milk would be carefully lifted from the table and placed on the ground—though on one occasion a 'Panchion was broken and the milk spilt'. Another mischievous trick was the hanging of a seven-pound weight on the spigot of a barrel of beer 'and the beer mingled with the sand and all spoiled'. Their stock of salt was 'mingled most perfectly with bran'. Flax contained in a box was repeatedly thrown out. Then the key of the box was turned, but immediately the spectators were not looking, the box unlocked itself and the flax jumped out. A loaf of bread tumbled off a form, 'a woman's patten[2] rose up in the house, and was thrown at them'. A comb broke itself against the window and the two pieces hurled themselves at the onlookers. 'A knife rose up in the window, and flew at a man, hitting him with the haft'. An ink-pot was thrown out of the window, followed by the stopper. Every day stones were thrown all over the house, windows were broken, and persons hit, but not hurt. 'But they were the less troubled because all this while no hurt was done to their persons'. Then wheat was showered over the assembled company, and the grandmother complained that she had lost 'half a strike of wheat' in this way. Something similar happened in the barn, where a quantity of 'fitches' (chickpeas) was scattered about. Even the baker's man did not get off scot-free. Calling at the house one day, a handful of crumbs suddenly left his basket and fell in the lap of a man who was sitting in the room.

In order to stop the annoyances, of course they had to find a 'witch'. One suspected old woman was arrested, convicted, and sent to gaol. But that did not deter the Poltergeists, because 'one night since, they heard great knockings and cruel noise, which scared them worse than all the rest, and once or twice that week the cheese was crumbled into pieces and spoiled'. That was about May 1, 1658.

Unfortunately, Glanvill does not tell us the end of the story, or

---

[1] A 'strike' is an instrument with a straight edge for levelling a measure of grain.

[2] A clog supported on an iron ring.

whether the Poltergeists grew tired of their tricks and sought fresh fields for their pranks, which, as is invariably emphasised in nearly every case of this sort, hurt the onlookers' feelings much more than their persons.

Glanvill's next case is an important one, and if only a tenth part of it is true, is valuable because of the evidence it supplies for the existence of what we now call Poltergeists and the phenomena we associate with them. The case is well-authenticated, and was recorded by James Sherring immediately after the disturbances. Sherring (who appears to have been an intelligent man) witnessed some of the phenomena, and received first-hand accounts of other strange occurrences. His evidence was taken down on June 23, 1677.

The site of the haunting was 'old Gast's house' at Little Burton, Somerset, and not far from Glanvill's own home at Bath. Glanvill, therefore, must have been cognisant of the manifestations at the time of, or shortly after their occurrence. At least, he would have been on the spot to check the evidence.

Because Sherring's account (which is partly in the first person and partly in the third) is so very much to the point, is so clear and concise, and withal so convincing, I will reproduce it, *literatim et seriatim*, from Glanvill's collection:

JAMES SHERRING'S REPORT ON THE BURTON POLTERGEIST

The first night that I was there with Hugh Mellmore and Edward Smith, they heard as it were the washing in water over their heads. Then taking a Candle and going up the stairs, there was a wet Cloth thrown at them, but it fell on the stairs. They, going up farther then, there was another thrown as before. And when they came up into the Chamber there stood a bowl of water, some of it sprinkled over, and the water looked white as if there had been sope used in it. The Bowl just before was in the Kitchin, and could not be carried up but through the room where they were. The next thing that they heard the same Night was a terrible noise as if it had been a slat of Thunder, and shortly after they heard great scratching about the Bedsted, and after that a great knocking with a Hammer against the Beds-head, so that the two maids that were in the Bed cried out for help. Then they ran up the stairs and there lay the Hammer on the Bed and on the Beds-head, there were near a thousand prints of the Hammer which the violent strokes had made. The Maids said that they were scratched and pinched with a hand that was put into the Bed which had exceeding long Nails. They said that the Hammer was locked fast up in the Cupboard when they went to Bed. This was that which was done the first Night, with many other things of the like nature.

The second Night that James Sherring and Tho. Hillary were there, James Sherring sat down in the Chimney to fill a Pipe of Tobacco. He made use of the fire-tongs to take up a Coal to fire his Pipe, and by and by the Tongs were drawn up the stairs, and after they were up in the Chamber, they were played withall as many times Men do, and then thrown down upon the Bed. Although the Tongs were so near him, he never perceived the going of them away. The same Night one of the Maids left her shoos by the fire, and they were carried up into the Chamber, and the Old Mans brought down and set in their places. The same Night there was a Knife carried up into the Chamber, and it did scratch and scrape the Beds-head all the Night, but when they went up into the Chamber the Knife was thrown into the Loft. As they were going up the stairs there were things thrown at them, which were just before in the low room, and when they went down the stairs the Old Mans Breeches were thrown down after them. These were the most remarkable things done that Night, onley there was continual knocking and pinching the Maids, which was usually done every Night.

The third Night, when James Sherring and Thomas Hillary were there, as soon as the people were gone to bed, their Clothes were taken and thrown at the Candle and put it out, and immediately after they cried out with a very hideous cry and said they should be all choaked if they were not presently helped. Then they ran up the stairs and there was abundance of Feathers plucked out of the Bolster that lay under their heads, and some thrust into their mouths that they were almost choaked. The Feathers were thrown all about the Bed and room. They were plucked out at a hole no bigger than the top of ones little finger. Some time after they were vexed with a very hideous knocking at their heads as they lay on the Bed. Then James Sherring and Thomas Hillary took the Candle and went upstairs and stood at the Beds feet, and the knocking continued. Then they saw a Hand with an Arm-wrist hold the Hammer which kept on knocking against the Bedsted. Then James Sherring going towards the Beds-head, the Hand and Hammer fell down behind the Bolster and could not be found. For they turned up the Bed-clothes to search for the Hammer. But as soon as they went down the stairs the Hammer was thrown out into the middle of the Chamber. These were the most remarkable things that were done that Night.

The fourth and fifth Nights, there was but little done more than knocking and scratching as was usually.

The sixth and seventh Nights, there was nothing at all, but as quiet as at other houses. These were all the Nights that they were there.

The things that do follow are what James Sherring heard the people of the house report.

There was a Saddle in the house of their Uncle Warrens of Leigh (which it should seem they detained wrongfully from the right owner) that as it did hang upon a Pin in the entry would come off and come into the house, and as they termed it, hop about the house from one place to another, and upon the Table, and so to another, which stood on the other side of the house. Jane Gast and her kinswoman took this

Saddle and carried it to Leigh, and as they were going along the broad
Common, there would be sticks and stones thrown at them, which
made them very much afraid, and going near together their Whittles[1]
which were on their shoulders were knit together. They carried the
Saddle to the house which was Old Warrens, and there left it and returned home very quiet. But being gone to Bed at Night the Saddle was
brought back from Leigh (which is a Mile and half at the least from
Old Gasts House) and thrown upon the Bed where the Maids lay.
After that, the Saddle was very troublesome to them, until they broke
it in small pieces and threw it out into the Highway.

There was a Coat of the same Parties, who was owner of the Saddle,
which did hang on the Door in the Hall, and it came off from the place
and flew into the fire and lay there some considerable time, before they
could get it out. For it was as much as three of them could do to pluck
it out of the fire, because of the ponderous weight that lay on it, as they
thought. Nevertheless there was no impression on it of the fire.

Old Gast sat at Dinner with a Hat of this Old Warrens on his Head,
and there was something came and struck it off into the Dish where his
Meat was.

There was a Pole which stood in the back-side about Fourteen or
Fifteen Foot in length, which was brought into the House, and carried
up into the Chamber and thrown on the Bed, but all the Wit they had
could not get it out of the Chamber, because of its length, until they
took down a light of the Window. They report that the things in the
House was thrown about and broken, to their great dammage.

One Night there were two of this Old Gast his Grand daughters in
Bed together, they were aged, One of them about Twelve or Thirteen
years, and the other about Sixteen or Seventeen. They said, that they
felt a Hand in Bed with them, which they bound up in the Sheet, and
took Bed-staves and beat it until it were as soft as Wool, then they took
a Stone which lay in the Chamber, about a quarter of a Hundred
weight, and put on it, and were quiet all the Night. In the Morning,
they found it as they left it the Night before. Then the eldest of the
Maids sware that she would burn the Devil, and goes and fetches a
Fuz[2] Faggot to burn it, but when she came again, the Stone was thrown
away, and the Cloth was found wet.

There were many other things which is too long and tedious to write,
it would take up a great deal of time.

This which follows is the Relation of Jone Winsor of long Burton,
she being there three Nights, taken the Third day of July, 1677.

She heard or saw nothing as long as the Candle did burn, but as
soon as it was out, there was something which did seem to fall down by
the Bed-side, and by and by it began to lay on the Beds-head with a
Staffe, and did strike Jone Winsor on the Head. She put forth her

---

[1] Blankets.—H.P.   [2] A kind of fungus; a puff-ball.—H.P.

Hand and caught it, but was not able to hold it fast. She got out of the Bed to light a Candle, and there was a great Stone thrown after her, but it missed her. When the Candle was lighted, they arose and went down to the Fire, and there lay a heap of Stones on the Bed whereon they lay just before. As soon as the Bed was made, and they laid down to take their rest, there was a scratching on the Form that stood by them in an extream manner. Then it came and did heave up the Bolster whereon they laid their heads, and did endeavour to throw them out. At last, it got hold on one end of the Pillow, and set it quite on end, and there it stood for some considerable time, at last falling down in its place, and they fell asleep, and so continued all that Night.

The Staff that was spoken of before was Jone Winsors, and she says, she left it below in the Kitchin. She says, that which troubled, did endeavour to kill the people, if it had power. She put them to it, to know the reason why they were troubled, and they said they knew nothing, unless it was about the business of Old Warren. She was there Three Nights, and the trouble was much after the same manner, nothing that was more remarkable.

That is the truth of what I heard them speak from their own Mouths, and they will attest it if called thereunto.

*   *   *   *

My last extract from *Saducismus Triumphatus* was not found among Glanvill's papers, but was an editorial addition to the work. The story is so much in keeping with the rest of the 'Relations', that Glanvill's editor makes no apology for including it. And neither do I.

The case was reported by a Mr. Andrew Paschal, 'formerly a Fellow of Queen's College, Cambridge', and relates to three nights' disturbances at his father's house in Soper Lane,[1] London, in August, 1661. He says:

During the first night's disturbance there were present my father and mother, my eldest brother, one of my sisters, with a young maiden gentlewoman, her bed-fellow (who seemed to be principally concerned), besides a maid that lay in the same chamber.

The gentlewoman before mentioned, being in bed with my sister in a chamber within that where my father and mother lay (the maid lying in another bed alone) there seemed to her then lying awake, to be one walking in the chamber, by a noise made as of a long gown or some trailing garment brushing and sweeping up and down the room.

By and by there was a noise of clattering their shoes under the bed, with a scratching and tugging of the mat under the bed likewise. This continued for some time, and my sister being awakened, heard it. So did the maid. After this, my mother, being called out of the next chamber where she was up (to prepare a chemical water which required

---

[1] Soper Lane, now Queen St., was in Cheapside. Many of its residents were wealthy merchants who dealt in drugs and spices.—H.P.

their being up all night[1]) came in, they being in a great fright. My brother went up also, he not having gone to bed, had sat up below. A candle was brought, and the noise ceased while they were in the chamber. Presently, after they were gone out again, and the light removed, the chamber door (which shuts with difficulty) flew to with a great bounce, it being wide open before. It shook the room where my mother was busied about the aforesaid preparation. After this, one of the shoes that was by the bedside, was flung over the bed with a mighty force against a press that stood on the other side. This put them to such a fright again that the gentlewoman rose. My brother went into the room again and sat up with them all night.

The above I received from my brother, who came to bed to me (who by reason of some illness had gone to bed first in the family) early the next morning. I was confirmed in it afterwards by my mother, upon whose bare assertion I dare confidently believe anything that shall be related.

The Second Night's Disturbance

The next evening as we sat at supper, we all heard a great noise above in the chamber, at the end of the house, as it were flinging of chairs and stools about the room or removing of great trunks. And going up to see, all was still till we came down again. However, the gentlewoman resolved to go to bed again that night in the same chamber. My sister went to bed with her, and the rest to their lodgings. Only my brother and I resolved to sit up some time and expect the event. Within a while after, we heard them knock earnestly above. We went both up and they told us there had been the same disturbance as the night before and something more. For besides the tugging of the mat under the bed, the bedclothes upon them were often tugged and pulled; insomuch as they were fain to hold them hard with their hands to keep them from being pulled off. All was quiet for a little time while we were in the chamber with a light, but we were no sooner out of the chamber with the candle, but the noise under the bed, the tugging of the mat, and the pulling of the bedclothes, began again. Moreover, something came into the bed, which the gentlewoman said ran up on her by degrees, and seemed little and soft like a mole. Upon this she shrieked out, and we came in again with the candle, when all was still again.

We retired often with the candle, and presently the same disturbance returned, together with a low whispering noise in many places about the bed, but chiefly towards the bed's-head which we all heard, staying in the chamber, and removing the candle into the next room. My father and mother rose, and there was none of us but heard all, or most part of this, but nothing appeared to us. The thing was continually moving and stirring in some part or other of the bed, and most commonly at

[1] Apparently Paschal *père* was a druggist, in that street of druggists.—H.P.

the feet, where it usually came up first. At last 'it came to that boldness that it would make the same disturbance while the candle was in the chamber, if but a little shaded behind the door, so that we could sometimes see the clothes pulled and tugged. And we frequently saw it heave and lift up the clothes upon the bed towards the feet, in a little hill or rising which my brother and I often clapped our hands on, perceiving it to move, and withall to make a little clacking noise, which cannot any more than the former whispering be expressed in writing. We could not perceive anything more than the clothes, as often as we saw them so moved and heaved up.

The shoes were laid up upon the bed's tester,[1] the second night, to prevent the clattering which was made with them the night before. And whilst we were standing talking in the chamber, as I was some distance from the bed, one of the shoes flew off and hit me lightly on the head, my hat being on. And another came presently tumbling down after it, none stirring the bed. Afterwards, the aforesaid little thing came upon the gentlewoman so frequently, that if we were the least removed, she could not lie quietly in her bed. Then she sat up in her bed with a mantle about her, which, when we were retired, was pulled at as if it would have been plucked from her. Whereupon she cried out again and I came into the chamber again, and was asked to hold fast upon the mantle about her, which notwithstanding upon removal of the candle, was tugged hard again, which I very sensibly perceived. Whereupon, we perceiving no cessation, my brother and I continued in the chamber all that night till break of day, with a candle in the room. The tugging of the mat under the bed, the heaving of the clothes about the feet, and the other whispering noise continued by fits, till light appeared. There was scarcely any of us, especially she herself, who did not conjure that whisperer by the most sacred names to speak out and tell us its intent. But nothing was to be seen, nor any answer made.

THE THIRD NIGHT'S DISTURBANCE

The gentlewoman resolved now to change her chamber, to try if the disturbance would follow. She did so, my sister still accompanying her. My brother and I sat up as before below stairs, expecting again what would follow. The same noise was heard this third night, as the night before, above in the chamber. We had not sat long below before we were summoned up with loud knockings again. They were in the same case as before, if not worse. A while after they were in bed in this other chamber, there was a clattering heard at the door; later, the same noise under the bed; the same heaving of the clothes, and the same whispering as before. But towards midnight, that thing which came into the bed before, came now so often with such ungrateful skippings up and down upon her that she often shrieked and cried out. It seemed cold and

---

[1] The top covering of a bed.—H.P.

Ragley Hall, Warwickshire, where Dr. Joseph Glanvill related his psychic adventures.

very smooth as she related, and would commonly come in at her feet, and run all up on her by her side to her shoulder. Once she desired me to clap my hand upon her back near her shoulder blade, as feeling it just then come up thither. I did so on a sudden, and there seemed a cold blast or puff of wind blow upon my hand just as I clapped it on her. And one thing more remarkable was this; when the whispering was heard at her bed's-head, after we had many times in vain conjured it to speak and tell us the intent of its whisperings and disturbance, I spoke to it very earnestly to speak out or whisper louder. Thereupon it hissed out much louder than before, but nothing intelligible to be heard. At last this disturbance with the thing in the bed being no longer tolerable to the gentlewoman, my mother rose (lying in the next chamber and hearing their perplexity) came into her chamber and prayed some time at her bedside just by her. Whereupon it pleased God within a very short time after to remove all those noises and that which disturbed her. After that night, I cannot tell certainly that there hath been anything of that nature heard in the house.

*   *   *   *

This case is strangely reminiscent of the unconvincing 'talking mongoose' that I investigated, with negative results, in the Isle of Man in 1935. There, too, was a young girl, Voirrey, who, with her parents, were alleged to have conversed *for years* with a little animal, 'like a ferret', but which called itself a mongoose, and who said its name was Gef.

In the seventeenth-century witchcraft trials, it often emerged that some poor old hag had a 'familiar' in the shape of a small animal (in one case the familiar was called Jeff), and in the Epworth Poltergeist case, the Wesley children called the 'little badger or cat' that was alleged to haunt the Parsonage, 'old Jeff'. In the Willington Mill haunting, one of the 'entities' was known as 'old Jeffrey'. 'Jeff ' and its variants are, apparently, popular nicknames for Poltergeists.

The reader's attention will not need to be drawn to the fact that in the Soper Lane manifestations, as in so many similar Poltergeist disturbances, a young girl was the *nexus*, or centre of attraction, or focus of the phenomena, real or alleged. And I think the 'young maiden gentlewoman' showed amazing fortitude in remaining in the Poltergeist-infested bed while the onlookers were calmly observing her reactions to the convolutions and the 'ungrateful skippings' of the peregrinating 'mole'. No wonder she shrieked! A normal girl would have been out of that bed in two seconds. And her bedfellow appears to have slept right through it all. Brave girl!

And the setting[1] of the Soper Lane séances is not new to those who study such things: the bedroom; the young girl in bed; the overcurious

---

[1] Compare Goldsmith's account of the bedroom séance in the Cock Lane affair, p. 125.

audience; the scratchings and draggings; the heaving and volatile bedclothes, is a *mise-en-scène* so *very* familiar in scores of houses where Poltergeist phenomena occur—or, shall I say, are said to occur?

I have not nearly exhausted Glanvill's stock of Poltergeist cases, but I have chosen some of the best of them—stories that, doubtless, were the subjects of much speculation and philosophical discussion between the contemplative Cambridge Platonist and his devoted friend and ex-pupil, Lady Conway, during their many strolls together through the lovely woods that surround Ragley Castle.

CHAPTER VII

The Ringcroft Poltergeist

I remarked in the last chapter that the Rev. Joseph Glanvill, F.R.S., could justly be regarded as the Father of Psychical Research in this country. The publication of his various tracts and works, especially *Saducismus Triumphatus* (1681) had a profound effect upon that section of the public interested in paranormal happenings. Especially, Glanvill's book stimulated those persons, fortunate enough to possess a 'ghost', to investigate the affair in a proper manner, to record the case systematically, and to have the phenomena attested by responsible witnesses.

There can be little doubt that Mr. Alexander Telfair, when he wrote up the amazing Poltergeist disturbances at Ringcroft in 1695, had Glanvill's book—and his methods—in mind. Even the title of this very rare tract, which I added to my collection some years ago, is suggestive of Glanvill's famous work: *A New Confutation of Sadducism. Being a true Narrative of the wonderful Expressions and Actions of a Spirit which infested the House of Andrew Mackie of Ringcroft in the County of Galloway in Scotland, from February to May 1695. Containing, amongst other things, Predictions as to future Times, in a Letter writ with Blood and dropt by the said Spirit. Writ by Mr. Alexander Telfair, Minister of the Parish; and attested by many other Ministers and Persons of Credit, whose Attestation and Names are subjoined.* London, Printed for Andrew Bell, at the Sign of the Cross-Keys in the Poultrey, 1696.

The chief fault of most ancient accounts of alleged abnormal happenings is that they are not well authenticated. The books or tracts containing these 'magic' memorials of a bygone age are valuable to a bibliophile, but are of little more than academic interest to the modern student of psychic phenomena. It is all the more refreshing, then, to find a book containing a summary of remarkable happenings that are thoroughly attested by a number of responsible persons. Moreover (and this fact is of extreme importance), each incident of the Ringcroft narrative is individually vouched for by the person or persons who witnessed the occurrence. This tract of nineteen quarto pages was written by the minister of the parish in which the manifestations took place, and the report is signed by the ministers of five neighbouring parishes; by the lairds of Colline and Milhouse; and by several other persons of repute, all of whom were eye-witnesses of the phenomena.

The disturbances—of true Poltergeist nature—took place in the household of Andrew Mackie of Ringcroft. As usual in such cases, there were a number of young children in the family, but all were under

75

observation when the major phenomena occurred. It is amusing to note that immediately the manifestations became known, a rumour was circulated to the effect that Mackie, a mason by trade, 'devoted his first child to the Devil, at his taking of the Mason-word,' i.e. upon his admission into the ranks of a society formed by Scottish working masons.

I will now give a few extracts from *A New Confutation*, describing the more interesting phenomena. It is stated that for some years previously, Mackie's house had a reputation for being haunted. But nothing unusual occurred until February, 1695, when Mackie discovered that, during the night, all his cattle had escaped from their sheds, and that their tethering ropes had been broken. The next night the same thing happened, and one of the beasts was found tied to a high beam in a shed, so that its feet barely touched the ground.

'Some nights after, a great quantity of Peat was brought into the middle of the House and set on fire, when all the family was asleep, and if the smoke had not awak'd them, they had certainly been consum'd in the Flames; but they extinguished the Fire, and though they made a narrow search, could neither hear nor see any Agent.'

On March 7, 1695, stones were thrown all over the house, and this phase lasted for several days. But no stones were then thrown on a Sunday. They were thrown night and day, but mostly during the night. An intensive search failed to solve the mystery.

'On Saturday, the Family being all without-doors, the Children coming in saw something like a Person sitting by the Fire, with a Blanket about it; which frightened all of them but the youngest, who being about Ten Years of Age, chid the rest for being afraid, telling them, that if they bless'd themselves they needed not fear; and perceiving the Blanket to be his own, blesses himself, and saying, Be what it will it hath nothing to do with my Blanket, he runs and pulls the Blanket away, but found nothing under it save a four footed stool turn'd up side down.'

On March 11, 1695, a number of pot-hooks and a hanger disappeared from the chimney corner and were found four days later in a 'cockloft'[1] which previously had been thoroughly searched. Attested by Charles Macklellan, laird of Colline and another witness.

'When it threw Stones at any Person, it was observed that they had not half their natural Weight: It threw them more frequently on the Sabbath than on other days, and more then too when any Body was at Prayer, and mostly at the Person praying.'

On the same Sunday, March 11, Telfair visited Mackie's home, 'and while I was at Prayer, it threw several small stones at me which did me no hurt.'

For a week, there were no phenomena and the Mackie family thought

[1] i.e., a garret.

the *Geist* had gone. But it returned, more violent than ever, on Sunday, March 18: 'It began to throw stones as before, but more frequently and of greater weight, so they hurt more when they hit'[1] than those it threw formerly; And thus it continued to the 21st, when I went again to the House, where it molested me mightily, threw stones and divers other things at me, and beat me several times on the Shoulders and Sides with a great Staff, so that those who were present heard the noise of the Blows. That same night it pull'd me off the side of a Bed, knock'd upon the Chests and Boards, as People do at a Door, And as I was at Prayer, leaning on the side of a bed, I felt something thrusting my Arm up, and casting my eyes thitherward perceived a little white Hand and an Arm, from the Elbow down, but it vanished presently.' Attested by three witnesses, including the laird of Colline.

The Poltergeist became more violent: on March 22 it beat the family 'with stones and staves', and drove some of them out of the house. Mackie, the head of the household, was wounded on the forehead, pushed by the shoulders several times, had his hair pulled, 'and he felt something like the Nails of one's Fingers scratch the Skin of his Head. And sometimes it would drag People about the House by their Clothes.'

The local miller 'was caught so fast by the side, that he cried out to his Neighbours for help, saying it would tear one of his Sides from him. That same Night it uncovered the Children as sleeping in Bed, and beat them on the Hips, the Noise whereof was distinctly heard by People in the House, as if it had been done by a Man's hand, yet nothing could be seen doing it.' During the 'spanking' of the children, various objects moved about the house of their own volition. Attested by many witnesses.

During family prayers[2] the spirit repeatedly cried, 'hush! hush!' at the close of every sentence and the dog, upon hearing the unfamiliar voice, would run to the door and bark. At other times during prayer the entity would whistle and groan. Several times the house was ignited; lumps of burning peat were thrown at the family during prayers; a 'sheep-house' was burnt to the ground; bundles of burning straw were found in the yard; 'fire-balls fell in and about the House, but the Fire

---

[1] A remarkable case of stone-throwing was recorded in *The Times* for April 27, 1872: 'From 4 o'clock, Thursday afternoon, until 11.30 in the evening, the houses, 56 and 58 Reverdy Road, Bermondsey, were assailed with stones and other missiles coming from an unseen quarter. Two children were injured, every window broken, and several articles of furniture were destroyed. Although there was a strong body of policemen scattered in the neighbourhood, they could not trace the direction whence the stones were thrown.' *The Times* (Sept. 16, 1841) also records that 'in the home of Mrs. Charton, at Sutton Courthouse, Sutton Lane, Chiswick, windows had been broken "by some unseen agent". Every attempt to detect the perpetrator failed. The mansion was detached and surrounded by high walls. No other building was near it. The police were called. Two constables, assisted by members of the household, guarded the house, but the windows continued to be broken "both in front and behind the house." '—H.P.

[2] This disturbance at prayers is paralleled in the Wesley case, p. 95.

vanished as it fell: It threw likewise an hot stone into the Bed between the Children, which burnt through the Bed-clothes.' Nearly two hours later, we are told, the stone was still too hot to hold in the hand.

'April the 7th, being Sabbath-day, it began again to throw Stones, and wounded William Mackminn a Blacksmith on the Head; it did also throw a Plow-share at him, and a Trough of above three stone Weight, which fell on his back, and yet did not hurt him.' That same night the house was set on fire twice and an 'extraordinary Light', seen outside the building, entered the house with one of the Mackie family.

On April 8, the local magistrate ordered that the laird of Colline should examine every person then alive who had ever lived in the house, built some twenty-eight years previously. The immediate cause of the inquiry was the finding of some human bones buried just outside the house. It was thought that a murder had been committed in the house and the body buried outside, the uneasy spirit of the victim being the cause of all the trouble. So they applied the test, so often mentioned in witchcraft trials, of making the tenants and ex-tenants of the haunted house 'touch' the bones. 'But no discovery was thereby made', says Telfair.

The next day five of the local Ministers formed themselves into an 'exorcising' committee in an attempt to lay the ghost. But, says Telfair, 'I no sooner began to open my Mouth, but it threw Stones at me, and all the rest that were in the House, but always most at him who was at Prayer. It did frequently make the whole House to shake, broke an Hole through the Roof, etc. and threw in great Stones, one of which being above a Quarter weight, fell upon Mr. James Monteith's Back, without doing him any Hurt'.

Some of the witnesses, including our author Telfair, the local minister, were levitated by something that gripped their legs or feet. Five ministers attested to that phenomenon.

During the whole of the month of April, the *Geist* threw stones, burnt outbuildings, set fire to furniture, disturbed the Mackie family at their prayers, pulled a child out of bed, hurled sieves, spades and other objects about the house, whistled and groaned, tied sheep together by their necks, cried out during prayers the words, '*Bo, Bo, Kick, Cuck*', at the same time 'pulling the Men backward and forward, and hoisting them up from their knees'; threw mud in the faces of those at prayer, etc. etc.

On April 26, after the usual stone-throwing and knocks, the *Geist* began to speak, 'and call those who were then in the House, *Witches* and *Rooks*, saying, *it would take them to Hell*'. It concluded with the words: 'Thou shalt be troubled till Tuesday.'

'On the 27th it set the House on fire seven times; and on the 28th, which was Sabbath-day, it continued setting fire to the House, from Sun-rising to Sun-setting; and as it was quenched in one part, it was instantly set on fire in another; and when it could not get its Design of burning the House accomplished, it pull'd down one end of it in the Evening, so that the People could not stay in it any longer, but went and kindled their Fire in the stable'.

Many fires were put out during the next day, Monday, and as soon as one was extinguished, another would flare up in some other part of the house.

'On Tuesday night, being the third [*sic*, i.e. 30th] of April, Charles Macklellan of Colline, with several Neighbours, being in the Barn at

'*He observed a black thing in the Corner of the Barn . . . .*'

Prayers, he observed a black thing in the corner of the same, which increased gradually as if it would have fill'd the whole House; he could not discern any distinct Form it had, but only that it resembled a black Cloud: it was very frightening to them all, and threw Barley-Chaff and Mud in their Faces. It did also gripe some of them by the Middle Arms, and other Parts, so hard, that for five days after they thought they felt those Gripes.'

Next day, May 1, 1695, the Poltergeist disappeared—for ever. Its last act was that 'it fired a little Sheep-house, which was intirely consumed, but the Sheep were got out safe, and since that time it never gave any farther trouble to Ringcroft.' At least, not up to the time of the printing of Telfair's tract, which was nearly twelve months later.

The tract concludes: 'The Particulars of this Relation are severally attested by those who were Witnesses to the respective Parts of it, *viz.*

> 'Mr. Andrew Æwart, *Minister of Kells*.
> 'Mr. James Monteith, *Minister of Borg*.
> 'Mr. John Murdo, *Minister of Carsmichael*.
> 'Mr. Samuel Spalding, *Minister of Partan*.
> 'Mr. William Falconer, *Minister of Kelton*.
> 'Charles Macklellan, *Laird of Colline*.
> 'William Lennox, *Laird of Milhouse*.
> 'Andrew Tait of Torr.
> 'John Tait of Torr.
> 'John Cairns of Hardhills.
> 'William Mackminn.
> 'Andrew Palin, etc.'

Is it conceivable that all the above-named witnesses, together with Andrew Telfair, the minister of the parish, and Andrew Mackie, the chief victim of the infestation, would conspire together to concoct this amazing story? I think not. And not all the witnesses could have been mistaken. I consider that the evidence for this case is extremely good. Probably Frank Podmore thought so too, as he does not mention it in his very critical *Modern Spiritualism*.

I reiterate that the chief value of the above report lies in the fact that it has been carefully drawn up and attested by a number of educated persons of repute, and that each manifestation is witnessed (sometimes by many observers) separately. This procedure is not common today; that such a document should have been published nearly 250 years ago is, I think, truly remarkable.

CHAPTER VIII

The Wesley Poltergeist

If the Rev. Samuel Wesley (1662–1735) had not happened to produce at least one famous son, it is extremely problematical whether the world would ever have heard of the Epworth Poltergeist. As it is, this case has become a classic—perhaps *the* classic of the early cases—amongst the best-authenticated ghost stories.

The available evidence for the haunting (that occurred during December and January, 1716–17) is based principally on the series of letters that Samuel (1690–1739), the Rector of Epworth's eldest son, received in London from his mother and other members of the family during the period of the 'visitation'. The Wesleys then occupied the Parsonage at Epworth, Lincolnshire, where the great preacher, John Wesley (1703–91), was born.[1] He, too, in 1726, received further accounts about the case, after inquiring into the matter in 1720.

The Rev. Samuel Wesley, the father, also wrote out an account of the haunting. This was transcribed by Samuel, the son, in 1730, from a copy made by John Wesley four years earlier. Finally, John Wesley later epitomised the whole story and published it in the *Arminian Magazine* for October, November, and December, 1784.[2]

It is to Dr. Joseph Priestley, F.R.S., that we are indebted for the publication[3] of the various accounts of the haunting received by young Samuel while he was at Westminster. They are included in Priestley's *Original Letters by the Rev. John Wesley*, the first[4] edition of which I have used for this chapter.

Priestley himself has some pertinent things to say about the letters, their writers, and the 'ghost', and I cannot do better than reproduce his remarks, which are contained in the Preface[5] to the *Letters*:

'To the letters which illustrate the early history of Mr. Wesley, I have subjoined (as part of the papers delivered to me by Mr. Badcock, in the handwriting of Mr. Samuel Wesley, and as being amusing in their way)

---

[1] John was the first child born to Mrs. Wesley when her husband returned to her after an estrangement—that lasted many months—due to political differences. John was aged thirteen and a half years when the disturbances began.

[2] John Wesley founded the *Arminian Magazine* in January, 1778. It was the earliest religious journal in these isles.

[3] In the year of John Wesley's death.

[4] *Original Letters by the Rev. John Wesley and his Friends, Illustrating His Early History, with other curious Papers, Communicated by the late Rev. S. Badcock*, Birmingham, 1791, pp. 118–166.

[5] pp. XI–XV.

an account of some strange noises, etc., which were never clearly accounted for, in the house of old Mr. Wesley. It consists of extracts from the old gentleman's journal, and various letters, written by several persons in the family at the time, some of them exceedingly lively and entertaining; so that this is perhaps the best authenticated, and the best told story of the kind, that is anywhere extant; on which account, and to exercise the ingenuity of some speculative persons, it seemed to me and others, not undeserving of being published.

'Mr. John Wesley . . . had no doubt of the noises being supernatural, and seems inclined to ascribe them to the judgment of God upon his father, for not observing a rash and ridiculous vow, made thirteen years before this event, in consequence of his wife's[1] refusing to say "Amen" to the prayers for King William, as believing him to be nothing more than the Prince of Orange, and no lawful King of England. It is amusing to observe, in how very weak a manner men of unquestionable good sense can sometimes reason.

'In favour of this story, it may be said, that all parties seem to have been sufficiently void of fear, and also free from credulity, except the general belief that such things were supernatural. But with respect to everything of this nature, it is to be observed, that, though the narratives of the most honest witnesses imply something supernatural, we are not to conclude that the facts cannot be accounted for in a natural way. Because the observers, being particularly struck with what appears most extraordinary, are apt to overlook the most important circumstances, the connection of which with the principal appearances they were not aware of. If any person, not in the secret, were to relate what he himself saw done by Breslau[2] and others, who amuse the world with tricks of legerdemain, he would tell the story in such a manner as to imply a real miracle, merely in consequence of his not having seen, or not having attended to, some particulars in the exhibition, which might either have served to explain the whole, or have sufficiently shewn that, extraordinary as it appeared, it *might*, at least, have been produced in a natural way.'

Priestley goes on to suggest that 'what appears most probable at this distance of time[3] in the present case, is that it was a trick of the servants, assisted by some of their neighbours, and that nothing was meant by it, besides puzzling the family, and amusing themselves'. Actually, there is not a shred of evidence to suggest that the servants played any part in the disturbances—in fact, if we are to believe the evidence, as supplied by the family's letters, it was quite impossible that the servants could have played a practical joke without the Wesleys immediately

---

[1] Mrs. Samuel Wesley was a violent Jacobite.—H.P.

[2] Philip Breslau, a famous British conjurer who flourished at the end of the eighteenth century. I have several of his books.—H.P.

[3] Priestley was writing more than seventy years after the disturbances.—H.P.

becoming aware of the deception. However, here is the complete correspondence, and other evidence, and the reader shall judge for himself:

LETTER I—TO MR. SAMUEL WESLEY, FROM HIS MOTHER

January 12, 1716–7.

Dear Sam,

This evening we were agreeably surprised with your pacquet, which brought the welcome news of your being alive, after we had been in the greatest panic imaginable, almost a month, thinking either you was dead, or one of your brothers by some misfortune been killed.

The reason of our fears, is as follows. On the First of December, our maid heard, at the door of the dining-room several dismal groans, like a person in extremes, at the point of death. We gave little heed to her relation, and endeavoured to laugh her out of her fears. Some nights (two or three) after, several of the family heard a strange knocking in divers places, usually three or four knocks at a time, and then stayed a little. This continued every time for a fortnight; sometimes it was in the garret, but most commonly in the nursery, or green chamber. We all heard it but your father, and I was not willing he should be informed of it, lest he should fancy it was against his own death, which, indeed, we all apprehended. But when it began to be so troublesome, both day and night, that few or none of the family durst be alone, I resolved to tell him of it, being minded he should speak to it. At first he would not believe but somebody did it to alarm us; but the night after, as soon as he was in bed, it knocked loudly nine times, just by his bedside. He rose, and went to see if he could find out what it was, but could see nothing. Afterwards he heard it as the rest.

One night it made such a noise in the room over our heads, as if several people were walking, then run up and down stairs, and was so outrageous that we thought the children would be frighted, so your father and I rose, and went down in the dark to light a candle. Just as we came to the bottom of the broad stairs, having hold of each other, on my side there seemed as if somebody had emptied a bag of money at my feet; and on his, as if all the bottles under the stairs (which were many) had been dashed to a thousand pieces. We passed through the hall into the kitchen, and got a candle, and went to see the children, whom we found asleep.

The next night your father would get Mr. Hoole[1] to lie in our house, and we all sat together till one or two o'clock in the morning, and heard the knocking as usual. Sometimes it would make a noise like the winding up of a jack, at other times, as that night Mr. Hoole was with us, like a carpenter plaining deals; but most commonly it knocked thrice and stopped, and then thrice again, and so many hours together.

[1] Rector of Haxey, a nearby village.—H.P.

We persuaded your father to speak, and try if any voice would be heard. One night about six o'clock he went into the nursery in the dark, and at first heard several deep groans, then knocking. He adjured it to speak if it had power, and tell him why it troubled his house, but no voice was heard, but it knocked thrice aloud. Then he questioned it if it were Sammy, and bid it, if it were, and could not speak, knock again, but it knocked no more that night, which made us hope it was not against your death.

Thus it continued till the 28th December, when it loudly knocked (as your father used to do at the gate) in the nursery, and departed. We have various conjectures what this may mean. For my own part, I fear nothing now you are safe at London hitherto, and I hope God will still preserve you. Though some times I am inclined to think my brother is dead. Let me know your thoughts on it.

S. W.

Letter II—To My Father

January 30, *Saturday*. [1716–17.]

HONOURED SIR,

My mother tells me a very strange story of disturbances in your house. I wish I could have some more particulars from you. I would thank Mr. Hoole, if he would favour me with a letter concerning it. Not that I want to be confirmed myself in the belief of it, but for any other person's satisfaction. My mother sends to me to know my thoughts of it, and I cannot think at all of any interpretation. Wit, I fancy, might find many, but wisdom none.

Your dutiful and loving Son,

S. WESLEY.

Letter III—From Mr. S. Wesley to His Mother

Dean's Yard, Westminster,
Jan. 19, 1716–7, *Saturday.*

DEAR MOTHER,

Those who are so wise as not to believe any supernatural occurrences, though ever so well attested, could find a hundred questions to ask about those strange noises, you wrote me an account of; but for my part, I know not what question to put, which if answered, would confirm me more in the belief of what you tell me. Two or three I have heard from others. Was there never a new maid, or man, in the house, that might play tricks? Was there no body above in the garrets, when the walking was there? Did all the family hear it together when they were in one room, or at one time? Did it seem to all to be in the same place, at the same time? Could not cats, or rats, or dogs be the sprights? Was the whole family asleep, when my father and you went down stairs?

84

Such doubts as these being replied to, though they could not, as God himself assures us, convince them who believe not Moses and the prophets, yet would strengthen such as do believe. As to my particular opinion, concerning the events forboded by these noises, I cannot, I must confess, form any—I think since it was not permitted to speak, all guesses must be vain. The end of spirits actions is yet more hidden than that of men, and even this latter puzzles the most subtle politicians. That we may be struck so as to prepare seriously for any ill, may, it is possible, be one design of providence. It is surely our duty and wisdom to do so.

> DEAR MOTHER,
> I beg your blessing,
> on your dutiful and affectionate Son,
> S. WESLEY.

I expect a particular account from every one.

LETTER IV—FROM MRS. WESLEY TO HER SON SAMUEL

Jan. 25, or 27, 1716–7

DEAR SAM,

Though I am not one of those that will believe nothing supernatural, but am rather inclined to think there would be frequent intercourse between good spirits and us, did not our deep lapse into sensuality prevent it; yet I was a great while e'er I could credit any thing of what the children and servants reported, concerning the noises they heard in several parts of our house. Nay, after I had heard them myself, I was willing to persuade myself and them, that it was only rats or weasels that disturbed us; and having been formerly troubled with rats, which were frighted away by sounding a horn, I caused a horn to be procured, and made them blow it all over the house. But from that night they began to blow, the noises were more loud, and distinct, both day and night, than before, and that night we rose, and went down, I was entirely convinced, that it was beyond the power of any human creature to make such strange and various noises.

As to your questions, I will answer them particularly, but withal, I desire my answers may satisfy none but yourself; for I would not have the matter imparted to any. We had both man and maid new this last Martinmas, yet I do not believe either of them occasioned the disturbance, both for the reason above mentioned, and because they were more affrighted than any body else. Besides, we have often heard the noises when they were in the room by us; and the maid particularly was in such a panic, that she was almost incapable of all business, nor durst ever go from one room to another, or stay by herself a minute after it began to be dark.

The man, Robert Brown, whom you well know, was most visited by it lying in the garret, and has been often frighted down bare foot, and almost naked, not daring to stay alone to put on his cloaths, nor do I think, if he had power, he would be guilty of such villainy. When the walking was heard in the garret, Robert was in bed in the next room, in a sleep so sound, that he never heard your father and me walk up and down, though we walked not softly, I am sure. All the family has heard it together, in the same room, at the same time, particularly at family prayers. It always seemed to all present in the same place at the same time, though often before any could say it is here, it would remove to another place.

All the family, as well as Robin, were asleep when your father and I went down stairs, nor did they wake in the nursery when we held the candle close by them, only we observed that Hetty trembled exceedingly in her sleep, as she always did, before the noise awaked her. It commonly was nearer her than the rest, which she took notice of, and was much frightened, because she thought it had a particular spight at her. I could multiply particular instances, but I forbear. I believe your father will write to you about it shortly. Whatever may be the design of providence in permitting these things, I cannot say. *Secret things belong to God*; but I intirely agree with you, that it is our wisdom and duty to prepare seriously for all events.

S. WESLEY.

LETTER V—FROM MISS SUSANNAH WESLEY TO HER BROTHER
SAMUEL

Epworth, Jan. 24. [1716–17.]

DEAR BROTHER,

About the first of December, a most terrible and astonishing noise was heard by a maid servant, as at the dining room door, which caused the up starting of her hair, and made her ears prick forth at an unusual rate. She said, it was like the groans of one expiring. These so frighted her, that for a great while she durst not go out of one room into another, after it began to be dark, without company. But, to lay aside jesting, which should not be done in serious matters; I assure you that from the first to the last of a lunar month, the groans, squeaks, tinglings, and knockings, were frightful enough.

Though it is needless for me to send you any account of what we all heard, my father himself having a larger account of the matter than I am able to give, which he designs to send you; yet, in compliance with your desire, I will tell you as briefly as I can, what I heard of it. The first night I ever heard it my sister Nancy and I were set in the dining room. We heard something rush on the outside of the doors that opened into the garden, then three loud knocks, immediately after other three, and in half a minute the same number over our heads. We enquired whether any body had been in the garden, or in the room above us, but there was nobody. Soon after my sister Molly and I were up after all the family were a bed, except my sister Nancy about some business. We heard three bouncing thumps under our feet, which soon made us throw away our work, and tumble into bed. Afterwards the tingling of the latch and warming pan, and so it took its leave that night.

Soon after the above-mentioned, we heard a noise as if a great piece of sounding metal was thrown down on the outside of our chamber. We, lying in the quietest part of the house, heard less than the rest for a pretty while, but the latter end of the night that Mr. Hoole sat up on, I lay in the nursery, where it was very violent. I then heard frequent knocks over and under the room where I lay, and at the children's bed head, which was made of boards. It seemed to rap against it very hard and loud, so that the bed shook under them. I heard something walk by my bedside, like a man in a long night gown. The knocks were so loud, that Mr. Hoole came out of their chamber to us. It still continued. My father spoke, but nothing answered. It ended that night with my father's particular knock, very fierce.

It is now pretty quiet, only at our repeating the prayers for the king and prince, when it usually begins, especially when my father says, 'Our most gracious Sovereign Lord,' etc. This my father is angry at, and designs to say *three* instead of *two* for the royal family. We all heard the same noise, and at the same time, and as coming from the same place. To conclude this, it now makes its personal appearance; but of this more hereafter. Do not say one word of this to our folks, nor give the least hint.

I am,
Your sincere friend and affectionate Sister,
SUSANNAH WESLEY.

LETTER VI—MR. S. WESLEY IN ANSWER

Dean's Yard, Feb. 9, 1716–7

DEAR SISTER SUKY,

Your telling me the spirit has made its personal appearance, without saying how, or to whom, or when, or how long, has excited my curiosity very much. I long mightily for a farther account of every circumstance by your next letter. Do not keep me any longer in the dark. Why need you write the less, because my father is to send me the whole story? Has the disturbance continued since the 28th of December? I understand my father did not hear it all, but a fortnight after the rest. What did he say remarkable to any of you when he did hear it? As to the devil's being an enemy to King George, were I the king myself, I should rather old Nick should be my enemy, than my friend. I do not like the noise of the night gown sweeping along the ground, nor its knocking like my father. Write when you receive this, though nobody else should, to your loving brother,

S. W.

LETTER VII—MR. S. WESLEY TO HIS MOTHER

Feb. 12. [1716–17.]

DEAR MOTHER,

You say you could multiply particular instances of the spirit's noises, but I want to know whether nothing was ever seen by any. For though it is hard to conceive, nay, morally impossible, that the hearing of so many people could be deceived, yet the truth will be still more manifest and undeniable, if it is grounded on the testimony of two senses. Has it never at all disturbed you since the 28th of December? Did no circumstance give any light into the design of the whole?

Your obedient and loving Son,

S. WESLEY.

Have you dug in the place where the money seemed poured at your feet?

LETTER VIII—MR. S. WESLEY TO HIS FATHER

Feb. 12. [1716–17.]

HONOURED SIR,

I have not yet received any answer to the letter I wrote some time ago, and my mother in her last seems to say, that as yet I know but a very small part of the whole story of strange noises in our house. I shall be exceedingly glad to have the entire account from you. Whatever may be the main design of such wonders, I cannot think they were ever meant to be kept secret. If they bode any thing remarkable to our family, I am sure I am a party concerned.

Your dutiful Son,

S. WESLEY.

LETTER IX—FROM MR. S. WESLEY TO HIS SISTER EMILY

Feb. 12. [1716–17.]

DEAR SISTER EMILY,

I wish you would let me have a letter from you about the spirit, as indeed from every one of my sisters. I cannot think any of you very superstitious, unless you are much changed since I saw you. My sister Hetty, I find, was more particularly troubled. Let me know all. Did anything appear to her? I am,

Your affectionate Brother,

S. WESLEY.

Letter X—From Old Mr. Wesley to His Son Samuel

Feb. 11, 1716–7.

Dear Sam,

As for the noises, etc. in our family, I thank God we are now all quiet. There were some surprising circumstances in that affair. Your mother has not written you a third part of it. When I see you here, you shall see the whole account, which I wrote down. It would make a glorious penny book for Jack Dunton: but while I live I am not ambitious for any thing of that nature. I think that's all, but blessings, from

Your loving Father,

Sam. Wesley.

Letter XI—From Miss Emily Wesley to Her Brother Samuel

[1716–17.]

Dear Brother,

I thank you for your last, and shall give you what satisfaction is in my power, concerning what has happened in our family. I am so far from being superstitious, that I was too much inclined to infidelity, so that I heartily rejoice at having such an opportunity of convincing myself past doubt or scruple, of the existence of some beings besides those we see. A whole month was sufficient to convince any body of the reality of the thing, and to try all ways of discovering any trick, had it been possible for any such to have been used. I shall only tell you what I myself heard, and leave the rest to others.

My sisters in the paper chamber had heard noises, and told me of them, but I did not much believe, till one night, about a week after the first groans were heard, which was the beginning, just after the clock had struck ten, I went down stairs to lock the doors, which I always do. Scarce had I got up the best stairs, when I heard a noise, like a person throwing down a vast coal in the middle of the fore kitchen, and all the splinters seemed to fly about from it. I was not much frighted, but went to my sister Sukey, and we together went all over the low rooms, but there was nothing out of order.

Our dog was fast asleep, and our only cat in the other end of the house. No sooner was I got up stairs, and undressing for bed, but I heard a noise among many bottles that stand under the best stairs just like the throwing of a great stone among them, which had broke them all to pieces. This made me hasten to bed; but my sister Hetty, who sits always to wait on my father going to bed, was still sitting on the lowest step on the garret stairs, the door being shut at her back, when soon after there came down the stairs behind her, something like a man, in a loose night gown trailing after him, which made her fly rather than run to me in the nursery.

89

'*There came down the stairs behind her, something like a man, in a loose nightgown trailing after him.*'

All this time we never told our father of it, but soon after we did. He smiled, and gave no answer, but was more careful than usual, from that time, to see us in bed, imagining it to be some of us young women that sat up late, and made a noise. His incredulity, and especially his imputing it to us, or our lovers, made me, I own, desirous of its continuance till he was convinced. As for my mother, she firmly believed it to be rats, and sent for a horn to blow them away. I laughed to think how wisely they were employed, who were striving half a day to fright away Jeffrey, for that name I gave it, with a horn.

But whatever it was, I perceived it could be made angry. For from that time it was so outrageous, there was no quiet for us after ten at night. I heard frequently between ten and eleven, something like the quick winding up of a jack, at the corner of the room by my bed's head, just the running of the wheels and the creaking of the iron work. This was the common signal of its coming. Then it would knock on the floor three times, then at my sister's bed's head in the same room, almost always three together, and then stay. The sound was hollow, and loud, so as none of us could ever imitate.

It would answer to my mother, if she stamped on the floor, and bid it. It would knock when I was putting the children to bed, just under me where I sat. One time little Kesy, pretending to scare Patty, as I was undressing them, stamped with her foot on the floor, and immediately it answered with three knocks, just in the same place. It was more loud and fierce if any one said it was rats, or any thing natural.

I could tell you abundance more of it, but the rest will write and therefore it would be needless. I was not much frighted at first, and very little at last; but it was never near me, except two or three times, and never followed me, as it did my sister Hetty. I have been with her when it has knocked under her, and when she has removed has followed, and still kept just under her feet, which was enough to terrify a stouter person.

If you would know my opinion of the reason of this, I shall briefly tell you. I believe it to be witchcraft, for these reasons. About a year since, there was a disturbance at a town near us, that was undoubtedly witches; and if so near, why may they not reach us? Then my father had for several Sundays before its coming, preached warmly against consulting those that are called cunning men, which our people are given to; and it had a particular spight at my Father.

Besides, something was thrice seen. The first time by my mother, under my sister's bed, like a badger, only without any head that was discernible. The same creature was sat by the dining-room fire one evening; when our man went into the room, it run up by him, through the hall under the stairs. He followed with a candle, and searched, but it was departed. The last time he saw it in the kitchen, like a white rabbit, which seems likely to be some witch; and I do so really believe it to be one, that I would venture to fire a pistol at it, if I saw it long enough. It has been heard by me and the others since December. I have filled up all my room, and have only time to tell you, I am,

Your loving sister,

EMILIA WESLEY.

LETTER XII—MISS SUSANNAH WESLEY TO HER BROTHER SAMUEL

March 27 [1717.]

DEAR BROTHER WESLEY.

I should farther satisfy you concerning the disturbances, but it is needless, because my sisters Emilia and Hetty write so particularly about it. One thing I believe you do not know, that is, last Sunday, to my father's no small amazement, his trencher danced upon the table a pretty while, without any body's stirring the table. When lo! an adventurous wretch took it up, and spoiled the sport, for it remained still ever after. How glad should I be to talk with you about it. Send me some news, for we are secluded from the sight, or hearing, of any versal thing except Jeffrey.

SUSANNAH WESLEY.

A PASSAGE IN A LETTER FROM MY MOTHER TO ME, DATED *March* 27, 1717

I cannot imagine who should be so curious about our unwelcome guest. For my part, I am quite tired with hearing or speaking of it, but if you come among us, you will find enough to satisfy all your scruples, and perhaps may hear, or see it for yourself.

S. WESLEY.

A PASSAGE IN A LETTER FROM MY SISTER EMILY TO MR. N. BERRY, DATED *April* 1. [1717.]

Tell my brother the spright was with us last night, and heard by many of our family, especially by our maid and myself. She sat up with drink, and it came just at one o'clock, and opened the dining room door. After some time it shut again. She saw as well as heard it both shut and open; then it began to knock as usual. But I dare write no longer, lest I should hear it.

EMILIA WESLEY.

MY FATHER'S JOURNAL, OR, DIARY, TRANSCRIBED BY MY BROTHER JACK[1] *August* 27, 1726, AND FROM HIM BY ME, *February* 7, 1730–1.

[1] i.e., John Wesley, who was at school during the Epworth disturbances. He entered Charterhouse at the early age of ten and a half years.—H.P.

An Account of Noises and Disturbances in my House, at Epworth, Lincolnshire, in December and January, 1716.

From the First of December, my children and servants heard many strange noises, groans, knockings, etc., in every story, and most of the rooms of my house. But I hearing nothing of it myself, they would not tell me for some time, because, according to the vulgar opinion, if it boded any ill to me, I could not hear it. When it increased, and the family could not easily conceal it, they told me of it.

My daughters Susannah and Ann, were below stairs in the dining room, and heard first at the doors, then over their heads, and the night after a knocking under their feet, though nobody was in the chambers or below them. The like they and my servants heard in both the kitchens, at the door against the partition, and over them. The maid servant heard groans as of a dying man. My daughter Emilia coming down stairs to draw up the clock, and lock the doors at ten at night, as usual, heard under the stair-case, a sound among some bottles there, as if they had been all dashed to pieces; but when she looked, all was safe.

Something like the steps of a man, was heard going up and down stairs, at all hours of the night, and vast rumblings below stairs, and in the garrets. My man, who lay in the garret, heard some one come glaring through the garret to his chamber, rattling by his side, as if against his shoes, though he had none there; at other times walking up and down stairs, when all the house were in bed, and gobling like a turkey cock. Noises were heard in the nursery, and all the other chambers; knocking first at the feet of the bed and behind it; and a sound like that of dancing in a matted chamber next the nursery, when the door was locked, and no body in it.

My wife would have persuaded them it was rats within doors, and some unlucky people knocking without; till at last we heard several loud knocks in our own chamber, on my side of the bed; but till, I think, the 21st night, I heard nothing of it. That night I was waked a little before one, by nine distinct very loud knocks, which seemed to be in the next room to ours, with a sort of a pause at every third stroke. I thought it might be somebody without the house, and having got a stout mastiff, hoped he would soon rid me of it.

The next night I heard six knocks, but not so loud as the former. I know not whether it was in the morning after Sunday the 23rd, when about seven my daughter Emily called her mother into the nursery, and told her she might now hear the noises there. She went in, and heard it at the bedsteads, then under the bed, then at the head of it. She knocked, and it answered her. She looked under the bed, and thought something ran from thence, but could not well tell of what shape, but thought it most like a badger.

The next night but one, we were awaked about one, by the noises, which were so violent, it was in vain to think of sleep while they continued. I rose, and my wife would rise with me. We went into every chamber, and down stairs; and generally as we went into one room, we heard it in that behind us, though all the family had been in bed several hours. When we were going down stairs, and at the bottom of them, we heard, as Emily had done before, a clashing among the bottles, as if they had been broke all to pieces, and another sound distinct from it, as if a peck of money had been thrown down before us. The same, three of my daughters heard at another time.

We went through the hall into the kitchen, when our mastiff came whining to us, as he did always after the first night of its coming; for then he barked violently at it, but was silent afterwards, and seemed more afraid than any of the children. We still heard it rattle and thunder in every room above or behind us, locked as well as open, except my study, where as yet it never came. After two, we went to bed, and were pretty quiet the rest of the night.

Wednesday night, December 26, after, or a little before, ten, my daughter Emilie heard the signal of its beginning to play, with which she was perfectly acquainted; it was like the strong winding up of a jack. She called us, and I went into the nursery, where it used to be most violent. The rest of the children were asleep. It began with knocking in the kitchen underneath, then seemed to be at the bed's feet, then under the bed, at last at the head of it. I went down stairs, and knocked with my stick against the joists of the kitchen. It answered me as often and as loud as I knocked; but then I knocked as I usually do at my door, 1—23456—7, but this puzzled it, and it did not answer, or not in the same method; though the children heard it do the same exactly twice or thrice after.

I went up stairs, and found it still knocking hard, though with some respite, sometimes under the bed, sometimes at the bed's head. I observed my children that they were frighted in their sleep, and trembled very much till it waked them. I stayed there alone, bid them go to sleep, and sat at the bed's feet by them, when the noise began again. I asked it what it was and why it disturbed innocent children, and did not come to me in my study, if it had any thing to say to me; Soon after it gave one knock on the outside of the house. All the rest were within, and knocked off for that night.

I went out of doors, some times alone, at others with company, and walked round the house, but could see or hear nothing. Several nights the latch of our lodging chamber would be lifted up very often, when all were in bed. One night, when the noise was great in the kitchen, and on a deal partition, and the door in the yard, the latch whereof was often lift up, my daughter Emilia went and held it fast on the inside, but it was still lifted up and the door pushed violently against her, though nothing was to be seen on the outside.

When we were at prayers for King George, and the Prince, it would make a great noise over our heads constantly, whence some of the family called it a Jacobite. I have been thrice pushed by an invisible power, once against the corner of my desk in the study, a second time against the door of the matted chamber, a third time against the right side of the frame of my study door, as I was going in.

I followed the noise into almost every room in the house, both by day and by night, with lights and without, and have sat alone for some time, and when I heard the noise, spoke to it, to tell me what it was, but never heard any articulate voice, and only once or twice two or three feeble squeaks, a little louder than the chirping of a bird, but not like the noise of rats, which I have often heard.

I had designed on Friday, December the 28th, to make a visit to a friend, Mr. Downs, at Normandy, and stay some days with him, but the noises were so boisterous on Thursday night, that I did not care to leave my family. So I went to Mr. Hoole, of Haxsey,[1] and desired his company on Friday night. He came, and it began after ten, a little later than ordinary. The younger children were gone to bed, the rest of the family and Mr. Hoole were together in the matted chamber. I sent the servants down to fetch in some fuel, went with them, and staid in the kitchen till they came in. When they were gone, I heard loud noises against the doors and partition, and at length the usual signal, though somewhat after the time. I had never heard it before, but knew it by the description my daughter had given me. It was much like the turning of a windmill when the wind changes. When the servants returned, I went up to the company, who had heard the other noises below, but not the signal. We heard all the knockings as usual, from one chamber to another, but at its going off, like the rubbing of a beast against the wall; but from that time till January the 24th, we were quiet.

Having received a letter from Samuel the day before, relating to it, I read what I had written of it to my family; and this day at morning prayer, the family heard the usual knocks at the prayer for the king. At night they were more distinct, both in the prayer for the king and that for the prince; and one very loud knock at the *Amen* was heard by my wife, and most of my children, at the inside of my bed. I heard nothing myself. After nine, Robert Brown sitting alone by the fire in the back kitchen, something came out of the copper hole like a rabbit, but less, and turned round five times very swiftly. Its ears lay flat upon its neck, and its little feet stood straight up. He ran after it with the tongs in his hands, but when he could find nothing he was frightened, and went to the maid in the parlour.

On Friday the 25th, having prayers at church, I shortened, as usual, those in the family at morning, omitting the confession, absolution, and prayers for the king and prince. I observed when this is done, there

[1] i.e., Haxey.—H.P.

is no knocking. I therefore used them one morning for a trial; at the name of King George, it began to knock, and did the same when I prayed for the prince. Two knocks I heard, but took no notice after prayers, till after all who were in the room, ten persons besides me, spoke of it, and said they heard it. No noise at all the rest of the prayers.

Sunday, January 27. Two soft strokes at the morning prayers for king George, above stairs.

Addenda to and from My Father's Diary [1716–17.]

Friday, December 21. Knocking I heard first, I think, this night; to which disturbances, I hope, God will in his good time put an end.

Sunday, December 23. Not much disturbed with the noises that are now grown customary to me.

Wednesday, December 26. Sat up to hear noises. Strange! Spoke to it, knocked off.

Friday, 28. The noises very boisterous and disturbing this night.

Saturday, 29. Not frighted, with the continued disturbance of my family.

Tuesday, January 1, 1717. My family have had no disturbance since I went.

Memorandum of Jack's[1]

The first time my mother ever heard any unusual noise at Epworth was long before the disturbance of old Jeffrey. My brother, lately come from London, had one evening a sharp quarrel with my sister Sukey, at which time my mother, happening to be above in her own chamber, the door and windows rung and jarred very loud, and presently several distinct strokes, three by three, were struck. From that night it never failed to give notice in much the same manner, against any signal misfortune, or illness of any belonging to the family.

Of the General Circumstances which follow, Most, if not All, the Family were Frequent Witnesses

1. Presently after any noise was heard, the wind commonly rose, and whistled very loud round the house, and increased with it.

2. The signal was given, which my father likens to the turning round of a windmill when the wind changes; Mr. Hoole (Rector of Haxey) to the plaining of deal boards; my sister to the swift winding up of a jack. It commonly began at the corner of the top of the nursery.

3. Before it came into any room, the latches were frequently lifted up, the windows clattered, and whatever iron or brass was about the chamber, rung and jarred exceedingly.

4. When it was in any room, let them make what noise they would, as

[1] i.e., John Wesley,—H.P.

they sometimes did on purpose, its dead hollow note would be clearly heard above them all.

5. It constantly knocked while the prayers for the king and prince were repeating, and was plainly heard by all in the room, but my father, and sometimes by him, as were also the thundering knocks at the *Amen*.

6. The sound very often seemed in the air in the middle of the room, nor could they ever make any such themselves, by any contrivance.

7. Though it seemed to rattle down the pewter, to clap the doors, draw the curtains, kick the man's shoes up and down, etc. yet it never moved anything except the latches, otherwise than making it tremble; unless once, when it threw open the nursery door.

8. The mastiff, though he barked violently at it the first day he came, yet whenever it came after that, nay, sometimes before the family perceived it, he ran whining, or quite silent, to shelter himself behind some of the company.

9. It never came by day, till my mother ordered the horn to be blown.

10. After that time, scarce anyone could go from one room to another, but the latch of the room they went to was lifted up before they touched it.

11. It never came once into my father's study, till he talked to it sharply, called it *deaf and dumb devil*, and bid it cease to disturb the innocent children, and come to him in his study, if it had anything to say to him.

12. From the time of my mother's desiring it not to disturb her from five to six, it was never heard in her chamber from five till she came downstairs, nor at any other time when she was employed in devotion.

13. Whether our clock went right or wrong, it always came, as near as could be guessed, when by the night it wanted a quarter to ten.

My Mother's Account to Jack[1]

August 27, 1726.

About ten days after Nanny Marshall had heard unusual groans at the dining room door, Emily came and told me that the servants and children, had been several times frighted with strange groans and knockings, about the house. I answered that the rats John Maw had frightened from his house, by blowing a horn there, were coming into ours, and ordered that one should be sent for. Molly was much displeased at it, and said, if it was anything supernatural, it certainly would be very angry, and more troublesome. However, the horn was blown in the garrets; and the effect was, that whereas before the noises were always in the night, from this time they were heard at all hours, day and night.

Soon after, about seven in the morning, Emily came and desired me to go into the nursery, where I should be convinced they were not

[1] i.e., John Wesley.—H.P.

startled at nothing. On my coming thither, I heard a knocking at the feet, and quickly after at the head of the bed. I desired, if it was a spirit, it would answer me, and knocking several times with my foot on the ground, with several pauses, it repeated under the sole of my feet, exactly the same number of strokes, with the same intervals. Kezzy, then five or seven years old said, let it answer me too, if it can, and stamping, the same sounds were returned that she made many times, successively.

Upon my looking under the bed, something ran out pretty much like a badger, and seemed to run directly under Emily's petticoats, who sat opposite to me on the other side. I went out, and one or two nights after, when we were just got to bed, I heard nine strokes, three by three, on the other side the bed, as if one had struck violently on a chest, with a large stick. Mr. Wesley leapt up, called Hetty, who alone was up in the house, and searched every room in the house, but to no purpose. It continued from this time to knock and groan frequently at all hours, day and night; only I earnestly desired it might not disturb me between five and six in the evening, and there was never any noise in my room after during that time.

At other times, I have often heard it over my mantle tree, and once, coming up after dinner, a cradle seemed to be strongly rocked in my chamber. When I went in, the sound seemed to be in the nursery. When I was in the nursery, it seemed in my chamber again. One night Mr. W. and I were waked by some one running down the garret stairs, then down the broad stairs, then up the narrow ones, then up the garret stairs, then down again, and so the same round. The rooms trembled as it passed along, and the doors shook exceedingly, so that the clattering of the latches was very loud.

Mr. W. proposing to rise, I rose with him, and went down the broad stairs, hand in hand, to light a candle. Near the foot of them a large pot of money seemed to be poured out at my waist, and to run jingling down my night gown to my feet. Presently after we heard the noise as of a vast stone thrown among several dozen of bottles which lay under the stairs; but upon our looking no hurt was done. In the hall, the mastiff met us, crying and striving to get between us. We returned up into the nursery, where the noise was very great. The children were all asleep, but panting, trembling, and sweating extremely.

Shortly after, on Mr. Wesley's invitation, Mr. Hoole staid a night with us; as we were all sitting round the fire in the matted chamber. He asked whether that gentle knocking was *it*? I told him yes, and it continued the sound, which was much lower than usual. This was observable, that while we were talking loud in the same room, the noise, seemingly lower than any of our voices, was distinctly heard above them all. These were the most remarkable passages I remember, except such as were common to all the family.

MY SISTER EMILY'S ACCOUNT TO JACK

[*August,* 1726.]

About a fortnight after the time when, as I was told, the noises were heard, I went from my mother's room, who was just gone to bed, to the best chamber to fetch my sister Suky's candle. When I was there, the windows and doors began to jar, and ring exceedingly, and presently after I heard a sound in the kitchen, as if a vast stone coal had been

'*We heard a noise as of a vast stone thrown among several dozen of bottles*'.

thrown down, and smashed to pieces. I went down thither with my candle, and found nothing more than usual; but as I was going by the screen, something began knocking on the other side, just even with my head. When I looked on the inside, the knocking was on the outside of it, but as soon as I could get round, it was on the inside again. I followed to and fro several times, till at last, finding it to no purpose, and turning about to go away before I was out of the room, the latch of the back kitchen door was lifted up many times. I opened the door and looked out, but could see nobody. I tried to shut the door, but it was thrust against me, and I could feel the latch, which I held in my hand, moving upwards at the same time. I looked out again, but finding it was labour lost, clapped the door to and locked it. Immediately the latch was moved strongly up and down, but I left it, and went up the worst stairs, from whence I heard, as if a great stone had been thrown among the bottles, which lay under the best stairs. However I went to bed.

From this time, I heard it every night, for two or three weeks. It continued a month in its full majesty, night and day. Then it intermitted a fortnight or more, and when it began again, it knocked only on nights, and grew less and less troublesome, till at last it went quite away. Towards the latter end it used to knock on the outside of the house, and seemed farther and farther off, till it ceased to be heard at all.

MY SISTER MOLLY'S ACCOUNT TO JACK

Aug. 27. [1726.]

I have always thought it was in November, the rest of our family think it was the 1st of December 1716, when Nanny Marshall, who had a bowl of butter in her hand, ran to me, and two or three more of my sisters, in the dining room, and told us she had heard several groans in the hall, as of a dying man. We thought it was Mr. Turpine, who had the stone, and used sometimes to come and see us. About a fortnight after, when my sister Suky and I were going to bed, she told me how she was frightened in the dining room, the day before, by a noise, first at the folding door, and then over head. I was reading at the table, and had scarce told her, I believe nothing of it, when several knocks were given just under my feet. We both made haste into bed, and just as we laid down, the warming pan by the bed side jarred and rung, as did the latch of the door, which was lifted swiftly up and down, presently a great chain seemed to fall on the outside of the door (we were in the best chamber) the door latch, hinges, the warming pan, and windows, jarred, and the house shook from top to bottom.

A few days after, between five and six in the evening, I was by myself in the dining room. The door seemed to open, though it was still shut, and somebody walked in a night gown trailing on the ground (nothing appearing) and seemed to go leisurely round me. I started up, and ran up stairs to my mother's chamber, and told the story to her and my sister Emily. A few nights after, my father ordered me to light him to his study. Just as he had unlocked it, the latch was lifted up for him.

The same, after we blew the horn, was often done to me, as well by day as by night. Of many other things all the family as well as me were witnesses.

My father went into the nursery from the matted chamber, where we were, by himself in the dark. It knocked very loud on the press bed head. He adjured it to tell him why it came, but it seemed to take no notice; at which he was very angry, spoke sharply, called it *deaf and dumb devil*, and repeated his adjuration. My sisters were terribly afraid it would speak. When he had done it knocked his knock on the bed's head, so exceedingly violently, as if it would break it to shivers, and from that time we heard nothing till a month after.

MY SISTER SUKEY'S ACCOUNT TO JACK

September, [1726.]

I believed nothing of it till about a fortnight after the first noises, then one night I sat up on purpose to hear it. While I was working in the best chamber, and earnestly desiring to hear it, a knocking began just under my feet. As I knew the room below was locked, I was frightened, and leapt into the bed with all my cloaths on. I afterwards heard as it were a great chain fall, and after some time, the usual noises at all hours of the day and night. One night hearing it was most violent in the nursery, I resolved to lie there. Late at night several strong knocks were given on the two lowest steps of the garret stairs, which were close to the nursery door. The latch of the door then jarred, and seemed to be swiftly moved to and fro, and presently began knocking about a yard within the room on the floor. It then came gradually to sister Hetty's bed, who trembled strongly in her sleep. It beat very loud, three strokes at a time, on the bed's head. My father came, and adjured it to speak, but, it knocked on for some time, and then removed to the room over, where it knocked my father's knock on the ground, as if it would beat the house down. I had no mind to stay longer, but got up and went to my sister Em and my mother, who were in her room. From thence we heard the noises again from the nursery. I proposed playing a game at cards, but we had scarce begun, when a knocking began under our feet. We left off playing, and it removed back again into the nursery, where it continued till towards morning.

SISTER NANCY'S ACCOUNT TO JACK

Sept. 10. [1726.]

The first noise my sister Nancy heard, was in the best chamber, with my sister Molly and my sister Sukey; soon after my father had ordered her to blow a horn in the garrets, where it was knocking violently. She was terribly afraid, being obliged to go in the dark, and kneeling down

on the stairs, desired that, as she acted not to please herself, it might
have no power over her. As soon as she came into the room, the noise
ceased, nor did it begin again till near ten; but then, and for a good
while, it made much greater and more frequent noises than it had done
before. When she afterwards came into the chamber in the day time, it
commonly walked after her from room to room. It followed her from
one side of the bed to the other, and back again, as often as she went
back; and whatever she did which made any sort of noise, the same
thing seemed just to be done behind her.

When five or six were set in the nursery together, a cradle would seem
to be strongly rocked in the room over, though no cradle had ever been
there. One night she was sitting on the press bed playing at cards with
some of my sisters, when my sister Molly, Etty, Patty, and Kezzy, were
in the room, and Robert Brown. The bed on which my sister Nancy sat,
was lifted up with her on it. She leapt down and said 'Surely old Jeffery
would not run away with her'. However, they persuaded her to sit down
again, which she had scarce done, when it was again lifted up several
times successively, a considerable height, upon which she left her seat
and would not be prevailed upon to sit there any more.

Whenever they began to mention Mr. S. it presently began to knock,
and continued to do so until they changed the discourse. All the time
my sister Suky was writing her last letter to him, it made a very great
noise all round the room, and the night after she set out for London, it
knocked till morning with scarce any intermission.

Mr. Hoole read prayers once, but it knocked as usual at the prayers
for the king and prince. The knockings at those prayers were only towards the beginning of the disturbances, for a week or thereabouts.

THE REV. MR. HOOLE'S ACCOUNT [TO JACK]
Sept. 16. [1726.]

As soon as I came to Epworth, Mr. Wesley telling me he sent for me
to conjure, I knew not what he meant, till some of your sisters told me
what had happened, and that I was sent for to sit up. I expected every
hour, it being then about noon, to hear something extraordinary, but
to no purpose. At supper too, and at prayers, all was silent, contrary to
custom, but soon after one of the maids, who went up to sheet a bed,
brought the alarm, that Jeffrey was come above stairs. We all went up,
and as we were standing round the fire in the east chamber, something
began knocking just on the other side of the wall, on the chimney piece,
as with a key. Presently the knocking was under our feet, Mr. Wesley
and I went down, with a great deal of hope, and I with fear. As soon as
we were in the kitchen, the sound was above us, in the room we had
left. We returned up the narrow stairs, and heard at the broad stairs
head, some one slaring with their feet (all the family now being in bed

beside us) and then trailing as it were, and rustling with a silk night gown. Quickly it was in the nursery, at the bed's head, knocking as it had done at first, three by three. Mr. Wesley spoke to it, and said he believed it was the devil, and soon after it knocked at the window, and changed its sound into one like the plaining of boards. From thence it went to the outward south side of the house, sounding fainter and fainter till it was heard no more.

I was at no other time than this during the noises at Epworth, and do not now remember any more circumstances than these.

Epworth, Sept. 1. [1726.]

My sister Kezzy says she remembers nothing else, but it knocked my father's knock, ready to beat the house down in the nursery one night.

Robin Brown's Account to Jack
[*August* 31? 1726.]

The first time Robin Brown, my father's man, heard it, was when he was fetching down some corn from the garrets. Somewhat knocked on a door just by him, which made him run away down stairs. From that time it used frequently to visit him in bed, walking up the garret stairs, and in the garrets, like a man in jack boots, with a night gown trailing after him, then lifting up his latch and making it jar, and making presently a noise in his room like the gobling of a turkey cock, then stumbling over his shoes or boots by the bed side. He was resolved once to be too hard for it, and so took a large mastiff we had just got to bed with him, and left his shoes and boots below stairs; but he might as well have spared his labour, for it was exactly the same thing, whether any were there or no. The same sound was heard as if there had been forty pairs. The dog indeed was a great comfort to him, for as soon as the latch began to jar, he crept into bed, made such an howling and barking together, in spite of all the man could do, that he alarmed most of the family.

Soon after, being grinding corn in the garrets, and happening to stop a little, the handle of the mill was turn round with great swiftness. He said nothing vexed him, but that the mill was empty. If corn had been in it old Jeffrey might have ground his heart out for him; he would never have disturbed him.

One night, being ill, he was leaning his head on the back kitchen chimney (the jam he called it) with the tongs in his hands, when from behind the oven stop, which lay by the fire, somewhat came out like a white rabbit. It turned round before him several times, and then ran to the same place again. He was frighted, started up, and ran with the tongs in the *parlour* (*dining room*).

D. R. Epworth, Aug. 31. [1726.]

Betty Massy one day came to me in the parlour, and asked me if I had heard old Jeffrey, for she said she thought there was no such thing. When we had talked a little about it, I knocked three times with a reel I had in my hand against the dining room ceiling, and the same were presently repeated. She desired me to knock so again, which I did, but they were answered with three more so violently it shook the house, though no one was in the chamber over us. She prayed me to knock no more for fear it should come into us.

Epworth, August 31, 1726.

John and Ketty Maw, who lived over against us, listened several nights in the time of the disturbance, but could never hear anything.

AN ACCOUNT OF THE DISTURBANCES IN MY FATHER'S HOUSE[1]

J. W.

When I was very young, I heard several letters read, wrote to my elder brother by my father, giving an account of strange disturbances, which were in his house, at Epworth, in Lincolnshire.

1. When I went down thither, in the year 1720,[2] I carefully enquired into the particulars. I spoke to each of the persons who were then in the house, and took down what each could testify of his of her knowledge. The sum of which was this.

2. On Dec. 2, 1716, while Robert Brown, my father's servant, was sitting with one of the maids a little before ten at night, in the dining room which opened into the garden, they both heard one knocking at the door. Robert rose and opened it, but could see nobody. Quickly it knocked again and groaned. 'It is Mr. Turpin', said Robert: 'he has the stone and uses to groan so'. He opened the door again twice or thrice, the knocking being twice or thrice repeated. But still seeing nothing, and being a little startled, they rose and went up to bed.

When Robert came to the top of the garret stairs, he saw a hand-mill, which was at a little distance, whirled about very swiftly. When he related this he said, 'Nought vexed me, but that it was empty. I thought, if it had been full of malt he might have ground his heart out for me.'

When he was in bed, he heard as it were the gobbling of a turkey-cock, close to the bed-side; and soon after, the sound of one stumbling over his shoes and boots. But there were none there; he had left them below.

3. The next day, he and the maid related these things to the other

---

[1] Copied, *Verbatim et literatim*, direct from the three original issues of the *Arminian Magazine* for Octr., Novr., and Decr., 1784. (Vol. VII, pp. 548–50, 606–08, 654–56.) The published copies of the 'Account' that I have consulted, are textually inaccurate. —H.P.

[2] John Wesley was then aged 17.—H.P.

maid, who laughed heartily, and said, 'What a couple of fools are *you*? I defy any thing to fright me.' After churning in the evening, she put the butter in the tray, and had no sooner carried it into the dairy, than she heard a knocking on the shelf where several pancheons of milk stood, first above the shelf, then below. She took the candle and searched both above and below; but being able to find nothing, threw down butter, tray and all, and ran away for life.

4. The next evening between five and six o'clock my sister Molly, then about twenty years of age, sitting in the dining-room, reading, heard as if it were the door that led into the hall open, and a person walking in, that seemed to have on a silk night-gown, rustling and trailing along. It seemed to walk round her, then to the door, then round again: but she could see nothing. She thought, 'It signifies nothing to run away: for whatever it is, it can run faster than *me*.' So she rose, put her book under her arm, and walked slowly away.

5. After supper, she was sitting with my sister Suky (about a year older than her) in one of the chambers, and telling her what had happened, she quite made light of it; telling her, 'I wonder you are so easily frighted: I would fain see what would fright *me*.' Presently a knocking began under the table. She took the candle and looked, but could find nothing. Then the iron casement began to clatter, and the lid of a warming-pan. Next the latch of the door moved up and down without ceasing. She started up, leaped into the bed without undressing, pulled the bed clothes over her head, and never ventured to look up till next morning.

6. A night or two after, my sister Hetty, a year younger than my sister Molly, was waiting as usual, between nine and ten to take away my father's candle, when she heard someone coming down the garret stairs, walking slowly by her; then going down the best stairs, then up the back stairs, and up the garret stairs. And at every step, it seemed the house shook from top to bottom. Just then my father knocked. She went in, took his candle, and got to bed as fast as possible.

7. In the morning she told this to my eldest sister, who told her, 'You know, I believe none of these things. Pray let *me* take away the candle to-night, and I will find out the trick.' She accordingly took my sister Hetty's place, and had no sooner taken away the candle, than she heard a noise below. She hastened down stairs, to the hall, where the noise was. But it was then in the kitchen. She ran into the kitchen, where it was drumming on the inside of the screen. When she went round it was drumming on the outside, and so always on the side opposite to her. Then she heard a knocking at the back-kitchen door. She ran to it, unlocked it softly, and when the knocking was repeated, suddenly opened it: but nothing was to be seen. As soon as she had shut it, the knocking began again: she opened it again, but could see nothing: when she went to shut the door, it was violently thrust against her: she let it fly

open; but nothing appeared. She went again to shut it, and it was again thrust against her: but she set her knee and her shoulder to the door, forced it to, and turned the key. Then the knocking began again: but she let it go on, and went up to bed. However from that time she was thoroughly convinced, that there was no impostor in the affair.

8. The next morning my sister telling my mother what had happened, she said, 'If I hear any thing myself, I shall know how to judge.'

Soon after she begged her to come into the nursery. She did, and heard in the corner of the room, as it were the violent rocking of a cradle; but no cradle had been there for some years. She was convinced it was preternatural, and earnestly prayed it might not disturb her in her own chamber at the hours of retirement. And it never did.

She now thought it was proper to tell my father. But he was extremely angry, and said, 'Suky, I am ashamed of you: these boys and girls fright one another: but you are a woman of sense, and should know better. Let me hear of it no more.'

At six in the evening, he had family prayers as usual. When he began the prayer for the king, a knocking began all round the room: and a thundering knock attended the *Amen*. The same was heard from this time every morning and evening while the prayer for the king was repeated.

As both my father and mother are now at rest, and incapable of being pained thereby, I think it my duty to furnish the serious reader with a key to this circumstance. The year before king William died, my father observed my mother did not say Amen to the prayer for the king. She said, she could not; for she did not believe the Prince of Orange was king. He vowed he would never cohabit with her till she did. He then took his horse and rode away, nor did she hear any thing of him for a twelvemonth. He then came back, and lived with her as before. But I fear his vow was not forgotten before God.

9. Being informed that Mr. Hoole, the vicar of Haxey, (an eminently pious and sensible man) could give me some farther information, I walked over to him. He said, 'Robert Brown came over to me, and told me, your father desired my company. When I came he gave me an account of all that had happened; particularly the knocking during family prayer. But that evening (to my great satisfaction) we had no knocking at all. But between nine and ten, a servant came in and said, Old Jeffries is coming; (that was the name of one that died in the house) for I hear the signal. This they informed me was heard every night about a quarter before ten. It was toward the top of the house on the outside, at the North-East corner, resembling the loud creaking of a saw: or rather that of a windmill, when the body of it is turned about, in order to shift the sails to the wind. We then heard a knocking over our heads, and Mr. Wesley catching up a candle, said, Come, Sir, now you shall hear for yourself. We went up stairs; he with much hope, and

I (to say the truth) with much fear. When we came into the nursery, it was knocking in the next room; when we were there, it was knocking in the nursery. And there it continued to knock, though we came in, particularly at the head of the bed, (which was of wood) in which Miss Hetty and two of her younger sisters lay. Mr. Wesley observing, that they were much affected though asleep, sweating and trembling exceedingly, was very angry, and pulling out a pistol, was going to fire at the place from whence the sound came. But I catched him by the arm, and said, Sir, you are convinced, this is something preternatural. If so, you cannot hurt *it*; but you give it power to hurt *you.* He then went close to the place and said sternly, Thou deaf and dumb devil, why dost thou fright these children, that cannot answer for themselves? Come to me to my study, that am a man? Instantly it knocked *his* knock (the particular knock which he always used at the gate) as if it would shiver the board to pieces, and we heard nothing more that night.'

10. Till this time, my father had never heard the least disturbance in his study. But the next evening, as he attempted to go into his study (of which none had any key but himself) when he opened the door, it was thrust back with such violence, as had like to have thrown him down. However he thrust the door open and went in. Presently there was knocking first on one side, then on the other: and after a time, in the next room, wherein my sister Nancy was. He went into that room, and (the noise continuing) adjured it to speak; but in vain. He then said, 'These spirits love darkness; put out the candle, and perhaps it will speak:' she did so: and he repeated his adjuration; but still there was only knocking, and no articulate sound. Upon this he said, 'Nancy, two Christians are an over-match for the devil. Go all of you down stairs; it may be, when I am alone, he will have courage to speak.' When she was gone a thought came in, and he said, 'If thou art the spirit of my son Samuel, I pray, knock three knocks and no more.' Immediately all was silence, and there was no more knocking at all that night.

11. I asked my sister Nancy (then about fifteen years old) whether she was not afraid, when my father used that adjuration? She answered, She was sadly afraid it would speak, when she put out the candle: but she was not at all afraid in the day-time, when it walked after her, as she swept the chambers, as it constantly did, and seemed to sweep after her. Only she thought it might have done it *for her*, and saved her the trouble.

12. By this time all my sisters were so accustomed to these noises, that they gave them little disturbance. A gentle tapping at their bed-head usually began between nine and ten at night. They then commonly said to each other, 'Jeffrey is coming: it is time to go to sleep.' And if they heard a noise in the day, and said to my youngest sister, 'Hark, Hezzy,[1]

[1] This is probably a misprint in the original text for 'Kezzy' (i.e., Keziah), the youngest girl of the family.—H.P.

Jeffrey is knocking above,' she would run upstairs, and pursue it from room to room, saying she desired no better diversion.

13. A few nights after, my father and mother were just gone to bed, and the candle was not taken away, when they heard three blows, and a second, and a third three, as it were with a large oaken staff, struck upon a chest which stood by the bedside. My father immediately arose, put on his nightgown, and hearing great noises below, took the candle and went down. My mother walked by his side. As they went down the broad stairs, they heard as if a vessel full of silver was poured upon my mother's breast, and ran jingling down to her feet.[1] Quickly after there was a sound, as if a large iron ball was thrown among many bottles under the stairs. But nothing was hurt. Soon after, our large mastiff dog, came and ran to shelter himself between them. While the disturbances continued, he used to bark and leap, and snap on one side and the other; and that frequently, before any person in the room heard any noise at all. But after two or three days, he used to tremble, and creep away before the noise began. And by this, the family knew it was at hand: nor did the observation ever fail.

A little before my father and mother came into the hall, it seemed as if a very large coal was violently thrown upon the floor and dashed all in pieces. But nothing was seen. My father then cried out, 'Suky, do you not hear? All the pewter is thrown about the kitchen.' But when they looked, all the pewter stood in its place. There then was a loud knocking at the back door. My father opened it, but saw nothing. It was then at the fore door. He opened that: but it was still lost labour. After opening first the one, and then the other several times, he turned and went up to bed. But the noises were so violent all over the house, that he could not sleep till four in the morning.

14. Several Gentlemen and Clergymen now earnestly advised my father to quit the house. But he constantly answered, 'No, let the devil flee from *me*: I will never flee from the devil.' But he wrote to my eldest brother at London, to come down. He was preparing to do so, when another letter came, informing him that the disturbances were over: after they had continued (the latter part of the time day and night) from the second of December to the end of January.[2]

JOHN WESLEY.

Hilton-Park,
  March 26, 1784.

The reader has now been presented with all the available evidence for the Epworth Poltergeist. I have reproduced it *in extenso* because it is a

[1] Compare a similar auditory impression in the Willington Mill and Tedworth cases.—H.P.

[2] Another Poltergeist case was reported from Epworth in 1905. In a house there, were heard strange sounds, 'lights', etc. See *Liverpool Echo*, Jan. 25, 1905.—H.P.

very important case. Even Frank Podmore, that arch-sceptic, admits[1]
that it is the 'most fully documented case in the history of the subject'.
Podmore, of course, had never heard of Borley.

It will hardly be necessary to point out that the phenomena centred
upon Hetty (Mehetabel) Wesley, who was then aged nineteen. We
read of her 'trembling strongly in her sleep', prior to and during a
'visitation'. 'Old Jeffrey' appeared to follow her about the Parsonage,
and the entity had a particular predilection for the bed on which she was
lying. In fact, this young girl seemed to attract or induce the phenomena,
as girls do in so many similar cases.

As Hetty was so much involved, why did she not write to her brother
Samuel, giving him her own personal experiences, as did most of the
other members of the family? I think she *did* write, but that her letters
have been lost or were suppressed. Hetty's sister, Susannah, when
writing to her brother Samuel (see Letter XII) makes the definite statement, 'I should farther satisfy you concerning the disturbances, but it is
needless, because my sisters Emilia and Hetty write so particularly
about it.' The implication is that Hetty was then writing, or *had* written
—not that she was *going* to write. Where are her letters?

And this brings me to the curious statements about the correspondence made by Joseph Priestly in the Preface[2] to his *Original Letters*.[3]
These letters, as we know, were given to Priestly by the Rev. S.
Badcock, who obtained them from the granddaughter of the elder
Samuel Wesley. Priestly says: 'Mr John Wesley, as I learned from
Mr. Badcock, was very desirous of getting these letters into his possession, but the daughter and granddaughter of Mr. Samuel, being offended
at his conduct, would never deliver them to him. It was taken for
granted that he would have suppressed them . . .' Of course, Priestly's
collection of Wesley letters is not comprised wholly of those relating
to the Epworth ghost. But the fact remains that John Wesley did not
want them published. This being so, was it because of what Hetty had
written to her brother Samuel about the Poltergeist, or the part she
herself had played in the disturbances? It is possible, of course, that
the Rev. Badcock or Joseph Priestly suppressed them—in order not to
give pain to any surviving members of the family. To sum up, Hetty
wrote a letter or letters; John did not want them published; Hetty's
letters have disappeared. Which is a pity.

That John Wesley believed[4] in the genuineness of the disturbances,
there can be no doubt. He would hardly have publicised the whole
story all over again in *The Arminian Magazine* in 1784 (when he was

---

[1] *Modern Spiritualism*, London, 1902, Vol. I, p. 32.
[2] pp. III and IV.   [3] *Op. cit.*
[4] W. Tyerman, in his *Life and Times of the Rev. John Wesley* (London, 1880, Fifth
Edition, Vol. 1, p. 22) says that 'Wesley was a firm believer in ghosts and apparitions',
his belief and interest dating from the time of the Epworth disturbances.

over eighty), had he felt that the affair was a hoax. And that he was a believer in paranormal phenomena is proved by the many instances of visions of angels, cases of obsession, veridical dreams, apparitions, etc., that he records in his *Journal*.[1]

[1] Miss Beatrice Pepper, of 1, Bentinck Street, Greenock, sends me a curious story of a Poltergeist that she thinks may be connected in some way with John Wesley. She says (May 17, 1944): 'Many years ago . . . I was staying with my aunt at [giving the full name and address of the house]. She occupied one quarter of the mansion, which had been divided into four—her portion containing the old hall and staircase. John Wesley was at one time reputed to have stayed in this house. One night I was awakened by a terrific noise as if all the furniture in the hall and dining-room was being moved. The hall floor being mosaic, the furniture simply scraped over it. The running about and noise continued for some time as if fighting was in progress. Finally, the noise ended abruptly with the sound of a man running up the staircase to within a few steps of the top, and shouting five words. What the words were I cannot tell, as I was too petrified with fright, my door being at the head of the stairs. Next morning, my cousin, several years younger than myself, independently repeated the same story to my aunt.' Miss Pepper, though on a holiday, cut short her visit because of the incident. She concludes her letter by stating that her aunt had to vacate the house on account of the disturbances, about which the other tenants also complained. Her young cousin seemed particularly troubled by the 'ghost'.

CHAPTER IX

Academic Poltergeists

Our universities, notably those of Oxford and Cambridge, can boast of many ghosts, but few Poltergeists. However, Shane Leslie and some friends managed to 'lay'—or frighten!—a terrifying monster in human shape when they were undergraduates at Corpus Christi College, Cambridge, in 1904.

The ghost was supposed to be in some way connected with a certain Doctor Bott, a Fellow of the College, who committed suicide in his rooms there just before he was due to preach the University sermon.

At the time of my story, there was in existence one of the numerous Cambridge Psychical Research Societies that are formed from time to time, and one evening certain members of this group were discussing Bott and his rooms, when an excited undergraduate from Corpus burst in upon them and implored them to go to the assistance of the then occupier of the rooms who was, he said, in great distress and was terrified at something that was in the room. I should have mentioned that the old rooms of Bott (originally part of Archbishop Parker's suite) had been closed some years previously by the authorities on account of the strange occurrences that had disturbed successive occupants. For example, the last man to occupy them was found one night in a state of terror, crawling about the rooms on his hands and knees!

Well, the authorities decided to re-open them, which they did in the winter term of 1904—just before the incident I am about to relate.

Upon receiving the appeal for help, Shane Leslie, a man named Wade, and a Kingsman rushed to Corpus to render what assistance they could. The King's Scholar, who was about to take up Holy Orders, said he would exorcise the ghost and took a phial of holy water with him. They arrived at Corpus just as the College clock was striking ten.

They found that the Corpus man was almost demented with fear. Although the rooms were *empty and locked*, he had seen a face at his window that looked on to the Old Court, and had heard footsteps in the room adjoining the one in which he slept, though he knew the apartment was empty.

In a corner of the Old Court they found Bott's rooms, outside of which was the terrified Corpus man who was too frightened, he said, to enter. However, the small group entered in single file, led by the Kingsman who held a crucifix in front of him. 'The Thing is watching me', he said. 'Push me slowly forward, hold up my arms, but do not get in

111

front of the crucifix, as you value your lives!' Suddenly the Kingsman exclaimed: 'The Thing is pulling me, hold me tight, or I shall lose the crucifix!' He continued: 'Limb of Satan, avaunt in the name of the All Holy!' and with that the crowd rushed into the Thing, and incidentally crashed into the panelling of the room—apparently, the Thing had gone.

Leslie and his friends poked the fire into a blaze and sprinkled the room with holy water. Then they waited for the next move. It wasn't long in coming! Suddenly the Kingsman exclaimed: 'The Thing is there!' at the same time pointing to the open doorway of the bedroom. Without a moment's hesitation, but minus his crucifix, which he had dropped, he sprang through the doorway into the bedroom—and was as rapidly hurled back, where he fell in a heap at the feet of his friends. Then he crawled about the room searching for the flask of holy water, of which there was still a little left.

Suddenly, to their horror, the Thing appeared in the doorway of the bedroom and began to advance towards them. They were petrified with fear. They could neither move nor speak.

Then something happened. There was a terrific crash behind them and a crowd of undergraduates, whose curiosity could no longer be restrained, burst open the door, letting in a flood of light. The Thing disappeared. The Kingsman declared that it had passed to the room above. 'We must follow it', he said. This room was occupied by a medical student, an atheist who, upon being informed of the reason for the sudden and unceremonial visit of the exorcists, laughed the whole thing to scorn. As the Kingsman advanced, crucifix in hand, towards a certain corner of the room, the sceptic darted in front of him. The next moment he was a helpless heap on the floor, murmuring 'I am cold, I am icy cold!'

Very little more happened. All the principals in this psychic drama were bordering on collapse. Those spectators who had witnessed the more terrifying incidents moved in a body to old Bott's rooms below, smashed the cupboards, tore down the ancient panelling and generally wrecked the place. Of course there was the usual inquiry and the Corpus authorities kicked up an awful row about the whole affair. They also closed Bott's rooms once more. I have seen these rooms; in fact, when lecturing at Cambridge University on one occasion, it was arranged that I should sleep the night there. However, the necessary accommodation could not be arranged in time and I slept in another college, also alleged to be haunted.

The story of Bott's ghost, or of the Corpus Poltergeist, if it be one, is well authenticated. The foregoing account has been extracted from the long and detailed story by Colonel Cyril Foley in the *Sunday Express* for December 5th 1927, which should be read in full. Mr. Shane Leslie agrees with Colonel Foley's description of the affair. By the way, I find that I have omitted to tell my readers what 'the Thing' was like. Well, each member of the terror-stricken party 'fortunate' enough to see the Thing found it impossible to describe accurately. But each one agreed that it was cut off at the knees!

Oxford, too, can boast of a legless ghost. (Are these truncated apparitions peculiar to seats of learning?) On October 23rd, 1929, Sir Charles Oman, M.P., gave a lecture to a revived Oxford University S.P.R. and was asked by Dr. R. H. Maret whether there was any truth in the story that Archbishop Laud still haunted St. John's College. He had been told that the level of the floor had been changed and now Laud was only to be seen from the knees upwards. Sir Charles replied that it was noises (thumps, bangs, and 'sounds of dragging') that had been heard—the ghost had not been seen. I was lecturing myself for the O.U.S.P.R. a few weeks later, and confirmed Sir Charles's statement.

The title of Sir Charles Oman's talk was 'Ghosts I have Known', and he mentioned those that are supposed to haunt, amongst others, Oriel and Wadham Colleges. If we can trust the evidence, the entity inhabiting the latter college was a Poltergeist—judging by the commotion it caused! Sir Charles was asked if he could say which Oxford College had the best—or the worst!—record for ghosts, and he replied that college ghost stories are not very good. I agree. Some of them are quite modern and many are merely traditional.

Undoubtedly, the best-authenticated Poltergeist case connected with any University is that recorded by Simon Ockley (1678–1720), Professor of Arabic in the University of Cambridge from 1711–1720, under the Sir Thomas Adams Foundation.

The data were collected and written up for me by Mr. H. O. Evennett, of Trinity College, Cambridge, and his account was published[1] by me in the *British Journal of Psychical Research* when I was editing that publication. I am much indebted to Mr. Evennett for the details of this very important case, which I reproduce herewith:

The chief authority for the life of Simon Ockley is the biography in Chalmers' *General Biographical Dictionary*, written by his grandson, Dr. Ralph Heathcote. The 'Life' in the *Dictionary of National Biography* adds a few odd references from Hearne's collections, etc., but is based entirely upon the older 'Life'. There are two volumes of his letters in the British Museum (Add. MSS. 15911 and 23204) which supply further details, and extracts from other letters (without references) are given by Isaac D'Israeli, *Calamities of Authors* (London, 1812–13). The *Introductions* to his various works may also be consulted, and Venn's *Alumni* . . . iii. 274.

These letters describing the Poltergeist are from the British Museum, Lansdowne MSS., 846ff. 44 etc. At the time the Professor was in Cambridge Castle for debt. He had just brought out his *History of the*

---

[1] *British Journal of Psychical Research*, London, March—Apl., 1929.

Saracens after a great deal of labour and worry, occasioned mainly by his financial difficulties from which he suffered severely all his life. He was a man of retiring and studious habits, who applied himself to his work with extreme intensity, to the detriment of his health. But no other account of him, printed or in MSS., refers to the experience of the Poltergeist.

'At last he gave such an explosion .... and rais'd both me and the bed with the force of it'.

Cambridge, May 6, 1718. S. Ockley to Dr. Keith.

Sir,

I do not remember myself to have been worse in my whole lifetime than I was on Sunday last, when to mend the matter I was plagued all night with a Caccodæmon that infests our castle after a very strange manner. He did not suffer me to get one wink of rest till after broad daylight, and not much then, for he is verily as troublesome in the day as the night at certain times.

I know these things are exploded as mere Chimeras in this (*si Diis placet*) discerning age; but they must give me leave to trust to my own experience rather than to their *Cui bonos*.

114

I felt him moving under the bed and heaving it up. I waited the event, whilst he entertained me with variety of sounds and capricious troublesome motions in different parts of the room. At last he gave such an explosion under the bed as seem'd to sound in my ears as loud as the largest cannon, and rais'd both me and the bed with the force of it.

I soon after heard him tapping at the top of my bed's head. I asked him what we were to have next? Immediately he flew through the boards that separate my bed chamber from the next room, and returned again with such violence that you would have imagined that he had shivered them all to pieces. Then giving a slight tap in the midst of a great boarded wooden chair that stands close by my bed's head, he seem'd to make such a noise as when a great cat leaps down upon the boards, but withall so hollow as if all his body except his feet had been made of copper. I look'd for him instantly the moon shining very bright, but there was no appearance; then moving a little while at a distance he returned to his old tricks again.

Once he was whisking about in the corner of the room and made such a noise suppose as a cat would do playing with a piece of paper. I snatched the curtain immediately to see him, which he took so ill that I thought my great wooden chair had been coming directly at me; such a suddain terrible jarring noise did he make with it.

So civil he is that tho' the parlour where I live all the daytime is a good bow's shot distant from the chamber where I lodge, yet he now and then makes me a visit here; and not long since as I was talking with an honest man about him, who is not over credulous in such cases, he made a proselyte of him at once by giving such a bounce as seem'd to shake the whole room and almost to blow me and my chair quite away, tho' I never could perceive anything stir.

Yesterday about one a'clock he entertain'd us with a multitude of hollow thumps exactly resembling the fire of cannon at a distance. In the afternoon it was more like thunder.

The last night I design'd to entertain him by candle light, but perceiving that some people in the street had got a notion that I was going to conjure down a spirit, and besides that he was not so active as in the dark; to humour him in his own way I put out my candle and put myself in a posture for his reception. The first I heard of him was a leap from the windows like a cat; then the noise of two able threshers upon a boarded floor. Afterwards he twisted a long line making the same noise that the ropemakers do. He whistles admirably well and drives a cart or a gang of packhorses. I have heard the sound of the bells as distinctly as ever I did in my life. After he had entertained me thus for a while, I having rebuked him after such a manner as I thought most proper, I was resolved to endeavour to compose myself to sleep in spite of him, which I did, but he would not let me rest long.

I fancy there is a gang of them, or else he is like the Old Man in

Scarron's comical Romance, that used to act three parts at once, viz: the King, the Queen and the ambasadour.

But, after all, it is no laughing matter. I am sure I do not find it so. It is exceedingly troublesome and terrible. There is something in the nature of those separated beings so different from flesh and blood as make their too near approach almost insupportable. God preserve us all from the Malignant influences of infernal powers for the sake of our blessed Lord the Saviour Jesus Christ.

Yesterday my daughter was here, and having confess'd that there were unaccountable sounds, she wished they were louder. The spirit did not stay a great while before he gratified her request, and gave us a peal like thunder.

If anyone doubts the truth of this I am ready to resign my chamber to him with all my heart.

(*Signed*) S. OCKLEY.

The next letter is dated Ascension Day, 1718 (May 23, O.S.) and in it Ockley apparently answers some remarks that Dr. Keith had made:

Dear Sir,

I perceive you are under a mistake. You are not aware how much I converse in my thoughts with the invisible world. I never make any ostentation of it, for if I ever mention anything that goes any farther than Mathematical demonstration our people know just as much of it as I do about the situation of the cities in the moon. But you are a Gentleman to whom I have such obligations that it is not, nor ought to be, in my power to refuse you anything; but notwithstanding all those obligations were they ten times greater, they should not induce me to communicate anything of this kind, unless I had that same assurance that I have of your being thoroughly qualified to judge of things of this nature.

Whether or no the spirit haunts the castle I am not certain. I believ'd so at first, but this I am fully assured of, that his last visit was a particular Dispensation of Providence to me.

I have heard him make noises at a distance some months ago. I am not so unacquainted with things of that nature as not to be able to distinguish those sounds from any other. I oftentimes said there was a spirit and was of course as often laughed at.

But once (I believe about 3 weeks ago) I had sent the keeper on an errand, it was about 9 o'clock at night, and my candle stood burning by my bedside, I heard upon the wall distinct rappings as if they had been upon wainscot; I anticipated your good advice. I recollected my spirits and resign'd myself into the hands of the Father of Spirits under the protection of his blessed Son our Lord and Saviour Jesus Christ.

I knew very well that that was but the beginning, and lived in constant expectation to hear more of it, which I did frequently; and the reason why I gave you a particular account of Sunday night was because it was the most remarkable.

I was indeed of your opinion first. I took it to be an uneasy departed spirit, and thought it an act of charity to assist it; but all my labour was lost; I had no remedy left but fervent prayer, in which I spent the greater part of the night.

Not that I was scared, for I defye anyone to convict me of anything that ever looked like cowardice,* if I have any fault with relation to such matters it lyes in the other extreme.

N.B. *So far as the asterisk was written as soon as I received your letter, since which time I have been under such a feverish indisposition as has made me incapable of anything and perfectly listless. I slept well for two or three nights and began to recover my strength and spirits but they must of necessity decay again unless my troublesome guest, as you very properly call him, either leave this habitation, or I be removed to another. He is come back again as it were with double force; for these two last nights he exercised me incessantly from ten till after four in the morning. Last night he gave near I believe an hundred strokes in the next room to me as loud as men make when they are rending timber or breaking down wainscot! besides variety of rappings, hideous, hollow, inarticulate voices, besides several other inimitable sounds. This morning between three and four a'clock he was very busy in rubbing down a long table that stands in my room, and as he was whisking about, he now and then stumpt like one that has a wooden leg.[1] You seem, Sir, to think that he is a ludicrous spirit, and that therefore he is never to be entertained or subdued in that way. I never did entertain him in that way, nor did he ever give me any reason.

I cannot yet be persuaded that he is a ludicrous spirit, nor the Soul of any person deceased. At present I take him to be a malignant evil Genius, of the same sort that I met with in Hand Alley, for the sounds and his manner are very much the same.

Nobody heard him but myself last night and let me have been in never so great distress, I could neither have awakened any of them nor have been able to gone out of my room.

I believe he would speak but cannot. I have thought sometimes to lay hold of some of his hollow tones but never could to any certainty. Whatsoever he is I do not desire to be farther informed by such conversation. If he is in any distress, nobody more ready than myself to serve him; but I do not desire he should distress me, which he do's exceedingly by robbing me of my rest, and exercising and debilitating my spirits. I have spoken to him several times, but he never returned a syllable of answer—a week's more such exercise would reduce me to a very bad condition.

(*Signed*) S. OCKLEY.

[1] Compare this 'stumping' effect with 'The Poltergeist that Stumbled'.—H.P.

Soon after this the Professor was released and returned to his family at Swavesey. It is to be supposed that his liabilities were finally met, thanks to the efforts of his friends, although a sentence in a letter of Dr. Keith's, presently to be given, would seem to imply that this was not so. Perhaps his release was on the score of ill-health, for it is certain that he was still very unwell on his home-coming. Moreover, the entity appears to have followed him, as is witnessed in the next letter, dated July 6, 1718, from Swavesey. It runs as follows:

Dear Sir,

. . . You ask me, Sir, whether my spirit has left me or not. I cannot say that he has. About an hour ago my second daughter and I sitting in the kitchen, I heard a very great noise above stairs. Now you are to understand that I am a man the most impatient of noise of any man breathing. I took it for granted that the maid had been cleaning the rooms or making a bed, and had flung something about by accident, but having occasion to go upstairs I found the coast clear, and upon enquiry was inform'd that the maid was sent on an errand; all the rooms were immediately search'd, no cat, no dog, nothing visible.

I cannot close my letter before I acquaint you with one memoir relating to the spirit in Cambridge Castle. One night when all the prisoners were lock'd up in their rooms except two or three innocents, I had occasion to go to the house of office. As soon as I sat down and placed my candle on my left hand, the spirit came down with such force as you would have imagined would have dashed the whole partition to pieces. Such things are so far from diminishing my courage that they encrease it, for immediately I summon up all my spirits, and make the most regular Christian opposition that I am able, but as I have told you before I am not able to bear the influence of their vehicles, and I owe my present indisposition to that malignant power (so much by way of parenthesis). I immediately snatch'd up my candle in one hand, and opened the door with the other, but nothing appeared.

I knew very well that there was none of the prisoners could or would impose on me, for tho' I do not design to make going to Jayl a habit, yet common sense taught me to secure the friendship of the most impudent fellow in the crew. I hate mortally to have a piss-pot emptied upon my head, and then be answered that nobody did it. He would not I'm sure play any tricks with me because I was his best friend; besides if he would he could not, for I defye all mortal powers to impose upon me in such a case.

The sounds that those spirits make are inimitable, and their accursed Influence insupportable. However, I went up and ask'd him why he made such a noise (tho' I knew it was not he, but I was resolved to be thoroughly satisfied). The poor man was asleep, but upon my waking him he answered that he had made no noise but had been composing himself to rest ever since he came to bed. I then took more particular notice of the building and observed that it was impossible for any of the prisoners (considering the situation of their lodgings) to have made any such noise in that place. I wrapt myself up in my gown and went thither again on purpose to see whether he would return. As soon as I was sat down he came with the same force, and gave such a jar to the door as if a man had kick'd at it with the utmost force. I saw the door jarr, as I did the first time, and opened it as quick as I could, but finding nothing went to bed.

(*Signed*) S. OCKLEY.

In reply to this letter Dr. Keith wrote on July 12, 1718:
Rev. and Dear Sir,

I received your very acceptable letter of the 6th and rejoyced to see it dated from Swavesey. I am sorry first of all to hear of your indisposition and listlessness and especially of the weakness and tremor of your nerves. I shall set down a prescription or two at the end of this, which I desire you would use for about ten days or a fortnight. You may send for the powders mentioned in the first two little vials, and weigh out 15 grains of each in the morning and evening when you take them. They will be the more effectual if you will add 5 grains of the Sal Succini to them, and therefore you may get one dram of this in a vial too. When you have weighed out the powders mix them in a little conserve of Rosemary flowers, and take it by way of Bolus, drinking a cupfull of sage or sassafras tea after it. Tho' you don't mention any disorder in your stomach yet I think it fit to order a general litter for you in order to help your digestion, which I reckon to be one-half of the cure. If you hav't an honest Apothecary that's your friend your daughter may get the ingredients and boil them at home, and also the two waters to add to the liquor when it is strained out and cold. I pray God to give his blessing that they may be a means of your recovery. When you are in any tolerable condition to use it, I would recommend to you gentle exercise, and especially riding on horse-back.

In the next place I cannot but lament the negligence and imprudence of your friends both at Oxford and Cambridge, and indeed am at a loss how to account for either. In the meantime, you must take good heart and do the best you can. And I hope you will especially since now you will be easier at home than ever. For I reckon the noise and disturbance that may come from the other spirit will be in all respects less sensible[1] ... cribed the whole of your three letters on the subject of the spirit in Cambridge Castle, and have here enclos'd them to be communicated to his Lordship at your leisure. I have not heard the least syllable of

---

[1] The hiatus that follows is due to the illegibility of the original MS.—H.P.

119

that of Hand Alley a great while. I often pass by the house and see it is still inhabited.

I remain very heartily,

Rev. Sir,

Your sincere humble servant,

(*Signed*) JAMES KEITH.

This letter (Add. MSS. 15911, f. 33) does not tell us how Ockley's financial affairs were settled. The doctor may be lamenting either that it was not due to the efforts of his friends that he was released, or may be only deploring that they took so long to do it. The professor appears, also, to have thought that the spirit which was now troubling him at home was a different one from that which had plagued him in prison. Did Dr. Keith really consider the whole affair simply a delusion of his friend's temporarily unbalanced mind? This is a question which may well be considered. Ockley was doubtless uncouth and abnormal. He may easily have overworked his brain, for he was indefatigable at his studies, allowing himself little or no leisure and working far into the night. The reaction which must have followed the completion of his history, coupled with his physical weakness, may quite possibly have deranged his mind for a while.

CHAPTER X

Dr. Johnson, Goldsmith, and the Cock Lane Ghost

I mentioned in the Foreword that I did not intend to include in this volume cases that were purely negative or entirely fraudulent. I have hesitated about giving an account of the sensational Cock Lane disturbances because there was in this case an element of fraud that was quite obvious even to the unscientific investigators of the eighteenth century.

And in the minds of many thinking psychists, the question has arisen as to whether the manifestations were fraudulent from beginning to end or whether there was a substratum of truth underlying this famous London ghost story. Such a brilliant and impartial writer and critic as Andrew Lang did not consider the Cock Lane 'ghost' the complete swindle the public—past and present—imagines it to be. And it is well known that even the best of mediums (and there *was* a medium in this classic Poltergeist case; as so often happens, it was a young girl) sometimes cheat when subjected to test conditions or when surrounded by a not too friendly audience who are waiting for things 'to happen.'

But there are other considerations that have prompted me to include the Cock Lane affair in my gallery of outstanding British Poltergeists. In the first place, Cock Lane produced London's most famous ghost— a ghost that, most unusually, has secured a niche for itself in the pages of such a very academic work as the *Encyclopædia Britannica*. Secondly, the literary giants of the day vied with one another in abusing it—or each other—or making capital out of it, or 'explaining' it. Dr. Samuel Johnson was very intrigued by the 'doings' in Cock Lane and attended more than one séance in the hope of witnessing miracles—which was unfortunate for the doctor as it gave Charles Churchill, the poet, the very opportunity he was looking for, and a venomous attack on the great lexicographer duly followed.

It was Oliver Goldsmith, however, who, among the *literati*, took the most active interest in the 'ghost' of Cock Lane, and it was he who bequeathed to us an unsigned tract—for which he was paid three guineas—describing what he saw and heard in a little girl's bedroom in the purlieus of Smithfield. This pamphlet is excessively rare.[1] I possess a copy, and I will give some extracts later.

---

[1] It is entitled: *The Mystery Revealed: Containing a Series of Transactions and Authentic Testimonials, Respecting the supposed Cock Lane Ghost....* London, 1742 (*recte* 1762). A copy sold for £900 at the Jerome Kern sale in New York a few years ago. It was published by Bristow, in St. Paul's Churchyard.

THE
MYSTERY REVEALED;

Containing a SERIES of

TRANSACTIONS

AND

AUTHENTIC TESTIMONIALS,

Respecting the supposed

COCK-LANE GHOST;

Which have hitherto been concealed from the
PUBLIC.

—— *Since none the Living dare implead,*
Arraign him in the Person of the Dead.

DRYDEN.

LONDON:

Printed for W. BRISTOW, in St. Paul's Church-yard;
and C. ETHRINGTON, York.
MDCCXLII.

Title-page of the pamphlet, written anonymously by Oliver Gold-
smith, dealing with his experiences of the 'Cock Lane Ghost'. It is
excessively rare. The date is a misprint: it was published in 1762.
From the author's collection.

The account of the haunting that now follows is compiled principally from my collection of original contemporary extracts cut from the *Gentleman's Magazine* for 1762, from Goldsmith's brochure, and from other works in my library.

The real trouble began in January, 1762, and, as usual, the first news of the sensation soon appeared in the periodical Press.

In 1756, a Mr. Kent married a young woman, a 'Miss E.L.' who came from Norfolk. Within twelve months she died in childbirth and her sister Fanny joined Mr. Kent in order to keep house for him. We hear little of the infant, though it is said to have lived a few minutes. The inevitable happened and Kent and his sister-in-law fell in love with each other. The law would not then—as it does now—permit a man to wed his deceased wife's sister, so they dispensed with the marriage ceremony. They took lodgings together and Kent was foolish enough to lend his landlord some money. Again the inevitable happened: Kent could not recover the loan; there was a row, and the couple sought fresh quarters. These they found in the house of a man named Parsons, who lived in Cock Lane, near Giltspur Street, Smithfield. Parsons was clerk of St. Sepulchre's Church. He had a daughter Elizabeth, aged eleven years.

One day, Kent was called to the country in order to attend a wedding. Fanny did not like to sleep alone, so she asked little Elizabeth to share her bed. Almost immediately, bumps, rappings and 'scratchings' occurred on the bedposts, under the bed and, according to one account, in various parts of the room. Upon complaining to Mrs. Parsons, Fanny was told that a cobbler next door sometimes worked all night and that perhaps it was he who was responsible for the 'manifestations'. But when these recurred on the Sunday night, this theory was discarded. Fanny was terrified and thought the strange sounds meant that she would soon die. She *did* soon die.

It was also suggested by ill-disposed persons that Kent's previous—and authentic—wife, in a burst of *post-mortem* jealousy, was trying to punish her erring sister by frightening her. The manifestations soon ceased.

Kent, apparently, had an incurable habit of lending his landlords money. Parsons, it is said, extracted a large sum from him. There was the usual failure to recover the loan, the usual row, the usual law case, and the usual migration to fresh lodgings on the part of Kent and Fanny. They went to Bartlet Court, Clerkenwell, where poor Fanny died on February 2, 1760.

Did Fanny succumb to her own potent powers of auto-suggestion, induced by the fright she received when sleeping with little Elizabeth during those exciting nights in Cock Lane? Perhaps. The local doctors said her death was due to small-pox, and her coffin was duly laid in the vault of St. John's Church, Clerkenwell.

There was now a lull in the manifestations—a lull that lasted for eighteen months. Then, early in January 1761-2, the disturbances in the Cock Lane house broke out afresh—again on and around the bed of Elizabeth Parsons. According to one of the papers, her father removed the wainscoting in the room, in case someone was playing a practical joke on the family.

Bedsteads and little girl sleepers are frequently the foci of Poltergeist activities. Mr. Mompesson's daughter, in the classic Drummer of Tedworth case; Hetty Wesley at Epworth Parsonage; Eleonore Zugun, the 'Poltergeist girl'—all were disturbed during their slumbers, or when lying in bed, by the mischievous *Geists*. Hetty, especially, was subject to these attacks: 'Her face would be flushed, she would moan, and turn over uneasily in her sleep.' And Elizabeth Parsons, too, 'was always affected with tremblings and shiverings at the coming and going of the ghost.' Of course, Elizabeth could have simulated these reactions.

Like Ann Robinson in the 'Astonishing Transactions at Stockwell', a change of bedroom, or even of house, made no difference to the peripatetic Poltergeist. It followed Elizabeth from her own home to those of her neighbours', and usually the 'scratchings', raps and bumps could be depended upon to put in an appearance, so to speak. The child was followed by the Poltergeist, and the Poltergeist was followed by the *élite* of London society, and less noted phenomena-hunters. At these bedroom 'séances' (as we should now call them) attended, as I have said, Dr. Johnson and Goldsmith. There were 'also present' on various occasions, the Duke of York, Lady Mary Coke, Horace Walpole, the Rev. Dr. Douglas, afterwards Bishop of Salisbury, and many more luminaries, legal, literary, and ecclesiastical. In fact, the Cock Lane ghost set all London—especially fashionable London—by the ears.

It would be interesting to learn at what period of the world's history ghosts first began to rap in order to attract attention, and when the 'sitters' or audience began to rap back in an effort to obtain intelligent answers to, I am afraid (I am speaking from experience), not very intelligent questions on the part of the investigators. There is no record as to when the first ghostly rap was heard and answered, but this séance technique must have been invented at a very remote period—probably in the Early Stone Age. And this method of 'communication' has persisted down to the present day, as all who attend modern séances are aware.

Anyway, Elizabeth Parson's attendant, Mary Frazer, re-invented the code and attempted to obtain from the ghost something more interesting than mere scratchings and raps. The technique is worked as follows: The sitters ask questions, and if the answer is in the affirmative, the ghost gives one knock; if the answer is 'no', the ghost gives two knocks. This arrangement has the advantage that you can 'lead' the ghost to say almost anything you wish, and can tie the entity into a knot

124

by skilful cross-examining. By these subtle means it was ascertained that the rapping ghost was the spirit of Fanny, and that her 'husband', Mr. Kent, had poisoned her with 'red arsenic' conveyed in a pint of purl which, I understand, is spiced beer. 'Fanny' added that she hoped Kent would be hanged! Much more information was forthcoming, but when it came to questions of provable facts, the rapping spirit rather broke down, as we shall see in a minute in studying Goldsmith's account of his séance.

It can be imagined that the fact that Kent had been accused of the murder of his dear departed by the lady herself, was soon noised abroad and he felt very uncomfortable. People pointed at him in the street. It was at this juncture that Goldsmith attended a séance in the little girl's bedroom, and the resultant brochure was written really in defence of Kent. I will now quote verbatim from *The Mystery Revealed*, a book that is remarkable for the description of a bedroom séance that might have been held yesterday in the parlour of a modern medium :

'To have a proper idea of this scene, as it is now carried on, the reader is to conceive a very small room with a bed in the middle, the girl, at the usual hour of going to bed, is undressed and put in with proper solemnity; the spectators are next introduced who sit looking at each other, suppressing laughter, and wait in silent expectation for the opening of the scene. As the ghost is a good deal offended at incredulity, the persons present are to conceal theirs, if they have any, as by this concealment they can only hope to gratify their curiosity. For, if they show either before, or when the knocking is begun, a too prying, inquisitive, or ludicrous turn of thinking, the ghost continues usually silent, or, to use the expression of the house, Miss Fanny is angry. The spectators therefore have nothing for it, but to sit quiet and credulous, otherwise they must hear no ghost, which is no small disappointment to persons, who have come for no other purpose.

'The girl who knows, by some secret, when the ghost is to appear, sometimes apprizes the assistants of its intended visitation. It first begins to scratch and then to answer questions, giving two knocks for a negative, and one for an affirmative. By this means it tells whether a watch, when held up, be white, blue, yellow, or black; how many clergymen are in the room, though in this sometimes mistaken; it evidently distinguishes white men from negroes, with several other marks of sagacity; however, it is sometimes mistaken in questions of a private nature, when it deigns to answer them; for instance: the ghost was ignorant where she dined upon Mr. K—'s marriage; how many of her relations were at church upon the same occasion; but particularly she called her father John instead of Thomas, a mistake indeed a little extraordinary in a ghost; but perhaps she was willing to verify the old proverb, that *it is a wise child that knows its own father* . . .' And so on.

It seems incredible that the above description of a séance was written

182 years ago. The preparation of the 'medium', the introduction of the sitters, the 'drying-up' of the manifestations if the sitters were too inquisitive, the assertion that scepticism inhibits phenomena, the 'two knocks for a negative, and one for an affirmative' are *exactly* what take place today at a spiritualist séance. Modern spiritualism is supposed to date from the American 'Rochester knockings' of 1848, with the Fox sisters as mediums. I suggest that it dates from the Cock Lane knockings of 1762.

The publication of Goldsmith's pamphlet attracted a good deal of attention, and things were rapidly approaching a crisis. People demanded that Elizabeth should be 'tested'. A Mr. Aldrich, a Clerkenwell clergyman, arranged a test séance at his house, and Dr. Johnson was present. The great moralist wrote up his experiences for the *Gentleman's Magazine*. Elizabeth was put to bed by a committee of ladies and the sitters watched the child for about an hour, during which period nothing happened. Then the male members of the audience decided to interview Parsons, who was waiting below stairs. They were suddenly interrupted by some of the ladies who declared that 'scratching Fanny', as the Poltergeist was then called, had started again, and that not only scratchings but also knocks were being heard. So everyone trooped upstairs again. This time they imposed the simplest condition on the 'medium': they compelled her to place her hands *outside* the bedclothes. Again nothing happened.

'Scratching Fanny' had promised to 'perform' in the absence of the medium, and, specifically, she said she would rap on her own coffin and give valuable information, if the company would adjourn, at one in the morning, to the vault in St. John's Church and make the test. So thither they went, accompanied by Dr. Johnson. They waited there a considerable time, and solemnly adjured the ghost to give the promised information. But it remained obstinately silent. There was not a single rap or scratch. Dr. Johnson published his account of the affair. It was then decided 'in the opinion of the whole assembly, that the child has some art of making or counterfeiting particular noises, and that there is no agency of any higher cause.' As a matter of fact, it proved nothing of the sort, though probably the investigators were becoming tired of the whole business.

These negative tests, plus Goldsmith's pamphlet, at last aroused the authorities to take some action in the matter. They decided to hold an inquiry, and some further tests were arranged. The girl was slung up in a hammock, 'her hands and feet extended wide', at two successive séances. Still nothing happened, which is not very surprising. A perfectly genuine medium could hardly be expected to produce phenomena under such uncomfortable conditions. Elizabeth was then threatened. She was told that unless something happened at a third and final séance she and her father would be committed to Newgate. This—naturally—

frightened the child, and she was detected secreting a small board and a piece of wood inside her dress. Scratches were now heard, but, (I am quoting the newspapers again), 'the concurrent opinion of the whole assembly was that the child had been frightened by threats' into this attempt to deceive the investigators, who also added: 'The master of the house and his friend both declared that the noises the girl had made this morning *had not the least likeness to the former noises.*'

This third negative séance was really the end of the Cock Lane Ghost. Parsons, Mary Frazer, a clergyman, a tradesman and others were tried at the Guildhall and convicted of a conspiracy. This was on July 10, 1762. Parsons was condemned to the pillory for having promoted it, but the public were not convinced. Their faith in ghosts was stronger than their belief in Parson's guilt, and instead of pelting him with dead cats, offal, etc., as was customary on these occasions, they pelted him with money. In fact, quite a lot of it. I am tempted to remark, with Cardinal Caraffa, *Populus vult decipi, decipiatur*—which can be roughly translated: The people wish to be fooled—let them!

Dr. Johnson was pilloried, too, in a different way. His enemy Charles Churchill wrote (1763) a terrible poem, *The Ghost*, around the Cock Lane affair. He mercilessly criticised and ridiculed Johnson ('Pomposo, insolent and loud, Vain idol of a scribbling crowd') for the part he had played in investigating the ghost.

He also attacked 'Johnson Pomposo' from a different angle. Johnson had taken large subscriptions for a new edition of Shakespeare that he had promised to edit. He had lived on these subscriptions for years, but the new work was not forthcoming. His friends repeatedly exhorted him to get on with the book, without avail. Churchill, in his poem, asked where the book was that had been so long promised and so liberally paid for, and directly accused Johnson of 'cheating'. This terrible word proved effectual, and in October, 1765, appeared, after a delay of nine years, the new edition of Shakespeare. So the Cock Lane Ghost has something to its credit.

James Boswell, Johnson's biographer, tells us that his hero 'expressed great indignation at the imposture of the Cock Lane Ghost, and related, with much satisfaction, how he had assisted in detecting the cheat, and had published an account of it in the newspapers. Upon this subject I incautiously offended him by pressing him with too many questions.' Of course, Johnson had nothing at all to do with 'detecting the cheat'— which never was detected. Elizabeth's performances with the pieces of wood were just silly attempts at cheating.

Was the Cock Lane Poltergeist a fraud from beginning to end? If so, what was the motive? As Andrew Lang points out, the manifestations began *before* the relations between Kent and Parsons (over money matters) became strained. And the eighteen months' quiet spell was a curious break in the Poltergeist disturbances.

In the many contemporary reports of this case that I have read, I note one very curious incident. At one of the séances, in addition to the usual scratchings, raps, bumps and knocks, there was heard an entirely new phenomenon: This was a whirring noise, 'or a sound as if a large bird was flying about the room'. This is a 'manifestation' *very difficult* or impossible to simulate in full light with a group of investigators standing around you. I think it would be impossible for any medium (especially for one so young as Elizabeth) to produce such sounds under the conditions I have named. Only once have I heard similar sounds and that was in a house, unoccupied for many years, near Minehead. There was no question about the phenomenon which reminded me of the sound made by a circular saw at full speed, a large bird flying, or the 'swish' of something being pulled rapidly through the air.

So I am inclined to think that perhaps, after all, there were some genuine phenomena in the Cock Lane affair. There was the usual young girl, so much in evidence in genuine Poltergeist cases, and it seems incredible that so many people of culture and intelligence could have visited Elizabeth's bedroom night after night without at once detecting imposture—as indeed they did on one occasion when the trick was so apparent. At dark séances fraud can remain undetected for long periods. But not when a girl is in bed with people crowding round her and under a good light. It would be interesting to know what became of the Parsons family, especially the medium, Elizabeth. There is no record of any further 'trouble' either in Cock Lane or elsewhere.

Another case, similar to that of Cock Lane, was investigated by the police of Port Glasgow, on the Clyde, in 1864. The disturbances occurred at the home of Hugh McCardle. The police tore up the floors; they examined the walls, ceilings, cellars, and tried to imitate the noises, etc., without success. A hand, 'moving up and down', was seen by various persons. 'We could not catch it', they said, 'it quietly vanished and we only felt cold air'. This case, detailed in the Dialectical Society's report,[1] is fully authenticated, and the names of witnesses, including the police, are given. Sworn statements were made at the time.

[1] *Report on Spiritualism of the Committee of the London Dialectical Society*. . . . London, 1871, pp. 200 ff.

CHAPTER XI

The Hinton Ampner Skull

One of the most detailed, convincing, and best-documented stories of Poltergeist haunting is that of the manor house at Hinton Ampner (or Amner), four miles south-by-east of Alresford, and nine miles east from Winchester, Hampshire.

It was built probably by Sir Thomas Stewkley some time before 1623, and he was, perhaps, the first occupant. Though a manor house, or mansion house, it was not, for a family seat, a particularly large residence. In due course, the house was occupied by his descendants, one of whom, Mary Stewkley, married (May 10, 1719) Edward Stawell. Her young sister, Honoria, lived with them. Mary died in July 1740, and Honoria continued to live with the widower, her brother-in-law. Of course the affair rapidly developed into a *scandalum magnatum*. It was alleged that a liaison existed between the two, and that a child was born. There were stories of dark deeds. The baby was supposed to have been 'done away with'. Whether true or not, this is the sort of story that, under the circumstances, was bound to originate in any small village, and doubtless the servants at the Manor fed the flames of curiosity that must have almost consumed the local rustics as to what was happening at the 'big house'. Honoria died on November 25, 1754, aged 66. There is a plaque to her memory in Hinton Ampner Church.

Edward Stawell became Lord Stawell on January 23, 1742, and on April 2, 1755, died through an apoplectic fit. He was aged about 56.

Very soon after Lord Stawell's death, phenomena were recorded. A groom declared that he saw the ghost of his old master, Lord Stawell, 'dressed in a drab coat', in his bedroom. It was bright moonlight.

Hinton Ampner Manor remained unoccupied, except by a few servants, for some years, though during each shooting season it was lived in for a few weeks. It was furnished, and in January, 1765, was let to the Ricketts family. I must now say something about Mrs. Ricketts, who is our chief witness in this case.

Mrs. Mary Ricketts was born in 1737–8 and came from a distinguished family. Like George Washington, she could not tell a lie. We read that 'her veracity was proverbial in the family'. Her father was Swynfen Jervis. Her favourite brother was Captain John Jervis who, later, was created[1] Baron Jervis of Meaford, Stafford, and Earl St. Vincent for his brilliant naval exploits.

Mary Jervis married (1757) William Henry Ricketts of Canaan,

[1] May 27, 1797.

129

Jamaica. His business took him frequently to the West Indies and his wife was therefore faced with the alternative of accompanying him on these journeys, or staying in England. When her husband was called away in 1769, as she then had three young children, she decided to stay at home.

As I have stated, the Ricketts entered into occupation of the Manor House in January, 1765, with an entirely new set of servants. They were brought from London, and were strangers to Hinton Ampner and its vicinity. Almost immediately, noises of slamming doors were continually heard, though no door was ever found open. A new set of locks was put on the doors, without result. In July of this same year, the 'gentleman in drab', alleged to have been seen by the groom some ten years previously, and believed by him to have been Lord Stawell, was seen towards evening. The same figure was seen again in the great hall, at night, by the groom, George Turner.

The following is a list, in chronological order, of further unexplained incidents:

In July, 1767, 'a woman dressed in dark clothes which rustled as though of very stiff silk' was seen. Soon after, other noises were heard, such as 'groans' and 'rustling'.

At the end of the year 1769, Mr. Ricketts went on one of his trips to Jamaica, leaving his wife and their three young children at Hinton Ampner. Mrs. Ricketts afterwards heard footsteps and the 'rustling of silk'.

1770. February. Mrs. Ricketts heard heavy men's footsteps in her room, which she changed. In the new room she heard music and, once, heavy knocks.

1771, at the beginning of the year, a frequent sound like the murmuring of the wind, was heard throughout the house. A maid, Elizabeth Godin, heard much 'groaning and fluttering' in her room.

On April 2, 1771 (the sixteenth anniversary of Lord Stawell's fatal seizure) was heard a variety of sounds, concluding with three heavy knocks. Heard by various persons. On May 7 of the same year, the disturbances grew worse. At midsummer they became much worse. 'A woman and two men talking' was a frequent phenomenon.

Mrs. Ricketts's brother, John Jervis (afterwards Lord St. Vincent) came to stay with her. The day after he left, a peculiar crash was heard, followed by piercing shrieks, dying away as though sinking into the earth. A nurse, Hannah Streeter, expresses a wish to hear more, and henceforth is troubled every night. Captain Jervis returns and he and his friend Captain Luttrell, and his own servant, agree to watch. They sit up night after night and hear the various phenomena.

Captain Jervis left the house before August 9, 1771, and his sister and her children very soon after. The Bishop of Winchester lent Mrs. Ricketts the old Palace at Winchester and thither she removed. Then the

Bishop of St. Asaph offered her his house in London, which she occupied for some time, afterwards renting one of her own in Curzon Street.

What finally determined Mrs. Ricketts to leave the house was an experience that terrified her. In one of her 'Narratives' that she left for posterity, she says: 'I was assailed by a noise I never heard before, very near me, and the terror I felt not to be described'. She gives no details.

Towards the end of the Ricketts's tenancy a reward of £50, then £60, and finally £100 was offered for the detection of the person or thing that was causing the disturbances. No information was forthcoming.

Some time during the year 1772, Hinton Ampner Manor was let to a family named Lawrence, 'who endeavoured, by threatening the servants, to stifle their statements'. An apparition of a woman was seen. The Lawrences left suddenly in 1773. The house was never again inhabited and was pulled down.

DOCUMENTATION

At the beginning of the chapter I said that the Hinton Ampner case was well-documented.[1] The testimony takes the form of letters from Mrs. Ricketts to her husband in Jamaica, and to the Rector of Hinton Ampner, the Rev. J. M. Newbolt; letters from her brother, John Jervis, to her husband; and letters from the servants to Mrs. Ricketts, etc., etc.

But the most moving evidence is that contained in an account, written in 1772, that Mrs. Ricketts left for her children and 'posterity'. I will reproduce this later.

Part of the story was published by R. H. D. Barham in his biography[2] of his father, the famous author of *The Ingoldsby Legends*. Mrs. William Henley Jervis, a great-granddaughter of Mrs. Ricketts, took exception to this incomplete account (and to one that appeared in the *Leisure Hour* for 1871, pp. 363 and 688), and as she possessed one of the two original manuscripts of Mrs. Ricketts's 'Narrative' (her aunt, Mrs. Edmund Palmer, possessed the other copy), she decided to give to the world the true facts.

She published the 'Narrative' in the *Gentleman's Magazine*[3] (always on the look-out for good ghost stories) under the title of 'A Hampshire Ghost Story', and it is this version I am going to use, as it is a verbatim copy of the manuscript as Mrs. Ricketts wrote it. But there are other versions, slightly different as regards names. For example, there was published a pamphlet on the case, and I imagine that this brochure was compiled from material that had appeared in the *Gentleman's Magazine*. I have not seen a copy of the pamphlet, and I cannot even find the title of it, or where published, etc.

[1] Sir Walter Scott mentions the case in *Letters on Demonology*, London, 1830, pp. 359–361.

[2] *Life and Letters of Richard H. Barham*, London, 1870.

[3] For Nov. and Dec. 1872. (Vol. IX, pp. 547–559 and pp. 666–678.)

In 1893, John, third Marquess of Bute, obtained a copy of the pamphlet, which he edited for the Society for Psychical Research. The Society published it.[1] Lord Bute not only edited it, but he appears to have altered the names of some of the persons mentioned therein, as they do not correspond with Mrs. Jervis's manuscript. Although the names of all persons and places are given *in full* in Mrs. Jervis's version (published in 1872), most of these have disappeared in the *S.P.R.* version, published twenty-one years later. This is very curious. As reproduced in the *S.P.R. Journal* (to which I am indebted for some of my information), with Lord Bute's notes, there are many blanks and dashes, and frequent references to 'Lord Z.', 'Mr. Y', and 'Mary X.', etc. (I counted thirty-nine *lacunæ* on one page!)—all very confusing and very infuriating. We are not told the name of the house, or where it is situated, or even the name of the county! I imagine that these omissions were in the original pamphlet edited by Lord Bute.

Mr. Sacheverell Sitwell includes the Hinton Ampner case in his book,[2] and has taken the trouble to find out and substitute proper names for many of the 'X's', blanks, and dashes. I, too, have filled in some more, so that the narrative I am presenting to the reader is, I think, complete as regards the real names of persons and places. As Mr. Sitwell remarks, the identification of the various persons in the case is an occupation in itself, due to the confusion caused by the way the documents, etc., were originally presented to the public. As I have stated, the best evidence for the haunting of Hinton Ampner comes from Mrs. Ricketts herself, who wrote out a true and first-hand account of the incidents for her children, to be read when they were old enough to appreciate such things. Here, then, is

MARY RICKETTS'S LEGACY TO HER CHILDREN

Hinton Ampner Parsonage,
July 7th, 1772.

To my dear children I address the following relation, anxious that the truths which I have so faithfully delivered shall be as faithfully transmitted to posterity, to my own in particular. I determined to commit them to writing, which I recommend to their care and attentive consideration, entreating them to bear in mind the peculiar mercy of Providence in preserving them from all affright and terror during the series of wonderful disturbances that surrounded them, wishing them to be assured the veracity of their mother was pure and undoubted, that even in her infancy it was in the family a proverb, and according to the testimony of that excellent person Chancellor Hoadley she was *truth itself*; she writes, not to gratify vanity, but to add weight to her relation.

[1] See the *S.P.R. Journal*, Vol. VI, 1893–94, pp. 52–74.
[2] *Poltergeists*, London, 1940.

To the Almighty and Unerring Judgment of Heaven and Earth I dare appeal for the truth, to the best of my memory and comprehension, of what I here relate.

(*Signed*) MARY RICKETTS.

Hinton Ampner, near Alresford, in Hampshire.

The Mansion House and estate of Hinton Ampner, near Alresford, Hampshire, devolved in 1755 to the Right Honourable Henry Bilson Legge in right of his lady, daughter and sole heiress of Lord Stawell, who married the eldest daughter and co-heiress of Sir Hugh Stewkeley, Bart., by whose ancestors the estate at Hinton had been possessed many generations and by this marriage passed to Mr. Legge on the death of the said Sir Hugh.

Mr. (who on the death of his elder brother became Lord) Stawell made Hinton his constant residence. Honoria, the youngest sister of his lady, lived with them during the life of her sister, and so continued with Lord Stawell till her death in 1754.

On the evening of April 2nd, 1755, Lord Stawell, sitting alone in the little parlour at Hinton, was seized with a fit of apoplexy; he articulated one sentence only to be understood, and continued speechless and insensible till the next morning when he expired.

His lordship's family at the time consisted of the following domestics: Isaac Mackrel, house steward and bailiff. Sarah Parfait, housekeeper, who had lived in the family nearly forty years. Thomas Parfait, coachman, husband to said Sarah, who had lived there upwards of forty years. Elizabeth Banks, housemaid, an old servant. Jane Davis, dairymaid. Mary Barras, cook. Joseph Sibley, butler. Joseph, groom. Richard Turner, gardener, and so continued by Mr. Ricketts. Lord Stawell had one son, who died at Westminster School, aged sixteen.

Thomas Parfait, his wife, and Elizabeth Banks continued to have the care of the house during the lifetime of Mr. Legge, who usually came there for one month every year in the shooting season. On his death in August, 1764, Lady Stawell, so created in her own right, since married to the Earl of Hillsborough, determined to let Hinton Ampner Mansion, and Mr. Ricketts took it in December following. Thomas Parfait was at that time lying dead in the house. His widow and Elizabeth Banks quitted it on our taking possession in January, 1765. We removed thither from town, and had the same domestics that lived with us there and till some time afterwards we had not any house-servant belonging to the neighbourhood. Soon after we were settled at Hinton I frequently heard noises in the night, as of people shutting, or rather slapping doors with vehemence. Mr. Ricketts went often round the house on supposition there were either housebreakers or irregularity among his servants. In these searches he never could trace any person; the servants were in their proper apartments, and no appearance of disorder. The noises continued to be heard, and I could conceive no other cause than that some of the villagers had false keys to let themselves in and out at pleasure; the only preventive to this evil was changing the locks, which was accordingly done, yet without the effect we had reasonably expected.

About six months after we came thither, Elizabeth Brelsford, nurse to our eldest son, Henry, then about eight months old, was sitting by him when asleep, in the room over the pantry, appropriated for the nursery, and, being a hot summer's evening, the door was open that faces the entrance into the yellow bedchamber, which, with the adjoining dressing-room, was the apartment usually occupied by the lady of the house. She was sitting directly opposite to this door, and plainly saw (as she afterwards related) a gentleman in a drab-coloured suit of clothes go into the yellow room. She was in no way surprised at the time, but on the housemaid, Molly Newman, coming up with her supper, she asked what strange gentleman was come. Upon the other answering there was no one, she related what is already described and desired her fellow-servant to accompany her to search the room; this they did immediately without any appearance of what she had seen. She was much concerned and disturbed, and she was thoroughly assured she could no ways be deceived, the light being sufficient to distinguish any object clearly. In some time after it was mentioned to me. I treated it as the effect of fear or superstition, to which the lower class of people are so prone, and it was entirely obliterated from my mind till the late astonishing disturbances brought to my recollection this and other previous circumstances.

In the autumn of the same year George Turner, son of the gardener of that name, who was then groom, crossing the great hall to go to bed, saw at the other end a man in drab-coloured coat, whom he concluded to be the butler, who wore such coloured clothes, he being lately come and his livery not made. As he passed immediately upstairs to the room where all the menservants lay, he was in great astonishment to find the butler and other men servants in bed. Thus the person he had seen in the hall remained unaccounted for, like the same person before described by the nurse; and George Turner, now living, avers these particulars in the same manner he first related them.

In the month of July, 1767, about seven in the evening, there were sitting in the kitchen, Thomas Wheeler, postilion; Ann Hall, my own woman; Sarah, waiting woman to Mrs. Mary Poyntz; and Dame Lacy; the other servants were out excepting the cook, then employed in washing up her things in the scullery.

The persons in the kitchen heard a woman come downstairs and along the passage leading towards them, whose clothes rustled as of the stiffest silk; and on their looking that way, the door standing open, a female figure rushed past, and out of the house door, as they conceived. Their view of her was imperfect; but they plainly

'*A female figure rushed past . . . . and instantly disappeared*'.

distinguished a tall figure in dark-coloured clothes. Dame Brown, the cook, instantly coming in, this figure passed close by her, and instantly disappeared. She described the person and drapery as before mentioned, and they all united in astonishment who or what this appearance could be; and their surprise was heightened when a man, coming directly into the yard and into the house the way she went out, on being asked who the woman was he met, declared he had seen no one.

Ann Hall, since married to John Sparks, now living at Rogate, near Petersfield, will testify to the truth of this relation, as will Dame Brown, now living at Bramdean. The postilion is since dead.

Meanwhile, the noises continued to be heard occasionally. Miss Parker's woman, Susan Maidstone, was terrified with the most dismal groans and rustling round her bed. At different times most of the servants were alarmed with noises that could no way be accounted for. In the latter end of the year 1769, Mr. Ricketts went to Jamaica; I continued at Hinton with my three infant children and eight servants, whose names and connections were as follows: Ann Sparks, late Ann Hall, my own woman, the daughter of very industrious parents. Sarah Horner, nurse, sister to a substantial farmer of that name, and of a family of integrity and property. Hannah Streeter, nursemaid, of reputable parents and virtuous principles. Lucy Webb, housemaid, of honest principles. Dame Brown, cook, quiet and regular. John Sparks, coachman. John Horner, postilion, aged sixteen years, eldest son to the farmer above mentioned. Lewis Chanson, butler, a Swiss of strict integrity. Richard Turner, gardener, but did not live in the house.

I have been thus particular in the description of those persons of whom my family was composed, to prove the improbability that a set of ignorant country people, excepting the Swiss alone, should league to carry on a diabolical scheme imputed to them so injuriously, and which in truth was far beyond the art and reach of man to compass.

Some time after Mr. Ricketts left me, I—then lying in the bedroom over the kitchen—heard frequently the noise of someone walking in the room within, and the rustling as of silk clothes against the door that opened into my room, sometimes so loud and of such continuance as to break my rest. Instant search being often made, we never could discover any appearance of human or brute being.

Repeatedly disturbed in the same manner, I made it my constant practice to search the room and closets within, and to secure the only door that led from that room on the inside in such manner as to be certain no one could gain entrance without passing through my own apartment, which was always made fast by a draw-bolt on the door. Yet this precaution did not preclude the disturbance, which continued with little interruption.

About this time an old man, living in the poor house at West Meon, came and desired to speak to me. When admitted, he told me he could not rest in his mind without acquainting me that his wife had often related to him that in her younger days a carpenter whom she had well known, had told her he was once sent for by Sir Hugh Stewkeley and directed by him to take up some boards in the dining-room, known in our time by the name of lobby, and that Sir Hugh had concealed something underneath which he, the carpenter, conceived was treasure, and then he was ordered to put down the boards in the same manner as they lay before. This account I repeated to Mr. Sainsbury, attorney to Lady Hillsborough, that if he thought it were a probability he might have the floor taken up and examined.

In February, 1770, John Sparks and Ann, his wife, quitted my service, and went to live upon their farm at Rogate. In the place of John Sparks I hired Robert Camis, one of six sons of Roger and Mary Camis, of the parish of Hinton, and whose ancestors have been in possession of a little estate there upwards of four hundred years—a family noted for their moral and religious lives. In the room of Ann Sparks I hired Ruth Turpin, but she being disordered in mind continued with me but few months. I then took Elizabeth Godin, of Alresford, sister to an eminent grocer of that place. Lewis Chanson quitted me in August, 1770, and I hired Edward Russel, now living with Mr. Harris, of Alresford, to succeed him.

I mention these changes among my domestics, though in themselves unimportant, to evince the impossibility of a confederacy, for the course of nearly seven years, and with a succession of different persons, so that at the time of my leaving Hinton, I had not one servant that lived with me at my first going thither, nor for some time afterwards.

In the summer of 1770, one night that I was lying in the yellow bed-chamber (the same I have mentioned that the person in drab-coloured clothes was seen to enter), I had been in bed half an hour, thoroughly awake, and without the least terror or apprehension on my spirits. I plainly heard the footsteps of a man, with plodding step, walking towards the foot of my bed. I thought the danger too near to ring my bell for assistance, but sprang out of bed and in an instant was in the nursery opposite; and with Hannah Streeter and a light I returned to search for what I had heard, but all in vain. There was a light burning in the dressing-room within, as usual, and there was no door or means of escape save at the one that opened to the nursery. This alarm perplexed me more than any preceding, being within my own room, the footsteps as distinct as ever I heard, myself perfectly awake and collected.

I had, nevertheless, resolution to go to bed alone in the same room, and did not form any conclusion as to the cause of this very extra-ordinary disturbance. For some months afterwards I did not hear any noise that particularly struck my attention, till, in November of the same year, I then being removed to the chintz bedroom over the hall, as a warmer apartment, I once or twice heard sounds of harmony, and one night in particular I heard three distinct and violent knocks as given with a club, or something very ponderous, against a door below stairs; it occurred to me that housebreakers must be forcing into some apartment, and I immediately rang my bell. No one hearing the summons and the noise ceasing, I thought no further of it at that time. After this, and in the beginning of the year 1771, I was frequently sensible of a hollow murmuring that seemed to possess the whole house; it was independent of wind, being equally heard on the calmest nights, and it was a sound I had never been accustomed to hear.

On the morning of the 27th of February, when Elizabeth Godin came into my room, I inquired what weather. She replying in a very faint tone, I asked if she were ill. She said she was well, but had never in her life been so terrified as during the preceding night; that she had heard the most dismal groans and fluttering round her bed most part of the night, that she had got up to search the room and up the chimney, and though it was a bright moonlight she could not discover anything. I did not pay much attention to her account, but it occurred to me that should anyone tell her it was the room formerly occupied by Mrs. Parfait, the old housekeeper, she would be afraid to lie there again. Mrs. Parfait dying a few days before at Kilmston, was brought and interred at Hinton churchyard the evening of the night this disturbance happened.

That very day five weeks, being the 2nd of April, I waked between one and two o'clock, as I found by my watch, which, with a rushlight, was on a table close to my bedside. I lay thoroughly awake for some time, and then heard one or more persons walking to and fro in the lobby adjoining. I got out of bed and listened at the door for the space of twenty minutes, in which time I distinctly heard the walking with the addition of a loud noise like pushing strongly against a door. Being thus assured my senses were not deceived I determined to ring my bell, to which I had before much reluctance on account of disturbing the nursery maid, who was very ill of a fever.

Elizabeth Godin during her illness lay in the room with my sons, and came immediately on hearing my bell. Thoroughly convinced there were persons in the lobby, before I opened my door, I asked her if she saw no one there. On her replying in the negative, I went out to her, examined the window, which was shut, looked under the couch, the only furniture of concealment there; the chimney board was fastened and when removed, all was clear behind it. She found the door into the lobby shut, as it was every night. After this examination I stood in the middle of the room, pondering with much astonishment, when suddenly the door that opens into the little recess leading to the yellow apartment sounded as if played to and fro by a person standing behind it. This was more than I could bear unmoved. I ran into the nursery and rang the bell there that goes into the men's apartments. Robert Camis came to the door at the landing place, which door was every night secured, so that no person could get to that floor unless through the windows. Upon opening the door to Robert I told him the reason I had to suppose that someone was intrenched behind the door I before mentioned, and giving him a light and arming him with a billet of wood, myself and Elizabeth Godin waited the event. Upon opening the door there was not any being whatever, and the yellow apartment was locked, the key, hanging up, and a great bolt drawn across the outside door, as usual when not in use. There was then no further retreat or hiding place. After dismissing Robert and securing the door, I went to bed in my son's room, and about half an hour afterwards heard three distinct knocks as described before; they seemed below, but I could not then or ever after ascertain the place. The next night I lay in my own room; I now and then heard noises and frequently the hollow murmur.

On the 7th of May, exactly the day five weeks from the 2nd of April, this murmur was uncommonly loud. I could not sleep, apprehending it the prelude to some greater noise. I got up and went in to the nursery, stayed there till half an hour past three, and then, being daybreak, I thought I should get some sleep in my own apartment; I returned and lay till ten minutes before four, and then the great hall door directly under me was slapped to with the utmost violence, so as to shake my room perceivably. I jumped out of bed to the window that commands the porch. There was light to distinguish every object, but none to be seen that could account for what I had heard. Upon examining the door it was found fast locked and bolted as usual.

From this time I determined to have my woman lie in a little bed in my room. The noises grew more frequent, and she was always sensible of the same sounds, and much in the same direction as they struck me. Harassed and perplexed, I was yet very unwilling to divulge my embarrassment. I had taken every method to investigate the cause, and could not discover the least appearance of a trick; on the contrary, I became convinced it was beyond the power of any mortal agent to perform, but knowing how exploded such opinions were, I kept them in my own bosom, and hoped my resolution would enable me to support whatever might befall.

After Midsummer the noises became every night more intolerable. They began before I went to bed, and with intermissions were heard till after broad day in the morning. I could frequently distinguish articulate sounds, and usually a shrill female voice would begin, and then two others with deeper and manlike tone seemed to join in the discourse, yet, though this conversation sounded as if close to me, I never could distinguish words.[1]

I have often asked Elizabeth Godin if she heard any noise, and of

[1] Compare a similar phenomenon in the 'Mill on the Eden.'—H.P.

what sort. She as often described the seeming conversation in the manner I have related, and other noises. One night in particular my bed curtains rustled, and sounded as if dragged by a person walking against them. I then asked her if she heard any noise and of what kind. She spoke of it exactly in the manner I have done. Several times I heard sounds of harmony within the room—no distinct or regular notes, but a vibration of harmonious tones; walking, talking, knocking, opening and slapping of doors were repeated every night. My brother, who had not long before returned from the Mediterranean, had been to stay with me, yet so great was my reluctance to relate anything beyond the

'*I heard . . . a tremendous noise which seemed to rush and fall with infinite velocity and force on the lobby floor*'.

bounds of probability, that I could not bring myself to disclose my embarrassed situation to the friend and brother who could most essentially serve and comfort me. The noises continuing in the same manner when he was with me, I wished to learn if he heard them, and one morning I carelessly said: 'I was afraid last night the servants would disturb you, and rang my bell to order them to bed.' He replied he had not heard them. The morning after he left me to return to Portsmouth, about three o'clock and daylight, Elizabeth Godin and myself both awoke—she had been sitting up in bed looking round her, expecting as she always did to see something terrible—I heard with infinite astonishment the most loud, deep, tremendous noise which seemed to rush and fall with infinite velocity and force on the lobby floor adjoining to my room. I started up, and called to Godin, 'Good God! did you hear that noise?' She made no reply; on repeating the question she answered with a faltering voice, 'She was so frightened she scarce durst speak'. Just at that instant we heard a shrill and dreadful shriek, seeming to proceed from under the spot where the rushing noise fell, and repeated three or four times, growing fainter as it seemed to descend, till it sank into earth. Hannah Streeter, who lay in the room with my children, heard the same noises, and was so appalled she lay for two hours almost deprived of sense and motion.

Having heard little of the noises preceding and that little she did not regard, she had rashly expressed a wish to hear more of them, and from that night till she quitted the house there was scarce a night passed that she did not hear the sound as if some person walked towards her door, and pushed against it, as though attempting to force it open. This alarm, so more than commonly horrible, determined me to impart the whole series to my brother on his return to Hinton Ampner, expected in a week. The frequency of the noises, harassing to my rest, and getting up often at unreasonable hours, fixed a slow fever and deep cough, my health was much impaired, but my resolution firm. I remained in anxious expectation of my brother, and he being detained a week longer at Portsmouth than he had foreseen, it occurred to me to endeavour, by changing my apartment, to obtain a little rest; I removed to that formerly occupied by Elizabeth Godin; I did not mention my intention till ten at night, when the room was prepared, and I went to bed soon after. I had scarce lain down when the same noises surrounded me that I before related, and I mention the circumstances of changing my room without previous notice, to prove the impossibility of a plan of operations being so suddenly conveyed to another part of the house were they such as human agents could achieve. The week following I was comforted by the arrival of my brother. However desirous to impart the narrative, yet I forebore till the next morning; I wished him to enjoy a night's rest, and therefore contented myself with preparing him to hear on the morrow the most astonishing tale that ever assailed his ears, and that he must summon all his trust of my veracity to meet my relation. He replied it was scarce possible for me to relate any matter he could not believe, little divining the nature of what I had to offer to his faith.

The next morning I began my narrative, to which he attended with mixed surprise and wonder. Just as I had finished, Captain Luttrell, our neighbour at Kilmston, chancing to call, induced my brother to impart the whole to him, who in a very friendly manner offered to unite his endeavours to investigate the cause. It was then agreed that he should come late in the evening, and divide the night watch between them, keeping profoundly secret there was any such intention. My brother took the precaution, accompanied by his own servant, John Bolton, to go into every apartment, particularly those in the first and attic storey, examined every place of concealment, and saw each door fastened, save those to chambers occupied by the family; this done, he went to bed in the room over the servants' hall.

Captain Luttrell and my brother's man with arms sat up in the chintz room adjoining, and my brother was to be called on any alarm.

I lay that night in Elizabeth Godin's room, and the children in the nurseries; thus every chamber on that floor was occupied. I bolted and locked the door that opened to that floor from the back stairs, so that there was no entrance unless through the room where Captain Luttrell kept watch.

As soon as I lay down, I heard a rustling as of a person close to the door. I ordered Elizabeth Godin to sit up a while, and if the noise continued, to go and acquaint Mr. Luttrell.

She heard it, and instantly Mr. Luttrell's room door was thrown open, and we heard him speak.

I must now give his account as related to my brother and myself the next morning.

He said he heard the footsteps of a person walking across the lobby, and that he instantly threw the door open, and called, 'Who goes there?' That something flitted past him, when my brother directly called out 'Look against my door.' He was awake, and heard what Mr. Luttrell had said, and also the continuance of the same noise till it reached his door. He arose and joined Mr. Luttrell. Both astonished, they heard various other noises, examined everywhere, found the staircase door fast secured as I had left it. I lay so near, and had never closed my eyes, no one could go to that door unheard. My brother and his man proceeded up stairs, and found the servants in their own rooms, and all the doors closed as they had seen just before. They sat up together, my brother and Mr. Luttrell, till break of day, when my brother returned to his own chamber. About that time, as I imagined, I heard the chintz room door opened and slammed to with the utmost violence, and immediately that of the hall chamber opened and shut in the same manner. I mentioned to Godin my surprise that my brother, who was ever attentive not to alarm or disturb the children, should hazard both by such vehement noise. An hour after I heard the house door open and slam in the same way, so as to shake the house. No one person was then up, for as I had never slept, I heard the servants rise and go down about half an hour afterwards. When we were assembled at breakfast, I observed the noise my brother had made with the doors.

Mr. Luttrell replied, 'I assure you Jervis made not the least noise; it was your door and the next I heard opened and slapped in the way you describe.'

142

My brother did not hear either. He afterwards acknowledged to me that when gone to bed and Mr. Luttrell and I were sitting below, he heard dreadful groans and various noises that he was then and after unable to account for. His servant was at that time with mine below.

Captain Luttrell declared the disturbances of the preceding night were of such a nature that the house was an unfit residence for any human being. My brother, though more guarded in his expressions, concurred in that opinion, and the result of our deliberations was to send an express to Mr. Sainsbury, Lady Hillsborough's steward, to request he would come over immediately on a very particular occasion, with which he would be made acquainted on his arrival.

Unluckily, Mr. Sainsbury was confined with the gout, and sent over his clerk, a youth of fifteen, to whom we judged it useless and improper to divulge the circumstances.

My brother sat up every night of the week he then passed at Hinton Ampner. In the middle of one of these nights, I was surprised with the sound of a gun or pistol let off near me, immediately followed by groans as of a person in agonies, or expiring, that seemed to proceed between my chamber and the next, the nursery. I sent Godin to Nurse Horner, to ask if she had heard any noise; she had not. Upon my enquiry the next morning of my brother, he had [not] heard it, though the report and groans were loud and deep.

Several instances occurred where very loud noises were heard by one or two persons, when those equally near and in the same direction were not sensible of the least impression.[1]

As the watching every night made it necessary for my brother to gain rest in the day, he usually lay down after dinner. During one of these times he was gone to rest, I had sent the children and their attendants out to walk, the dairymaid had gone to milk, the cook in the scullery, my own woman with my brother's man sitting together in the servants' hall; I, reading in the parlour, heard my brother's bell ring with great quickness. I ran to his room, and he asked me if I had heard any noise, 'because', said he, 'as I was lying wide awake an immense weight seemed to fall through the ceiling to the floor just by that mahogany press, and it is impossible I should be deceived'. His man was by this time come up, and said he was sitting underneath the room as I before mentioned, and heard not the least noise. The inquiry and attention my brother devoted to investigate this affair was such as from the reach of his capacity and ardent spirit might be expected; the result was his earnest request that I would quit the place, and when obliged to return to Portsmouth, that I would permit him to send Mr. Nichols, his Lieutenant of Marines, and an old friend of the family, to continue till my removal with me.

One circumstance is of a nature so singularly striking that I cannot

[1] A common phenomenon in Poltergeist cases.—H.P.

143

omit to relate it. In one of our evening's conversations on this wonderful train of disturbances I mentioned a very extraordinary effect I had frequently observed in a favourite cat that was usually in the parlour with me, and when sitting on table or chair with accustomed unconcern she would suddenly slink down as if struck with the greatest terror, conceal herself under my chair, and put her head close to my feet. In a short space of time she would come forth quite unconcerned. I had not long given him this account before it was verified to him in a striking manner. We neither then, nor I at other times, perceived the least noise that could give alarm to the animal, nor did I ever perceive the like effect before these disturbances, nor afterwards when she was removed with me to another habitation. The servants have the same account of a spaniel that lived in the house, but to that, as I did not witness it, I cannot testify.

There is another copy, and no more to be taken unless either be destroyed.

(Signed) MARY RICKETTS.

As happened at Borley, Willington, and Battersea, the Poltergeists at Hinton Ampner made the continued occupancy of the Manor House an impossibility. So they pulled it down! I see from Kelly's *Directory of Hampshire* that the new Hinton Ampner House[1] was built in 1793, and that the occupant (1931) was Henry John Dutton, Esqre., J.P., lord of the manor. I have heard of no disturbances there.[2]

During the demolition of the old Manor the house-breakers made a curious discovery. Under the floor of one of the rooms was found 'a small skull, said to be that of a monkey'. Some said it was the skull of a baby! 'But the matter was never brought forward by any regular inquiry, or professional opinion resorted to as to the real nature of the skull'— which we will hope *was* that of a monkey.

Well, if a crime was actually committed at the Manor, as rumour averred, the chief actors—or culprits—were beyond the reach of the law or human punishment by the time they found the chief 'exhibit'. Was it the uneasy Lord Stawell who was compelled to wander around his old house in his 'drab coat', frightening unsuspecting grooms? Was it the fair—but frail?—Honoria, whose rustling silks so terrified Mrs. Ricketts and her servants? Perhaps—but perhaps not. We have no evidence. But I wish they had cleared up the mystery of that skull!

[1] Which stands in a park of 66 acres on an eminence near the Church, with lovely views of the surrounding country.

[2] Since this was written, I have found a letter from Mr. C. J. P. Cave, M.A., J.P., F.S.A., of Stoner Hill, Petersfield, who informs me (October 14, 1941) that 'in the new house some curious noises used to be heard that have never been explained. They were usually heard just before dawn'. The new house was built fifty yards from the old site.

CHAPTER XII

'Astonishing Transactions at Stockwell'

If I were asked to choose an example of Poltergeist activity that best represented the popular conception of what a Poltergeist is, and does, I would unhesitatingly single out the case of what became known as the Stockwell Ghost. This extraordinary affair created a sensation in London comparable only with that caused by the Cock Lane Ghost, of some ten years earlier.

The case is remarkable in many ways: The manifestations lasted for a few hours only, and were witnessed by a number of credible people. The instrument of the disturbances knew perfectly well that it was she who was the *nexus* or prime-mover that was causing all the trouble, but she also knew that she was absolutely helpless in the matter. This is very unusual; these young people are invariably ignorant of the fact that they are responsible for all the bother.

Another facet of the case is that the popular mind usually associates an adolescent—often a young girl—with Poltergeist phenomena, and in this classic Stockwell haunting we have a striking example of this; there was nothing ambiguous about who or what was responsible for all the trouble. Ann Robinson, a young woman aged twenty, knew quite well that, in some curious way, the manifestations were occurring through her, and she was very sorry. This case goes far to illustrate the theory that there is some psychical-physiological connection between Poltergeists and pubescency. There are other examples cited in this volume, which the reader will note.

But perhaps the outstanding feature of the Stockwell ghost affair is the way in which the case was recorded. The report was drawn up immediately after the cessation of activities—I almost wrote hostilities—and the report would do credit to a modern investigator. Few accounts of such things published today are so well presented and witnessed. The only criticism that one can make is that it would have made the report more interesting if one had been told something of the past history of this Poltergeist subject; and it is a pity we know nothing of her subsequent adventures. Of course fraud was alleged by persons who were not present, but there is no evidence whatever that Ann Robinson cheated the good people of Stockwell, which in 1772 was a country district on the outskirts of London. A careful study of the report convinces me that Ann did not resort to trickery, and that we here have an early—and therefore valuable—account of a well-recorded and authenticated Poltergeist case running true to type.

When I decided to include this case amongst the important Poltergeist hauntings of England, my intention was to epitomise the story in the usual way. But a study of the contemporary record convinced me that I could not improve upon it, so I reproduce it in its entirety.

The report was published in the form of a tract entitled: *An Authentic, Candid, and Circumstantial Narrative, of the Astonishing Transactions at Stockwell, in the County of Surry, on Monday and Tuesday, the 6th and 7th Days of January, 1772, Containing a Series of the most surprising and unaccountable Events that Ever happened, which continued from first to last, upwards of Twenty Hours, and at different Places. Published with the Consent and Approbation of the Family and other Parties concerned, to Authenticate which, the original Copy is signed by them. LONDON: Printed for W. Bailey, No. 42 Bishopsgate Street. MDCCLXXII.*

The above tract must be excessively rare, as I have seen only one copy—my own, which I acquired some years ago. Here then is the account of the 'astonishing transactions':

A Narrative, Etc.

Before we enter upon a description of the most extraordinary transactions that perhaps ever happened, we shall begin with an account of the parties who were principally concerned, and in justice to them give their characters; by which means the impartial world may be enabled to form some judgment what credit is due to the following narrative.

The events indeed are of so strange and singular a nature, that we cannot be at all surprised the public should be doubtful of the truth of them, more especially as there have been too many impositions of this sort; but let us consider, here are no sinister ends to be answered, no contributions to be wished for, nor would be accepted, as the parties are in reputable situations and good circumstances, particularly Mrs. Golding, who is a lady of an independent fortune: Richard Fowler and his wife might be looked upon as an exception to this assertion, but as their loss was trivial, they must be left out of the question, except so far as they appear corroborating evidences.

Mr. Pain's maid lost nothing.

How or by what means these transactions were brought about, time only will discover, if that ever happen: We have only now to rest our confidence on the veracity of the parties, whose descriptions have been most strictly attended to, without the least deviation; nothing here offered is either exaggerated or diminished, the whole stated in the clearest manner, just as they occurred, and as such only we lay them before the candid and impartial public.

Mrs. Golding, an elderly lady, at Stockwell, in Surry, at whose house the transactions began, was born in the same parish (of Lambeth) has lived in it ever since, and has always been well known, and respected as a gentlewoman of unblemished honor and character.

Mrs. Pain, a niece of Mrs. Golding, has been married several years to Mr. Pain, a farmer at Brixton-Causeway, a little above Mr. Angel's, has several children, are well known and respected in the parish.

Mary Martin, Mr. Pain's servant, an elderly woman, has lived two years with them, and four years with Mrs. Golding, where she came from.

Richard Fowler, lives almost opposite to Mr. Pain, at the Brick-Pound, an honest, industrious and sober man.

Sarah Fowler, wife to the above, an industrious and sober woman.

The above are the subscribing evidences that we must rest the truth of the facts upon: yet there are numbers of other persons who were eye-witnesses of many of the transactions, during the time they happened, all of whom must acknowledge the truth of them.

Another person who bore a principal part in these scenes was Ann Robinson: Mrs. Golding's maid, a young woman, about twenty years old, who had lived with her but one week and three days.

I shall not take up any more of the reader's attention from the narrative, but begin as follows.

On Monday, January the 6th, 1772, about ten o'clock in the forenoon, as Mrs. Golding was in her parlour, she heard the china and glasses in the back kitchen tumble down and break; her maid came to her and told her the stone plates were falling from the shelf; Mrs. Golding went into the kitchen and saw them broke. Presently after, a row of plates from the next shelf fell down likewise, while she was there, and nobody near them; this astonished her much, and while she was thinking about it, other things in different places began to tumble about, some of them breaking, attended with violent noises all over the house; a clock tumbled down and the case broke; a lanthorn that hung on the staircase was thrown down and the glass broke to pieces; an earthen pan of salted beef broke to pieces and the beef fell about; all this increased her surprise, and brought several persons about her, among whom was Mr. Rowlidge, a carpenter, who gave it as his opinion that the foundation was giving way and that the house was tumble-ing down, occasioned by the too great weight of an additional room erected above: so ready are we to discover natural causes for every thing! But no such thing happened as the reader will find, for whatever was the cause, that cause ceased almost as soon as Mrs. Golding and her maid left any place, and followed them wherever they went. Mrs. Golding run into Mr. Gresham's house, a gentleman living next door to her, where she fainted.

In the interim, Mr. Rowlidge, and other persons were removing Mrs. Golding's effects from her house, for fear of the consequences he had prognosticated. At this time it was quiet; Mrs. Golding's maid remaining in her house, was gone up stairs, and when called upon several times to come down, for fear of the dangerous situation she was thought to be in, she answered very coolly, and after some time came down as deliberately, without any seeming fearful apprehensions.

Mrs. Pain was sent for from Brixton-Causeway, and desired to come directly, as her aunt was supposed to be dead;—this was the message to her. When Mrs. Pain came, Mrs. Golding was come to herself, but very faint.

Among the persons who were present, was Mr. Gardner, a surgeon, of Clapham; whom Mrs. Pain desired to bleed her aunt, which he did; Mrs. Pain asked him if the blood should be thrown away; he desired it might not, as he would examine it when cold. These minute particulars would not be taken notice of, but as a chain to what follows. For the next circumstance is of a more astonishing nature than any thing that had preceded it; the blood that was just congealed, sprung out of the bason upon the floor, and presently after the bason broke to pieces; this china bason was the only thing broke belonging to Mr. Gresham; a bottle of rum that stood by it broke at the same time.

Amongst the things that were removed to Mr. Gresham's, was a tray full of china, etc., a japan bread-basket, some mahogany waiters, with some bottles of liquors, jars of pickles, etc. and a pier glass, which was taken down by Mr. Saville, (a neighbour of Mrs. Golding's) he gave it to one Robert Hames, who laid it on the grass-plat at Mr. Gresham's; but before he could put it out of his hands, some parts of the frame on each side flew off; it raining at that time, Mrs. Golding desired it might be brought into the parlour, where it was put under a sideboard, and a dressing glass along with it; it had not been there long before the glasses and china which stood on the side-board, began to tumble about and fall down, and broke both the glasses to pieces. Mr. Saville and others being asked to drink a glass of wine or rum, both the bottles broke in pieces before they were uncorked.

Mrs. Golding's surprise and fear increasing, she did not know what to do or where to go; wherever she and her maid were, these strange destructive circumstances followed her, and how to help or free herself from them, was not in her power or any other persons present: her mind was one confused chaos, lost to herself and every thing about her, drove from her own home, and afraid there would be none other to receive her; at last she left Mr. Gresham's, and went to Mr. Mayling's, a gentleman at the next door, here she staid about three quarters of an hour, during which time nothing happened. Her maid staid at Mr. Gresham's, to help put up what few things remained unbroke of her mistress's, in a back apartment, when a jar of pickles that stood upon a table turned upside down, then a jar of rasberry jam broke to pieces, next two mahogany waiters and a quadrille-box[1] likewise broke to pieces.

[1] i.e., a box bearing a pattern of small squares; or one in which were kept forty playing-cards used in a game called Quadrille.—H.P.

Mrs. Pain, not chusing her aunt should stay too long at Mr. Mayling's for fear of being troublesome, persuaded her to go to her house at Rush Common, near Brixton-Causeway, where she would endeavour to make her as happy as she could, hoping by this time all was over as nothing had happened at that gentleman's house while she was there. This was about two o'clock in the afternoon.

Mr. and Miss Gresham were at Mr. Pain's house, when Mrs. Pain, Mrs. Golding, and her maid went there. It being about dinner time they all dined together; in the interim Mrs. Golding's servant was sent to her

'One of the eggs flew off, crossed the kitchen, and struck a cat on the head'.

house to see how things remained. When she returned, she told them nothing had happened since they left it. Some time after Mr. Gresham and Miss went home every thing remaining quiet at Mr. Pains: But about eight o'clock in the evening a fresh scene began, the first thing that happened, was, a whole row of pewter dishes, except one, fell from off a shelf to the middle of the floor, rolled about a little while, and then settled, and what is almost beyond belief, as soon as they were quiet, turned upside down; they were then put on the dresser, and went through the same a second time: next fell a whole row of pewter plates from off the second shelf over the dresser to the ground, and being taken up and put on the dresser one in another, they were thrown down again.

149

The next thing was two eggs that were upon one of the pewter shelves, one of them flew off, crossed the kitchen, struck a cat on the head, and then broke to pieces.

Next, Mary Martin, Mrs. Pain's servant, went to stir the kitchen fire, she got to the right hand side of it, being a large chimney as is usual in farm houses, a pestle and mortar that stood nearer the left hand end of the chimney shelf, jumped about six feet on the floor. Then went candlesticks and other brasses: scarce any thing remaining in its place. After this the glasses and china were put down on the floor for fear of undergoing the same fate, they presently began to dance and tumble about, and then broke to pieces. A tea pot that was among them, flew to Mrs. Golding's maid's foot and struck it.

A glass tumbler that was put on the floor jumped about two feet and then broke. Another that stood by it jumped about at the same time, but did not break till some hours after, when it jumped again and then broke. A china bowl that stood in the parlour jumped from the floor to behind a table that stood there. This was most astonishing, as the distance from where it stood was between seven and eight feet but was not broke. It was put back by Richard Fowler, to its place, where it remained some time and then flew to pieces.

The next thing that followed was a mustard pot, that jumped out of a closet and was broke. A single cup that stood upon the table, (almost the only thing remaining) jumped up, flew across the kitchen, ringing like a bell, and then was dashed to pieces against the dresser. A candlestick that stood on the chimney shelf flew across the kitchen to the parlour door, at about fifteen feet distance. A tea kettle under the dresser, was thrown out about two feet, another kettle that stood at one end of the range, was thrown against the iron that is fixed to prevent children falling into the fire. A tumbler with rum and water in it, that stood upon a waiter upon a table in the parlour, jumped about ten feet and was broke. The table then fell down, and along with it a silver tankard belonging to Mrs. Golding, the waiter in which had stood the tumbler and a candlestick. A case bottle then flew to pieces.

The next circumstance, was a ham that hung in one side of the kitchen chimney, it raised itself from the hook and fell down to the ground. Some time after, another ham that hung on the other side of the chimney, likewise underwent the same fate. Then a flitch of bacon which hung up in the same chimney fell down.

All the family were eye witnesses to these circumstances as well as other persons, some of whom were so alarmed and shocked that they could not bear to stay, and was happy in getting away, though the unhappy family were left in the midst of their distresses. Most of the genteel families around were continually sending to enquire after them, and whether all was over or not. Is it not surprising that some among them had not the inclination and resolution to try to unravel this most intricate affair, at a time when it would have been in their power to have done so; there certainly was sufficient time for so doing, as the whole from first to last continued upwards of twenty hours.

At all the times of action, Mrs. Golding's servant was walking backwards and forwards, either in the kitchen or parlour, or wherever some of the family happened to be. Nor could they get her to sit down five minutes together, except at one time for about half an hour towards the morning, when the family were at prayers in the parlour; then all was quiet: but in the midst of the greatest confusion, she was as much composed as at any other time, and with uncommon coolness of temper advised her mistress not to be alarmed or uneasy, as she said these things could not be helped. Thus she argued as if they were common occurrences which must happen in every family.

This advice surprised and startled her mistress, almost as much as the circumstances that occasioned it. For how can we suppose that a girl of about twenty years old (an age when female timidity is too often assisted by superstition) could remain in the midst of such calamitous circumstances (except they proceeded from causes best known to herself) and not be struck with the same terror as every other person was who was present. These reflections led Mr. Pain, and at the end of the transactions, likewise Mrs. Golding, to think that she was not altogether so unconcerned as she appeared to be. But hitherto, the whole remains mysterious and unravelled.

About ten o'clock at night, they sent over the way to Richard Fowler, to desire he would come and stay with them. He came and continued till one in the morning, and was so terrified that he could remain no longer.

As Mrs. Golding could not be persuaded to go to bed, Mrs. Pain at that time (one o'clock) made an excuse to go upstairs to her youngest child, under pretence of getting it to sleep, but she really acknowledges it was through fear, as she declares she could not sit up to see such strange things going on, as every thing one after another was broke, till there was not above two or three cups and saucers remaining out of a considerable quantity of china, etc. which was destroyed to the amount of some pounds.

About five o'clock on Tuesday morning Mrs. Golding went up to her niece, and desired her to get up, as the noises and destruction were so great she could continue in the house no longer. At this time all the tables, chairs, drawers, etc. were tumbling about. When Mrs. Pain came down, it was amazing beyond all description! their only security then was to quit the house for fear of the same catastrophe, as had been expected the morning before, at Mrs. Golding's: in consequence of this resolution, Mrs. Golding and her maid went over the way to Richard Fowler's: When Mrs. Golding's maid had seen her safe to Richard Fowler's, she came back to Mrs. Pain, to help her to dress the children in the barn, where she had carried them for fear of the house falling. At this time all was quiet they then went to Fowler's, and then began the same scene as had happened at the other places. It must be remarked, all was quiet here as well as elsewhere, till the maid returned.

When they got to Mr. Fowler's, he began to light a fire in his back room. When done he put the candle and candlestick upon a table in the fore room. This apartment Mrs. Golding and her maid had passed through. Another candlestick with a tin lamp in it that stood by it were both dashed together, and fell to the ground. A lanthorn with which Mrs. Golding was lighted with cross the road, sprung from a hook to the ground, and a quantity of oil spilled on the floor. The last thing was the basket of coals tumbled over; the coals rolling about the room; the maid then desired Richard Fowler not to let her mistress remain there, as she said, wherever she was the same things would follow. In consequence of this advice, and fearing greater losses to himself, he desired she would quit his house; but first begged her to consider within herself, for her own and the publics sake, whether or not she had not been guilty of some atrocious crime, for which providence was determined to pursue her on this side of the grave, for he could not help thinking, she was the object that was to be made an example to posterity, by the all seeing eye of providence, for crimes which but too often none but that providence can penetrate, and by such means as these bring to light.

Thus was this poor gentlewoman's measure of affliction complete not only to have undergone all which has been related, but to have added to it the character of a bad and wicked woman, when till this time, she was esteemed as a most deserving person. In candour to Fowler, he could not be blamed; what could he do? what would any man have done that was so circumstanced? Mrs. Golding soon satisfied him; she told him she would not stay in his house or any other persons, as her conscience was quite clear, and she could as well wait the will of providence in her own house as in any other place whatever; upon which she and her maid went home. Mr. Pain went with them. After they had got to Mrs. Golding's the last time, the same transactions once more began upon the remains that were left.

A nine gallon cask of beer, that was in the cellar, the door being open, and no person near it, turned upside down.

A pail of water that stood on the floor, boiled like a pot.

A box of candles fell from a shelf in the kitchen to the floor, they rolled out, but none were broke.

A round mahogany table overset in the parlour.

Mr. Pain then desired Mrs. Golding to send her maid for his wife to come to them, when she was gone all was quiet; upon her return she was immediately discharged, and no disturbances have happened since; this was between six and seven o'clock on Tuesday morning.

At Mrs. Golding's were broke the quantity of three pails full of glass china, etc.

At Mrs. Pain's they filled two pails.

Thus ends the narrative; a true, circumstantial, and faithful account of which I have laid before the public; for so doing I hope to escape its censure; I have neither exaggerated or diminished one circumstance to my knowledge; and have endeavoured as much as possible throughout the whole, to state only the facts, without presuming to obtrude my opinion on them. If I have in part hinted any thing that may appear unfavourable to the girl, it proceeded not from a determination to charge her with the cause, right or wrong, but only from a strict adherence to truth, most sincerely wishing this extraordinary affair may be unravelled.

The above narrative is absolutely and strictly true, in witness whereof we have set our hands this eleventh day of January, 1772.

MARY GOLDING.
JOHN PAIN.
MARY PAIN.
RICHARD FOWLER.
SARAH FOWLER.
MARY MARTIN.

The original copy of this narrative, signed as above, with the parties own hands, is in the hands of J. Marks, Bookseller, in St. Martin's Lane, to satisfy any person who chuses to apply to him for the inspection of the same.

FINIS

A ridiculous sequel to this case appeared in William Hone's *Everyday Book* (London, 1826, Vol. I, p. 62). A certain Braidley declared that, years after the Stockwell disturbances, Ann Robinson had confessed that she deceived Mrs. Golding and her friends, and had produced the phenomena by affixing horse-hairs, wires, etc., to the various articles of crockery, thus causing them to fall. It was also stated that 'she employed some simple chemical secrets'!

Of course, this story is sheer invention, and there is no evidence to support it. The greatest conjurer living could not produce the Stockwell effects by means of wires, etc., surrounded by people on the look-out for tricks, and in a well-lighted room, without instant detection. I know what can, and cannot, be done in this way.

If the reader complains that the Stockwell story is 'rather ancient', I will cite a brand-new one, only a few days old, that is on all fours with it. I picked up my *Evening Standard* recently (December 8, 1943), and read how 'The Ghost Wrecked a Room', a story sent by the journal's correspondent. A Madame Aucher and her daughter Geneviève, aged sixteen, went to sleep in a house at Frontenay-Rohan-Rohan, near

153

Poitiers, France. 'During the night the girl was lifted by what is said to be a supernatural agency and thrown to the foot of her bed. The bed-clothes were raised up to the roof and suspended in mid-air. Plates and ornaments were thrown violently across the room.' So Mme Aucher and her daughter tried another room. They sat down on some chairs 'which were whisked away from under them and then overturned.' The girl left the house.

As so often happens, a priest was called in. He exorcised the place—and all was quiet. Then the girl returned, and an oaken dresser moved away from the wall and crashed to the floor, and 'a table nearly crushed Gen-darme Pillon—according to his sworn statement.' The marble top of a table was cracked by a violent, unseen blow. As neither prayers nor police could stop the phenomena, all the occupants moved out of the house.

Madame Aucher and her daughter went to visit relatives at the other end of the village; and, as in the case of Ann Robinson, at Stockwell, *immediately*, a box of spices on the mantelpiece was lifted by something unseen and emptied itself over the table where the women sat. Then furniture began to move about; tables overturned; chairs were hurled across the room; curtains were torn down and the entire contents of the house were wrecked *in a matter of minutes*. Again the police were called in, and had to admit themselves baffled. Then the mother and daughter left the district and went to another house. 'And there have been no more disturbances,[1] even in their new home'. Poltergeists are like that.

A few weeks later (January 10, 1944), another strange Poltergeist case was reported in the *Evening Standard* by its Halifax (Nova Scotia) correspondent. In the home of Mrs. Ethel Hilchie was a typical infesta-tion, which began with knockings on Christmas eve. When the reporter was actually interviewing the lady 'the outhouse door locked itself and a metal hoop came sailing through the air from an unknown source. A pair of scissors on the shelf opened and closed. A bowl of soup spilled itself into a child's lap; a soap box flew down a flight of stairs; a kettle of boiling water upset itself on the stove; and an alarm clock took off in flight from a dresser'. A Halifax photographer visited the Hilchie home in an attempt to get some pictures of the *Geist*. 'He said nothing hap-pened until leaving, when a flash bulb jumped out of his bag and smashed itself on the floor'.[2]

[1] There has been a sequel to this case since I wrote the above. In the *Evening Standard* (December 18, 1943), it is stated that the police took Geneviève back to the house near Poitiers, 'to see what would happen'. Immediately, a coffee-mill was thrown at a gendarme, and another policeman was hit by a heavy box. The police then made the girl sit down at a table and write. While she was thus occupied, a lampshade was thrown at their heads. As they could not solve the mystery, Geneviève was taken to an asylum. That is exactly what happened to Eleonore Zugun in her own village. (See p. 257.)

[2] As this book goes to press, I have received from Mr. R. S. Lambert a full account of the Hilchie case in a series of cuttings from the *Toronto Daily Star*, beginning January 8, 1944. The phenomena lasted for several weeks.

CHAPTER XIII

The Poltergeist of Stamford Street

From my collection of rare works on Poltergeists, I select another tract dealing with London 'infestations'. I am including this in the present volume because (*a*), the case is intrinsically good; (*b*) the tract must be extremely rare because I have neither seen nor heard of another copy; (*c*) to my knowledge, the tract has never been reprinted, and the case is quite unknown among students; and (*d*) it gives me an excuse for reproducing the delightful title-page—which is a story in itself. There are so few London Poltergeist cases that I could not resist the temptation to include the account of the 'mysterious house' in this collection.

The tract is a large octavo of eight pages, published in London about 1820. It is not difficult to fix the date of the pamphlet, because there is an allusion to gas-lighting. It was very early in the nineteenth century that a German named F. A. Winsor[1] came all the way from Frankfort to London to demonstrate his process of making gas at the Lyceum Theatre. This was in 1804. In the year 1807 Pall Mall was lighted by gas. Then followed Westminster Bridge (1813); the whole of Westminster (1814); and by 1816 gas-lighting was common all over London. From the allusion to gas in the text, and to other indicia, I regard the tract as having been printed about the year 1820.

The title of the tract is *The History of the Mysterious House and Alarming Appearances at the Corner of Stamford St., Blackfriars Road* . . . and was published by W. Jenkinson, 91, Leather Lane, Holborn. The site of our 'mysterious house' is today occupied by the Blackfriars branch of the Midland Bank, No. 1, Stamford St., S.E.1, and Poltergeists there must be few and far between. But in 1820 the house was one of those old, rambling, derelict places that look haunted if they are not. It probably acquired an evil reputation simply because it was empty for many years and had fallen into disrepair. However, someone took the trouble to investigate both house and the stories connected with it, and left for posterity a history of the strange occurrences, some of which (the reverberating knocker, the shower of halfpence, the sudden disappearance of pies and joints, the lights at the window, etc.) are true Poltergeist stuff. I wish our historian had told us what the 'ladies who tarry at the corner' thought about it all.

However, I can throw a little light on the subsequent history of the haunted house—or should it be houses? In Edward Walford's *Old and New London*[2] it is stated: 'At the corner of Stamford Street and Black-

---

[1] Who started what is now the Gas Light and Coke Company.

[2] London, 1872–78, Vol. VI, p. 382.

THE HISTORY OF THE

Mysterious House

And alarming Appearances

AT THE CORNER OF STAMFORD ST., BLACKFRIARS ROAD,

Well known to have been unoccupied for many Years, and called

The Skeleton's Corner !

ALSO THE PARTICULARS OF THE

FEMALE SPECTRE

Which appeared at the Window ;

And an account of who are the

VICTIMS OF SEDUCTION AND MURDER.

The wonder and excitement caused by the appearance of the house, and also
by the curious and

Extraordinary Disappearance of the Inmates.

Alarming noises and strange shadows ; the curiosity exited on passing the house, and an
account of what has been reported to have been seen of the

Skeleton and Apparitions.

THE REPORT OF THE BUTCHER, BAKER, AND THE PIEMAN,

And other interesting particulars.   Spectre visit of that strange Female in Black, and

FATE OF THE YOUNG LADY

Supposed to be a tenant many years ago ; also an account of an old haunted Mansion
in the country, and the courage displayed by a young Officer.

LONDON : PUBLISHED BY W. JENKINSON, 91, LEATHER LANE, HOLBORN,
And Sold by all Booksellers.

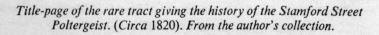

Title-page of the rare tract giving the history of the Stamford Street
Poltergeist. (Circa 1820). From the author's collection.

friars Road, on the spot now occupied by the Central Bank of London[1] and three or four large houses adjoining it, stood, till 1874, a row of tenements, which for many years previously, owing to the eccentricity of their owner, a Miss Angelina Read, had been allowed to remain unoccupied. They had long been windowless, and the dingy rooms encumbered with dirt and rubbish and overrun with rats; indeed, such a forlorn and desolate aspect had they assumed that they became generally known as the "haunted houses". In the above year, Miss Read having bequeathed them to the Consumption Hospital at Brompton, they were demolished, and some fine buildings have been erected in their place.'

Walford, in 1878, mentions 'haunted houses'. But the 1820 tract refers only to a 'large old house', a 'commodious dwelling of two stories'. I suggest that, in 1820, the tenements contiguous to the house were in good repair and occupied. And that in 1878, the 'old house' had disintegrated into rubbish, and that the tenements were then fast disappearing, too—hence they also acquired a reputation for being haunted.

The 'strange looking lady enveloped entirely in black', mentioned in the tract, could hardly have been the eccentric Angelina Read who bequeathed the 'house' to the Brompton Hospital in 1874. So there may have been *two* strange female owners of the strange house. Perhaps that 'induced' the Poltergeist! Well, then, here is the story (slightly abridged), complete with 'anilisation' by the author, of the Poltergeist house at 'Skeleton's Corner':

THE MYSTERIOUS HOUSE

In the Blackfriars Road

Description of the House.—The house is a very commodious dwelling of two stories, the front in Stamford Street; its frowning dingy appearance strikes at once any one with a notion that it is a pity such a building should be left to decay and go to ruin.

The many accounts prevalent of the strange things seen and heard render them worthy of being recorded.

Large old houses are apt from the length of their timbers and being greater in quantity than in modern buildings to give, their joists to settle, and at various times to crack and split, so as to cause an alarming noise and stir up the imagination to fancy the most horrible and terrifying visions; even the bricks in the chimnies at times get loose and rolling down into an empty room would mightily disturb any timid person.

The windows below are terribly shattered, and whether done by visible or invisible hands they present a strange and singular appearance.

[1] The Central Bank of London, Ltd., established 1863. In 1891 it amalgamated with the Birmingham and Midland Bank, Ltd., under the title of the London and Midland Bank, Ltd., now the Midland Bank, Ltd.—H.P.

It is the common notion from the noises which are at times heard that the house is in the possession of ghostly hands, and from what has been seen it might truly be thought to be the case.

At one time it was considered to be frequented by the ladies who tarry at the corner, (hence called the unfortunate skeletons' corner, of which an account will be given hereafter,) however let who inhabit it that dares for a feeling always prevails of getting past it as soon as possible.

It is said that no one could stand and watch it at night but what something or other was sure to create astonishment and surprise, and the many attracted to the spot at times is very great.

Singular shadows are also very frequently seen, sometimes in one part and then in another, but always varying and changing, with the usual mysterious sounds attendant, which are as indescribable as the shadows themselves.

Whoever did last occupy it seems not be be known, and their mysterious disappearance noticed, till the look of the house and other strange things brought it under the eye of the public.

The following is the earliest account that caused notice to be taken of this mysterious building—

Some time since, about midnight, the passengers were suddenly surprised by flashes of light appearing at each window, and being known as an empty house of course could not be accounted for, their astonishment was however increased as they became more frequent, and between each flash a low moaning sound like a being in distress struck upon the ear; this was repeated at intervals, and a mist was also seen to rise and invelope the house as almost to hide it from the sight, but this clearing off it seemed at rest and as peaceable as ever.

The number of atrocious deeds committed in some buildings and never brought to light except by accident or the demolition of them, is enough to awaken any one to be cautious of where they enter, and the number of skeletons found at different times without any account being able to be given of how they came in the places found render it natural when a place looks suspicious to be circumspect.

It is not to be supposed that anything of this wicked kind was ever enacted within these walls, but the reports about the above would cause any one to believe it to be of the most horrible and grave character.

The following is an account of things said to have taken place and seen :—

The astonishment and consternation created one night may be better imagined than described when the spectre of a woman in white without a head was seen at full length at one of the windows, there being no light it could not be so well seen, but it was plain enough to be described; how the head was taken off could not be told, but dressed in a winding sheet it presented a hideous appearance, and scared many away at the time; it soon gradually disappeared, and the figure of a murderous looking villain with a razor in one hand and the head of a female apparently in a handkerchief was seen as if in the act of making an escape.

The singular shadow of a female without a head was enough to alarm any individual, and the figure seen afterwards would seem to reveal some shocking tragedy. In the day time all the shutters appear to be shut, but this cannot be the case at night, when such sights are seen. It is almost impossible to describe all that has been said to have been seen in or about this mysterious dwelling. One account is related of it being once the residence of a rich heiress, who being left without a guardian, was overwhelmed by suitors, and many was the duels fought in her behalf. How many victims fell through their violent passion cannot be told, but the house is supposed to be haunted with their spectres. A very slight clue was ever got to trace the steps of this young lady, and being missed suddenly, whether she died by the hands of her desperate lovers or naturally was never known.

Among the reports of spectres seen is that of a skeleton with a light, which at any time would be enough to scare many timid persons away; it is also observed how quiet the place seems in the day, which but from the state in which it is in would create no astonishment, though at night when such scenes as the above are seen, renders it an object of curiosity and wonderment.

Another report states that some nights is heard a continual tapping at the windows, but nothing visible; it has even been said that the knocker has kept knocking at the door, but this would be singular indeed. A strange looking figure has also been seen to bob its head up the iron-plate hole in the street; if such queer looking visitors were often seen no doubt they would be soon in possession of more premises than these, and many a scared face would tell other strange accounts of what had been seen, but fortunately its respect adheres only to this place.

It will be in the recollection of the reader, that a strange looking lady, enveloped entirely in black, used to saunter about the Blackfriars road, and who she was or where she came from nobody ever knew; from one year's end to the other her dress was always the same. A year or so since it was reported that this individual died, but it is said that her spirit still hovers about these premises, and frequently appears at the windows. It is not known whether this individual was in any way connected with the proprietorship of these premises, or it might be surmised that some singular attachment still adhered her to them; a restless spirit is not unfrequently to be met with in this life, therefore it is not to be supposed but it may exist in the other.

But, again—This Old House is not situated in a crowded neighbourhood but in a large open thoroughfare and before the eyes of every passer by—and as may be said—the strange appearance of the rolled up blinds would lead one to think that the supposed inmates had a care that they should be preserved and kept clean, but when we see the inside shutters shut may be they are not aware of the demolition of the glass; indeed what can be thought when such singularities take place as described, and moreover who can doubt the character of the inhabitants who choose to live in such a circumscribed space.

It has been known for an individual to be so venturesome as to make a descent into the front area, but it must be the temptation of what curiosities may be found that could induce anyone to show such courage.

Some still more mysterious things have been said to have happened, which it will be as well to relate. A scraper placed at the door and suddenly disappearing would create but little astonishment, as the prowlers about often take a fancy to that useful article; neither can it be wondered at that quartern loaves disappear when a baker happens to leave his barrow at the door for the same purpose; but what can be said when a butcher passing the door should suddenly miss the weight of meat from his shoulder, sure enough he would exclaim, 'somebody has prigged the beef', but who—who;—well might he exclaim who, when just before the baker's boy had lost the savoury minced pies and never discovered it till about to deliver them. The butcher said he seed nobody take it, so did the baker's boy—but it was a scurvy trick to take the man's milk and fill his pails with chalk and water.

The pieman at the opposite corner has long wondered how his pies kept so hot, as not thinking the warmth from the gas light above him could have that effect, but he always continued his cry of pies hot! pies hot! till a coming customer, when upon serving he found there was not the shadow of a pie left, lawks, says he, how is this? when a shower of halfpence from no one knew where put an end to his astonishment and his customer disappeared.

Among other singular tales told of these premises is that of the invisible postman for certain it is that he is never seen; but more than that no landlord is ever known to apply for his rent, a truly uncommon occurrence; but something more astonishing than either of the above, is the fact of no taxgatherer venturing to poke his sagacious nose at the door, these truly singular circumstances must show that they have a fear in applying that it may be in vain; for whoever heard of ghosts paying any rent or taxes, but ghostly letters are to be seen often enough in the hands of silly creditors. Another startling fact is also said to be that no tallyman has ever been seen to call, a notorious oversight in the arrangements of the inmates. Whoever knew a house to represent peace and plenty without all the above visitants. It is well known that hundreds of other houses are equally as much haunted as the above, for the meagre forms and emaciated countenances fully develop the ghostly meals they partake of daily; and yet the landlord and taxgather have no repugnance in calling upon them, and in the event of their not being able to comply to their demands, take care not to leave them the ghost of a stick.

What an excellent opportunity for a courageous individual to undertake the battle with the sprites and clear the place; and how many would be glad to have the job?

It would be certainly much better if no one has any claim to the place, for the inhabitants to be charitable and endeavour to make a little more revenue to the parish, by their having better tenants than are reported; and there is no doubt that such would be found who would be ready enough to shelter themselves withour fear of molestation on the parts of the ghosts—The winter is fast approaching and with shame let it be said, that during the last inclement season, so spacious a tenement should be empty while so many poor creatures were prowling the streets. It is not wished that the inhabitants should be annoyed by having a receptacle for the distressed so close to their sensitive noses, and yet they would be much gratified at the good done; and poverty is not (much to their credit,) deemed such an unpardonable crime in that as in other localities.

Having detailed all the reports of these mysterious premises in as near a form as possible to their relating, it will generally be supposed that a great deal of fiction is here introduced, but in order to dispel as much as possible any doubts on the subject an anilisation of the different parts will be as well to be made.

It is certainly possible as the eye being at all times likely to be deceived, that second sight developing supernatural antics was brought into practice; but it would be as well to endeavour to fathom the causes of such mysterious accounts, and the following is adduced,—

How startled and surprised we should be to find ourselves brushed by and yet not see the cause. According to one report the house is suddenly illuminated; could this have been by the magic influence of glaring lightning, and the ugly figures might have been the reflection on the glass of the lookers on themselves?

At another time is seen the appearance of a skeleton, this would scare timid persons enough at any time, but persons of stronger nerves would be apt to enquire into the cause of such an appearance. Who knows but at the doctor's opposite an anatomical subject may be for surgical science placed in a room opposite to where the identical figure was seen, and the light moved about by the parties pursuing their studies.

There is also the frightful apparition of a female without a head and a monster afterwards; this looks like the pranks of a being in human form amusing themselves at the credulity of the lookers on, for who would suppose but what the Magic Lantern was instrumental in creating such terrifying scenes.

The noises and tapping at the windows perhaps are more difficult to be accounted for, as it is not supposed that any Old Organ for the wind to whistle through its pipes exists here, and unless caused by the wind blowing over the chimnies which at times will make a noise to astonish anyone, it evades conception.

The coalhole visitant was without doubt one of the courageous individuals who stole over into the area, and perhaps the sight of a policeman's hat saved the iron-plate from decamping with the mysterious visitor.

The singular circumstances of the pieman will cause many to stare with astonishment and his pies being noted for their superiority always gains him good custom, and well he deserves to be supported for his standing within such a curious locality; he braves all weathers, and let any pass him when they will he will always supply them with a pie all hot.

It may be remarked that this House is tenanted by rats which play such fearful and mischievous pranks, but however true this can be they must be rats of unusual size and strange formations.

It is well known the sagacity of those animals is very great, but no credit could be given to their doing what has been before described; as (although carnivorous animals) their united strength would not have enabled them to have taken the beef, and as their taste for pastry (not a whit the less,) would have led them to have taken the dishes; or by their power have transferred the milk; besides many other strange doings than even these.

It cannot be suspected that the windows were broken by these little creatures either; indeed a casual observer would be inclined to believe that some explosion had taken place so completely are they demolished; no doubt some alarmed persons on the outside had at some time raised a siege and battled at the glaze believing it was possible to scare away what had scared them.

Persons in the present century are generally supposed not to be very superstitious, but sometimes the mind acted upon by a sudden calamity or aroused by a fearful dream or vision, that cannot be dispelled seizes and oftimes makes a prey on the most robust.

Many stories are told of castle spectres and ghosts, but such were merely written as tales, to divert and amuse, not that such existed; but here we have the house and within the sight of any who choose to bestir themselves to go and see it.

The End

I will take this opportunity of introducing another London 'Poltergeist', also represented in my collection by a rare tract: *The Tyburn Ghost; or, The Strange Downfall of the Gallows. A most true Relation How the famous Triple-Tree Neer Paddington was on Tuesday-night last* (*the third of this instant September*) *wonderfully pluckt up by the Roots and demolisht by certain Evil-Spirits* . . . London, 1678.

I cannot add much to the title of this rare first edition except to say that the good people near where the Marble Arch now stands awoke one morning to find that their gallows had disappeared from its site at the junction of the present Edgware and Bayswater Roads. On some occasions its two uprights and cross-beam are said to have actually spanned Edgware Road. The 'demolisht' gallows was re-erected, and the following were afterwards hanged on it: Jack Sheppard (1724), Earl Ferrars (1760), and many more famous—and infamous—criminals. Seventeen years before this tract was printed, the skeletons of Cromwell, Ireton, and other regicides were hung on Tyburn Tree or, as it was sometimes called, the 'Deadly Never Green'.

CHAPTER XIV

'Ring Out, Wild Bells'

There is a belief—that is quite erroneous—that Official Science, as represented by the Fellows of the Royal Society, looks askance at Psychical Research and ignores the whole field. Actually, the reverse is the case. Very many Fellows have taken—and take—an active and sustained interest in our subject, or have contributed to it important works and papers on the various facets of this fascinating and important science. It would take too long to enumerate all those Fellows who have helped in the way I have indicated, but off-hand, I can mention the names of Joseph Glanvill, Robert Boyle, Reid Clanny, Sir William Crookes, A. R. Wallace, Sir Oliver Lodge, William McDougall, Julian Huxley, R. J. Tillyard, W. R. Bousfield, E. W. MacBride, Lord Rayleigh, A. O. Rankine, and Sir William Barrett. One Fellow, Edward Heron-Allen, even wrote a book[1] on palmistry that ran into several editions.

Another Fellow, Sir Richard Gregory, Bart., the mouthpiece of Official Science in this country (in 1939 he was elected President of the British Association for the duration of the war), has always taken the keenest and most sympathetic interest in psychical research, an interest that is reflected in the pages of *Nature*, of which he was the distinguished editor for many years.

As for psychical research in the universities, well, we are progressing slowly in this direction. There is a Studentship in Psychical Research at Trinity College, Cambridge; and London and Oxford are definitely interested. My own successes—and rebuffs—in the fight for academic recognition have been detailed elsewhere.[2]

This digression concerning orthodoxy and psychics has been occasioned by the fact that another distinguished Fellow of the Royal Society, Major Edward Moor (1771–1848), has put on record his convincing account of a Poltergeist visitation that has become a classic. And no story of paranormal bell-ringing (such as occurred at Borley and many other places); in fact, no mention of a major haunting anywhere would be complete without some reference to the inexplicable—and noisy—Poltergeist disturbances that occurred at Great Bealings, a village two and a half miles from Woodbridge in East Suffolk, and twenty miles from Borley. At the time of the manifestations, Great Bealings had a population of some 200 souls.

On February 25, 1834, Major Moor sent a letter to the *Ipswich Journal* describing the most extraordinary bell-ringing that had occurred

---

[1] *A Manual of Cheirosophy*, London, 1885. I possess the original holograph MS.

[2] See *Search for Truth*, London, 1942, pp. 97–132.

in his house,[1] and for which no normal explanation could be found. The letter (which appeared in the issue of the *Journal* dated March 1, 1834) was as follows:

'Sir,

A circumstance of an unaccountable nature has recently occurred at my house, and I shall be obliged by your giving insertion to this, my account of it. On Sunday, the 2nd. instant, returning from afternoon service, I was told that the dining-room bell had been rung three times, at intervals, between two and five o'clock. At this, the servants left in the house, a man and woman, were surprised; no person or cause being

'*All the bells in the kitchen had been ringing violently*'.

perceptible, though sought. This passed; and, had nothing more happened, would probably have been soon forgotten. The next day, Monday, the same bell rang three of four times in the afternoon—the last time within my hearing, shortly before 5 p.m. This too might have passed; for I fancied I could discern a cause sufficient for such an effect, although the room was not in use, and certainly no one was within reach of the bell-pull: but the proceedings of yesterday (Tuesday, the 4th) have, I confess, completely baffled me.

[1] According to Kelly's *Directory of Suffolk*, 1929, Bealings House is a'Georgian mansion of brick, surrounded by park-like grounds'. The west window of St. Mary's Church is dedicated to Charlotte, Lady Hatherley, who was the only daughter of Major Moor. She died in 1878 and is buried in the churchyard. Major Moor's son, the Rev. Ed. James Moor, was Rector of Great Bealings from 1844 to 1886.

'I left home early, and returned before five in the afternoon. I was immediately told that "all the bells in the kitchen had been ringing violently". A *peal* at that moment sounded in my ears. I proceeded thither, and learned from the cook, that "the five bells on the right" had, since about three o'clock, been frequently so affected. There are nine bells in a row, about a foot apart, 10 feet from the floor, and 12 from the fire; not over it. While I was intently looking at the bells, and listening to the relation that the ringings had occurred at intervals of about a quarter of an hour, the same five bells rang violently; so violent was it that I should not have been surprised if they had been shaken from their fastenings. My son was beside me, also watching: he had witnessed one peal before, and had heard more than one. The cook and another servant were then in the kitchen. Although expecting a ringing, the suddenness and violence of the effect, with the agitation of the bells, rather startled me. My son said he had been startled at his first-witnessed peal; so had the cook, but she had heard and seen so many that she was now unmoved. After about ten minutes, I intently watching the while, another similar phenomenon was witnessed; but we thought not quite so loud as that preceding, and we were in some doubt if more than four bells actually rang. With an accession of observers, we continued watching during another quarter of an hour, when a third peal, by the five, occurred—very like those preceding, but some of us thought less loud. The five bells, whose pealing I have mentioned, are those of the dining-room, drawing-room over it, an adjacent bed-room, and two attics over the drawing-room.

'We are now arrived at the time of before six, of Tuesday, the 4th. Dinner was then taken into the breakfast-room, when sitting down, the bell of that room rang singly, as if it had been pulled. No one was near the pull, it having rung after we sat down to dinner. During dinner the same five bells rang, perhaps every 10, 12, or 15 minutes, say four times, and continued to do so, with nearly uniform violence, while the servants, six in number, were at dinner in the kitchen; and with longer intervals, till 7.45, when the last peal of Tuesday sounded.

'The nine bells have been hung 28 years, and so well hung that they have never, I think, required any repair, save that of the breakfast room; the wire of which broke, and was repaired a month or six weeks ago by a tradesman of Woodbridge, who assisted at the original hanging. All the bells in the house—12 in number—except one, have thus rang, without apparent cause. The one is the front door bell, which hangs between the five *pealers* and the three.

'Now, Sir, is this not a strange relation? At the first gentle, single tinkling, I was disposed to think that I could account for it. But the boisterous clang and agitation of my first witnessed peal of five at once showed its fallacy. You and your readers may be assured that there is no hoax in the matter. I do not mean by me, but by any one. I am thoroughly convinced that the ringing is by no human agency. How then is it? I cannot say. A satisfactory solution is beyond the reach of my philosophy. At *this moment*, 11 a.m. Wednesday, the 5th, comes a peal. I, my son, and grandson in the breakfast room, three or four persons in the kitchen. At *this instant*, an interval of three minutes, comes another peal, like the last. I go into the kitchen. I return and note that three minutes after, I intently looking, the five rung very violently; again, in four minutes, more violently than ever. One actually struck against the ceiling.

'I repeat that I am baffled as to a sufficient cause of what I have thus seen, and heard, and described. The weather has been calm. The known laws of the electric theory seem inadequate in their ordinary operation, as are those of the expansion of metals by change of temperature. I think, Sir, this strange relation will amuse you and your readers. And if you or any of them can give a satisfactory explanation of it, I farther think it will be instructive to many—and among them to your very obedient Servant,

'EDWARD MOOR'.

In my collection I have a little book[1] that Edward Moor published about the strange manifestations at his house, and in it he gives a detailed account of the hanging of the bells, and shows the impossibility of their being rung by any person in or outside the house. He says: 'The bells rang scores of times when no one was in the passage or backhouse, or grounds, unseen. I have waited in the kitchen for a repetition of the ringings, with all the servants present, when no one, so much as a mouse, could be in concealment. Neither I, nor the servants, singly or together, nor any one, be he whom he may, could or can, I aver, work the wonderment that I and more than half a score of others saw . . . I will here note, once for all, that after much consideration, I cannot reach any procedure by which they have been, or can be produced.'

In a footnote to this book (which, by the way, was published to raise funds for the building of a church at Woodbridge, just as at Borley a 'psychic fête' was organised to get money for Borley Church), Edward Moor states that the bell-ringing at Bealings persisted from February 2 to March 27, 1834, a period of fifty-four days. The ringing ceased as abruptly as it started, and the cause was never discovered. No other phenomena appear to have happened, and the story of the noisy bells of Bealings is today a classic of a rather common phase of Poltergeist activity.

In order—as he admits—to increase the size of his book, Major Moor began collecting other accounts of paranormal bell-ringing and there are detailed in *Bealings Bells* some twenty cases, most of which are

[1] *Bealings Bells. An Account of the Mysterious Ringing of Bells at Great Bealings, Suffolk*, Woodbridge, 1841. The book is rare.

interesting, and some inexplicable. These phenomena—real or alleged—occurred at such places as Derbyshire, Ramsgate, Chelmsford, Cambridge, Oxford and London. Most of them are well authenticated, especially the 'ringing' at Greenwich Hospital (now Greenwich Naval College). Another London case was connected with 9, Earl Street, Westminster, in which the ringing was so loud and persistent that it sent one of the maidservants into convulsions!

As I have stated, bell-ringing by Poltergeists is a common diversion, and they seem unable to resist the temptation of pulling a bell-wire in any house in which they have taken up their abode. And if Poltergeists can *pull*, it seems curious that they seem usually unable to *push*. I cannot, at the moment, recollect a single example where an electric bell-push has been paranormally operated. And yet there are many cases where Poltergeists have infested houses fitted with electric bells.

I have mentioned that Poltergeists cannot resist bell wires. But at Borley, when the Rev. G. E. Smith cut most of the wires, in an attempt to stop the annoyance, the bells still rang. And this was not due to 'rats' or 'atmospheric effects'! It was at Borley that Dom Richard Whitehouse, O.S.B., saw the bells ringing of their own volition. He said: 'I have stood in the kitchen passage and watched the bells moving to and fro, the only people in the house often standing alongside of me, witnessing the same performance.'[1] The large yard bell[2] used to ring, too. Yet it was out of reach of any human hand, and no rope was attached.

Other bell-ringing phenomena noted in this volume include the cases of Mrs. Mara Mack's seaside home; Watton Priory, the Cambridge Poltergeist, Berkeley Square, 'Poltergeist Manor', etc. And at Willington Mill, the *Geist* rang a hand-bell!

I could cite the performances of many more bell-ringing Poltergeists, but all these cases have a family likeness. However, two of the more remarkable were those at Plymouth and Cambridge. In the former, in 1885, disturbances were witnessed in the home of a Mrs. Serpell. Rappings, noises, etc., and apparitions were heard and seen; objects mysteriously disappeared (as at Borley); dogs were terrified (also as at Borley), and bells rang, and rang, and rang! The cause was never discovered.[3] At Cambridge, something similar happened in the house of a Mrs. Jephson. There were several witnesses. In addition to the bell-ringing nuisance, objects were moved, and the usual Poltergeist disturbances were experienced.[4] All these cases are interesting, but not comparable with the classic ringing of Bealings' bells. And I must not forget the strange affair at Blackheath, where a door-bell continued ringing of its own volition though the police stood and watched it. No trickery

[1] *Most Haunted House in England*, p. 97.
[2] Now in my garden at Pulborough. I am waiting for it to ring—paranormally.
[3] *Journal, S.P.R.*, Vol. III, pp. 249–52, 322–32.
[4] *Journal, S.P.R.*, Vol. X (1895–96), pp. 43–7.

was discovered.[1] A few weeks previously, at Brighton, a musical instrument 'played of its own accord'.[2] Poltergeists like discord.

The reader is perhaps wondering whether we have induced the Poltergeists to ring bells experimentally. We have, but not those activated by wires. During our Borley investigation, Dr. H. F. Bellamy, his son, and a friend used a piece of apparatus that worked successfully. It had been constructed by Mr. S. H. Glanville. Under a pile of books on a mantelpiece in the dining-room was placed a spring contact-maker that rang an electric bell when the books were removed. The window was sealed, and all doors in the house were locked. During an observational period upstairs, Dr. Bellamy and his friends heard the bell suddenly ring. They ran downstairs and as they approached the dining-room, the ringing ceased. When they entered, 'the books were displaced, no book occupying its original position, and the bottom one was right off the contact-maker. Nothing else in the room had been disturbed and the window was still sealed.' No one was in the house except the three experimenters, who were satisfied that the displacement of the books (and consequently the ringing of the bell) was due to paranormal action. The experiment is fully recorded in the Borley book.[3]

The 'Poltergeist mediums', Miss Stella C. and the Schneider brothers, rang bells experimentally on many occasions. Bells in sealed wooden cages were rung under conditions that precluded fraud. They were rung at request, and intelligently, when they were feet away from either medium or sitters. Not only were hand-bells rung, but zithers were twanged, a hoop of sleigh-bells shaken, and a musical-box started and stopped to order—many times.[4] These induced phenomena were under control, unlike the spontaneous manifestations of the true Poltergeist.

[1] *Daily Mirror*, February 13, 1905.   [2] *Daily Mail*, December 24, 1909.
[3] *Op. cit.*, pp. 123, 214–15.
[4] See my *Rudi Schneider* (London, 1930); *Stella C.* (London, 1925), etc.

CHAPTER XV

The Willington Poltergeist

This case needs little introduction from me, as the narrator, Mr. Edmund Procter, so fully describes the conditions under which the phenomena were observed; the chief actors concerned; and the quite unpicturesque and unromantic *mise-en-scène* in which the prolonged drama was enacted.

Willington Mill is at Willington Quay, Northumberland, a small town on the River Tyne, two miles south-west of North Shields. Robert Stephenson (1803-1859), the famous engineer, was born there and the story of the haunting must have been familiar to him. The Procters vacated the mill house in 1847, some twelve years after the haunting began, and the place was let to employees of the firm. Then the building was converted into workmen's dwellings which, I understand, are still standing.

The case is very important for several reasons. The account has been prepared from the contemporary diary kept by our chief witness, Mr. Joseph Procter, who was a God-fearing man and a well-known Quaker. Verbatim extracts from the diary are given, and they bear the stamp of truth. Very few Poltergeist cases are so fully documented, and fewer still are the contemporary diaries, by responsible persons, that can be brought in as evidence. There are day-to-day diaries relating to the disturbances at Borley Rectory, Ballechin House, the 'Mill on the Eden' and one or two more good cases, but such invaluable records are of rare occurrence.

The Willington Mill case is also important because the disturbances, which began in 1835, persisted for so many years. This is remarkable, as Poltergeist visitations are usually of short duration. But there are outstanding exceptions, some of which are included in this volume.

The narrator of the story is Mr. Edmund Procter, son of Mr. Joseph Procter, the owner and occupant of the mill house and our chief witness. As he points out, many versions of the haunting have appeared in a number of books and journals. In order to leave to posterity an authentic account of the strange happenings, he edited his father's diary and sent (1892) the manuscript to the Society for Psychical Research for publication.[1] I am indebted to the Society for permission to reproduce those extracts I have quoted. Mr. Edmund Procter's interpolations are in square brackets. Here, then, is

[1] In the *S.P.R. Journal*, Vol. V, 1891–92, pp. 331–352.

MR. JOSEPH PROCTER'S DIARY

The 'Haunted House at Willington' has been a familiar theme on Tyneside for half a century, and the general public have been made acquainted with it in William Howitt's *Visits to Remarkable Places*, Catherine Crowe's *Night Side of Nature, The Local Historian's Table Book*, Stead's *Ghost Stories*, and other publications. I was myself born in this 'haunted house', and have vivid recollections of many singular occurrences. As my parents, however, ceased to reside there when I was but a child of seven, any evidence of my own can be but of trifling value. On my father's death in 1875, a diary that he had kept almost from the outset of the disturbances, and during many years of their occurrence, was found among his papers. The publication of this diary has been delayed for two reasons: first, my mother's objection to their publicity during her lifetime; secondly, because the manuscript breaks off suddenly, and I have long hoped, but in vain, to find the continuation and conclusion. To such readers as were not personally acquainted with the writer of this diary I may briefly state that he was a member of the Society of Friends, belonging to a family which had been attached members of that body from its very foundation. During many years he was an 'overseer' or 'elder', and was frequently appointed to offices of trust in church matters. Like many other Quakers, he took an active interest in the Peace Society, the Anti-Slavery Society, and other philanthropic organisations. He was also among the earliest teetotallers in the north of England.

His reading was fairly extensive, the *Quarterly* and *Edinburgh* being sandwiched with George Fox's *Journal* and the old *Examiner*, and Ebenezer Elliott taken alternately with some French author or the *British Friend*. I mention these details solely to place outsiders in a position to judge of the character and the reliability of the writer of the diary, and will only add my own testimony that a man with a more delicate sense of what it means to speak the truth I have yet to meet.

It only remains to add that throughout the narrative 'J.P.' stands for my father himself, and 'E.P.' for my mother, and that the paragraphs between brackets are my own additions. The earliest statement I can find is the following, in his own handwriting:

Particulars relating to some unaccountable noises heard in the house of J. and E. Procter, Willington Mill, which began about three months prior to the present time, viz., 1 mo. 28th, 1835, still continuing, and for which no adequate natural cause has hitherto been discovered.

About six weeks ago the nursemaid first told her mistress of the state of dread and alarm she was kept in, in consequence of noises she had heard for about two months, occurring more particularly nearly every evening when left alone to watch the child [my eldest brother, then about two years old] to sleep in the nursery, a room on the second floor; she declared she distinctly heard a dull heavy tread on the boarded floor of the unoccupied room above, commonly pacing backwards and forwards, and, on coming over the window, giving the floor such a shake as to cause the window of the nursery to rattle violently in its frame. This disturbance generally lasted ten minutes at a time, and though she did not heed it at first, yet she was now persuaded it was supernatural, and 'it quite overset her'. The latter was indeed evident from the agitation she manifested.

The kitchen girl said that the nursemaid had called her upstairs sometimes when frightened in this manner, and that she had found her trembling much and very pale. On examining her further in reference to this improbable tale, she did not vary in her statement, but on searching the rooms above and finding nothing to cause such results, but little credit was attached to the story.

Before many days had elapsed, however, every member of the family had witnessed precisely what the girl described, and from that time to the present, nearly every day, and sometimes several times in the day, the same has been heard by one or more of the inmates, varying unimportantly in the nature of the sound. A few particular instances may here be selected, in which imagination or fear could have no influence.

On sixth day, 1st month 23rd, 1835, my wife had in the forenoon requested one of the servants to sweep out the disturbed room in the course of the day, and being herself in the nursery [the room below] after dinner, heard a noise in the room like a person stirring about, which she took for granted was the maid cleaning out the chamber, when, to her surprise, she afterwards found that neither of the girls had been upstairs at all. The next day one of the maids, being in the nursery, supposed, from the noise she heard, that the other was lighting the fire in the room above, as had been desired, which proved a similar mistake to that on the preceeding day. It may be remarked that the nursemaid first mentioned had left, and another engaged, from whom the affair was carefully concealed. A day or two after her arrival the noise was observed by her fellow servant whilst they were together in the nursery, but she apparently did not observe it herself, from her companion talking and using the rocking-chair. Later, however, the same evening, it began suddenly when she was present, and she, somewhat alarmed, inquired who or what was in the room above.

On First day, the 25th, being kept at home by indisposition, my wife was in the nursery about eleven o'clock in the forenoon, and heard on the floor above, about the centre of the room, a step as of a man with a strong shoe or boot going towards the window and returning. The same day, when we were at dinner, the maid, being with the child in the nursery, heard the same heavy tread for about five minutes; she came into the sitting-room to satisfy herself that her master was there, thinking it must have been he who was upstairs. The following day the dull sound was resumed, and up to this day the boots have not done duty again. It may be noted that frequently the room has been examined immediately after the occurrence of the noise; it has been sat in, in one instance slept in all night, and in every case nothing has been elicited. Several of our friends who have waited to hear the invisible disturber have all, with one exception, been disappointed.

My brother, John Richardson Procter, remained in the room below some time after the usual period of operation, fruitlessly, but within ten minutes of his departure the nurse was so terrified by the loudness of its onset that she ran downstairs with the child half asleep in her arms. My cousin, Mary Unthank, stayed two nights and was much in the room without being gratified. All the persons who have heard, and six have been so far privileged, are confident that the noise is within the room on the third floor, as the precise part of the floor above on which the impression is made is clearly distinguishable through the ceiling below, and the weight apparently laid on, shaking violently the window in the room below, when no other window in the house is affected, and during a dead calm, is of itself a proof of this.

It seems impossible there can be any trick in the case; there is a garret above, and the roof is inaccessible from without; the house stands alone, and during most of the time the window was built up with lath and plaster, whilst the only other communication with the outside, by the chimney, was closed by a fireboard which was so covered over with soot as to prove that not a pebble or a mouse had passed. The room is devoid of furniture, and for some time the door was nailed up. Not a rat has been seen in the house for years, nor at any time anything heard like a scratch or squeak, or running between the floor and ceiling; nor, it is conceived, could a hundred rats so shake the floor by their weight as to cause the window below to rattle as it does.

The noise has been heard at every hour of the day, though oftenest in the evening, rarely in the night; has no connection with weather nor with the going of the mill; [the mill was contiguous but there was a road between it and the house] in short, it is difficult to imagine a natural cause having a shadow of pretension to belief.

Those who deem all intrusion from the world of spirits impossible in the present constitution of things will feel assured that a natural solution of the difficulty will still be obtained on further investigation; whilst those who believe with the poet 'that millions of spiritual creatures walk the earth unseen', and that, even in modern times, amidst a thousand creations of fancy, fear, fraud, or superstition, there still remain some well-attested instances in which good or evil spirits have manifested their presence by sensible tokens, will probably deem it possible that this may be referred to the latter class—especially when they learn that several circumstances tending to corroborate such a view are witheld from this narrative.

[Whether the 'several circumstances withheld' are disclosed in the written narratives which follow I am unable to say. I find the following consecutive:]

Additional particulars relating to unaccountable noises, etc. heard at Willington Mill, containing the most remarkable from first month 25th, to the present time, second month 18th, 1835.

On First day night, the 31st of first month, soon after retiring to bed, before going to sleep, my wife and I both heard ten or twelve obtuse deadened beats as of a mallet on a block of wood, apparently within two feet of the bed curtain, on one side by the crib in which the child was laid. The next night, before undressing, I had hushed the child asleep in his crib, and while leaning over it with one hand laid upon it and listening to some indistinct sounds overhead, which had just ceased. I heard a tap on the cradle leg as with a piece of steel, and distinctly felt the vibration of the wood in my hand from the blow. This might be a sudden crack not infrequent when wood is drying in, but it sounded like a knock on the outside. Since this time the walking in the empty room has not been heard oftener than twice or thrice, of which this afternoon was the last time.

On the same evening I heard that Thomas Mann, the foreman of the mill—a man of strict integrity and veracity, who has been two years in Unthank and Procter's employ—had heard something remarkable, and on questioning him elicited the following statement. It may be premised that U. and P. have a wooden cistern on iron wheels to bring water for their horses, which stands in the mill yard. When in motion, drawn by a horse to be filled, it makes a very peculiar noise which may be heard a considerable distance, especially when the wheels want greasing, and by any person accustomed to it the noise of its going could not be mistaken for that of any other vehicle. The mill was going all night, and T.M.'s place was to attend the engine till 2 a.m. Going out to fill the barrow with coals about one o'clock, he heard this machine, as he thought, going along the yard, which did not at the moment strike him as out of the usual course; but remembering the hour, the apprehension that it was being stolen flashed on his mind; it was creaking excessively, from want of oil as might be supposed, and was then drawing near the yard gates, towards which he pursued after it, when, to his astonishment, he found it had never stirred from its place near where he at first was, and looking round everywhere all was still and not a creature to be found. He afterwards searched round the premises with a lantern, but descried nothing. He was much puzzled, but it was not till the next day that he felt himself compelled to attribute the phenomenon to a supernatural cause.

More than once I have, on coming through the garden at night heard a sound like someone stepping down the gravel walk and have not been able to discover anyone. This step on the gravel[1] has been heard by one or two others, but nothing seen.

On First day, 2 mo., 15th [1835], my wife and I were informed by our cousin Unthanks that they understood that the house, and that room in particular in which the noises now occurred, was said to be haunted before they entered it in 1806, but that nothing that they knew of had been heard during their occupancy of 25 years.

[On the same page as the above, and in my father's handwriting, is the following memorandum below the above recital; there is a line drawn through them, however, whether by himself I am unable to say, and the sentence is apparently unfinished:]

An infirm old woman, the mother-in-law of R. Oxon, the builder of the premises, lived and died in the house, and after her death the haunting was attributed . . .

[I have heard my father speak of this circumstance, but the evidence appeared to be of a slight and hearsay character.]

[I find the following occurence described on a separate sheet of paper, but believe, although it is not dated, that this is the correct sequence of the manuscript. I have myself heard all the particulars from the lips of all the parties concerned, which completely agreed with this account in my father's handwriting.]

For about two months previously there had rarely been 24 hours without indications by noises, etc. not in any other way accountable, of the presence of the ghostly visitant, to some or all of the inmates. A few days previously a respectable neighbour had seen a transparent white female figure in a window on the second storey of the house. On the 13th of last month [November], early in the evening, two of the children in the house, one aged about 8, the other under two years, both saw, unknown to each other, an object which could not be real, and which went into the room where the apparition was afterwards seen and disappeared there. A near connection of the family on a visit [my mother's sister], but for whom, for obvious reasons, a lodging was obtained at the house of Thomas Mann [the foreman of the flour mill adjoining, and much respected by his employers] went out as usual to sleep about 9.30 p.m. Soon after going to her bedroom, T.M.'s wife went out of the house for some coals, and was struck with a figure in the window previously referred to [nothing being between the two houses but a kitchen garden and a road]; she called her husband, who saw the same figure passing backwards and forwards and then standing still in the window. It was very luminous and likewise transparent, and had the appearance of a priest in a white surplice. T.M. then called out the relative of the family and his own daughter. When they came the head was nearly gone and the brightness somewhat abated, but it was

[1] Compare this with my experience of the footsteps on the gravel path that surrounded the cottage at Horley. (See p. 26).—H.P.

fully ten minutes before it quite disappeared by fading gradually downwards. Both when standing and moving it was about 3 feet from the floor of the room. T.M. went down close under the window, and also went to inform the inmates of the circumstances, but finding they had locked-up for the night did not accomplish it. It was a dark night, without a moon, and there was not a ray of light, nor any person anywhere near the house. The window blind was close down, and the figure seemed to come through both it and the glass, as had the brightness been all inside of the glass the framing of the window would have intervened, which was not visible. In walking the figure seemed to enter

'The figure was very luminous and likewise transparent and had the appearance of a priest in a white surplice'.

the wall on each side. The occupier of the house [my father] slept in that room, and must have gone in shortly after the disappearance of the apparition.[1]

[My aunt, the 'near connection' referred to above, Mrs. Christiana Wright of Mansfield, who was still living, has read the manuscript of this incident this year (1892). She has corrected it in two or three unimportant details, but otherwise confirms it as strictly according to her own observation.]

[1] Compare this figure at the window with what Miss Rosemary Williams saw at Borley (p. 297).—H.P.

[The following account of my father's has no year stated, but it appears to be about this time. J.C. is my mother's sister, Jane Carr, of Carlisle.]

On the 16th of 12th mo., a little before twelve o'clock at night, J.C. and her bedfellow were disturbed by a noise similar to the winding up of a clock,[1] apparently on the stairs where the clock stands, which continued for the space of ten minutes. When that ceased footsteps were heard in the room above, which is unoccupied, for perhaps a quarter of an hour; whilst this was going on the bed was felt to shake, and J.C. distinctly heard the sound like a sack falling on the floor above.[2] On the 3rd of 1st month, about 12 o'clock at night, J.C. being quite awake, was disturbed by a noise similar to a person knocking quickly and strongly five times on a piece of board in the room; when that ceased she distinctly heard the sound of a footstep close by the side of her bed. About the beginning of the year J.B. was awoke by a sound like a bullet lodged in the floor above or in the wall of his bedroom, and looked at his watch to ascertain the time; he found next morning that his wife in the next room was awoke by the same sound.

About the 21st inst. E.P. and nurse Pollard both felt themselves raised up and let down three times. [My mother has described this experience to me; she said the bed was lifted up as if a man were underneath pushing it up with his back. She did not speak to nurse Pollard, nor the nurse to her, each thinking the other was asleep; this not being disclosed until breakfast time.] On the 15th, about 8 p.m., J.P., jun., who had been in bed about half an hour, called of someone to come to him and begged for a light; he said that something under the crib raised him up very quickly many times, and wished to know what it could be. On the 11th of 1st mo., whilst the servants were at dinner, E.P. was lying on the sofa in her lodging-room when she felt the floor to vibrate as from a heavy foot in an adjoining room; in the writing room underneath J.C. at the same time heard the sound of a person walking backwards and forwards in the room above. Soon after this E.P. heard the sound of a closet door in the room above shutting three times, after which footsteps came into the middle of the room and then all was silent. E.P. feels assured there was nobody upstairs at the time. On the 17th, at 7 p.m., the two elder children and two nursemaids were in the nursery when a loud clattering or jingling was heard in the room; it sounded from the closet; the girls were very much terrified as also was Jane P., who is four years and a half old. Little Joseph, perceiving his sister affrighted, endeavoured to calm her by saying, 'Never mind, Jane, God will take care of thee.' Some weeks before this little Joseph

---

[1] The Epworth Poltergeist made a noise 'like the winding up of a jack'.—H.P.

[2] Compare this phenomenon with the 'immense weight seemed to fall through the ceiling to the floor' heard by Captain Jervis in the Hinton Ampner case, p. 143.—H.P.

said in the morning to his aunt, Jane Carr, who was sleeping with him, that he was a long time in getting to sleep the night before from some people walking very fast in the room above; he wondered who it could be. This was an unoccupied room. One night, whilst sleeping in a crib in his parents' room, he awoke his father to say that someone had stepped close to his bed. One night about this time J.P. heard early in the morning a noise as of wood moving from the middle to one side of the boarded floor of the empty room above; after which he heard a loud beating in the mill yard. Another night he heard two very peculiar sounds as of whistling or whizzing. [I have sometimes heard my father imitate this peculiar and horrid sound.] About 11 o'clock on the night of the 23rd, J.C. and her little bedfellow heard a succession of thumps or blows in the empty room above which continued for the space of ten minutes. A little after one o'clock the same night J.P. was awakened by a single beat or blow in the room above, after which one of the chairs in his own room seemed shifted.

On the night of the 26th J.P. heard the sound of footsteps in the attic, and afterwards as of setting things down in the room above, from about 11.30 p.m. to 2 a.m. A little after eleven he had heard several prolonged and peculiar whistles which were also heard by the nurse in another room; they seemed to come from the landing; she had described it without knowing that J.P. had heard it. Joseph was shaken in his crib early the same night.

On the 27th no one slept in the third storey; about eleven o'clock Jane C. and the nursemaid heard in the room above the sound of some person with strong shoes sometimes walking, sometimes running backwards and forwards, moving chairs and clashing down box lids, and sometimes thumping as with a fist. These sounds also moved on to the stair-head. About midnight J.C. felt the bed raised up on one side as if to turn her over, giving two lifts. Nurse Pollard in another room on the same floor heard a noise which roused her as she was going to sleep; something then pressed against the high part of the curtain and came down on to her arm, which was weighed down with the same force; in great terror she called out, 'Lord have mercy upon me!' Nothing further occurred to her that night, nor was the maid who slept with her aroused.

2nd month 3rd. On nearly every day or night since the last entry more or less has been heard that could be referred to no other than the same cause; amongst them the following may be noted: Joseph and Henry have been several times disturbed in their cribs during the evening; once they heard a loud shriek which seemed to come from near the foot of the bed. On going up Joseph was found trembling and perspiring from the fright. One evening J.P. heard a very peculiar moan or cry in the same room; also J. and E.P. and Jane C. heard footsteps and noises which ceased on running upstairs to prevent the children being frightened. Another time Joseph said his bed moved backwards and forwards; also a voice by the foot of the bed said, 'Chuck'[1] twice, and then made a noise like a child sucking. He describes other voices; he is very inquisitive as to the origin of these noises, and says he never heard or felt anything like it whilst we lived at Shields.

It may be proper to mention that neither he nor any of the children have any idea of anything supernatural. Jane sleeps in another room; she told her mother that she felt the bed go up and down, and other things of that kind, not having heard of her brother Joseph, or any of us, having felt anything of the same kind.

About the 30th J. and E.P. heard loud thumps in the room above, also footsteps in the night, when they knew no one was upstairs, as the cook was at that time sleeping for company with the nurses on the second floor. A day or two later, about six in the evening, whilst the servants were at tea in the kitchen, E.P. and J.C., whilst in the nursery on the second floor, heard what seemed to be heavy pieces of wood jarring on the floor above.

2nd mo., 1st. About 11 p.m., some little time after all had gone to bed, the sound of chairs etc., being moved about on the kitchen floor was heard.

2nd mo., 4th. Jane C. had been poorly, and was awake about 4.30 a.m., as well as her companion, when they heard footsteps descending from the upper storey which passed their door and went down into the kitchen; they thought it was the cook and wondered at her being so early. They then heard the sound of the kitchen door opening and then of the kitchen window being thrown up and the shutters opened with more than usual noise. About seven o'clock they were surprised by the cook calling at their room for a light; having been up early to do the washing the previous morning she had this time over-slept herself. She had clearly not yet been downstairs.

In the afternoon of the same day Jon. D. Carr [my mother's brother of Carlisle] came to the house and stayed all night, sleeping alone on the second storey. Soon after going to bed he heard noises in the room above, as of a piece of wood or a balance rapidly striking each end of the floor; afterwards many beats as with a mallet, some very loud; also like a person stamping in a passion. He also heard a peculiar whistle, which he imitated so as exactly to resemble what J.P. heard some time before; he further heard a noise on the stairs and landing, and for some time felt his bed to vibrate very much; he put his hand down to the stock and felt it shaking. This suddenly ceased. He was quite awake and collected, indeed did not sleep till two o'clock though unusually disposed to it. He said in the morning he would not live in the house for any money.

[1] Compare the *Bo, Bo, Kick, Cuck.*, heard in the Ringcroft disturbances, p. 78.— H.P.

The account he gave to Jonathan Carr [his father] induced the latter to come over from Carlisle next morning to see if he could assist with his advice under such disagreeable and dangerous disturbances.

[I can find no other allusion to my grandfather's visit among my father's papers.]

On 2nd mo., 5th, between 11 and 12 at night, Jane C. heard a thump on the landing near the bedroom door, upon which she awoke her companion, Mary Young. [This was the cook whom my aunt had to sleep with her, not daring to sleep alone in such a house; she was a most respectable and intelligent woman whom I well remember; she was eight years in my mother's service when she married the principal tradesman in the village.] Mary Young heard the slot in the door apparently slide back, the handle to turn and the door to open. A rushlight was burning on the dressing-table, but the bed was an old four-poster, and the curtains being drawn nothing could be seen. A step then went to the rushlight and appeared by the sound to snuff it and then lay down the snuffers. In the act of snuffing the light was transiently obscured, as when that act is customarily performed. Jane C. then felt it raise up the clothes over her twice; then they both heard something rustle the curtains as it went round the bed; on getting to Mary Young's side she distinctly saw a dark shadow on the curtain. On getting to the bed-board where Jane C. lay a loud thump as with a fist was heard on it; something was then felt to press on the counterpane on M. Young's side of the bed, the bed curtain being pushed in but nothing more seen. Whatever the visitor might be was then heard to go out, seeming to leave the door open. In the morning they found the door still bolted as it was left when they went to bed. In this occurrence Jane C. heard and felt everything described, but having her head under the bedclothes could not see the shadow as her companion did. [I have on three or four occasions heard a graphic account of this night of horror both from my aunt Jane Carr in later life, and from Mary Young some years after her marriage. The description they both gave exactly agreed with the above narrative from my father's pen except that one or both of them stated that a few minutes after the unknown dreadful visitor left the room they arose, found the door locked as when they came to bed, and searched the room in every way. This is the only discrepancy I notice. One would naturally expect that my aunt would refuse to stay longer in the house after such an experience, but such was not the case; she was as I remember her to be, a woman of strong nerve, of very cheerful temper, and not easily disturbed. She died on board the steamer *Prussian Eagle*, in Plymouth Sound, in 1859.]

On the 7th J.C. heard the noise of a box trailed over the floor above the nursery when she was certain no one was upstairs, the servants being at dinner in the kitchen and the rest of the family in the parlour downstairs.

On the previous night there had been unaccountable thumpings and bed shakings but nothing of special note.

From 2nd mo., 6th to the 20th, nothing particular has been heard; but Jane, about 4½ years old, told her parents that when sleeping with her aunt she one night saw by the washstand at the foot of the bed where the curtains were open, a queer looking head, she thought of an old woman; she saw her hands with two fingers of each hand extended and touching each other; she had something down the sides of her face and passed across the lower part of it. She saw it plainly though it was darkish in the room. She was afraid and put her head under the clothes and by-and-bye fell asleep. On the 17th, about dusk, she described having seen a head on the landing as she was coming downstairs, and appeared to be very much terrified.

About the 25th, pretty late at night, whilst J.P. was asleep, E.P. felt a heavy pressure which unnerved her very much; it seemed to take her breath away and she felt quite sick after it, but did not tell J.P. of it until the morning. Some night previous E.P. was awoke by feeling a pressure on the face over the eye, of icy coldness; it was suddenly laid on with a good deal of force and as suddenly withdrawn. [I have heard my mother describe this on different occasions 20 or 30 years after it occurred; her face always had a pained expression when she related this experience, which I think was more distressing to her than anything she underwent in the house.]

3rd mo., 3rd. About 5 a.m. E.P. was awake when several beats were felt on one side of the room, which awoke J.P.; a vibration was felt in the room, the bed shook considerably and the curtain rings rattled. The knocks were repeated on the floor above.

On the night of the 5th E.P. heard what appeared to be a heavy box turned over twice in the room above, where no one was sleeping, and the entire household being asleep except herself, and everything still.

[I omit several memoranda about this time as to the children and servants hearing voices and sounds of various descriptions.]

3rd mo., 13th, 1840. Since the last entry Joseph has heard the sound of a thick stick being broken in his room; of a stepping backwards and forwards; of his name being called, etc. About the same date J. and E.P. heard unaccountable drummings and vibrations; also the sound of someone stirring in the closet.

On the 21st J. and E.P. heard a handbell rung upstairs; they were quite satisfied at the time that no one was there. On the 28th heavy thumps in the middle of the night, and after breakfast the next morning E.P. heard a handbell rung upstairs when she was quite certain everyone was downstairs. J. and E.P. are sure it is no actual bell in the house that is rung, the tone being altogether different. Joseph has been disturbed nearly every night lately; he says when there is nobody upstairs the voices are loud; he is now afraid of going into his room in the daytime.

The words he reports as being uttered, such as 'Never mind'—'Come and get', seem to have no particular application. Tonight he has heard footsteps twice, and felt a bat on his pillow. At the time two of the servants were at a temperance meeting, the other in the kitchen. [The inference that my brother was simply dreaming, or else shamming, so as to get someone to come beside him, will no doubt readily occur to some minds. I can only say that a more truthful boy, or one more transparently honest I do not think ever breathed. He was six years of age at this time, and died eleven years afterwards from an accidental blow on the head at a boarding-school.]

On the 30th Henry (3 years old) was awakened by his brother Joseph ringing the bell at his bedside, saying his bed was shaking, and that he heard someone talking in the room; Henry being asked if he did not think it was Joseph that spoke, said No, and showed where the sound came from; they both heard it again about ten minutes later on.

4 mo., 6th. During the last nine days J. and E.P. have often heard something stirring in the night, and knocks in the servants' room above; these they afterwards found the girls had not heard, being very sound sleepers.

4 mo., 4th. This evening E.P. plainly heard someone or something stirring and rustling about in a room she knew no one was in, and there and then found that no one was in it.

6th. During last night there seemed to be but little quiet in the house till daylight; noises as of a shoe dragged over the boards just outside the door, and as though the servants had got up and were going about; knocks loud and knocks gentle, indeed all sorts of knocks.

[It may be well to mention here that the Newcastle and North Shields Railway, which passes about a quarter of a mile from the house, was opened on June 19th, 1840.]

[A gap occurs in the diary here, but the following letter written by my father to my mother on July 4th, 1840, illustrates a striking incident of which full particulars are given by William Howitt and Mrs. Crowe. The hero, Dr. Drury, a practitioner then well known in Sunderland, had obtained leave to sit up all night on the stairs with a friend, during the absence of the family except my father and one servant. He had wished to bring a loaded musket and a dog with him; my father objected to firearms, but consented to the dog.]

Willington. Seventh day, evening.

Dear Elizabeth, . . . Last night Dr. Drury came with T. Hudson, a shopman of Joseph Ogilvie, chemist, and no dog. After a long chat they sat on the high landing; I went to my own bed; Bell in the Camp room. About one o'clock I heard a most horrid shriek from E.D., slipped on my trousers and went up. He had then swooned, but come to himself again in a state of *extreme nervous excitement*, and accompanied with

'Drury ... had been struck speechless as the ghost advanced from the closet'.

183

much coldness and faintness. He had seen the G.; had been struck speechless as it advanced from the closet in the room over the drawing-room to the landing, and then leapt up with an awful shriek and fainted. The other young man had his head laid against the easy-chair and was dozing, and as the G. made no noise in coming up he did not wake till the yell of his friend called him to his help.

I called up Bell to make on the fires, get coffee, etc. but he continued in a shocking state of tremour for some hours, though not irrational. He had a ghastly look and started at the smallest sound—could not bear to see anything white; he had not been in the least sleepy, and was not at all frightened till the moment when the G. met his gaze. They had both previously heard several noises, but all had been quiet for about a quarter of an hour, and E.D. was thinking of getting his companion to go to bed, not expecting anything more that night. . . . E.D. has got a shock he will not soon cast off. I go to Shields tonight and I question I come back at present.

[The diary resumes as follows:]

5 mo., 17th, 1841. Since the latter end of 12 mo., 1840, we have been entirely free from those very singular disturbances which had been occurring with some intermissions for about 14 months before; and as we now appear to be threatened with a renewal of them, I here make some memoranda of the circumstances. Our servants for some time have shown no symptoms of timidity, and seemed to have no appre-hension of any recurrence of former visitations. E.P. has not been well lately, and has thought she observed something in the demeanour of the servants indicative of fear within a day or two past; on questioning them this afternoon they said the ghost had come back, but they wished to keep it from her if possible, as she was poorly. On the 29th, about 9 p.m., J.P., hearing Joseph call, and going upstairs, heard a rustling, like a female running out of the room, but saw no one and was satisfied no one was there. Joseph said his name had been called several times from near the foot of the bed in a voice like his own. That night J. and E.P. heard a drumming and tapping in different parts of their room; at one moment it seemed to be something heavy falling on the floor of the room above, then on the floor of the room adjoining where it awoke the youngest child, and then to pounce down in the room below on the ground floor. [I have frequently heard my father describe this peculiar case.]

6 mo., 1st. The two maids, Davis and E. Mann, report they were unable to sleep before 2 a.m. from constant noises, particularly the apparent treading of bare feet backwards and forwards at the foot of their bed, the noise several times awaking the youngest child; some-times the tread seemed to pass out on to the landing and run up and down stairs. The nursery door was of course bolted.

7th day, 11 mo., 13th, 1841. About 4.30 p.m. Joseph, now eight

years old, was in the nursery with his brothers and sisters; he had
seated himself on the top of a chest of drawers and was making a
pretended speech to them, when he suddenly jumped down, and the
nursery door being ajar, J.P., who was in his own bedroom adjoining,
heard him exclaim there was a monkey, and that it had pulled his leg
by his shoe-strap. J.P. did not himself see the monkey, but coming out
of his room saw the children peering under the curtains of the bed in the
Blue-room where, they alleged, the animal had disappeared. Joseph
afterwards stated that the monkey had given a sharp pull at his shoe-
strap, and had tickled his foot; he did not suppose any other but it was
a real monkey. Edmund, who is under two years old, was frightened a
short time before by what he called a 'funny cat', and showed a good
deal of timidity the rest of the evening, looking under chairs, etc., lest
it should be lurking there, and it is to be noted that he has no fear of a
cat.

[Now it so happens that this monkey is the first incident in the lugu-
brious hauntings, or whatever they may be termed, of which I have any
recollection. I suppose it was, or might easily be, the first monkey I had
ever seen, which may explain my memory being so impressed that I
have not forgotten it. A monkey, and upstairs in the nursery, that is
the business. My parents have told me that no monkey was known to
be owned in the neighbourhood, and that after diligent inquiry no
organ-man or hurdy-gurdy boy, either with or without a monkey, had
been seen anywhere about the place or neighbourhood, either on that
day or for a length of time. Although I freely admit the evidence of an
infant barely two years old is of very small import, yet I may say I have
an absolutely distinct recollection of that monkey, and of running to
see where it went to, as it hopped out of the room and into the adjoining
Blue-room. We saw it go under the bed in that room, but it could not
be found or traced anywhere afterwards. We hunted and ferretted
about that room, and every corner of the house, but no monkey, or any
trace of one, was more to be found. I don't know what to make of such
a visitation, and have no explanation to offer; but that it was a monkey,
that it disappeared under the bed in the Blue-room that Saturday afternoon, and was never seen or heard of again—of this not merely from
my own childish recollection, but from the repeated confirmation of
my brothers and sisters in after life, I am perfectly certain. I am merely
recording facts as simply as I can; readers may smile or mock as seemeth
good unto them—I cannot alter what has taken place to suit either
them or any one else.]

On the 26th of 10th mo., 1841, about 9 a.m., Joseph and Henry were
playing at the foot of the stairs; they both saw a white face looking
down upon them over the stair rails leading to the garret. Joseph called
for his aunt, Christiana Carr, to come and see it, but just as she was
coming he saw it hop away. Henry heard it give a great jump, but

Joseph, being very dull of hearing, did not. They both agreed in the description of what they saw.

On First day evening, 19th of 12th, 1841, about 8 o'clock, E.P. and her sister, Christiana Carr, were in the nursery with the infant, and heard a heavy step coming up the stairs. They at first thought it might be J.P., but recollected that he had put on his slippers, and the step was with heavy shoes; it seemed to pass into the adjoining room in which were some of the children asleep. They soon heard sounds in that room as of something heavy falling, and by-and-bye Henry, about five years old, began to cry as if afraid. The only maid then at home came up to him, when he could not speak for a length of time for sobbing; at last he said something spoke to him, and had also made noises with the chairs.

About the middle of 11th mo., 1841, Christiana Carr went with Eliz. Mann into a bedroom about 10 p.m. They heard a heavy labouring breathing, first at the far side of the room and then very near them, the floor at the same time shaking with a constant vibration. They hastily retired.

On the 24th of 11th mo. Joseph, who had gone to bed about 8 o'clock, presently called of his father in some alarm; he said a man had just been in who went to the window, threw up the sash, put it down again and then walked out; he had light or grey hair and no hat on. He was astonished J.P. had not met him. Within a few minutes he called out again; he had heard a step from the door to the closet at the far side of the room where he heard something like a cloak fall. He durst not look up to see who it was. [If any readers exclaim that these are but the dreams and nightmares of children, I will only remind them that I am simply transcribing from my father's diary, written on the dates given by his own hand, and that they must form their own conclusions.]

[The diary goes on to say that my mother had her own mother staying with her and sleeping with her at this time for about a fortnight.]

One night, when E.P. was asleep, Jane Carr [her mother] heard a sound like a continued pelting of small substances[1] which at first she took for cinders from the fire; afterwards, as she sat up in bed, with a light burning, and seeing nothing, she heard the sound of somebody going gently about the floor, the dress rustling as it passed from one part of the room to another. On or about the 1st of 11th mo. E.P. awoke at night, heard the sound of an animal leaping down off the easy-chair which stood near the bed; there was no noise of its getting up and running off, but a dead silence.

7 mo., 14th, 1841.—J. and E.P. heard the spirit in their own room, and in the room overhead, making a noise as of something heavy being hoisted or rolled, or like a barrel set down on its end; also noises in the

---

[1] Compare this effect with the 'happering of peas upon boards,' mentioned by Mr. Mompesson in his letter. (See Appendix A.)—H.P.

Camp-room of various and most unaccountable character. Edmund, who is about a year and a half old, roused up with every symptom of being dreadfully frightened; he screamed violently, was a very long time in sleeping again, and frequently awoke in a fright; he became feverish and continued so all the following day, seeming frightened at the sight of his crib, and alarmed at any noise he did not understand.

8 mo., 3rd.—Since the last date there have been few nights during which some branch of the family has not heard our visitor. One night J.P. was awoke and heard something hastily walk, with a step like that of a child of 8 or 10 years, from the foot of the bed towards the side of the room, and come back seemingly towards the door, in a run; then it gave two stamps with one foot; there was a loud rustling as of a frock or night-dress. I need scarcely say the door was locked, and I am quite certain there was no other human being in the room but E.P., who was asleep. The two stamps roused E.P. out of her sleep. About this time Joseph, on two or three occasions, said he had heard voices from underneath his bed and from other parts of the room, and described seeing on one occasion a boy in a drab hat much like his own, the boy much like himself too,[1] walking backwards and forwards between the window and the wardrobe. He was afraid but did not speak.

Noises as of a band-box falling close at hand, as of someone running upstairs when no one was there, and like the raking of a coal rake, were heard about this time by different members of the family.

8 mo., 6th. On the night of the 3rd, just after the previous memorandum was written, about 10.30 p.m., the servants having all retired to bed, J. and E.P. heard a noise like a clothes-horse being thrown down in the kitchen. Soon the noises became louder and appeared as though some persons had burst into the house on the ground floor and were clashing the doors and throwing things down. Eventually J.P. got one of the servants to go downstairs with him, when all was found right, no one there, and apparently nothing moved. The noises now began on the third storey, and the servants were so much alarmed that it was difficult to get them to go to bed at all that night.

8 mo., 6th to 12th. My brother-in-law, George Carr, was with us. He heard steppings and loud rumblings in the middle of the night, and other noises.

[At this point the diary abruptly comes to an end. I know, however, that disturbances of a varied character continued more or less, perhaps less rather than more, for years. One episode during the period has been frequently told to me by my father, and I think no account of it has been published. All his family were in Cumberland and he was sleeping alone, only one servant being in the house. He had retired about 10.30. Owing to the disturbances he and my mother, as well as the domestics,

[1] Is it possible that Poltergeists sometimes appear in the likeness of those young children whom they use as a *point d'appui* for their manifestations?—H.P.

usually burnt a rushlight during the night, a description of candle at that time in common use; but on this occasion he had no light whatever. He had not been two minutes in bed when suddenly, seemingly close to the bedside, there was an awful crash as of a wooden box being wrenched open with a crowbar with terrific force; he started up and cried out with a loud voice, 'Begone! thou wicked spirit!' As if in defiance of this adjuration the fearful crash was almost immediately repeated, and if possible, louder than before. Cool-headed as my father was, and inured to unwelcome surprises from the unknown, he was painfully agitated by this ostentatious outburst of ill-will or wanton devilry; he arose, struck a light, searched the room, opened his bedroom door, listened on the stairs, looked into the other rooms, and explored the house generally, but found everything perfectly quiet. There was no wind, and indeed there seemed no explanation, but one only, of this horrid visitation.]

[Finding life in the house to be no longer tolerable; fearing also an unhappy effect, if not a permanent injury on the minds of their children should they remain longer in such a plague-ridden dwelling, they finally left it in 1847, and went to reside at Camp Villa, North Shields, social and other reasons also influencing them to take this step. My parents have both repeatedly told me that during the last night they slept in the old house, the rest of the family having preceded them to the new one, there were continuous noises during the night, boxes being apparently dragged with heavy thuds down the now carpetless stairs, non-human footsteps stumped on the floors, doors were, or seemed to be, clashed, and impossible furniture corded at random or dragged hither and hither by inscrutable agency; in short, a pantomimic or spiritualistic repetition of all the noises incident to a household flitting.[1] A miserable night my father and mother had of it, as I have often heard from their own lips; not so much from terror at the unearthly noises, for to these they were habituated, as dread lest this wretched fanfaronade might portend the contemporary flight of the unwelcome visitors to the new abode. Fortunately for the family, this dread was not realised. So far as I know, and in this I am confirmed by my elder brother and sisters, the eight years' residence in the new home was absolutely free from all forms of the annoyances and uncomfortable knockings, the stealthy steps and the uncouth mutterings that for ten or eleven years had disturbed the even tenor of a quiet Quaker family in the old house at Willington Mill.]

*   *   *

The subsequent history of the house may be briefly told. The foreman and chief clerk in the flour mill, less sensitive perhaps to the dis-

---

[1] Compare this phenomenon with a similar one recorded by Mrs. Mara Mack in her old home (page 342).—H.P.

turbances, and with families of maturer years,[1] raised no objection to occupying it after a time, and it was divided into two separate dwellings, and inhabited by them for nearly twenty years. They were occasionally disturbed by unaccountable noises, and Thomas Mann, the foreman, on one or two occasions saw what appeared to be apparitions, but both families were designedly reticent on the subject, and I believe suffered but little throughout their occupancy. About 1867 the mill and house were let for a few months to a firm of millers in an adjoining town whose mill had been burnt down; I have been informed that those then occupying the house were much troubled, one family declining to stay on any terms. Not long afterwards my father sold the entire premises to a firm of guano merchants, and information reached us that two machinists, one of them a German, who were fixing machinery in the mill, spent some restless evenings and unhappy nights in the house in fruitlessly trying to discover the origin of fitful and exasperating disturbances. No effort was made, so far as I know, to test the accuracy of these rumours. On one occasion, whilst the house was unoccupied shortly before its sale, I was one of a party of four or five young men, one of them a doctor, who spent an entire night in the house, upstairs, in the hope of hearing or seeing something, but absolutely without result. Some little time after this I was one of another and larger party, including two ladies, who spent an evening in another upstairs room, accompanied by a 'medium' of repute at that time well known in Newcastle; no person whatever being in the house besides our own party. The séance was not without incidents, well understood by those acquainted with such proceedings, and which it would be useless, at the moment, to describe, to those who are not, but absolutely futile as to establish any communication with the alleged spirit or spirits supposed to haunt or to have formerly haunted the premises. My father never made any attempt to open up communication in this way; his experiences were prior to the time when the modern developments of Spiritualism made the lingo of the séance familiar to the public ear, and although he took an earnest interest in the subject, he never attended a séance and laid stress upon the application of the well-known text about 'seducing spirits and doctrines of demons'. The mill is now only used as a warehouse. The house has been divided into small tenements; I understand the owner, recognising the doubtful repute of the house, offered the apartments free for a short term. About two years ago I interviewed three or four of the tenants, and was told that no disturbances had been experienced. Although of modest pretensions, it was formerly a comfortable, old-fashioned house of ten or twelve rooms, but the untidiness of its present aspect is a painful spectacle to those who remember it at its best; the stables and adjoining out-buildings

[1] With the departure of the young Procter children, it is possible that the Poltergeists could no longer produce the same effects, with the older 'material'.—H.P.

have been pulled down, the garden wall has disappeared, the jargonelle pear trees that formerly blossomed up to the third storey are represented by the mere ghosts of blackened stumps, the large old thorn tree of red blossom, and the abundance of iris and auricula that were wont to bloom in the garden are as far off as the snows of last winter.

The singular record of the house gives it an interest nevertheless, even in its squalid present and its ungracious decay.

Some may think the whole affair altogether a very paltry story. I admit it is not a very picturesque 'ghost'; but whatever its merit it is at least authentic, and that is rather an important feature in a ghost. The truth has been told without extenuation or reserve, and if the recital points to the conclusion that the spirit or spirits, or whatever you choose to call them, belonged to the residuum of the spirit world, I hope my family may not be held responsible.

[*Signed*] EDMUND PROCTER.

Newcastle-on-Tyne, October, 1892.

*   *   *

There remains little for me to add to Edmund Procter's convincing narrative. But I must mention that the correspondence between Dr. Edward Drury, who collapsed when he saw the ghost, and Mr. Joseph Procter, was published in *The Local Historian's Table Book*.[1] It will be remembered that the doctor and a friend obtained permission from Mr. Procter to spend a night in the house.

Mr. Joseph Procter, in a letter to his wife, said he heard Dr. Drury give 'a most horrid shriek'. In the book I have cited is a letter to Mr. Procter from the doctor, who describes what he saw on that exciting night:

Sunderland, July 13, 1840.

'About ten minutes to twelve we both heard a noise as if a number of people was pattering with their bare feet upon the floor; and yet, so singular was the noise that I could not minutely determine from whence it proceeded. A few minutes afterwards, we heard a noise, as if someone was knocking with his knuckles among our feet; this was immediately followed by a hollow cough from the very room from which the apparition proceeded. The only noise after this was as if a person was rustling against the wall in coming upstairs. At a quarter to one, I told my friend that, feeling a little cold, I would like to go to bed, as we might hear the noises equally well there. He replied that he would not go to bed till daylight. I took up a note which I had accidentally dropped, and began to read it, after which I took out my watch to ascertain the time, and found that it wanted ten minutes to one. In taking my eyes from the watch they became rivetted upon a closet door, which

[1] By M. A. Richardson, London, 1843, Vol. I.

I distinctly saw open, and saw also the figure of a female attired in greyish garments, with the head inclining downwards, and one hand pressed upon the chest, as if in pain, and the other, viz., the right hand, extended towards the floor, with the index finger pointing downwards. It advanced with an apparently cautious step across the floor towards me; immediately as it approached my friend, who was slumbering, its right hand was extended towards him; I then rushed at it, giving at the time, as Mr. Procter states, a most awful yell; but instead of grasping it, I fell upon my friend, and I recollected nothing distinctly for nearly three hours afterwards. I have since learned that I was carried downstairs in an agony of fear and terror.

'I hereby certify that the above account is strictly true and correct in every respect.

(*Signed*) 'EDW. DRURY.'

The reader will note correspondences between the Willington Mill case and those of Borley and Ballechin, and very curiously, each of the three houses had a much-haunted 'Blue Room'. (Are all 'Blue Rooms' haunted?) There are also similarities between the phenomena witnessed at Willington and those seen and heard in the mill on the Eden. In both cases the chief witnesses kept diaries, in which the principal manifestations were recorded. Can it be doubted that at least some of these manifestations were of a paranormal nature?

191

CHAPTER XVI

The 'Electric Horror' of Berkeley Square

Haunted May Fair! What volumes could be written about the great ones, whose shades are perhaps at this moment flitting hither and thither through the purlieus of Berkeley Street and Square, Hay Hill, Shepherd Market, and those streets named Curzon, Bruton, Grafton, Dover and Clarges. If it is true that any part of us persists after death, then the spirits of such men as John, the 'great' Duke of Argyll; the impecunious Sheridan; unhappy Chopin (who lodged in Dover Street); Lord Brougham, Lord Granville, Edmund Kean, Lord Beaconsfield, the Butes and the Lansdownes, are surely haunting the scenes of their trials and triumphs. And such famous 'characters' as Beau Brummell, Martin Van Butchell (the quack doctor who sold hairs from his beard at a guinea apiece to ladies who wanted to become the mothers of fine children); Tiddy Dol, the gingerbread seller, immortalised by Hogarth; Mrs. Saraband, the puppet-show woman; the Rev. Dr. George Keith, at whose 'shop' in Curzon Street, one—or rather, two—could be married at any hour of the day or night for a guinea; and many other Mayfair oddities. Is it so very unreasonable that their eccentric and intangible *manes* should still revisit their earthly abodes and survey the modern scene? That is, if the *Blitz* has not driven them away!

But it is not of these 'ghosts of Mayfair' that I am going to write, but rather of those unquiet spirits that take up their abode in houses and other places which, in consequence, become what we are pleased to call haunted. Contrary to popular belief, London has few haunted houses: that is, few in comparison with its vast size and rich history. Of course, there are some famous ghosts: the Hampton Court spectre, the boy princes who haunt the Tower of London, where is also to be seen—if one is lucky!—the lady who roams a certain tower with her head tucked underneath her arm. Then there is the Cock Lane Ghost—partly a fraud!—the Stockwell ghost, not a fraud, and in reality a Poltergeist; and the famous Tyburn ghost—all of which have been introduced to the reader.

There are very few reputed haunted houses in Mayfair. My old offices in Berkeley Street were once occupied by the Empress Eugénie and were supposed to be troubled by the spirit of that unhappy lady, and I have met persons who declared that they have heard soft footsteps pattering along the passages and in the rooms where the widow of Napoleon III once nursed her sorrows. Also, a tenant on the same floor declared that she frequently heard knocks. Surely her ghost must be hard put to it to cope with the blasé motor salesmen, the *grands couturiers*, the *midinettes*, the pompous hotel porters and the vendors of *postiches de ville* and *coiffures de soirées*—all so exceedingly mundane that the life of a Berkeley Street ghost can hardly be worth living. Another reputed ghost is that of the highwayman, 'Galloping Tom', who was shot in the Rope Walk just as he was leaping the steps leading to Curzon Street, after holding up a coach on Hay Hill.

But in Berkeley Square it is different. Not all of it is in the hands of the vandals and much of the place has altered little during hundreds of years. In this quiet backwater one can still cool oneself in the shade of the plane trees and see the old link-extinguishers attached to the railings of some of the houses, reminiscent of sedan-chairs and cumbrous family coaches with their famous running footmen. Fortunately, the equestrian statue of George III (in the character of Marcus Aurelius!) which stood in the centre of the Square, has disappeared.

Some distinguished people have lived in Berkeley Square. Horace Walpole resided at No. 11, and the Marquis of Hertford at No. 13. Lord Clive had a house at No. 45 and Earl Grey lived at No. 48. The Earl of Jersey occupied No. 38 for half a century, and it was here that one of the queens of Almack's—Lady Jersey, widow of the fifth earl—held her nightly riots of noisy revelry. Many other famous residents or visitors to the Square could be named: William Pitt, Dr. Johnson, Colley Cibber, Edmund Burke, Lord Erskine, the Earl of Chatham, Joshua Reynolds, David Garrick, Madame D'Arblay, Georgina, Duchess of Devonshire, and many more.

I have mentioned some well-known houses, but not the best-known house in Berkeley Square. Undoubtedly, this is No. 50, famous for its ghost—or perhaps ghosts—which has intrigued investigators for nearly a century. The owners or occupiers of this house do not here concern us except that Messrs. Maggs Brothers, Ltd., the well-known antiquarian booksellers, have now taken a lease of the premises. If the intangible occupants of the house resent this fresh intrusion on their privacy, at least they will be able to retaliate to the extent of acquiring new ways of terrifying us mortals by the simple process of browsing amongst the ancient tomes on magic when the place is locked up for the night.

It is difficult to determine when the ghost first 'appeared' in No. 50, Berkeley Square, once the home of George Canning. It is probable that the place acquired a reputation for being haunted as early as the beginning of the nineteenth century. Though most of the other houses in the Square have associations, both honourable and historical, No. 50 can boast little in the way of 'background' for the simple reason—I believe— that the place was so often empty and deserted. Jessie Adelaide Middleton quotes[1] a letter she received from Mr. Ralph Nevill (a relative of Mr. Myers mentioned in this narrative) who states that in his opinion

[1] *The Grey Ghost Book*, London, 1912, pp. 49–50.

No. 50, Berkeley Square, London, W.1, the eighteenth-century home of many ghosts and Poltergeists.
(By courtesy of Messrs. Maggs Bros., Ltd.)

the Berkeley Square ghost may date from the eighteenth century, when the house, complete with some beautiful Adam fireplaces, and link extinguishers, was built.

But in the 'seventies people began to get really curious about the house. In November, 1872, someone wrote to *Notes and Queries* to ask if the place were indeed haunted. It was Lord Lyttelton who replied[1] and he said that: 'It is quite true that there is a house in Berkeley Square [No. 50] said to be haunted, and long unoccupied on that account. There are strange stories about it, into which this deponent cannot enter'. As Lord Lyttelton was averse to publicising the pranks of the Poltergeists, the present writer will endeavour to relate some of the various tales associated with the house. I have been to considerable trouble in collecting this information.

There are many versions of the Berkeley Square Ghost. In her book,[2] Jessie Adelaide Middleton says: 'I remember, years ago, hearing a weird story connected with the house, in which the ghost of a child, in a Scotch plaid frock, played the chief part. The poor child was supposed to have been either tortured or frightened to death in the nursery there, and its pathetic little wraith, sobbing and wringing its hands, used to appear to the inmates until nobody dared to live in the house'.

Another story tells how a man went mad in one of the upper rooms waiting for a certain message which never came. These 'messages' appeared on the walls, written by a ghostly hand, but the right one never appeared. This drove the occupant out of his mind and he, too, haunted the place. What the vital message was, history does not relate. This curious wall-writing story has its parallel in the Borley Rectory hauntings, as the reader will discover.

A further legend relates how a young girl named Adeline or Adela threw herself out of the window of a certain top room in order to escape the attentions of a most unavuncular and wicked uncle and guardian who resided in the same house. It has been stated that, sometimes, the wraith of the screaming girl can still be seen clinging to the window ledge, once more about to drop to its doom. Another story, no less picturesque, but much more material, is related by the author of *The Grey Ghost Book*[3] and is to the effect that 50, Berkeley Square was the home of a gang of coiners who made weird noises at night in order to scare away too inquisitive investigators.

Still another story, that I acquired from one of the residents in the Square, tells how sometimes pandemonium broke out in the house— which was still empty—in or about the year 1840, and always at night. Although the house was not furnished in any way, the sounds of massive furniture, or heavy boxes, being dragged across bare floors were heard periodically—perhaps once in two months. Sometimes, bells were heard ringing. On more than one occasion, local investigators entered

[1] Nov. 16, 1872.   [2] *Op. cit.*, p. 16.   [3] *Op. cit.*, p. 17.

the house during these manifestations and invariably saw nothing, except the still swinging bells. Then a curious development occurred. During the height of some such disturbance a window would be flung open and small objects such as stones, old books, a pair of spurs, etc., would be hurled into the street. Where did the objects come from, and who hurled them? No one ever discovered. Something similar happened at Borley, and I have a collection of these so-called 'apports' (Roman Catholic medallions, a French medal struck during the Revolution, a wedding-ring etc.) that appeared as mysteriously as they did in Berkeley Square. All this is good Poltergeist stuff running true to type. And now for the climax: One morning after a particularly noisy night, the good people of Berkeley Square found that *every window* of No. 50 had been smashed—at least, every window that looked on to the Square. Who did it, Poltergeists or small boys? Well, the terms are almost synonymous and the culprits were never discovered.

But to return to Lord Lyttelton. A few weeks after his reply in *Notes and Queries*, a correspondent wrote to this journal and stated that he had visited the house in order to make a personal investigation. The door was opened by an old woman caretaker who refused any information, but admitted that the 'place was occupied'—but whether by ghosts or humans, she would not say. Pursuing his inquiries in the neighbourhood, he learnt that the houses adjoining No. 50 had been troubled by strange noises and in one of them, it was stated, a woman had gone out of her mind after having slept one night there. Perhaps she, too, slept in a top room!

It is to *Notes and Queries* that the curious inquirer must turn for most of the information concerning the haunting of 50, Berkeley Square, as this journal appears to have taken a singular and sustained interest in the 'ghost'. In the issue of August 2, 1879, W. E. Howlett cites a reference which appeared in *Mayfair* of the previous May 10:

'The mystery of Berkeley Square still remains a mystery. We were in hopes that during the last fortnight a full, final, and satisfactory answer would have been given to our questions; but we have been disappointed. The story of the haunted house in the heart of Mayfair is so far acquiesced in by the silence of those who alone know the whole truth, and whose interest it is that the whole truth should be known. That story can be recapitulated in a few words. The house in Berkeley Square contains at least one room of which the atmosphere is supernaturally fatal to body and mind. A girl saw, heard, or felt such horror in it that she went mad, and never recovered sanity enough to tell how or why. A gentleman, a disbeliever in ghosts, dared to sleep in it, and was found a corpse in the middle of the floor after frantically ringing for help in vain. Rumour suggests other cases of the same kind, all ending in death, madness, or both, as the result of sleeping, or trying to sleep in that room. The very party-walls of the house, when touched, are found saturated with electric horror. It is uninhabited save by an elderly man and woman who act as caretakers; but even these have no access to *the* room. This is kept locked, the key being in the hands of a mysterious and seemingly nameless person, who comes to the house once every six months, locks up the elderly couple in the basement, and then unlocks *the* room, and occupies himself in it for hours. Finally, and most wonderful of all, the house, though in Berkeley Square, is neither to be let nor sold. Its mere outside shows it to be given up to ghosts and decay. Readers who feel curious about the matter are referred to our issue of a fortnight ago for the details of which the above account is a *résumé*.'

For some months the 'ghost' was left in peace so far as *Notes and Queries* was concerned. Then suddenly a Mr. T. Westwood of Brussels writes[1] suggesting that 'a legal inquiry' should be held into the facts of the case. This drew a reply[2] from a 'doubting Thomas', J.C.M., who writes:

'This mystery vanishes the moment we use ordinary means of arriving at truth instead of indulging our imaginations. I pledge myself for the accuracy of the following facts: The house in question belonged to an eccentric gentleman. He was in good circumstances, but chose to spend no money on it. For many years soap, paint, and whitewash were never used. He was occasionally visited by a sister, the only person seen to enter the house except his two maidservants. Then by degrees began the stories—"insanity", "murder", "walls saturated with electric horror", etc. He died. The sister sent in an estate agent to see whether it would be worth while to put the house in order for the remainder of the lease. The agent, an intelligent and cultivated man, told me that he found the house in hideous disrepair. He asked the maids if they ever heard any strange noises. They said "No". "Do you ever see ghosts?" They laughed: "We never seed none." '

A humorist who signed himself 'Clarry' next called attention to the fact that an account of the Berkeley Square Mystery had appeared in *Twilight Stories*. After giving a vivid picture of the German bands and itinerant players who pestered the residents in the Square, he concludes: 'Mr. Westwood expresses himself somewhat virtuously indignant that the matter is not legally investigated. If he has had the authority of the proprietor or can give evidence to justify such a proceeding, by all means let him do so; if not, I do protest against anyone's castle being besieged, and the owner's privacy invaded, through the morbid imagination of a young authoress [Miss Rhoda Broughton] or the tittle-tattle and gossip of the kitchen and the Servants' Hall'.

Another correspondent, 'C. C. M.', writing from the Temple, took the trouble to see who was supposed to live at No. 50. He says:[3] 'The last name appearing in the *London Directory* as the occupier was that

[1] *Notes and Queries*, Nov. 20, 1880. [2] Nov. 27, 1880.
[3] Dec. 11, 1880.

197

of an Honourable Miss Curzon, who died in 1859, aged ninety. From that date, twenty-one years ago, to the present its external appearance has been that of an occupied house'. Miss Curzon took the house from Esther, Lady Bromley.

He then recalls that in the *Weekly Times* for May 4, 1873, a certain Mr. Myers, then occupying 50, Berkeley Square, was sued by the local council for taxes due. The summons was taken out by the tax-collector Knox, and the case was tried by the magistrate Knox—and the other 'knocks' (in the haunted house) were, very appropriately, discussed at the hearing. Collector Knox said 'that the house in question is known as the "haunted house", and has occasioned a good deal of speculation among the neighbours'. He believed 'that the neglect to pay the taxes arose on the part of the occupier, from eccentricity'. They call it by other names today! So much for the Knoxes and the knocks.

'Clarry' throws some light on the life of the eccentric Mr. Myers. He says:[1] 'The case, as related to me, was that Mr. Myers being engaged to be married, he took the house, No. 50, Berkeley Square, which was furnished, and that every preparation was made for, as he supposed, his future happiness; but just before the time appointed for the wedding the lady jilted him. This disappointment is said to have "broken his heart and turned his brain". He became morose and solitary—would never allow a woman to come near him. A male servant only was allowed occasionally to see him, and he lived alone. Sometimes, but very rarely, could he be seen in the back yard. At night he would "keep his assignation with his woe", and flit about the house. At this time doubtless "strange noises would be heard by the neighbours". And thus, upon the melancholy wanderings of this poor lunatic, was founded that story of the ghost by which so much space in your columns has been from time to time occupied. Those whom so many persons persist in calling "mad doctors" could tell of hundreds of cases of mind diseased and conduct similar to that of poor Myers. His sister was, it was said, his only relative, and she was too old or too great an invalid to interfere. About two years ago I saw his hatchment[2] up at No. 50 and I then hoped that the poor unhappy man's story, together with his ghost, would have been interred with his bones. But fondness for, and craving after, the marvellous have, I am sorry to say, revived the present discussion. The house having now been treated to "soap, paint, and whitewash", and all that can be gathered of the wretched and lonely eccentric being told, let no one seek further "to draw his frailities from their dread abode"; and let no one believe that there was ever the slightest foundation for the existence of a ghost'. So that's that! But let the disappointed reader continue!

Mr. J. F. Meehan records some tragic happenings at 50, Berkeley

[1] Dec. 25, 1880.
[2] A frame bearing the escutcheon of a dead person.—H.P.

Square. He says[1] 'The following particulars of this affair may perhaps be of some interest. They are extracted from an original letter (lately in my possession) addressed to the late Bishop Thirlwall. It was written on January 22, 1871:

"Ghosts remind me that I never told you a story Mrs. X. related to us when she was here last, about the haunted house in Berkeley Square; S. pointed it out to me last spring. One side of it looks towards the street which, crossing Mount Street, runs into the Square itself. The dilapidated, forsaken, dusty look of this house quite suits a reputation for ghosts. By the way, I am not sure whether it is the corner house or next door to the corner house, but Lady M. declares that the real site is at the end of Charles Street, where the street opens into Berkeley Square. This house, she says, is watched strictly by police. None of its inhabitants ever cross its doorstep, and *false coining* is supposed to be carried on there, but has never been detected. Miss H. (who repeated the tale to Mrs. X.) was told by some R.C. friends of hers that a family they knew hired the haunted house—wherever it is—in Berkeley Square for a London season, as there were daughters to be brought out, one of whom was already engaged. They spent a short time in the house without finding anything amiss; then they invited the young lady's lover to join them, and the next bedroom, which they had not occupied, was made ready for him, and the housemaid was either sleeping there, or else still busy with her preparations at twelve o'clock the night before his arrival. The hour had no sooner struck than piercing shrieks were heard, loud enough to rouse the whole household. They rushed upstairs, flung open the door of the haunted room, and found the unfortunate housemaid lying at the foot of the bed in strong convulsions. Her eyes were fixed, with a stare of expressive terror, upon a remote corner of the chamber, and an agony of fear seemed to possess her, yet the bystanders saw nothing. They took her to St. George's Hospital, where she died in the morning, refusing to the last to give any account of what she had seen; she could not speak of it, she said; it was far too horrible. The expected guest arrived that day. He was told the story, and it was arranged that he should not occupy the haunted room. He voted it all nonsense, and insisted upon sleeping there. He, however, agreed to sit up until past twelve, and to ring if anything unusual occurred. 'But', he added, 'on no account come to me when I ring first; because I may be unnecessarily alarmed, and seize the bell on the impulse of the moment: wait until you hear a second ring.' His betrothed expostulated in vain. He did not believe in apparitions, and he would solve the mystery. She listened, in a misery of suspense, when the time of trial drew near. At last the bell rang once, but faintly. Then there was an interval of a few dreadful minutes and a tremendous peal sounded through the house. Every one hurried breathless to the haunted room. They found the

[1] Dec. 25, 1880.

199

guest exactly in the same place where the dead housemaid had lain, convulsed as she was, his eyes fixed in horror upon the same spot where hers had been fixed the night before, and, like her, he never revealed his experiences. They were too awful, he said, even to mention. The family left the house at once." '

Mr. Meehan's lurid accounts of the Berkeley Square ghost brought forth a number of letters from correspondents, some of whom confirmed the stories, though a few demanded 'real evidence'. He decided[1] to hand over the case to the Rev. C. F. S. Warren, of Farnborough, Banbury, who was asked to make a thorough investigation. Mr.

'His eyes fixed in horror on the same spot'.

Warren's report duly appeared in *Notes and Queries*, and this is what he says:[2]

'My researches into this mystery have, as I suspected they would, led to little real result; nevertheless, it may interest the readers of *Notes and Queries* to hear how I have tried and failed.

'1. I began, of course, on the lines laid down in the letter to Bishop Thirlwall which Mr. Meehan quotes. Here I got as far as "Miss H.", and there ran aground. Miss H., it appears, is now in a sisterhood, and her sister states that she "knows" that for this reason Miss H. would refuse to give any information as to the story, even if she remembered it, "which I am sure she does not". I pressed for the address of the sisterhood, that I might prove the matter for myself; but this was refused me. The husband of "Mrs. X." hinted to me, not at all obscurely, that the story probably had no other source than the narrative published by Miss Broughton, which I shall come to directly; and Miss H.'s sister referred me to this same narrative as if it were a most unimpeachable authority, and all that could possibly be necessary.

'2. To investigations in this new direction I therefore betook myself. I ascertained from the publishers of *Temple Bar* that Miss Broughton's form of the story appeared in February, 1868, and was afterwards reprinted in her *Twilight Stories*. For this book I sent, and having read the story, and found it almost identical with that given in *Notes and Queries* (the differences are that the housemaid is taken to the doctor's house instead of to the hospital and—certainly a very important one—that the lover is killed instead of saved alive). I wrote to Miss Broughton to ask whether she could give me any information on the subject. Her answer was this, and I have her leave to publish it:

' "27, *Holywell Street, Oxford, Feb. 2nd*, 1881.

' "Dear Sir, You are mistaken in supposing that my story has anything to do with the so-called Berkeley Square Mystery. Its incidents happened, as I was told by my informant, in the country, and I clothed it in fictitious characters and transposed it to London, which I have since regretted, as so many people have thence assumed that it must refer to the house in Berkeley Square. The slip you enclose is clearly my story mistakenly applied to a wrong house. I am sorry to be unable to assist you in your search, but I can at least divert you from a wrong track.

' "(*Signed*) R. BROUGHTON."

'3. With regard to the general question of the house's reputation, I have the evidence of Mr. George Vincent, Head Porter of Brasenose College. He had already written to *Notes and Queries* that while he lived in the house as servant to the Hon. Elizabeth Curzon, from 1851 till her death at a great age in 1859, he saw no ghost; and in answer to a letter I addressed to him, he added to this that during that time the house (so far as he knew) was not said to be haunted in any way, and that about four or five years later, i.e. 1863–4, Lord de la Zouche, nephew to Miss Curzon, coming down to Oxford to enter his son, the present lord, at Christ Church, informed him that the reputation had then arisen. This date I thought too early, as the present lord was then about eleven or twelve years old; but Mr. Vincent said men were often entered at Christ Church some years before coming into residence.

'4. Two others whom I addressed on the subject were the present Lord de la Zouche and Sir Charles Young, Bart., the latter of whom, Mr. Vincent told me, succeeded Miss Curzon in the house; but the former letter remained unanswered, and the other came back from the Dead Letter Office. I hardly think, however, they could have thrown much light on the matter.

'To sum up, therefore since the only distinct legend told of Berkeley Square has been shown not to belong to it, there remains only the general belief, to all appearance unfounded, that the house is "haunted", which it seems to me may be well accounted for by its neglected condition when empty and the habits of the melancholy and solitary hypochondriac, already mentioned in *Notes and Queries*, when it was occupied by him. With respect to the story, I undertook to inquire into it as connected with Berkeley Square; and as Miss Broughton, doubtless for that reason, has given me no evidence or authority for it, I have made no attempt to gain it from her or others. I think I have done my part; and to any one else who chooses to follow me I heartily wish good luck'.

One more story of the Berkeley Square ghost, and I have finished. K.H.B., writing in *Notes and Queries* for 1881, records an interesting variant of the haunting. He says: 'In the season of 1880 a ball was given at No. 49. A lady and her partner were sitting against the partition wall of No. 50, when on a sudden she moved from her place and looked round. The gentleman was just going to ask the reason when he felt impelled to do the same. On comparing their impressions, both had felt very cold, and had fancied someone was looking over their shoulders from the wall behind! From this it would appear that "brick walls do not a prison make" for these uncomfortable ghosts, who can project themselves right through them, to the great discomfort of their next-door neighbours. The inhabitants of No. 49, who very likely never gave a ball last season, could say what ground there is for this story —unless the ball-givers lived on the other side of No. 50, in Charles Street'.

And so we must leave the 'Ghost of Berkeley Square', not without regret that so little evidence for its existence is available. If there is no ghost, surely there ought to be, on account of the intense interest which, for so many years, its alleged activities has aroused. To say nothing of all the trouble that curious inquirers—including myself!—have been put to. Ghost or no ghost, the 'Berkeley Square Mystery' is a good story and so thought Bulwer Lytton, whose *The Haunted and the Haunters*[1] is supposed to have been founded on the doings at No. 50, which has altered little since it was built. It is well known that occupied haunted houses produce more phenomena than empty ones; so if Messrs. Maggs Brothers find their First Folios and *incunabula* all higgledy-piggledy one morning, after leaving the books in perfect alignment overnight, then the Poltergeists will have been up to their old tricks again, or acquiring new ones. Or should they hear soft patterings

[1] In *Blackwood's* for Aug., 1859, afterwards published in book form.

behind the wainscoting, or strange footsteps overhead, or are disturbed by the sweet Adeline moaning from the awful top room (perhaps still 'saturated' with the electric horror'), then No. 50 is undoubtedly *still* infested—and I hope they will send for me![1]

[1] Charles G. Harper, in *Haunted Houses* (London, 1907) remarks: 'The famous "haunted house in Berkeley Square" was long one of those things that no country cousin coming up from the provinces to London on sight-seeing bent, ever willingly missed'.

CHAPTER XVII

The Mill on the Eden

The clergy are my friends. I have received much support—both practical and moral—from such men as Dr. W. J. Phythian-Adams, Canon of Carlisle; the Rev. J. J. Fynes-Clinton; Canon Harold Anson; the late Father Herbert Thurston, S.J.; the Very Rev. F. A. Iremonger, D.D., Dean of Lichfield (formerly Director of Religious Broadcasts, B.B.C.); and many others. These gentlemen have reported cases to me, they have elucidated problems connected with my work, and have assisted me in many ways. I will remark in parentheses that the clergy, as a whole, take a profound interest in psychical research. Many of them are good 'percipients' or are themselves 'psychic', and some are the fortunate possessors of 'haunted rectories'.

Nearly all my clerical friendships were formed through the medium of my books, especially the Borley report, and many scores of parsons have been made known to me in that way. A few of my correspondents desire to remain anonymous, though at the same time wishing to put interesting information into my hands. This was the case with a certain clergyman who wrote to me after having read my *Search for Truth*.[1] He was particularly interested in my chapter on Poltergeists and informed me that he was in possession of the records—or rather copies of them— of one of the strangest Poltergeist cases he had ever heard of. He sent me a brief outline of the case and, on his next visit to London, called on me at the Savage Club, where he told me the whole story in detail.

My new friend informed me that, as a young man, he was a curate at one of the Manchester churches and, during his summer vacations, used to tour the Lake District, Westmorland, Cumberland and those central highlands south of the Tyne that are the joy of the pedestrian and the lover of the picturesque. All his tours were made on foot.

My friend was particularly fond of the Eden, that beautiful river that rises on the east border of Westmorland, and flows north-west past Kirkby Stephen, Appleby, Kirkoswald, and Carlisle to Solway Firth at Rockcliffe Marshes—a distance of some sixty-five miles.

The curate usually made his headquarters at Appleby, that little capital of Westmorland, and explored the river up and down for many miles. Into the Eden, near Appleby, several small rivers and becks empty themselves, and on one of these tributaries stood—or rather stands, for the mill house is still there—a small flour mill, the power for which was supplied by the tumbling stream which, turning a large wooden water-wheel, ground the corn, etc.

[1] London, 1942.

204

But this was some years before the occurrence of the incidents I am about to relate. Growing foreign competition in the shape of 'port wheat' killed the little industry, the wheel fell to pieces, the mill house itself was vacated, and looked like sharing the same fate as the wheel. This was in 1884.

At the time when my friend got to know the place, it was a sort of farm-house, where milk and eggs, and the lightest of refreshments, were sold to the very few tourists whose walks happened to take them in that direction. The curate visited the house during three consecutive summers and became friendly with the owner and his wife, from whom he learnt the previous history of the mill, and the story of the strange occurrences that at one time threatened to drive the family to distraction. My friend's visits were during the summers of 1904, 1905 and 1906.

As I have stated, the mill wheel and house fell into disuse in 1884. The place remained empty for three years, and in the spring of 1887 was bought by a Mr. Fowler, whose family then consisted of his wife and two daughters, 'Teddie' and Jessica, aged twelve and fourteen years respectively. Mr. Fowler spent some £200 in doing the place up, in removing the remains of the old wheel, and in making the place habitable. And now a word must be said about the wheel itself.

The wheel was an old-fashioned one, made partly of wood, of which there are still a few left in this country. One end of the axle was extended into a large room in the house, known as the 'wheel-room', which contained the mill-stones, the cog-work grinding mechanism, and several grinding machines, such as a chaff-cutter, turnip-cutter, grindstone and a churn. These implements could be connected with the water-wheel outside, and were continually in use during the mill's prosperous days. A part of the wheel-room overhung the stream.

The wheel-room was also partly furnished as a living room, with a truckle bed, chairs, a table, etc. and was occupied night and day by the man whose duty it was to grind the corn, oil the machinery, adjust the paddles of the wheel according to the head of water or a spate, and generally look after the place. His name was Tom Watkins. He was assisted in the daytime by a youth, who appears to have no bearing on the story.

When Mr. Fowler bought the place, his first job was to get rid of such machinery and shafting as remained in the wheel-room. In the room were a door, from which stone steps led to the stream, and a large window, protected by iron bars, which also looked on to the stream. Having removed the remains of the wheel, he did away with the steps, bricked up the door aperture, but retained the window—the only source of light. In order to increase the accommodation of his home, he added a large portion of the wheel-room to his kitchen. This was accomplished by removing the brick wall that divided them, and putting up a match-board wall or partition across the wheel-room with a communicating door between. This arrangement doubled the size of Mr. Fowler's kitchen, at the same time reducing the cubic area of the wheel-room by two-thirds. When the alterations to the wheel-room were completed, there was no access to the wheel-room except through the kitchen. The room could not be entered on the stream side *via* the window owing to the bars; and, in any case, as I have remarked, the room itself jutted out over the stream—the projection extending to some four feet. All this must be emphasised.

The alterations were completed early in May, 1887, and the Fowler family moved in. In the general disposition of their belongings, it was decided to use what remained of the old wheel-room as a lumber room, where boxes and packing cases could be stored. The enlarged kitchen was used as a principal living room and nearly all the meals were taken there.

The first untoward incident occurred about a fortnight after the family moved in. They were having their evening meal, time about 6.30. Teddie had been put to bed owing to a feverish cold, and only the elder daughter and her parents were at table.

Half way through the meal, there was a sound of breaking glass: obviously the noise came from the wheel-room, the door of which was always kept closed. Jumping up, Mr. Fowler opened the door in the partition and at once saw that one of the panes of glass in the window overlooking the stream had been smashed. His first thought was that a big bird had flown into it, but upon a closer examination he concluded something had been thrown at the window and he peered through the glass to the trees that fringed the opposite bank of the stream, but he could see no one. Then he went out of the house, along his garden path that ran parallel with the stream, where he could get a good view up and down the river. But no one was in sight; in fact it was rather difficult for a stranger to reach that portion of the bank that lay under the wheel-room window without traversing his property or using a boat.

Mr. Fowler returned to the wheel-room and began to hunt for the missile. He soon found it, between two packing cases. It was a large, roundish pebble from the bed of the stream and was *still wet*. So no doubt remained as to where the stone came from. But who threw it?

About ten days later, when Mr. Fowler and his family were finishing their evening meal, an incident occurred that almost paralysed them with fear. Mr. Fowler had actually finished his supper and was lighting his pipe, when a series of terrific blows rained on the partition from the far side—blows that were transferred to the communicating door after the first onslaught. Fowler, almost petrified, was sitting opposite this door and plainly saw it shake with each bang. The children were terrified. After the first shock of surprise was over, Fowler ran to the door and opened it, thinking that someone had managed to secrete himself in the wheel-room amongst the boxes, etc. and was playing a practical joke on them. But no one was there. Every box and case was removed, but nothing was discovered that could account for the disturbance.

More puzzled than frightened, when the element of surprise had more or less disappeared, the family made another search of the wheel-room, with negative results. One thing was quite certain: not a living thing, not even a rat, could enter the wheel-room without first passing through the kitchen. The Fowlers stayed up till past midnight, apprehensive that something else might happen. But nothing did happen, so they went to bed and to an undisturbed, if sleepless rest.

Three days later, as Mrs. Fowler and Jessica were tidying up the kitchen after breakfast, they thought they heard voices. Mr. Fowler was on the small-holding he had purchased near his house and Teddie was at school. The voices sounded clear, yet indistinct, but it was obvious that they came from the wheel-room. For a moment Mrs. Fowler thought that her husband had returned with a friend, and was conversing with him in the wheel-room. Then a chill ran down her spine as she recollected that neither she nor her daughter had left the kitchen since her husband departed after breakfast, and therefore it could not be he. Though terrified, she still had the courage to place her ear hard up against the partition, and she afterwards declared that the voices sounded louder, though not more distinct. Fearing that either she or Jessica might be attacked, and afraid to enter the wheel-room to investigate, mother and daughter ran out of the house and remained standing in the road until a man from a neighbouring cottage passed by and assisted them to investigate. The voices had ceased, and of course there was no one visible in the wheel-room. When Fowler returned home to lunch he pooh-poohed the whole thing, believing that the incidents experienced a few days previously had upset their nerves.

But that same night, just as they were beginning their meal, the voices were heard again. This time they were louder, and sounded like an altercation between a man and a woman. Fowler placed his ear to the partition and could hear the voices more plainly. Suddenly, they all heard a sound as if a saucer had been dropped and broken. Fowler instantly opened the communication door, and the voices ceased abruptly. No one was in the room, and nothing appeared to be broken. But a flaming piece of paper was found in a corner. Were the Poltergeists trying to burn the house down?

By this time Fowler was becoming disturbed. He knew nothing of these things or of paranormal happenings, and was afraid to make inquiries in the village as he did not want crowds of curiosity-mongers besieging his home. His children were becoming nervous wrecks, afraid to go to bed or to be left by themselves. His wife bore the incidents bravely, but he could see that even her health was being undermined.

What perturbed him, too, was the fact that his business took him often to Manchester, and he did not like leaving his family alone during his absence. However, as some measure of security, he screwed two iron bars right across the communicating door, so that it could be opened neither from the inside of the wheel-room nor from the kitchen. While he was actually doing this job, another stone was hurled through the wheel-room window from the river, smashing another pane of glass. So, procuring a long ladder, he nailed some half-inch mesh wire netting over the outside of the window, thus protecting it from the river side.

'*Pandemonium broke loose in the kitchen*'.

The above precautions were completed on the Saturday, and, as he was due in Manchester the following Monday, he asked his only employee, a man named Dick Carter, and his wife, to sleep in the house while he was away. He had to give some reason for this, and gave the real reason, swearing Carter and his wife to secrecy.

Whether the barring of the door and the window offended the Poltergeists is a matter for conjecture, but on the night of Fowler's departure pandemonium broke loose *in the kitchen*. Cups and saucers fell off the dresser; a jug of beer that was being mulled on the range was upset; the fire-irons clattered; coal 'leapt out of the bucket'; some glass-cloths that were drying on a line were snatched off, and similar occurrences were witnessed. All the above incidents happened immediately after the evening meal and terrified Mrs. Fowler and the children, though Carter and his wife kept calm—fortunately.

Suddenly the commotion ceased, at the same time as a terrific clatter was heard coming from the wheel-room. Apparently, packing cases were being flung about, or dragged along the floor, and a sound, as of hammering, was heard intermittently. After twenty minutes of this pandemonium, the five occupants of the house left the building, crossed the stream by means of a boat, and watched the wheel-room window from the opposite bank. From this view-point they could still hear the clatter in the wheel-room, and could actually *see* some of the things being moved. Packing cases and boxes passed and re-passed the window, as if being carried on the shoulders of someone—but what it was that was carrying them could not be seen. Stored in the room was an old perambulator and the top portion of it was seen slowly to *pass the window five times*! The wheels, being hidden by the brickwork, could not be seen. Then came a lull for a few minutes, then a terrific crash was heard (cause unseen) and then all was quiet again. The scared spectators waited for about fifteen minutes, but nothing further happened, so they re-entered the house, fearful that the unwelcome guests had transferred their activities to other rooms in their home. But all was quiet inside.

Nothing further happened that night. Carter remained on guard after the other inmates had retired to their beds, and he, too, got some sleep in the early hours of the morning. But it was a peaceful night for all concerned, including the Poltergeists.

Next morning Carter thought he would remove the bars from the communicating door and examine the wheel-room. Then it occurred to him that he might 'release' something if he did this, so refrained. Instead, he procured a long ladder and peered into the room through the window. A curious sight met his eyes: all the boxes, parcels, cases, etc. had been *piled up on one side of the room*—the side containing the door leading to the kitchen. This door, exactly opposite the window, was completely hidden. The perambulator was perched on top of the pile. If Carter had removed the bars from the door, and had opened it, half the contents of the wheel-room would have tumbled into the kitchen.

Nothing untoward occurred on the Tuesday, or the Wednesday, until Mr. Fowler returned from Manchester on the evening of the latter day. About ten o'clock the commotion in the wheel-room began afresh—the banging and dragging of packing cases; intermittent hammering; the smashing of glass (the window attacked from inside the room); thumps on the door, as if the entities were signalling to be let out; loud voices, as if in altercation, and so on. These manifestations lasted about one hour and then suddenly ceased. Fowler had, of course, heard all the news from Carter, and was not surprised at what had taken place. He remained on guard in the kitchen for a couple of hours, but nothing further happened, so he went to bed.

Mr. Fowler was now rather easier in his mind. He had been to Manchester—home of spiritualism—and on inquiry had heard all about the strange entities that smash and crash and throw things about, and had been assured that the trouble would cease as suddenly as it began. He was also assured that Poltergeists[1] never hurt anyone, though this is not literally true.[2]

He was also informed that these curious cases of haunting were often connected in some way with a child or adolescent, and he was strongly advised to send his children away. This was difficult as, in the first place, he could not afford it; and, secondly, the elder girl was wanted at home in order to assist her mother.

However, the more he thought of the idea, the more he became convinced that at least Teddie, the younger child, should have a long holiday. She was a delicate girl, and the manifestations were not exactly conducive to good health.

Fowler had a married sister in the Isle of Man and he wrote to her, not telling her too much about the 'ghosts', but explaining that Teddie was run down and that he proposed visiting her later in the summer with his family in order to discuss with her the possibility of the girl's staying with her for a few weeks. His sister's reply was satisfactory and the holiday was duly arranged for the following September.

It would be tedious to relate all that happened in the wheel-room and kitchen, *and nowhere else*, during the summer of 1887. There is a sameness about the phenomena, and the Poltergeists were neither very intelligent nor very imaginative. They stuck to the well-tried tricks, time-honoured through the centuries, and appeared to invent few new horrors to frighten Fowler and his family. But what is interesting is the fact that Fowler, being a very methodical man, kept a sort of journal or diary, in which he recorded daily all his business deals and household expenses and, incidentally, the doings of his unwelcome visitors. Phenomena and potato prices were mentioned on the same page, together with how many piglets his sows produced. I have seen copies of many pages of this interesting diary, extracts from which were made by my clerical informant, such extracts forming the basis of this story. I will reproduce a few of Fowler's notes, with dates:

1887.
Sat. Aug. 13. Four jugs broken in kitchen, several knocks on door.
   Scraping on wheel-room window.
Mon. Aug. 15. Cat frightened at something in kitchen, and has run
   away.

[1] I doubt if he heard this term used in 1887.
[2] In the Borley case, people were injured.

Thurs. Aug. 18. Five spoons found on floor of kitchen this morning. On dresser over night. Jess had a plate thrown at her. Noises in room [wheel-room].

Sun. Aug. 21. Quiet, except for jug of water upset, and knives found in sink.

Fri. Aug. 26. A noisy night last night [in wheel-room]. On guard outside room. They kept it up for nearly two hours. Ink bottles thrown to floor [in kitchen].

Mon. Sept. 5. No sleep last night. On guard all night. Hell's in the room [wheel-room]. Wife stayed up part of time.

I have quoted only a very few extracts from Fowler's common-place book, as the entries that concern us all record similar happenings: displacement of objects, knocks, bangs, and smashing of the wheel-room window, every pane of which was destroyed. In the light of present-day prices,[1] the value of commodities in 1887 is interesting. For example, a bottle of claret cost a shilling; six chickens cost 6/6d. the lot; a pint of gin cost from 1/8d. to 2/-; cider 3d. a pint; pork sausages 4d. a pound, and so on.

Mr. Fowler and his family left for the Isle of Man on Saturday, September 24, and remained a week. It was arranged that Teddie should live with her aunt for a month or so—actually she stayed three years. During his week's holiday Fowler, his wife, and Jessica, boarded out near his sister's house in Peel, and their board and lodging cost them 5/6d. a day each. For tea on their first day, as Fowler records in his diary, they had cold lamb, ham, lobster salad, cake, preserve, etc. One wonders what the principal meals were like. The entire week's holiday, for four people, including fares, board and lodging, amusements, presents, and all incidental expenses, cost Fowler £11 14s. 6d. Halcyon days!

Mr. Fowler had locked up the mill house before leaving, and when he returned he made a thorough examination of every room—including the wheel-room. Nothing had been disturbed. His man had kept an eye on the place, and had noticed nothing amiss.

Well, that was the end of the haunting—or nearly the end. Certain strange noises were heard periodically, but it was never certain that they were—as we should now term it—of paranormal origin. Nothing was ever again displaced, and the new panes in the wheel-room window ceased to be an attractive target for the Poltergeists.

The fact that the disturbances ceased when little ailing Teddie quitted the premises seems to support the theory that, at least, certain Poltergeist manifestations are induced in some obscure way by a child or adolescent. Anyway, Fowler, at least, was convinced that there was actually a *nexus* between Teddie and the ghosts and, as I say, she never

[1] I am writing this in May, 1943.

visited her home for three years. And there is no record of disturbances having been experienced in her aunt's house at Peel. However, Teddie did return home eventually, but apparently the Poltergeists had lost interest in her—or were plaguing someone else. There was no further trouble.

With the exception of Teddie, all the chief actors in the mill house drama are dead. Teddie, now aged nearly seventy, married a smart young farmer and, in due course, came into the property—including the Poltergeists, if they still exist. Jessica also married and went to Canada, where she did not survive the birth of her first baby.

All this information was given to me by my clerical friend who has more or less kept in touch with the family since his first visit in 1904, when Fowler—then in the early fifties—told him the whole story and showed him the old diaries, from which my friend made extracts. Jessica was not alive in 1904, but Teddie was married and living in the district, and my informant saw her once only.

As a postscript, I ought to give some account of Tom Watkins, the factotum who looked after the diminutive mill in its palmy days. He was a swarthy Welshman, morose, taciturn, and with a fiery temper. As has been stated, he lived in the wheel-room by himself, and had no friends except a middle-aged Irishwoman who periodically visited him. This woman was the widow of a man whom Watkins had killed in a street brawl many years previously. I suspect that the quarrel concerned the woman. Anyway, after a short term of imprisonment, Watkins and the woman remained friendly.

Did Watkins convey an 'evil influence' to the wheel-room? Did the defunct Irishman—or his ethereal remains—follow him thither? Had the Poltergeist disturbances any connection whatsoever with the slayer or the slain? These are matters for speculation, and the reader can amuse himself in attempting to supply the answers. I will only remark in closing that there is no record whatever of any manifestations having occurred *before* the Fowler family took up their abode in that very exciting mill on the Eden.

CHAPTER XVIII

The Poltergeist that Stumbled

Are Poltergeists 'ghosts in solid form'? Are they tangible, three-dimensional entities? Though able to cause noises, do they, too, make sounds when in impact with non-resisting bodies? Some of these queries are answered in the following adventure I had when I was very young, proving, I think, that Poltergeists can indeed solidify themselves on occasion.

My very first 'ghost' was made of cardboard. I will hasten to explain that it was the 'property' spectre of a three-act psychic play, *The Sceptic*, which I wrote and produced[1] when I was still a schoolboy. Of course I took the principal part myself, and I am sure I played the hero with considerable histrionic verve!

The reason I mention my early attempt at portraying the paranormal is because *The Sceptic* was the dramatised record of a remarkable experience that befell me when I investigated my first haunted house.

As a member of an old Shropshire family, I spent nearly all my holidays and school vacations in a little village—in fact, a hamlet—which I will call Parton Magna. In Parton Magna is the old Manor House, *circa* A.D. 1600. It had been purchased by a retired canon of the Church of England, and his wife. There were rumours that the place was haunted—but popular tradition provides a ghost for every old country house, especially if a tragedy has taken place within it.

Within a very few weeks of the canon's settling down with his household in their new home, reports were received of curious happenings in the stables and out-buildings. Though fastened securely overnight, stable doors were found ajar in the morning. Animals were discovered untethered and wandering; pans of milk were overturned in the dairy, and utensils scattered about. The woodshed received the attentions of the nocturnal visitant nearly every night. Piles of logs neatly stacked were found scattered in the morning, in spite of the fact that the door of the shed was kept locked. The manifestations in the woodshed became so frequent and troublesome that it was decided to keep watch. This was done on several evenings, a farm-hand secreting himself behind a stack of logs. Upon every occasion when a watch was kept on the wood, nothing happened *inside* the shed. On those nights when the shed was watched from within, pebbles were flung on to the corrugated iron roofing, the noise they made rolling down the metal being plainly heard.

[1] At the Amersham Hall, Lewisham, on Friday, December 2, 1898. For description, see *South London Press*, December 10, 1898.

213

Then a watch was kept both inside and outside of the shed, but no one was seen, though the pebbles were heard as before. Here is another Poltergeist case running true to type.

The disturbances around the house continued with unabated vigour week after week until even local interest waned somewhat. Then, quite suddenly, they almost ceased, the disturbing entity transferring its activities to the inside of the mansion, which I will now describe.

The Manor House was built for comfort, though it has been restored at various times. From the large hall a wide staircase leads to a landing. At the top of the stairs (of which there are about fifteen—but I am speaking from memory) is, or was, a solid oak gate placed across to prevent dogs from roaming over the whole house. The staircase I have mentioned leads to the more important rooms opening out of a short gallery.

The first indication received by the canon and his family that the entity had turned its attention to the interior of the house was a soft pattering sound, as of a child's bare feet running up and down the wide passage or gallery. The noises were at first taken to be those caused by a large bird or small animal out of the fields; a watch was kept, but investigation proved fruitless. These same noises were heard night after night, but nothing could be discovered. Then the maids began complaining that the kitchen utensils were being disturbed, usually during their absence, in the daytime especially. Pots and pans would fall off shelves for no ascertainable reason when a maid was within a few feet of them, but always when her back was turned. I do not remember its being proved that a person actually saw a phenomenal happening of any description, though many were heard. Another curious circumstance connected with this case was the disturbing entity's fondness for raking out the fires during the night. The danger of fire from this cause was so obvious that, before retiring to rest, the canon's wife had water poured on the dying embers.

Like every old country house worthy of the name, the Manor, Parton Magna, had a history, which at the period of my story was being sedulously discussed by the villagers. The story is that the house was built by a rich recluse who, through an unfortunate love affair, decided to retire from the world and its disappointments. A niece, who acted as chatelaine, looked after the old man and managed his servants. One night, some few years after their settlement at the Manor House, the recluse became suddenly demented, went to his niece's apartment, and, with almost superhuman strength, strangled the girl in bed. He then left the house, spent the night in the neighbouring woods, and at daybreak threw himself into the river that runs through the fields near the house. The legend, like the Poltergeist, also runs true to type. Like most traditions, there is a grain of truth in the story, the fact being that many years previously a girl named Mary Hulse had died at the Manor under suspicious circumstances.

It can be imagined that the canon's health was suffering under the anxiety caused by the disturbing events I have recorded above, and he was persuaded to leave the house for at least a short period. This was in the early autumn. On my way back to school for the Michaelmas term I broke my journey at Parton Magna in order to stay with our friends, who then made me acquainted with the state of affairs at the Manor House; in fact, it was the principal topic of conversation. The canon and his household had by then vacated their home temporarily, the premises being looked after by the wife of one of the cowmen. What really drove the family out was the fact that the nocturnal noises were becoming greater; in particular, a steady thump, thump (as of someone in heavy boots stamping about the house), disturbing the rest of the inmates night after night. I decided I would investigate and invited a boy friend to join me in the adventure.

I must confess that I had not the slightest idea what we were going to do, or going to see, or what I ought to take with me in the way of apparatus. But the last question was very soon settled because all I had with me was a ¼-plate 'Lancaster' stand camera. On the morning of the adventure I cycled into the nearest town and bought some magnesium powder, a bell switch, a hank of flex wire, two Daniell's batteries and some sulphuric acid. A big hole was made in my term's pocket money! In the afternoon I assembled my batteries and switch and prepared the flash powder by means of which I hoped to photograph—*something*! So that there should be no unwillingness on the part of the magnesium to go off at the psychological moment, I extracted the white smokeless gunpowder from four or five sporting cartridges and mixed it with the magnesium powder. By a lucky chance I had with me a delicate chemical balance that I was taking back to school. With the weights was a platinum wire 'rider', which I inserted in the electrical circuit in order to ignite the magnesium flash-powder. With the above-mentioned impedimenta, a box of matches, some candles, a stable lantern, a piece of chalk, a ball of string, a box of rapid plates, a parcel of food, the camera and accessories and (forbidden luxury!) some cigarettes, we bade a tender farewell to our friends and made our way across the fields to the Manor House, where we arrived at about 9.30 p.m.

The first thing we did when we reached our destination was to search every room and attic, and close and fasten every window. We locked all the doors we could and removed the keys. The doors leading to the exterior of the house were locked, bolted and barred, and chairs or other obstacles piled in front of them. We were determined that no material being should enter without our knowing it. After we had searched every nook and cranny of the building, we established ourselves in the morning-room, locked the door and waited for something—or somebody—to turn up. Our only illumination was the light of the stable lantern which we placed on the table.

215

At about half-past eleven, when we were beginning to get very sleepy and wishing (though we did not admit it) that we were in our beds, my friend thought he heard a noise in the room overhead (the traditional apartment of the unfortunate Mary Hulse). I, too, had heard a noise, but concluded it was caused by a wandering rodent or the wind. It did not sound an unusual noise. A few minutes later there was a thud in the room above that left nothing to the imagination. It sounded as if someone had stumbled over a chair. I will not attempt to describe our feelings at the discovery that we were not alone in the house: for a moment or so we were almost paralysed with fear. But, remembering what we were there for, we braced up our nerves and waited. Just before midnight we again heard a noise in the room above; it was as if a heavy person were stamping about in clogs. A minute or so later the footfalls sounded as if they had left the room and were traversing the short gallery. Then they approached the head of the stairs, paused at the dog-gate (which we had securely fastened with string), and commenced descending the stairs. We distinctly counted the fifteen thumps corresponding to the number of stairs—and I need hardly mention that our hearts were thumping in unison. 'It' seemed to pause in the hall when the bottom of the stairs was reached, and we were wondering what was going to happen next. The fact that only a door intervened between us and the mysterious intruder made us take a lively interest in what its next move would be. We were not kept long in suspense. The entity, having paused in the hall for about three minutes, turned tail and stumped up the stairs again, every step being plainly heard. We again counted the number of thumps, and were satisfied that 'it' was at the top of the flight—where again a halt was made at the dog-gate. But no further noise was heard when this gate had been reached. My friend and I waited at the door for a few minutes more, and then we decided to investigate the neighbourhood of the dog-gate and Mary Hulse's room. But we had barely formed this resolution before we heard the thumps descending the stairs again. With quickened pulse I again counted the fifteen heavy footsteps, which were getting nearer and nearer and louder and louder. There was another pause in the hall, and again the footsteps commenced their upward journey. But by this time the excitement of the adventure was making us bolder; we were acquiring a little of that contempt which is bred by familiarity. We decided to have a look at our quarry, if it were visible, so with my courage in one hand and the camera in the other, I opened the door. My friend was close behind with the stable lantern. By this time the 'ghost' was on the fifth stair, but with the opening of the door leading into the hall the noise of its ascent stopped dead.

Realising that the 'ghost' was as frightened of meeting us as we were of seeing it (although that is what we had come for), we thought we would again examine the stairs and the upper part of the house. This we did very thoroughly, but found nothing disturbed. The dog-gate was still latched and tied with string. To this day I am wondering whether 'it' climbed over the gate (easily accomplished by a mortal), or whether it slipped through the bars. I think we were disappointed at not seeing anything we could photograph, so decided to make an attempt at a flashlight picture if the Poltergeist would descend the stairs again.

For my stand for the flash-powder I utilised some household steps about six feet high which we found in the kitchen. I opened out the steps and placed them about twelve feet from the bottom of the stairs. On the top of the steps, in an old Waterbury watch-case, I placed a heaped-up eggcupful of the magnesium-*cum*-gunpowder mixture—enough to photograph every ghost in the county! But in my simple enthusiasm I was running no risks of under-exposure. I placed the Daniell's batteries in the morning-room, and connected them up with the magnesium powder on the steps and the bell-push on the floor of the room, the wire flex entering the room under the door. In the heap of powder I had buried my platinum 'rider' which was interposed in the electrical circuit.

The exact position as to where we should photograph the entity presented some difficulty. We were not quite sure what happened to it when it reached the hall, so we decided to make an attempt at photographing it when it was ascending or descending the stairs. We decided on the former position, arguing (which shows how simple we were!) that the ghost would have become less suspicious of us by the time it was on its return journey! I stationed my friend on the seventh or eighth stair (I forget which), and he held a lighted match which I accurately focussed on the ground-glass of my Lancaster *Le Méritoire* camera, that I placed on one of the treads of the steps. I inserted the dark-slide, withdrew the flap, uncapped the lens, and then all was ready. The whole thing was rather mad, of course, but the reader must remember that we were very young, with no experience of Poltergeist photography.

By the time we had fixed up the camera and examined the connections it was about half-past one. During the time we were moving about the hall not a sound was heard from above-stairs. Having arranged everything to our satisfaction, we returned to the morning-room, locked the door again and extinguished the lantern. Then we lay upon the carpet near the door, with the pear-push in my hand, and commenced our vigil.

It must have been nearly an hour before we heard anything, and again it was from the Mary Hulse room that the noises emanated. The sounds were identical to those we had previously heard: as if someone in clogs were treading heavily. Shortly after, the 'thumps' could be heard approaching the dog-gate and again 'it' paused at the top of the stairs. The pause was greater than the previous one, and for a minute or so we thought the Poltergeist had come to the end of its journey; but no, it passed over—or through—the dog-gate and commenced stumping down the stairs again. Having reached the hall the visitant stopped, and in my mind's eye I could picture it examining the arrangements we had made for securing its photograph. Then we thought we heard the steps moved. In order to get the camera square with the stairs I had taken a large book—using it as a set-square—and drawn on the tiled floor a chalk line parallel with the stairs. Exactly against this line I had placed the two front feet of the steps.

During the next five or six minutes we heard no movement in the hall. Then suddenly 'it' started its return journey. With our hearts beating wildly and with suppressed excitement, we lay on the floor counting the slow, measured thumps as they ascended the stairs. At the seventh

'The Manor House continued to be the centre of psychic activity for some months'.

thump I pressed the button of my pear-push and—a most extraordinary thing happened, which is rather difficult to describe on paper. At the moment of the explosion the ghost was so startled *that it involuntarily stumbled* on the stairs, as we could plainly hear, and then there was silence. At the same moment there was a clattering down the stairs as if the spontaneous disintegration of the disturbing entity had taken place. The flash from the ignition of the powder was so vivid that even the morning-room from which we were directing operations was lit up by the rays coming from under the door, which was rather ill-fitting.

It would be difficult to say who was the more startled—the Poltergeist

218

or myself, and for some moments we did nothing. After our astonishment had subsided somewhat, we opened the door and found the hall filled with a dense white smoke in which we could hardly breathe. We re-capped the camera, relit our lantern, and made a tour of inspection. The first thing we noticed was that the steps were shifted slightly out of the square. Whether 'it' moved the steps (as we thought at the time), or whether the shock of the explosion was responsible (which is doubtful), we could not determine. The Waterbury watch-case had disappeared with my platinum 'rider', and I have never seen the latter from that day to this. The watch-case we found eventually on the second stair from the bottom. What happened to it was apparently this : through the extremely rapid conversion of the gunpowder and magnesium into gases, and the concavity of the interior periphery of the case tending to retain the gases, the case was converted into a projectile, the very active propellant shooting it towards the stairs (the force of the explosion happening to send it in that direction), which it must have hit at about the spot where the entity was ascending—surely the only recorded instance of a ghost having a watch-case fired at it : it has been suggested that I call this narrative 'How I "shot" my first Poltergeist'! The sound of the watch-case falling was the rattling noise we heard when we thought we should find our quarry lying in pieces at the foot of the staircase. We immediately developed the plate, but nothing but an over-exposed picture of the staircase was on the negative.

The Manor House continued to be the centre of psychic activity for some months after our curious adventure, but the disturbances became gradually less frequent, and eventually ceased. Fate decreed that some years later I should spend many happy weeks in the house. If sometimes during that period my heart beat faster than its accustomed rate, the cause was *not* a paranormal one! Suffice it to say that I did not see or hear anything of the alleged spirit of Mary Hulse, though I will candidly admit that I was not looking for her—my interest in the diaphanous maiden having been transferred by that time to one of a much more objective nature!

CHAPTER XIX

The Ballechin House Controversy

This classic case, apart from its intrinsic value to psychical researchers, is remarkable for two reasons : (a) its curious correspondences with the Borley mystery; and (b) the fact that in 1897 the house and its phenomena started a long and acrimonious squabble that filled the correspondence columns of *The Times*[1] for nearly a month. Lord Onslow, Andrew Lang, Henry Sidgwick, F. W. H. Myers and many others took part in the discussion, during which the S.P.R., then a young society of some fifteen summers, was subjected to much criticism. The letters created an interesting *divertissement*, sandwiched as they were between the colourful accounts of the Diamond Jubilee, then in full swing.

Ballechin House, Perthshire, is situated at Strathtay, near Dunkeld (famous for a distillery producing spirits of a different order) and is a large modern seat, then the property of Captain J. M. S. Steuart, built on the site of a much older mansion, dating back at least to the sixteenth century. It acquired a reputation for being haunted as long ago as 1878.

In 1892, John, third Marquess of Bute, heard of the hauntings from a Jesuit priest, Father Hayden, S.J., who had stayed at the house. Lord Bute, who was deeply interested in psychic matters, induced Father Hayden to give him an account of his experiences, which were as follows :

While he was sleeping in one of the rooms reputed to be haunted, loud noises occurred between his bed and the ceiling 'like continuous explosion of petards' so that he could not hear himself speak. He changed his room, but the noises followed him. Other sounds that he heard he likened to that of a 'large animal throwing itself violently against the bottom of the door, outside'. He also heard raps, and a shriek or scream. Later, Father Hayden wrote out a short account of his experiences. He said : 'I went to Ballechin on Thursday, July 14th, 1892, and I left it on Saturday, July 23rd. So I slept at Ballechin for nine nights, or rather *one* night, because I was disturbed by very queer and extraordinary noises every night except the last, which I spent in Mr. Steuart's dressing-room. At first I occupied the room to the extreme right of the landing, then my things were removed to another room. In both these rooms I heard the loud and inexplicable noises every night, but on two or three nights, in addition to these, another noise affrighted me—a sound of somebody or

[1] See *The Times* for June 8, 9, 10, 12, 13, 14, 15, 16, 18, 19, 21, 22, 23, 24, 1897. The references are headed 'On the Trail of a Ghost'.

something falling against the door outside. It seemed, at the time, as if a calf or big dog would make such a noise. Why those particular animals came into my head I cannot tell. But in attempting to describe these indescribable phenomena, I notice now I always do say it was like a calf or big dog falling against the door. Why did I not hear the noises on the ninth night? Were there none where I was? These are questions the answers to which are not apparent. It may be there *were* noises, but I slept too soundly to hear them. One of the oddest things in my case, in connection with the house, is that it appeared to me that (1) somebody was relieved by my departure; (2) that nothing could induce me to pass another night there, at all events alone, and in other respects I do not think I am a coward.' Father Hayden sprinkled the rooms with holy water and recited the *Visita quæsumus*, a prayer for the divine protection of a house and its occupants, but all to no purpose.

In August, 1893, Father Hayden met by accident a young woman who some twelve years previously used to be governess in the Steuart family. Without his telling her that he had even been to Ballechin, she volunteered the statement that she had left her employment because 'so many people complained of queer noises in the house'. She became frightened and left. When questioned, it was learnt that the noises had occurred in the two identical rooms successively occupied by Father Hayden.

Further evidence for the haunting of Ballechin House came from the villagers and others in the neighbourhood, and a Catholic Archbishop tried to exorcise the ghost at about this time.

In August, 1896, Ballechin House, with the shooting, was let to a wealthy family of Spanish extraction, for twelve months. They stayed exactly eleven weeks and forfeited more than nine months' rent. Their English butler, Mr. Harold Sanders, wrote a long letter to *The Times*,[1] giving an account of the phenomena that drove the family away. He stated that the manifestations included various kinds of noises, such as rattling, knocking, 'tremendous thumping' on the doors, heavy footsteps along the passages and similar disturbances heard by every inmate of the house, including the servants.

Mr. Sanders continues: 'The same thing happened with variations almost nightly for the succeeding two months that I was there, and every visitor that came to the house was disturbed in the same manner. One gentleman (a colonel) told me he was awakened on several occasions with the feeling that someone was pulling the bedclothes off him: sometimes heavy footsteps were heard, at others like the rustling of a lady's dress; and sometimes groans were heard, but nearly always accompanied with heavy knocking: sometimes the whole house would be aroused. One night I remember five gentlemen meeting at the top of the stairs in their night-suits, some with sticks or pokers, one had a revolver, vowing vengeance on the disturbers of their sleep. During the two months after

[1] For June 21, 1897.

I first heard the noises I kept watch altogether about twelve times in various parts of the house, mostly unknown to others (at the time), and have heard the noises in the wing as well as other parts.

'When watching I always experienced a peculiar sensation a few minutes before hearing any noise. I can only describe it as like suddenly entering an ice house, and a feeling that someone was present and about to speak to me. On three different nights I was awakened by my bed-clothes being pulled off my feet. But the worst night I had at Ballechin was one night about the second week in September, and I shall never forget it as long as I live. I had been keeping watch with two gentlemen, one a visitor, the other one of the house. We heard the noises I have described about half-past two. Both gentlemen were very much alarmed; but we searched everywhere, but could not find any trace of the ghost or cause of the noises, although they came this time from an unoccupied room. (I may mention that the noises were never heard in the daytime, but always between twelve, midnight, and four in the morning—generally between two and four o'clock.) After a thorough search the two gentlemen went to bed sadder, but not wiser, men, for we had discovered nothing. I then went to my room, but not to bed, for I was not satisfied, and decided to continue the watch alone. So I seated myself on the service stairs. . . .

'I had not long to wait (about twenty minutes) when the knocking recommenced from the same direction as before, but much louder than before, followed, after a very short interval, by two distinct groans, which certainly made me feel very uncomfortable, for it sounded like someone being stabbed and then falling to the floor. That was enough for me. I went and asked the two gentlemen who had just gone to bed if they had heard anything. One said he had heard five knocks and two groans, the same as I had; while the other (whose room was much nearer to where the sounds came from) said he had heard nothing. I then retired to my bed, but not to sleep, for I had not been in bed three minutes before I experienced the sensation as before, but instead of being followed by knocking, my bedclothes were lifted up and let fall again— first at the foot of my bed, but gradually coming towards my head. I held the clothes around my neck with my hands, but they were gently lifted in spite of my efforts to hold them. I then reached around me with my hand, but could feel nothing. This was immediately followed by my being fanned as though some bird was flying around my head, and I could distinctly hear and feel something breathing on me. I then tried to reach some matches that were on a chair by my bedside, but my hand was held back as if by some invisible power. Then the thing seemed to retire to the foot of my bed. Then I suddenly found the foot of my bed lifted up and carried around towards the window for about three or four feet, then replaced to its former position. All this did not take, I should think, more than two or three minutes, although at the time it seemed hours to me. Just then the clock struck four and, being tired out with my long night's watching, I fell asleep.'

Some of the guests confirmed the butler's story. A Miss B. wrote: 'I wakened suddenly in the middle of the night, and noticed how quiet the house was. Then I heard the clock strike two, and a few minutes later there came a crashing, *vibrating* batter against the door of the outer room. My sister was sleeping very soundly, but she started up in a moment at the noise, wide awake.'

Miss B., who slept with her sister, again heard the 'battering' noise two nights later, when the two young women, with their host's daughter, remained in the latter's bedroom, waiting for the 'ghost'. Another member of the house party, Major B., also experienced some startling phenomena. His room was the one next to that occupied by a colonel. The major writes: 'August 24th, 1896, about 3.30 a.m., I heard very loud knocking, apparently on Colonel A.'s door, about nine raps in all —three raps quickly one after the other, then three more the same, and three more the same. It was as if someone was hitting the door with his fist as hard as he could hit. I left my room at once, but could find nothing to account for the noise. It was broad daylight at the time. I heard the same noises on the 28th and 30th August at about the same hour, viz. between 3 and 4 a.m.'

Colonel A., in a letter to the major, confirms the account of the bangings. He says: 'What I heard was what you heard, a terrific banging at one's bedroom door, generally about from 2 to 3 a.m., about two nights out of three.' So here we have good evidence of paranormal bangings on a door, from two men who were on either side of it.

Another member of the house party, a Mrs. G., recorded her experiences. She says: 'I, my daughter, and my husband were put in rooms adjoining, at the end of the new wing. . . . At 2 a.m. a succession of thundering knocks came from the end of our passage, re-echoing through the house, where it was heard by many others. About half an hour afterwards my husband heard a piercing shriek; then all was still . . . The next night and succeeding ones we heard loud single knocks at different doors along our passage. The last night but one before we left I was roused from sleep by hearing the clock strike one, and immediately it had ceased six violent blows shook our own door on its hinges, and came with frightful rapidity, followed by deep groans.'

An old Spanish nurse, employed by the new tenants, was greatly disturbed by the noises on the door, which was actually burst open one night by the blows rained upon it.

It can be imagined that Lord Bute was deeply interested in the various accounts of the haunting of Ballechin House and decided (as I did in the case of Borley Rectory) to rent the mansion. He could not personally conduct the investigation, so delegated the work to two well-known psychical researchers of the period, Colonel Lemesurier Taylor and Miss A. Goodrich-Freer (i.e. Mrs. Hans Spoer). Actually the house was taken in the name of Colonel Taylor; and he and Miss Freer and her friend, Miss Constance Moore (daughter of the Rev. Daniel Moore, Prebendary of St. Paul's and Chaplain to Queen Victoria) took up their residence at Ballechin House on February 3rd, 1897. They had engaged a staff of servants in Edinburgh.

I will now interpolate that the whole of this chapter has been compiled from the contemporary correspondence in *The Times*, already alluded to, and from the official report of the hauntings that was published by Miss Freer and Lord Bute under the title of *The Alleged Haunting of B—— House*.[1] In many ways it is an infuriating book. Nearly every proper name, including that of the house, was suppressed, initials, blanks and dashes taking their place. Here is a specimen (p. 56): '. . . the house being tenanted by Mr. J. R. H—— of K—— Court, C——, G——shire. The household consisted of Mr. and Mrs. H——, three sons, Miss H——, my sister and I, and two other guests, Colonel A—— and Major B——.'

Ordinarily, such a report would hardly be worth the paper it was written on. The editors of the book recognised this fact, but they were so desperately afraid of starting another row about the investigation, that they resorted to initials and blanks instead of real names, except in the case of their own immediate friends who accompanied them to Ballechin.

What made this procedure even more ridiculous is the fact that, *before the book was published*, most of the people concerned, including the owner of the mansion, sent letters to *The Times*, giving their full and proper names, with no attempt at anonymity. With the help of *The Times*, and my own general knowledge of the case, I have managed to substitute real names for many of the blanks and dashes. Nearly fifty years have elapsed since 'Mr. H.' had his exciting house-party, so there is little likelihood that my remarks will cause any heart-burning in any quarter.

The Alleged Haunting of B—— House is divided into two parts, and large portions of it are devoted to the *Times* controversy. But the more valuable section of the book is a day-to-day journal of what happened at Ballechin, and the precautions—rather crude, as the investigation was conducted in the pre-scientific days of psychical research—taken to guard against fraud or errors in observation. Miss Freer was the moving spirit in the investigation, and it was she who was responsible for keeping the diary of events.

In the early morning after their arrival she was 'startled by a loud clanging sound, which seemed to resound through the house'. It was as

[1] London, 1899. My copy formerly belonged to Lord Halsbury. A revised edition appeared in 1900.

if a long metal bar was being struck with a wooden mallet. The clanging was repeated at frequent intervals during two hours. At 4.30 a.m. Miss Freer and her friend heard sounds of talking coming from the same floor. Her maid also heard the voices, together with 'footsteps and the sound of things dragged about'—typical of Poltergeist phenomena.

The next night the maids heard sounds as of continuous reading aloud —a phenomenon experienced repeatedly during the investigation. 'The sound was always that well known to Roman Catholics as that of a priest "saying his office".' A new kitchen-maid arrived later in the day and refused to stay even one night. She became frightened, and left the house at 11 p.m.

'Against the snow I saw a slight black figure . . . dressed as a nun'.

Miss Freer and her friends experimented—as we did in the Borley case—with the Ouija board, and amongst the 'messages' received was one telling them to go, at dusk, to 'the glen in the avenue, up by the burn'. The communicator said her name was 'Ishbel' and she repeated this several times. So the experimenters journeyed to the place indicated, and Miss Freer tells us what she saw: 'Against the snow I saw a slight black figure, a woman, moving slowly up the glen. She stopped, and turned and looked at me. She was dressed as a nun. Her face looked pale. I saw her hand in the folds of her habit. Then she moved on, as it seemed, on a slope too steep for walking. When she came under the tree she disappeared.' In a later account she gives a fuller description of the phantom nun which was seen by Miss Freer on many subsequent occasions. Once the 'nun' was in tears : 'Her weeping seemed to me passionate and unrestrained', and 'She speaks upon rather a high note, with a quality of youth in her voice'.

Although Miss Freer saw the 'nun' (which she supposed to be 'Ishbel') no other member of her party could see the ghost at that time. It was invisible to them—which proves, I think, that the nun was purely a subjective image, 'seen' only by Miss Freer. Though the figure was seen many times by Miss Freer, it was very seldom visible to other observers. Apparitions in various forms were alleged to have been seen by other members of Miss Freer's group, but the evidence is rather weak.

It would be tedious to make further extracts from Miss Freer's journal, and the interested reader should consult her book. But the following audible phenomena were heard by many observers during the three months' investigation :

Footsteps, voices, dragging of heavy objects, pattering sounds, explosive bangs, reading in monotone, knockings, crashes, 'movements of animals', groans, falls of some heavy object, rappings, metallic sounds, thumps on doors, etc., footsteps in locked and empty rooms, and once a dog reacted to sounds of invisible shuffling footsteps and strange voices.

Mr. F. W. H. Myers and a party visited the house and so did Sir Oliver (then Professor) Lodge, who arrived on April 12, 1897. In a letter to Lord Bute, he said : 'We have not heard the loud bang as yet. Knocks on the wall, a sawing noise, and a droning and a wailing are all we have heard.' To Miss Freer he wrote : 'There has been nothing for me to do here as a physicist, and I return home tomorrow, but nevertheless the phenomena, taken as a whole, have been most interesting . . . some of the raps seemed intelligent.'

As to the causation of the phenomena, many legends were current that might account for the manifestations—if they (the legends) were true. Murder, suicide, and sudden death enter into these stories, just as they did in the Borley case. Also, as at Borley, an eccentric and deceased former owner threatened, when alive, to come back and haunt the place when he was dead. Both men were believers in survival. I have mentioned more than once the really remarkable parallelisms that exist between Ballechin and Borley. I will enumerate a few of them :

Both houses have Roman Catholic associations, or the owners were originally Catholics. Both buildings are large and rambling sort of places, set in lonely districts. Similar legends—and scandal—have grown up around the two hauntings, and the phantoms include, in each case, a legless figure. Attempts to exorcise the ghosts of both Borley Rectory and Ballechin have been made by Roman Catholic priests, and in each house has been seen the phantasm of a parson. And each house boasted a 'Blue Room'.[1] And in each house, an early occupant (at Borley, the Rev. Harry Bull and at Ballechin, a Major Steuart) threatened to come back and haunt the place.

Both buildings were respectively rented by psychical researchers for the purpose of prolonged investigation: Lord Bute took Ballechin for three months; I rented Borley for a year. Every one of my observers said that Borley was the coldest and the quietest house they had ever been in; Miss Freer writes: 'The house looked very gloomy . . . it felt like a vault . . . The room was so cold that we had to cover our faces.' The investigators both at the Essex Rectory and in the Scotch mansion 'felt a sensation of cold' on many occasions.

A 'nun' haunted the grounds of both buildings, but *never* the houses, and was seen on many occasions. In the case of Borley, the figure was seen by many people over more than half a century, under good conditions. In each case, in 'automatic' messages *via* the Ouija board or Planchette, the supposed nun 'communicated' and gave her name: 'Marie Lairre' in the case of Borley, 'Ishbel' at Ballechin. The appearance of the two nuns was almost identical, and both gave the impression of being 'sad, and in trouble'. Miss Freer saw the Ballechin nun weeping.

Many of the phenomena at both Borley and Ballechin were identical, and this applies particularly to the audible and Poltergeist manifestations. In addition, dogs reacted strangely to unusual sounds. Bedclothes were removed from sleepers at both houses—typical Poltergeist pranks. And I could name many other correspondences between the Borley and Ballechin hauntings, monographs on which were issued after the respective investigations. I will add in parentheses that I am quite certain that, excepting myself, *not one* of the hundred observers who reported on Borley had ever even heard of the Ballechin case, which is really very little known, and Miss Freer's book—now rare—does *not* reveal the name or the exact whereabouts of the house!

Though there are so many correspondences between Borley and Ballechin, the cases are not comparable from the evidential standpoint. And Miss Freer's monograph covers little more than the three months' investigation of herself and friends—and those infuriating anonymous witnesses. On the other hand, we have first-hand evidence of what has happened at Borley for more than sixty years—a continuity most unusual—and perhaps unique—in the history of any haunted house.

And now I come to the question: 'Was Ballechin *really* haunted?' On the evidence, poor as it is, the answer must be 'Yes'. Looking at the case in retrospect, I don't think we can come to any other conclusion, and if

[1] There was also a haunted 'Blue Room' at Willington Mill, one at Tackley, Oxon., and another in Calvados Castle. And in a famous Blue Room at Dunedin, New Zealand, the Poltergeist-medium, Pearl Judd, performed her 'miracles'. See *The Blue Room*, by Clive Chapman, Dunedin, 1927. On Dec. 22, 1944, the B.B.C. broadcast a ghost-story, *The Fiddler* (by Richard Hearne), in which all the murders were committed in the 'Blue Room'.

the case had been handled to-day by modern methods, the result would, I am sure, have been much more convincing. *The Times* controversy began a week or so after Lord Bute relinquished his tenancy. It was a pity that the report had not then been published. When Miss Freer's book eventually became available, some two years later, public interest in Ballechin House and the strange doings there had subsided. Which, perhaps, was just as well.

CHAPTER XX

The Battersea Poltergeist

Having told the story of some old London Poltergeists, I will now relate my adventures with a comparatively new one—an amazing affair exhibiting many unusual features; so unusual, in fact, that in some respects the case is unique.

The focus of the manifestations was centred in a small villa in Eland Road, Lavender Hill, Battersea, a bustling working-class district of London with no attractions, one would have thought, for a Poltergeist.

This villa was inhabited by Mr. Henry Robinson, an invalid of 86, who had lived there twenty-five years, and who was removed to the infirmary at the request of the family when the disturbances commenced. With Mr. Robinson senior, lived his twenty-seven-year-old son Frederick, and his three daughters: Miss Lillah Robinson, Miss Kate Robinson, and Mrs. George Perkins, a widow, who had a fourteen-year-old son, Peter. The Misses Robinson were school teachers and their brother was a tutor.

The house in Eland Road is of a type of which tens of thousands can be found scattered all round the Metropolis. It has two floors and a small garden at front and rear. It is the typical abode of the London artisan. From the garden can be seen the back windows of some premises then occupied by a medical practitioner who kept a private asylum or mental home. I was told that men suffering from shell-shock were his principal patients. From the doctor's windows to the back of the 'mystery house', as the Press dubbed it, is about eighty yards. It would be possible for a person standing at the windows of the private asylum to propel, by means of a catapult, small objects such as coins, pieces of coal, etc. with sufficient force to break the windows of the houses in Eland Road.

It was just before Christmas that, from a private source, I first heard of the strange happenings in Eland Road; but I attached no importance to the report, which differed little from many others that I receive. I heard nothing further until the week commencing January 15, 1928, when reports of alleged extraordinary happenings began to appear in the Press. I decided I would investigate.

On Thursday, January 19, at 9.30 a.m., I paid my first visit. I thought I was fairly early on the scene but a garrulous female free-lance journalist—who opened the door—had arrived there earlier and tried to bluff me into abandoning my investigation. Not being easily bluffed, I successfully negotiated the outer defences of the 'mystery house' and entered the building. I found the family at breakfast, and my first impression was distinctly favourable as regards the family and the improbability that the inmates of the house were responsible for the destruction of their own home. For I at once saw that someone or something had caused considerable damage to the Robinson *ménage*. Broken windows, smashed furniture, and the *débris* of ornaments were much in evidence. After a few minutes' chat I withdrew and promised to call again.

On my return to the National Laboratory I found a message from the news editor of the London *Evening News* asking if I would allow a reporter of that paper to accompany me to the house. I consented and at three o'clock the same afternoon a car was sent for me, and for the second time that day I found myself in Eland Road—this time with a Press representative. Miss Kate Robinson and Mr. Fred Robinson were the only members of the family who were in the house on this occasion, and from them we obtained the complete story of the disturbances.

'Except for Percy', said Mr. Robinson, 'we lived in the house for twenty-five years, happily and peacefully. Then on November 29, lumps of coal, pieces of soda and pennies began to fall on the conservatory—a lean-to building at the back of the house.

'It stopped for a few days. It began again early in December. It struck me as being extremely curious at the time that, although the pieces of coal were very small, they broke the glass.

'Things became so serious that I decided to call the police. I had no other idea except that some person was throwing things over the garden wall.

'A constable came along, and together we stood in the back garden and kept watch. Pieces of coal and pennies crashed on to the conservatory roof, but we could not trace their flight. One lump of coal hit the constable's helmet. He ran to the garden wall, but there was nobody there.

'On December 19 our washerwoman said she would not work any longer in the house. She came to me in a state of terror and pointed to a heap of red-hot cinders in the outhouse. There was no fire near. How could they have got there?

'Again I called a constable, and we decided to watch in the kitchen. Two potatoes were hurled in while we were sitting there.

'It was on Monday that the climax came—at nine o'clock in the morning—and for an hour the family was terror-stricken. There were loud bangings in all parts of the house. My sister ran to tell the magistrate. The window panel in my father's bedroom was smashed, and as he was in such a state of fear I decided to remove him from the house. I called in a man from the street, and together we carried him from the room. Just as we were taking him out a heavy chest of drawers crashed to the floor in his bedroom.

The house in Eland Road, Battersea, the scene of extraordinary Poltergeist manifestations. (See Chapter XX.)

'Previously, my sister had seen the hall stand swaying and had called me. I caught it before it fell, but some strange power seemed to tear it from my hands, and it fell against the stairs, breaking in two parts.'

Mr. Bradbury, the man who was called in to help move the old gentleman, confirmed Mr. Fred Robinson's account. He said:

*'I caught it before it fell, but some strange power
seemed to tear it from my hands . . .'*

'Mr. Robinson called me to his house, and when I arrived there at about ten o'clock there were a fishmonger and a greengrocer discussing with him what had happened. I saw several women in the house and they appeared to be very frightened. Mr. Robinson took me up to a bedroom, where he said his father had been sleeping, and showed us an overturned chest of drawers.

'One of the women said that she was afraid to stop in the house, and that she was also afraid to go into her room to pack up her clothing. We went with her into her room, and she told us that she had been awakened by loud bangings on the door, and the crashing of glass. We stayed there until she had packed her bag and then returned to the back bedroom, where Mr. Robinson showed us pennies and coal on the conservatory roof.

'The four of us—all men—were watching these, when suddenly from another bedroom came a great crash and downstairs we heard a woman scream. We ran to the room and there we saw a chest of drawers lying on the floor. It was all very strange, and Mr. Robinson then took us to the kitchen and showed us the damage done there.'

After we had heard the history of the disturbances from their commencement, the Press representative and myself made a tour of the house and carefully inspected the damage, which was considerable. Several of the windows were broken, some with small holes in them as if stones had been fired at them. Some of the panes of glass of the conservatory roof were also shattered, and, lying on the roof, were pebbles, pennies, lumps of coal, potatoes, pieces of soda, etc., which had been thrown there. A door inside the house had also one of its glass panels broken. In the back bedroom we found the panels of the door shattered; a heavy chest of drawers was splintered as if from a fall; and the remains of several smashed ornaments were scattered about. In the hall we saw a smashed hat-stand in two pieces and we viewed the remains of two broken bedroom doors, a tea tray with one of its sides ripped off, and a number of pictures that had fallen to the ground. In the small garden were strewn lumps of soda, coal, etc., and Mr. Robinson pointed out two windows of neighbouring houses which had received the unwelcome attention of the alleged *Geist*: both had small holes in them as if caused by stones shot from a catapult.

After our tour of inspection we returned to the kitchen where the four of us—Miss Kate Robinson, Mr. Fred Robinson, Mr. Grice, the *Evening News* representative, and myself—stood chatting. We were the sole occupants of the house. Mr. Grice and I were just about to leave when some hard object fell with a resounding thwack in the passage at the back of us.

The kitchen is connected with the scullery by a short passage. The scullery leads directly to the garden by a door which we had just closed.

Upon the fall of the object we four at once proceeded into the passage and found that a metal ferro-cerium gas-lighter, with a wooden handle, overall length about eight inches, was lying mid-way between the kitchen and scullery. Undoubtedly it had been projected from behind us and had, apparently, struck the wall in its flight. We immediately went back through the scullery and into the garden but no one was visible.

Miss Robinson told us that the gas-lighter—weight about two ounces —was always kept on the gas stove in the scullery. Certainly no one was in the scullery, garden, or passage when the lighter was thrown or fell. I say 'fell' because it is just possible that it may have been placed on the top of the open door that separates the kitchen from the passage. But experiment proved that a considerable push on the door was needed to displace the lighter, which, however, might have been so balanced that a touch would bring it down. But the Robinsons declared that the lighter was on the gas stove when we first visited the scullery. I did not see it there myself; neither did the *Evening News* representative. It was a curious incident and made an excellent stop-press paragraph for the evening papers!

The *Evening News* representative and I again visited Eland Road the next morning (Friday) and were told that a number of phenomena had been witnessed since our previous visit. Pieces of coal, pennies, lumps of soda and stones had been thrown about and one more window had been smashed. We stayed about an hour but witnessed nothing unusual.

I arrived back at the National Laboratory about 11.30 and half an hour later was rung up by the editor of the *Evening News*, who told me that the authorities had removed young Robinson for observation as to his mental state. I was astounded at this fresh development. I had had an hour's conversation with Mr. Fred Robinson on the previous day and had found him quite normal and very intelligent. It is alleged that the police had formed a theory that Mr. Robinson, junior, was responsible for the manifestations and had decided to examine him at St. John's Hospital, Battersea.

I again visited the house on Monday afternoon (Jan. 23) and had a long interview with Mrs. Perkins, the widowed sister. Mr. Grice of the *Evening News* again accompanied me to Eland Road, and again went over the house with me.

The fact that Mr. Frederick Robinson was not now in the house made no difference to the alleged phenomena. Mrs. Perkins told us that during the week-end the manifestations had been both violent and varied. Besides the usual arrival of pieces of coal, etc., there had been 'great activity amongst the furniture'. Chairs, of their own volition, 'had marched down the hall single file' and three times Mrs. Perkins attempted to lay the table for Saturday's dinner. On each occasion the chairs had piled themselves up on the table, making it impossible for the woman to proceed with the preparation of the meal. At the third attempt, she went out into the road and asked a police officer who was on duty there to enter the house and examine the 'phenomenon' for himself. The stolid London policeman naturally accused Mrs. Perkins of piling up the furniture herself. A London policeman knows little about Poltergeists! (See the drawing from *Punch*, page 3.)

Mrs. Perkins's sister, Miss Robinson, stated that after her brother

233

had left the house an *attaché* case 'flew' from a kitchen chair to the floor; an umbrella sprang from the stand in the hall to the kitchen floor; a cruet crashed to the ground; and the table fell over after it had been prepared for dinner.

She continued: 'We were so frightened that we went outside. Through the kitchen window we saw all the kitchen chairs fall over. We went upstairs and found stones on the roof. An extraordinary part about it is that the furniture seemed *heavy*[1] to pick up again'.

Three persons appear to have witnessed the alleged spontaneous movement of the furniture, viz. Mrs. Perkins, Miss Robinson, and Peter Perkins, the fourteen-years-old boy who was so frightened—it was stated—that he could hardly be induced to sit on a chair in case it should move. He was afterwards sent to the country to recuperate.

After we had heard the story of what had happened during the weekend, we made another examination of the house. It appeared to be in much the same state as when we left it on the previous Friday. We then returned to the kitchen and the four of us (Mrs. Perkins, Miss Robinson, Mr. Grice and myself) stood chatting in the kitchen when suddenly there was a sound as if a heavy object had fallen behind us, in the kitchen, but near the passage leading to the scullery, *the door of which was shut*. To me the noise sounded like the fall of a heavy boot or brush and I at once began to look for such an article; so did the *Evening News* representative. In a minute or so I saw something dark under a chair in the corner and putting my hand on it I found it was a pair of lady's black shoes. Actually I put my hand on a hard object which was in the right shoe and brought it to light. It was a small bronze ornament in the form of a cherub, weighing about four ounces.

The cries of astonishment—real or simulated—with which the ladies greeted my 'find' were renewed when it was discovered that the ornament was missing from the mantelpiece of the front sitting-room, where, I was informed, it had reposed (together with its fellow-cherub) for twenty-five years. We were assured that these cherubim had *never* been removed from the front room. I continued my search of the kitchen but could discover nothing else which could have fallen. If the bronze ornament really came from the next room it must have made two right-angled turns and travelled over our heads. It is conceivable that the ornament may have been thrown by one of the women, but I was within a few inches of both Mrs. Perkins and her sister and saw no suspicious movement on the part of either. Mr. Grice also declares that he saw nothing that could account for the flight of the ornament, which was quite cold when I picked it out of the shoe; if it had been held in the hand, it would, of course, have retained some of the heat.

We searched the house once more but satisfied ourselves that we

[1] It is often alleged that objects displaced by Poltergeists acquire extra weight.—H.P.

were the only occupants. Mr. Grice and I arranged to spend the next night in the house. The next day I was informed that the Eland Road house had been shut up, so that I gave up the idea of staying all night. The strange occurrences were driving the family to distraction. With both of its male members away, one daughter ill, and the little boy dispatched to the country, the two remaining sisters determined to quit the house of evil associations. The crowds, too, were frightening them. During the week-end mounted police were necessary in order to keep back the gaping mob which all day and night stood in the road and gazed, open-mouthed, at nothing more thrilling than a couple of broken panes of glass. On the Saturday evening the Battersea hooligans threatened to break into the house if they were not permitted to 'investigate' the phenomena for themselves. As I was leaving on Monday a burly ruffian with a Russian accent accosted me and asked if he could 'mind the place' for me. He would have looked—and felt—much more at home in a *vodka* bar at Minsk. I declined his services—without thanks.

During the early part of the week Miss Robinson and her sister decided to return to the house. On the Tuesday the news editor of the *Daily Express* asked me if I would make the experiment of taking a medium to the house in order to see if she could get any 'impressions'; I consented.

The psychic was a Miss X., the daughter of a well-known London professional man and, of course, an amateur. The *Daily Express* representative was Mr. F. G. H. Salusbury, a gentleman with whom I was already acquainted. We visited Eland Road on Wednesday afternoon, January 25, arriving at the house about three o'clock. Mrs. Perkins was there—the only member of the Robinson family who entered the place that afternoon.

We took Miss X. to every room in the house in order to discover if she received any impression. She at once declared that the place made her feel 'miserable'. This was not particularly illuminating, as many suburban houses have the same effect upon me. But in the kitchen Miss X. declared she felt 'chilly'. There was a good fire burning in the room—in fact, the kitchen was the only apartment which was heated. Neither Mr. Salusbury nor I felt cold in this room; on the contrary, we felt much warmer. But Miss X. continued to get colder and positively shivered. Her respiration slowed down, and her hands were distinctly cold. We left her sitting by the fire watching Mrs. Perkins do her household duties. We then continued our search of the house, carefully closing the kitchen door behind us.

We again examined the upper rooms of the house, inspecting and examining minutely every article of furniture, ornaments, etc., and noting their exact position. Hardly had we reached the top floor when Mr. Salusbury thought he heard something fall down below. I heard nothing myself, but we visited the lower rooms and could find nothing that had moved. The kitchen door was still closed. In reply to our query we were informed that the ladies in the kitchen had heard nothing. We returned to the upper story after again closing the kitchen door.

The rooms on the top floor of the Eland Road house are divided by a passage which runs from the back to the front of the building. During our inspection of these rooms we must have traversed this narrow and well-lighted passage at least six or seven times. Neither of us noticed anything on the floor of the passage. At this juncture we were in the front room when we both heard an object fall in some part of the house. We immediately turned to go once more to the lower part of the building and simultaneously saw in the passage, with the light falling full on it, a piece of common yellow soap as used for washing clothes. It was lying right in our path, about six feet from the door of the room we had just entered. We both declared that it was utterly impossible for us to have passed that soap without seeing it; to do so seven times without noticing it or treading on it would have been a miracle. Curiously enough, we did not hear it fall—if it did fall.

Without touching the soap, we made our way downstairs to the kitchen, the door of which was still closed. Both Mrs. Perkins and Miss X. declared that neither had moved during our tour of inspection; the door of the kitchen had not been opened and no one could have entered the house except by the front door (which opened only on the inside) or through the garden, scullery and kitchen.

Mrs. Perkins accompanied us to the top floor again and examined the soap, which she said belonged to the scullery. She could not account for its appearance on the top floor. The ladies also had heard something fall in the house, but we all agreed that it did not sound at all like a piece of soap falling. We then carefully examined the soap, which showed no signs of having had a blow or of falling heavily. Miss X. was still cold and shivering, though she had just come from a warm kitchen. We stayed in the house for another half-hour, but nothing further happened.

Mr. Frederick Robinson returned home a few days after the incident of the soap and I have heard of no phenomena there since. As I surmised, Mr. Robinson was found to be perfectly normal, and it was preposterous that he should have been compelled to leave his home. The Battersea 'mystery house' affair died a natural death and so another 'Poltergeist case' ended in a very unsatisfactory and inconclusive manner. The elder Mr. Robinson died in the infirmary. The Robinsons vacated the house.

It is obvious that the occurrences which I have described were either genuine phenomena, or were due to some mischievous person or persons with a very powerful motive for disturbing the peace of the locality.

My own first impression was that the ex-soldiers at the mental home had discovered that the Eland Road house was an excellent target for their missiles. The angle at which portions of the house were struck originated this theory in my mind. There had also been 'friction' between the Robinsons and the inmates of the mental home. But no normal exterior force could have smashed crockery and broken the furniture inside the house. I was then faced with the alternative of suspecting the Robinson family of deliberately destroying the home that had sheltered them for twenty-five years, or attributing the phenomena to a paranormal origin.

I at once acquitted the boy, Peter, of having any guilty knowledge of the disturbances, assuming they were caused normally. In the first place, he was absent when many of the phenomena occurred; secondly, he had not the physical strength to inflict the damage which some of the furniture sustained. And with a house full of people any suspicious action on his part would have been noticed instantly. And on the one occasion when I saw him, he looked thoroughly scared. Though phenomena of the so-called Poltergeist type are often associated with adolescents I am not certain that in the case under review there was any connection between the boy and the manifestations.[1]

More than one visitor to the 'mystery house' has suggested to me that the disturbances were deliberately planned by some of the members of the Eland Road family in order to frighten Robinson *père* out of the house—for what reason is not stated. But that theory will not stand analysis. Though the most violent of the alleged phenomena occurred when Mr. Robinson, senior, was in residence, the manifestations were afterwards so numerous and disturbing that, as we have seen, Mr. Robinson, junior, was suspected of originating them and was subjected to considerable annoyance and personal discomfort after his father had *left* the house. And no family would deliberately smash up their home for the purpose of driving out one of their number, especially when that member is the head of the family and the responsible tenant. And it was *after* Mr. Robinson senior's departure that the remainder of the family were subjected to the distracting attention of the public, police and Press.

The incidents of the gas-lighter, the cherub and the soap are still puzzling me. On the three occasions when I witnessed the movements of the objects I could never be *quite* certain that a normal explanation could not be found for the supposed phenomena.

It must be admitted that the problem presents some very unusual features. The removal of the two members of the household, and the suggestion that the early disturbances were caused by the inmates of the sanatorium at the rear of the house, mark the Battersea mystery as being decidedly out of the ordinary run of such cases. I feel convinced,

[1] But see Mr. F. Robinson's view, p. 238.

though I have no evidence, that the disturbances were started originally by some of the soldiers who were receiving treatment at the private mental home. That the worry and anxiety caused by these disturbances may have reacted on some of the Robinson family seems obvious. Whether this reaction was a normal or extranormal one is, in the absence of further evidence, a matter for speculation. But I consider that the evidence for the abnormality of the occurrences is much stronger than that for the theory that the Robinson family were wholly responsible for the trouble.

In 1941, Mr. Frederick Robinson himself gave the world an account[1] of what happened in Eland Road. What I was not aware of at the time is what he calls the 'most wonderful piece of psychic phenomena anyone could observe, i.e. the dropping of small white slips of paper on the stairs, and about the rooms. This, by the way, never appeared in the Press for some unknown reason. Held up to the light these slips revealed writing as if done with a pin—the messages were sometimes threatening, and sometimes more sober in character. I recall one night after an unusually loud series of rappings seeing a message on a slip of paper come down from nowhere to fall on my bed. Upon elucidation, I read this : "I am having a bad time here. I cannot rest. I was born during the reign of William the Conqueror". The message was signed by the gruesome name of "Tom Blood". Sometimes it was "Jessie Blood".' Those readers who have read the story of the Borley hauntings, will remember that similar messages were found on slips of paper that were found scattered all over the house. And the Borley wall writings are, in many ways, unique.

What supports the theory that Poltergeist phenomena are frequently associated with children or adolescents is the fact that 'these occurrences only took place when my young nephew was in the house. . . . I was an actual witness of the happenings nearly one hundred times, often when the lad was under observation, and at other times when we were sure he was safely in his room upstairs'. Something similar occurred in the famous Epworth Parsonage case, in which the Wesleys were concerned, as the reader is aware. I think we can be sure that Miss Hetty Wesley was the unconscious prime-mover or focus of the manifestations. She was then about nineteen years old. The phenomena would continue even during her slumbers. Her face would be flushed, she would moan and turn over uneasily in her sleep. The Wesley case has certain correspondences with the Battersea affair in that the disturbances were associated with a child or adolescent—as so often happens.

Well, so much for the Battersea Poltergeist. As I said at the beginning of this chapter, the case was very unusual, particularly the intervention of the police and their extraordinary treatment of Mr. Frederick Robinson.

[1] *Two Worlds*, March 14th, 1941.

While I am on the subject of modern London Poltergeists I will
mention a curious case that Professor J. C. Flugel, Dr. C. E. M. Joad
and I investigated in 1935 and 1940. The disturbances were in a house
at Woodside, Wimbledon, and were originally reported to Joad, who
called me in. We visited the place one night and heard the whole story
from the occupants—a professional man and his family, including
some young children.

The usual phenomena had occurred: raps, bangs, sounds as of heavy
furniture being moved, something walking up and down the stairs,
doors opening of their own volition, maidservants being locked in their
rooms (as frequently happened at Borley), etc. Many of these manifestations were experienced when all the inmates were under observation,
and even when the children were away from home.

But we neither heard nor saw anything. The manifestation ceased
suddenly, and, *five years later*, recommenced. Then they again stopped
abruptly. I have heard nothing of this case since 1940.

CHAPTER XXI

'Poltergeist Manor'

Another Scotch Poltergeist case which, if not on all fours with the Ballechin House mystery, at least presents some correspondences with it, is now engaging my attention. The house is in Fifeshire and, like the Ballechin mansion, is a very large one, a family seat with many rooms. It was built about 150 years ago, and a large staff was necessary to run the household, which included a young girl in her 'teens, the daughter of the owner, and another young lady. The family was of the upper middle class, of course educated and cultured. The place became known as 'Poltergeist Manor', on account of the extraordinary occurrences that were witnessed there.

I cannot, at the moment, reveal the exact location of the house because I am hoping to make an extensive investigation of the phenomena after the War, and I sincerely hope that the Poltergeists will not also 'cease hostilities' with the lifting of the black-out ban and our return to normality—and sanity.

The case was first reported to me by a well-known professional man, and what follows is the report I drew up at the time, and which I recorded in my case-book. This was some two or three years ago. Since then, developments have taken place which I will mention in their proper place. Here, then, is my original record:

The gentleman who reported the case to me has himself done some 'investigating' and he sent me a pretty full account of his inquiries. The damage done by the Poltergeist up to the beginning of the War was considerable: more than £100. Furniture, china and bronzes were the chief 'sufferers'. Some of this furniture, that could not be moved normally by two men, slid about of its own volition, and could not be held while in motion. Some old and heavy fire-irons that were constantly rattling and moving about were tied up with string. As they were put back in the fender 'they all leapt apart and there was not one knot in the piece of string.' The witnesses to this phenomena will swear to this on oath.

On another occasion a bronze vase weighing about fifteen pounds went hurtling through the front-door at an incredible speed, and at an angle of ninety degrees shot into the front garden where it came to rest against the garage. Two witnesses vouch for its strange flight.

The phenomena are running true to type as in so many Poltergeist cases. The following incident is reminiscent of what occurred in the Great Amherst Mystery, where a young girl was the focal point of the manifestations. As the daughter of the house went to bed with her sister-in-law, 'the pillow and bolster jumped up and hit her, and the bed lifted and shook violently.' The girls shouted for help. The mother rushed in just as the bedclothes 'floated' off the bed on to the floor. She joined the girls in bed and *her* pillow was switched from under her and a chest of drawers moved into the centre of the room. She jumped out of bed, pushed the chest up to the wall again, and with a pillow in her back, leant against the drawers. Both she and the chest were pushed into the centre of the room.[1] She sent her daughter and daughter-in-law into another room, but queer things happened there too.

On one occasion, in under five minutes, every picture in the drawing-room, hung near a very high ceiling, was taken off the walls and dumped in a heap in the centre of the room. Not one was broken. It would have taken a man twenty minutes at least, and with a step-ladder, to have reached the pictures. In fact, some of the frames were almost impossible to reach, as large articles of furniture would have prevented the use of a ladder at all.

It was impossible to keep water in the bedrooms as the ewers were constantly emptied on to the middle of the beds. On one occasion, when the lady of the house left her boudoir for a few minutes, she found on her return that a heavy Victorian mirror, together with half a dozen pots of face-cream, etc., on it, had completely disappeared. Immediate search revealed that the mirror had been 'transported' to a bedroom below, and the pomade pots suddenly appeared in their original positions. A heavy wardrobe, which it was almost impossible for one man to move, suddenly shifted of its own volition, leant forward at an angle of about forty-five degrees, without striking the ground (thus apparently defying the laws of gravity), recovered itself and restored itself to its original position. This phenomenon was seen and vouched for by two witnesses.

Upon another occasion a chest of drawers, in broad daylight, moved itself across a passage. As some members of the household were struggling to put it back, they saw another chest of drawers, on which were eight valuable china boxes, fall right over. All the ornaments—except one—were smashed to smithereens. This chest of drawers was ten feet away from the nearest person. (Vouched for by three witnesses.)

The professional man who first drew my attention to the case, and who sent me the relevant documents concerning it, described what happened at his first visit. As he entered the house, he was asked to go into the library: 'It was turned upside down, the pictures on the walls turned to their faces, the fire-irons were on the mantelpiece.' All this happened, he was informed, as his car sped up the drive to the house. 'We had tea, and I went back to the library with my host. An ash-tray flicked past my head and struck the wall. I left the room and saw a

[1] All the details I am quoting concerning this case are taken from the signed statements of witnesses, who are prepared to swear on oath that they are true.

bronze pot in mid-air falling from a high wardrobe. A minute later, a tumbler smashed in a corner behind us. . . . After dinner there was a crash and I found our host on the stairs mixed up in a chair and badly shaken. At about midnight I went to bed, after a bath. When drying myself, I heard a bump and came out to find, on the half-landing opposite my bedroom, a large Delft vase smashed to smithereens, though it fell on a soft carpet. It had come from the upper landing. Its companion was standing in the middle of the upper stair. A terrified servant appeared and my hostess and I pacified her. I went to bed. In ten minutes there was a crash. I leapt out of bed in one second and there was a large heavy chair lying outside my door. It had come from

' . . . *a large vase crashed past me and smashed with terrible power.*'

the upper landing. I went to bed again. In a few minutes there was a knock. It was my hostess, who said: 'Come here and look!' I went. All the pictures on the upper stairs with their faces to the wall! We put them back and for the next quarter of an hour we were chasing bronzes and vases which disappeared from one place upstairs, down two flights. As we turned one corner, all the rest of the pictures were found, this time, lying on the stairs. After that we had a quiet night.'

On the next day a friend called in. He had been shooting, and had two pigeons in a game-bag, which he placed in the hall. When he got up to go, the bag had disappeared and was eventually found outside in the area. The report continues: 'I went upstairs to my room when there was a whizz and a crash and a large vase crashed past me and smashed with *terrible* power. In under a second I was round the corner—dead silence. It had come from upstairs above my bedroom. Later, a large bronze was found in the w.c., head down. Later, in the drawing-room, we heard a rumble in the hall, which turned out to be a billiard ball. My hostess said she had hidden a white one and a red one (which had been 'tiresome') in the drive some days before, and had told no one. She went to the place; only the red one was there. The rest of the night was quiet.'

A few days later, seventeen fires broke out in the house, much to the amazement of the police, who investigated. (These conflagrations remind me of those spontaneous outbreaks of fire at Borley Rectory and in the Great Amherst Mystery.) There was some trouble with the insurance company, who were incredulous that ghosts caused the fires, but they eventually paid up.

The fires broke out while my informant was actually in the house. While he was sitting in a heavy antique chair, he was gently deposited on the floor with the chair on top of him. Two minutes later he went back to the chair, which had on its arm an ash-tray with weighted leather flaps to keep it in position. He was quietly reading and smoking. Happening to look up, he was amazed to find that the used matches had come out of the tray and had spaced themselves out at two-inch intervals along the arm of the chair, like a regiment of soldiers! There were only three persons in the house: his host and hostess, and himself. Terrified, the family and staff had gone to live in the cottage on the estate. After the match incident, a hanging lamp outside his bedroom door was struck and swung violently. No one was near it. Large chests that he could not shift with all his strength moved out from the wall, and leant over at an angle of forty-five degrees, with no visible means of support. The dogs in the house were terrified.

It can be imagined that occasionally life becomes so unbearable in the house that the family has to move out periodically in order to get a little peace. Then things quieten down a bit, and they and their staff then return. There is some danger, too, during these 'bad' periods, as members of the family have been repeatedly struck—and injured—by flying missiles. Both Anglican and Roman Catholic priests have tried to exorcise or 'lay' the Poltergeist, without success. When someone was saying prayers for the supposed uneasy spirit, books were hurled at him.[1]

*   *   *   *

Since I compiled the above report, the case has been mentioned in the national and local Press, especially in connection with the claim on

[1] It will be remembered that in the Drummer of Tedworth case, a bedstaff was hurled at the local minister after he had said prayers in Mompesson's house.

the insurance company for damage caused by the spontaneous outbreaks of fires due, it was alleged, to Poltergeist activities. In the *Daily
Telegraph* for April 8, 1942, under the heading 'Mansion Fires
Mystery', it is stated: 'An insurance company has paid £400 for damage
alleged to have been done by a Poltergeist or mischievous spirit. . . . In
a mansion in Fife twenty rooms had been set on fire, furniture had been
heaped in the drawing-room, and ewers of water left in the bedroom
were emptied over the bed immediately the room was vacated. Faced
with a claim for £400 fire damage, the insurance company had investigated the matter. It was certain the fire had not been started by the
occupants, and that it had not been caused accidentally. So the claim
was paid.' A similar report was published in the *Daily Mail* for the
same date, and other national newspapers gave the same very interesting
news.

The fact that insurance companies now recognise the existence of
Poltergeists, and that they can cause material damage, is proof of the
change that is taking place in official circles as regards paranormal
phenomena. If hard-headed insurance men now accept Poltergeist
incendiaries as a 'risk' to be reckoned with, it is proof positive of the
progress that scientific psychical research has made during recent years.
And a possible sequel to the Fife case is that insurance companies will,
in future, insert a 'Poltergeist clause' and disclaim all liability for loss
or injury due to 'occult means'—or they will charge a higher premium
if 'damage caused by paranormal entities' is to be covered. This will be
a triumph for the Poltergeists!

I had hardly begun this chapter when my professional friend wrote
and informed me that certain developments, which I mentioned previously, had occurred since he sent me his preliminary report in 1940.

In the first place, the owner of 'Poltergeist Manor' died soon after
my friend wrote me, and the owner's wife followed him to the grave
twelve months later. The house became vacant and was taken over by
the military authorities. Then the soldiers declared that they had seen
the ghost of the owner both in the house and in the very extensive
grounds. This may, or may not, be true. In this same letter my friend
gives details of some further phenomena that he witnessed, that could
not have been produced normally by any person. The fires were exceptionally interesting. He says: 'The fires were the *weirdest* things. Heaps
of matches were in the rooms. On a bare wall of white enamel in my
bedroom, six feet up, were three large burnt blisters, finger size, and I
cannot think what human instrument could have raised such. I had a
huge Victorian bed with a wide strip of wood at the sides, down to
within an inch of the floor. Well, there was a heart-shaped burn there,
larger than my hand. A blow-lamp might have done it, but no matches
or such-like. In the dining-room, which was very high-ceilinged, the
rolled-up blind was burnt through. I am six feet tall and I had to stand

on a chest to reach up to it! In the bath-room, a footling little hand-towel was burnt, and the flimsy inflammable curtains unharmed. A shovel-full of coals was on the library sofa. All this, for a human, would take time, and there wasn't any time. Then—I forgot to mention it—smoke ‘was seen emerging from a wardrobe, and inside a hat was burning. Wherever X. [a young maidservant] went (*with* the firemen, after they turned up), apparently the fires automatically broke out, and the firemen accused her, and there was, as you can imagine, a terrible rumpus!'

So there we have another version of the old story of a girl adolescent being the unconscious prime-mover in a Poltergeist-infested house; the unwilling *nexus* between the psychical invisibles and their effect upon matter. Well, if the firemen were not satisfied, the insurance people were—at least, they were fifty per cent. satisfied, as I understand that the original claim was for £800. A very expensive Poltergeist! It is only fair to add that many of the phenomena were witnessed when the young girl, mentioned above, was not even on the premises. But there certainly appeared to be some affinity between her and the fires.

I will conclude this brief summary of the Fifeshire manifestations by relating a few more strange incidents, all vouched for by reliable witnesses, that occurred in the mansion.

The owner was lying awake one night. He could not sleep, when suddenly he saw a flame, like that of spirits of wine, on the carpet. He says: 'I got up and flogged it with a pillow. It just moved aside. I put my hand on it and it did not burn, and it then disappeared.' There was no trace of a burn on the carpet. His bed also, he said, jumped up and down and moved about.

The flame phenomenon is curious and was paralleled at Borley. If the reader has perused my *Most Haunted House in England*, he will remember that Mr. S. G. Welles, Rhodes Scholar of University College, Oxford, when investigating at Borley Rectory, was stationed in the dark in the Blue Room when he saw a remarkable luminous phenomenon. In his report he said: 'I became aware of a luminous patch of light on the ceiling, about six inches from the moulding that ran round the top of walls. This luminous patch, perhaps a foot by five inches, moved slowly from its original position, poised there a moment, moved as slowly back, disappeared for an instant, again appeared just where it had been before, and then disappeared a second and last time.' Mr. Welles and his friends tried many experiments in an attempt to reproduce the same effect normally, but they found that this was not possible.

But to return to 'Poltergeist Manor'. On one occasion, when the owner was away, an amateur dramatic society held a rehearsal in the large drawing-room. During an interval, *when no one was in the room*, two pastels fell from the wall. They heard the noise, went to see what it was, left the pictures *in situ*, and returned to their tea—or whatever they were doing. When, later, they resumed their rehearsal, the *pastels had been restored to the walls*. They made the positive statement that no one had entered the room during their absence.

Poltergeists are not usually beneficent and obliging—just the contrary in fact. But there was a bell in the hall at the Manor that occasionally rang of its own volition, and *always* when lunch was ready, and *always* when the owner was out in the grounds somewhere. He used to hear the bell and return to the house. But he was never sure, until his wife informed him, whether the rope had been pulled by a maid or a Poltergeist!

I do not know what the reader's reaction to the 'Poltergeist Manor' will be, but so far as I am concerned there is a *primâ facie* case for serious—and scientific—investigation. Many credible people have signed statements as to what they have seen, and heard. And the sceptic has his work cut out to explain away the very material £400 paid by the insurance company. The case impressed me from the start because of the *first-hand* evidence of my friend, the very hard-headed professional man who is used to solving 'mysteries' and assessing evidence. And I repeat that I am sorry that I cannot, at this juncture, give the exact name and location of the house. The case is *sub judice* and the reader must wait. But perhaps in a future edition of this book I may be able to relate my own experiences in this very strange dwelling north of the Tweed.[1]

[1] In the *American Weekly* for July 12, 1942, is a long account, with many illustrations, of alleged happenings at the Fifeshire manor. The article, 'No Rest in the Mansion', does *not* reveal the exact location of the house.

CHAPTER XXII

Poltergeist Mediums

Actually no such people as Poltergeist mediums are known to investigators, but some psychics do produce phenomena comparable with those witnessed during Poltergeist disturbances. In fact, one girl was known, and is known to this day, as the 'Poltergeist girl' on account of the fact that phenomena, indistinguishable from true Poltergeist movements, occurred spontaneously in her presence.

Of course, many mediums, under good conditions, have been able paranormally to displace objects at séances, usually *when in trance*. The brilliant exception to this general rule was the late Frau Maria Silbert, whom I tested at Graz, Austria, and in London. Maria did *not* go into a trance, and sat usually in a good light—often the ordinary illumination of a well-lit room. But, alas! the phenomena occurred—or at least originated—under a heavy table at which she sat, and which was part of the séance technique. So, if she actually sat in the light, the manifestations occurred in what amounted to darkness. This was unsatisfactory. But with her 'raps' it was different.

Frau Silbert's phenomena consisted of brilliant lights, most of which appeared to come from her finger-tips; innumerable raps, which appeared to emanate from the séance-table, chairs and sometimes from behind the medium; the apparent spontaneous transit of objects from below the séance-table to some point above it, finally resting in the medium's hands; the billowing of the cabinet curtains; the spontaneous engraving of metallic objects (placed under the table for that purpose) with the word 'Nell' (her alleged 'spirit control') and similar manifestations.

There were some good phenomena seen at the London séances with Frau Silbert. My heavy penknife (weight 3½ ounces), which I placed on the floor under centre of the table, was, a few moments later, instantly precipitated into her right hand, which was *above* the table. All this occurred in the ordinary electric lighting of the room. I sat next to her, and helped to control her. The phenomena were impressive and interesting—and very puzzling. I will remark in parentheses that at a later London séance, Clive Maskelyne, of the famous conjuring family, was present in order to discover the *modus operandi* of the 'tricks'. He completely failed.[1] By the way, the spontaneous paranormal displacements of objects at séances given by physical mediums are known as *telekinetic* phenomena—though Poltergeists produce the same effects.

[1] 'Evoe', in *Punch* (Jan. 27, 1926), had some amusing verses about this.

Other movements I saw at this particular London séance included the flight of a small bell, many raps in various parts of the room—and our own raps, of varying number and intensity, were instantly duplicated, at request, on pieces of furniture, etc.

I had often wondered what Maria's phenomena would be like in her own house, if they were so good in a foreign country, and among strangers. The opportunity to visit her home occurred in 1925. I journeyed thither with some friends and in her cosy flat in Waltendorf, a suburb of Graz, we saw more 'miracles'. But curiously, the phenomena were not so impressive as those I had seen in London, notwithstanding the fact that she was in her own home and surrounded by her family. But we saw the spontaneous flight of a number of objects: my own gilt petrol lighter (which was also inscribed with the word 'Nell'), a gold cigarette case, and one of the sitters even risked his gold watch and fob! And the heavy table was levitated and dropped to the floor with a terrific bang. This effect might have been due to trickery. But what was not due to trickery were the magnificent succession of raps that occurred all over the room, in various selected places on the walls and furniture to order, and at command. The raps were almost continuous throughout the séance, which was lighted by a 20-watt electric bulb over the centre of the table.

We held another séance on the following evening (November 4) and similar phenomena occurred. But on this occasion, by calling over the alphabet, the 'entity' rapping at certain letters, we managed to get intelligent messages (in German) that informed us that we were leaving for London on the following morning (a fact known to the medium), etc. All very interesting, but not very enlightening. I paid a second visit to Graz in the summer of 1931 as the guest of Professor Haslinger of Graz University, who arranged a séance with Maria at his flat. The medium was ill but, under a brilliant electric light, she produced raps in profusion all over the room and furniture. Any kind of rap called for was given, at the place requested. Our own raps were imitated and altogether it was a most convincing demonstration of some sort of power that the medium possessed.[1]

Other mediums have produced displacements of objects by paranormal means. The Austrian boys, Willi and Rudi Schneider, have some brilliant examples of 'telekinesis' to their credit. I have tested these lads in Munich, Vienna, Braunau-am-Inn (their birthplace, and that of Hitler) and London, always with the same result—the most convincing telekinetic phenomena, in addition to the most varied manifestations, from materialisations to 'pseudopods'. And they convinced practically every scientist who sat with them.

Miss Stella C., the young English medium, produced 'Poltergeist

---

[1] Frederica Hauffe, the 'Seeress of Prevorst', when in the 'magnetic sleep', could rap at a distance. See *Die Seherin von Prevorst*, by Justinus Kerner, Stuttgart, 1832.

phenomena' under perfect conditions of control, including movements of objects in a locked and sealed cage. And I could name other psychics who have been equally successful. For example, another young woman, Mlle Stanislawa Tomczyk (now Mrs. Everard Feilding), a Polish medium, was tested by Dr. Julien Ochorowicz, in 1908-09 at Wisla, Poland, with positive results. She was controlled by an 'entity' known as 'Little Stasia' which probably emanated from her subconscious mind. It was claimed that she could produce movements of objects at a distance; stop the pendulum of a clock in a glass case (as Anna Rasmussen has been proved to do); control the spinning of a roulette wheel, so that certain numbers turned up more frequently than chance would account for, and similar telekinetic movements. Dr. Ochorowicz concluded that certain rays emanating from her fingers acted as rigid rods.

And, of course, some mediums have been able to *move themselves*! I mean paranormally. Did not D. D. Home on Sunday, December 13, 1868, 'float' out of a third-floor window of Ashley House, Victoria Street, hover in the air for some seconds, and then float back into the same suite of rooms through another window, none the worse for his aerial adventure? It is true that this alleged levitation occurred almost in total darkness. But it was witnessed by some credible (and credulous?) observers, including Lord Adare, afterwards the Earl of Dunraven; the Master of Lindsay, and others. D. D. Home produced many Poltergeist effects, which were ascribed to the spirits. See *The Heydey of a Wizard*, by Jean Burton (New York, 1944). It is a biography of Home.

But the greatest feat, of the Poltergeist order, connected with any medium, was that of Mrs. Samuel Guppy who, in 1871, was instantly precipitated from her home at Highbury to a house in Lamb's Conduit Street, some three miles away, where she came down bump right in the middle of a séance. Of course the whole thing was a swindle; but this modern 'transit of Venus' (who was wearing only her underclothes and weighed seventeen stone) was never proved to be a swindle.

But I am not concerned in this volume with mediums who are levitated, or with those who float over London in deshabille. I am trying to link up the telekinetic or 'displacement' phenomena of some mediums with typical Poltergeist manifestations. And, for my argument, I can cite two outstanding examples with whom I have experimented. They are Anna Rasmussen, a Danish private medium (who has been tested in London), and Eleonore Zugun, a young Rumanian peasant whom I brought to London in 1929. She actually became known as the 'Poltergeist Girl'. It will come as a shock to those uninformed critics who declare that physical phenomena occur only in the dark, to learn that both Anna and Eleonore never sat in the dark, and that their phenomena occurred often in brilliant sunlight or under the glare of 500-watt electric lamps.

249

The 'transit of Venus'. Mrs. Samuel Guppy being 'transported' across London (1871).

I first heard of Anna Rasmussen through my friend Professor Christian Winther of Copenhagen University, who had been experimenting with her for many years. As I had arranged to give a talk at the University during my second Scandinavian lecture tour, the Professor invited me to two séances with Anna. The first was held in one of the University's laboratories, the other in Professor Winther's own home on the outskirts of the Danish capital. This was in June, 1927. Anna was then twenty-nine years old.

At 2.45 p.m. we seated ourselves round the heavy, oblong, plain oak laboratory table, weighing eighty pounds. The sun was streaming through the windows. The sitters, whose chairs were well away from the table, included the Professor, his wife, the medium, her boy friend named Melloni, and another lady. All the sitters joined hands in light contact.

On top of the séance-table was a tabourette or stool, 27½ inches high, of plain wood, with four legs with supporting struts some third of the distance from the bottom. On the under side of the stool-top were screwed two hooks, 90 mm. apart. From these hooks were suspended (by means of threads) two steel balls such as are used for ball-bearings in machinery. The weight of the balls was about one ounce each, though the weights were not identical. They reached nearly to the table-top. To exclude draughts or conscious or unconscious blowing by the medium or sitters, sheets of plate glass were firmly clamped to the four sides of the tabourette—thus forming it into a glass chamber containing two pendulums of dissimilar weights.

Like most mediums, Anna has a 'control' or trance personality named 'Dr. Lasaruz', who appears to direct the proceedings either by raps on the table or tabourette, or by inspiring the medium, who goes into a very light trance, to write automatic messages on pieces of paper, telling us what he wants done, the order of the sitters, etc. By these means, 'he' suggested where we should sit, and stated what phenomena would occur.

Up to this point the psychic had been quite normal; that is, so far as I could judge from the demeanour of a person whom I had met for the first time. But Anna now underwent some subtle change. She did not go into trance or appear sleepy, but her manner altered and she seemed 'different'. Her right wrist began to swell slightly—always a sure sign that she is about to produce some automatic script. Her respiration also grew more rapid. Dr. Winther told me that in a fairly deep trance the respiration rate increases to 244 to the minute.

3.03 p.m. A series of quick raps from the table demanded our attention, and we ascertained by question and answer that I was to change places with Melloni. This was done and I now sat on Anna's right hand, helping Mrs. Winther to control the medium. We now suggested to the 'doctor' that he should try to swing one of the pendulums in the en-

251

closed tabourette. Frau Rasmussen picked up the pencil and in a listless manner (suggestive of the early stages of the trance state) wrote on a piece of paper a message that purported to come from the control. It read: 'I do not know what you mean by "the pendulum." (Signed) Dr. Lasaruz.' At which we all laughed heartily, this being a favourite joke of the 'doctor's.' We then asked the control whether he would swing the right pendulum. Three knocks from the table indicated that he would *not*, at which we expressed our disappointment. Immediately two quick raps from the table informed us that the control had changed his mind and would oblige us—for which we thanked him.

3.14. Anna now picked up the pencil and in *mirror writing* produced a message, signed by 'Lasaruz', to the effect that we should sing. This we did somewhat inharmoniously, and afterwards I suggested to the control that after such an exhibition of our vocal powers he should produce some good phenomena. 'No!' was at once rapped out on the table. Dr. Winther remarked that 'Lasaruz' *would* have his joke! Immediately after, the right pendulum quivered slightly, and in two minutes commenced swinging. About a minute later the left pendulum began to swing, at the same time as the right bobbin was damped down. The right bobbin then increased its arc, and almost—but not quite—touched one of the glass sides. The total swing was about eight inches. For three or four minutes the arc described by the right pendulum (the heavier of the two) never varied, and we sat fascinated by the swing of the steel ball which we imagined *must* hit the glass next time—but which did not actually do so. I remember thinking that Galileo must have been fascinated in a similar manner, when watching that famous swinging lamp in the church at Pisa, whose oscillations are said to have suggested to him the isochronism or 'equal-timeness' of the pendulum.

In nine minutes the right pendulum was tapping regularly on one of the glass sides of the tabourette. It then slackened somewhat, for no apparent reason. Dr. Winther then called out the letters of the alphabet and at certain letters the right bobbin tapped the glass. In this manner we obtained messages and directions. We asked whether conditions were now good, and 'Yes' was given in reply. During the whole of this activity on the part of the right pendulum, its fellow bobbin was swinging very slowly, describing an arc of about half an inch.

3.30 *to* 3.45. For fifteen minutes the right-hand ball was swinging steadily, the left bobbin merely oscillating slightly. Occasionally Professor Winther would request 'Dr. Lasaruz' to damp the right pendulum or to increase its arc. This was always done, very gradually, but the change was at once noticeable. Once it practically ceased moving, and Dr. Winther then asked that the bobbin should be swung at right angles to its previous motion. This was done at once.

In my notes I have a query to the effect whether any magnetic emanation from the medium would affect the balls. But as the emanation would have to be intermittent (in order to allow for the return swing of the balls) and controllable, this theory will not stand much analysis. And any magnetic or electrical emanations would affect both balls equally. This also applies to any secreted powerful electro-magnet that might be employed for moving the balls normally; both or neither of the steel bobbins would react to any extraneous magnetic influence.

4.03. Dr. Winther says: '*Bankibord*', a catch-phrase which means that 'Dr. Lasaruz' is requested to 'bang the table'. This was done two or three times by the control. The following are the verbatim notes that I made of the latter part of the séance:

4.08. Left pendulum swings at request of Dr. Winther.

4.10. Medium complains of headache. This is regarded as a sign of good phenomena.

4.12. Left-hand ball changes course at suggestion of Dr. Winther. Arc: 2½ inches. Right ball stationary.

4.17. Anna now writing (mirror writing). 'Dr. Lasaruz' says, 'Be patient and you will have good phenomena in the evening.'

4.19. Left-hand ball swinging. Arc: 4 inches. Right ball still motionless.

4.23. Arc of left pendulum now extended to 4¾ inches. A lady remarks that she feels very cold. The medium, too, is obviously cold; her hands extremely cold, as I confirm. The hand I am controlling is very cold. Left bobbin now slowing down and almost stationary. We had no means of measuring the temperature, as it was purely a demonstration séance for my benefit. But it certainly felt cooler. Professor Winther has repeated my Rudi Schneider and Stella C. thermometric experiments with Anna Rasmussen and appears to have definitely confirmed the fact—first instrumentally demonstrated by me—that at the moment of telekinetic action the normal rise of the temperature in the medium's immediate vicinity appears to be checked, or that the temperature apparently falls. He is convinced 'that the production of telekinetic energy is accompanied by a drop in the room temperature.'

4.27. Arc made by left pendulum now increased to 5 inches. Right bobbin stationary.

4.30. Swing of left pendulum now 6 inches. The medium's hand which I am holding becomes moist and clammy, but still cold. Left bobbin is being damped rapidly, and becomes quite stationary. Right bobbin now moving.

4.33. Right pendulum swinging steadily. Arc described: 8 inches. Has appearance of being 'pulled.' [This remark in my notes accurately describes the impression I received at the time. It was a *different* swing from that of the left ball—or *appeared* different. It seemed more jerky, with less regular phase. Other sitters noticed it.]

4.34. Right pendulum gradually increases its swing to 9 inches.

4.36. Right ball rapidly increasing its arc, and touches glass. At request it gives twenty-two taps on the glass side of stool; then slows down for half a minute; then strikes four on the glass.

4.41. Right pendulum slowing down. Left pendulum suddenly comes into action.

4.43. Both pendulums swinging. Arcs: Right, 3 inches; left, 5 inches. Both balls swinging very steadily.

4.46. Right pendulum is damped and stops. Left pendulum increases its swing to 8 inches.

4.53. Left pendulum slowing down (to 2-inch arc). Right pendulum again starts swinging. When both balls swinging 2 inches, Dr. Winther asks that their movements be reversed. Without actually coming to rest, both balls then commence to swing at right angles to their previous motions. This continues for some minutes.

5.01. A number of raps on the table attract our attention and we ascertain that 'Dr. Lasaruz' wishes the Professor to bring the pendulums to rest. Dr. Winther removes one of the glass panels and damps the balls.

5.06. Anna Rasmussen picks up pencil and automatically writes 'We have to prepare for this evening, but now this will take too long for now. Goodbye, Dr. Lasaruz.' A series of rapid raps on table denote end of séance. (The message itself appeared very ambiguous, but its meaning was quite clear.) The medium, or her control—or both—required a rest before the evening sitting. I was not then aware of the fact that Frau Rasmussen knew we were having another séance, but it afterwards transpired that she did.

At the next séance a much more elaborate set-up was used. In his own home, Professor Winther was able to make the conditions of the séance, and the control of the medium, even more scientific. The sitters included members of the Professor's family, a Dr. P. Borberg, Melloni, and myself.

The set-up used at the evening séance was a very different proposition from the one we used in Professor Winther's laboratory. As much of the experimental work had been carried out in his own home, Dr. Winther had had constructed a most elaborate form of table, quite vibration-proof, with apparatus for photographically recording the oscillation periods of the pendulums by means of a tiny pencil of light emitted by the special bobbins.

I will not describe in detail this special set-up, beyond saying that it is an oblong, rectangular table, supported on, and bolted to a concrete pillar, the whole clamped to a concrete floor. Firmly fixed to the table-top is a form of tabourette, the lower portion enclosed by red glass, like a dark-room lamp. From the top of the enclosed upper portion of tabourette are hung bobbins of various weights and sizes suspended by means of thin electrical flex, which is connected to pea-lights contained in the bobbins. A tiny lens in each bobbin traces, by means of a pencil of light, its pendulatory motion on to an electrically-rotated strip of bromide paper. When developed, the path of the pendulum is clearly shown on the sensitised emulsion and makes a permanent record. I need only add that in my opinion the table is entirely fraud- and vibration-proof.

I will not detail the phenomena we witnessed that evening, as they were very similar to those we had seen in the afternoon. But they were produced under perfect conditions of control. And the paranormal movements of the bobbins were photographically recorded by means of the pea-lights and travelling bromide strip. Professor Winther has published a very full, illustrated monograph on his experiments, in the *Journal* of the American S.P.R., New York, January-March, 1928.

At supper-time we were entertained to some striking phenomena of true Poltergeist character. At request, 'Dr. Lasaruz' gave us excellent imitations of the sounds made by 'sawing', 'weaving', 'running water', 'bouncing of a ball', etc. Just before nine o'clock, we asked the 'doctor' whether he would bang the underside of the table when the clock struck the hour, keeping time with the strokes. By means of raps somewhere in the table, the doctor said he would. And he did! But he gave only five bangs, synchronising with the last five strikes of the clock, instead of nine.

These supper-table phenomena were very impressive and convincing. They occurred in a brilliant light, and frequently I looked under the table during the progress of the manifestations, and could see the sitters' feet. Their hands were on the table during the whole of the demonstration, which could *not* have been produced normally by any person present.

In Eleonore Zugun we have a girl whose psychic life-story is known almost from her cradle to the present day. This is very unusual in the case of a medium, and her history is a curious one. She was born at Talpa, Rumania, on May 24, 1913. Talpa is a village and her parents are peasants. At the age of twelve she went to live with her grandparents at a village named Buhai. A few days after Eleonore's arrival a shower of stones entered their cottage, smashing several windows. Then in full sunlight a big stone, a piece of porcelain, and half a brick also entered the house, breaking more windows. No one was seen to throw the missiles, which invariably fell at the child's feet. Then observers saw an iron ring fall from a stove and that, too, fell near Eleonore. Then a small mug fell off the dresser—all these phenomena being reminiscent of the Stockwell manifestations. The simple peasants thought that the girl was 'bewitched', or possessed by the Devil, and sent her back home.[1]

Home once more, the Zugun family were having a meal in their kitchen when a stone from outside came crashing through the window

[1] For the early history of Eleonore, and account of the phenomena, see *Der Spuk von Talpa*, by Countess Wassilko, Munich, 1926.

pane. The stone was wet[1] and round—similar to those found in the river Seret, a few yards from their cottage. A priest was called. He marked the stone with a cross, and threw it back into the river. Then he returned to the house. A little later, the *same* stone, recognised by the priest's mark, was flung into the house again.

Then her parents became frightened and sent the child to a neighbour's house. The villagers were more and more convinced that *Dracu*, the Devil, was the cause of all the trouble, especially as the manifestations followed the girl from place to place. They threatened to put her in an asylum. Frightened, the child returned to her parents, and, immediately following her home-coming, large potatoes came from under the bed and fell violently upon her father's shoulders. Her father then resolved to take the child to a priest, and next morning he, together with fourteen other peasants, conducted Eleonore to the old priest of Zamostea, named Macarescu, a bedridden old man of about eighty. Soon after Eleonore had entered his room, an iron vessel, which had before been placed on a stand, suddenly burst into many pieces. Immediately afterwards, an earthen vessel which had been on the hearth, also burst. The splinters were thrown into the court. Scarcely had the people recovered from the shock, when both inner windows broke, and one of the splinters fell into the room. The outside windows remained intact. During these events the old priest, his son, and the school teacher, Teodorescu, were all present. All, startled, ran out of the room. The teacher looking through the window, alone saw a big chest, which stood against the wall, move backwards and forwards, as well as from side to side, of its own volition. Only one young man, Joan Ostafi, had remained in the room. When he saw the chest moving, he stopped it, saying: 'Wait, devil, I see you cannot do it alone, I will help you.' At this very moment, a plank, hidden in a corner, sprang upon the young man and injured him. Then all again entered the room and one of them proposed going on a pilgrimage to St. Johannes at the Convent of Suczava. The name of the saint being pronounced, a stone was thrown against a picture of him that hung on the wall, destroyed the picture, and remained lodged in the wall. Only the teacher was sufficiently courageous to remain in the room. He sat opposite a bench on which was a can of water. Suddenly this can of water was levitated eighteen inches, described a half circle, and came down on the other end of the bench without spilling a single drop of water. The peasants begged the priest to hold a mass, in order to cast out the 'devil' that was supposed to be in possession of Eleonore—as the villagers believed. This ritual was without success, and the pilgrimage was accordingly performed, also without any success; on the contrary, the phenomena grew more and more violent and frequent.

[1] An identical phenomenon heralded the outbreak of hostilities in the 'Mill on the Eden', p. 206.

As the pilgrimage was not successful, the girl was sent to the Convent of Gorovei, near Talpa. The most amazing phenomena happened—or were alleged to happen, at Gorovei. The priests said masses for her; she was exorcised; she was examined by psychiatrists; she was experimented with—and on—and she was hypnotised. But the phenomena still occurred. Then the University of Czernowitz became interested, but failed to do anything. Finally the case got into the Press—as was inevitable.

It was various articles in the *Czernowitzer Morgenblatt* and the *Allegemeine Zeitung* that attracted the notice of my friend, the late

'*A plank . . . . sprang upon the young man and injured him.*'

Fritz Grunewald, the well-known Berlin engineer and psychical researcher. He was interested not only in the girl, but in the controversy that was raging in the Press. Certain papers declared that the whole thing was a swindle; others were convinced that Eleonore was mad; while those newspapers which had investigated for themselves, said the phenomena were genuine. However, the girl *was* declared insane, and was incarcerated in the local asylum—where she was confined, alone, in a dark room—treatment comparable with the witchcraft persecutions of the seventeenth century.

It was at this juncture that Grunewald came on the scene. In the true spirit of investigation, he visited every place where Eleonore had stayed;

interviewed hundreds of people; saw many phenomena for himself; and was convinced that a thorough and scientific investigation was necessary. He persuaded Eleonore's father to withdraw her from the asylum. Having obtained possession of the girl, he returned her to the Convent of Gorovei, where he observed her for three weeks. All the major phenomena were confirmed. He returned to Berlin to make arrangements for the reception of the girl in the family of some friends of his—and then suddenly dropped dead. He lived by himself, and the body lay in the hall of his flat in the Spandauerstrasse for twelve days before it was discovered.[1]

With the death of Grunewald, Eleonore was again left to the tender mercies of the superstitious villagers of Talpa, and the Countess Wassilko-Serecki,[2] a Rumanian lady living in Vienna, decided to rescue her. She, too, was interested in psychical research.

Eleonore arrived in Vienna in September, 1925, and at once puzzled the Austrian scientists, especially the physicists. Her phenomena grew stronger and more spectacular. My friend, Professor Hans Thirring, the distinguished physicist of Vienna University, was especially interested and wrote to me about the girl. I had already received Grunewald's report,[3] so was acquainted with the case. Dr. Thirring invited me to investigate the girl, and arranged for me to give a talk on psychical research at his University.

I arrived in Vienna on April 30, 1926, and began my observational periods next day. I found Eleonore installed in the Countess's charming flat in the Josefstadterstrasse and I at once set about arranging a test. I decided to utilise the Countess's bedroom-study for my experiments. This room was divided longitudinally by a matchboard partition, about six feet high, with an opening at one end for communication between the two divisions. A pair of French windows, leading to a balcony overlooking a quiet wooded garden, provided ample illumination for both study and bedroom.

I have already intimated that the apartment was divided into a study and bedroom and these I minutely examined after I had carefully fastened both doors and windows. A bed, toilet table, chairs, etc. comprised the bedroom furniture; and a low bookcase, filled with books, a couch, a writing table, chairs, etc. were placed in conventional positions in the study portion of the room.

Having completed my examination of the room, I now turned my attention to Eleonore and the Countess who, not without amusement,

[1] Curiously, I had an appointment in Berlin with Grunewald, who was going to write a preface to a German edition of one of my books. I called at his flat early in July, 1925, and because I could get no answer, hammered at his door. I little knew that his body lay a few inches from me, on the other side of the door.

[2] See her 'Early History and Phenomena of Eleonore Zugun', *British Journal of Psychical Research*, Jan.–Feb., 1927.

[3] *Psychische Studien*, Munich, July, 1925.

were watching my precautionary measures. I had already met the Countess on a previous visit to Vienna.

I found Eleonore to be an intelligent, well-developed, bright girl with a sunny disposition. She was then nearly thirteen years old. Though physically strong and healthy, she was 'young' mentally. In many ways, she was more like a girl of eight: her shyness; her extreme fondness for simple toys; her simple games and childish ways. But she could read and write well and was even something of an artist. She was five feet tall and weighed 123 pounds. The Countess and I seated ourselves on the couch and watched Eleonore playing with a toy that fascinated her: a spring gun that projected a celluloid ping-pong ball, which was caught in a sort of conical wire basket that was attached to the gun. Suddenly, as we watched, the ball came to pieces, its component halves falling at our feet. The girl ran to the Countess and asked her to mend it. She jumped up, and so did I. As I watched my hostess examining the join, a steel stiletto with handle, used for opening letters, the whole about ten inches long, shot across the room from *behind* me and fell against the closed door. I instantly turned round and a minute investigation revealed nothing—and no one—that could have projected the stiletto, which was normally kept on the writing table behind us, against the wall farthest from where we stood.

Let me say at once that no one in that room, and certainly not Eleonore, could have thrown the paper-knife. We were at least ten feet from the table; I had both Eleonore and the Countess in full view. Eleonore had one half of the ball in her right hand, and the gun in her left; the Countess had the other half of the ball in *her* hand, and I was actually watching both my hostess and the child; the stiletto came from *behind* and to the right of us, and I was between the missile and the door. It was a brilliant introductory phenomenon.

I will not describe the many other manifestations I witnessed during the days I spent in Vienna, as they have been detailed elsewhere.[1] But the phenomena included the precipitation of a small mirror over the partition *from the bedroom side*, while we three were in the study portion. Then a metal cap followed the mirror. A large black cloth dog, that Eleonore used to cuddle, shot from the study side of the room, over the partition, and fell on to the coal-scuttle near the bed. No one was nearer to the dog (which was lying on a chair near the French windows) than ten feet, and Eleonore, at the moment of the flight, was pushing a table against a wall, using both her hands. Then I saw a cushion on one of the chairs *begin* to move. As I watched, it slid *slowly* off the chair and fell to the floor. No one was near it. After each of these phenomena, and many others, I examined the room, the furniture, etc. but everything was normal. I reiterate that there were no wires, threads, spring releases, rubber bands, compressed air tubes, springs released by the

---

[1] *Leaves from a Psychist's Case-Book*, by Harry Price, London, 1933.

gradual expansion of a viscous substance, or similar contrivances: things difficult to hide and easy to find in this sunlit room. We also witnessed another type of phenomenon—stigmata—but a description of these I am leaving for another chapter.

Well, I was much impressed with what I had seen. So impressed in fact, that I decided to import both the 'Poltergeist girl' and her bene-factress—and, I hoped, the phenomena—to London in an attempt to witness again the wonders I had seen in Vienna. The girl and the Countess accepted my invitation with joy.

Countess Wassilko and Eleonore arrived in London on September 30, 1926. A number of phenomena, I was told, had been witnessed on the long journey from Vienna. They were delighted to be in London. Eleonore looked even more robust than when I saw her in the previous spring; and, although she was now turned thirteen years of age, there was no sign of the menses.

The first alleged phenomenon that occurred was that a silver finger-ring, suddenly missed from Eleonore's dressing-table on the first night of their arrival, tumbled from nowhere as the girl was playing with a Cairn terrier that used to visit my Kensington laboratory.

Soon after the ring incident, two or three Press representatives came to see me. One of them, Mr. E. Clephan Palmer, had brought Eleonore a large package of toys, including a wonderful clockwork black cat, with eyes that spat fire, if not brimstone; a fit plaything for *Dracu*. It was a pleasure to watch the child's face as she undid the parcel. When she came to the clockwork toy her eyes sparkled almost as much as the cat's. She at once wound up the cat and placed it on the floor. We were all watching with amusement the glee with which she was handling the toy, and were interested to see how the thing would work. Eleonore wound it up, stooped down, and placed the cat on the floor—at the same instant as something fell upon her head and dropped to the floor. I immediately picked up the object and saw that it was an L-shaped piece of metal (size 14 × 11·5 mm., weight 24 grains), enamelled white. I at once thought it was a part of one of the toys which Mr. Palmer had brought for the girl, but upon closer inspection it was quite obvious that the object was a small metallic sign such as is used for affixing to notice-boards. I then remembered that I had seen a notice-board in the hall on the ground floor on which were a number of similar letters which are magnetic, thus easily attaching themselves to the metal sur-face of the board. We naturally thought that the L had come from the board and that its absence would at once be noticed. We accordingly rang through by means of the house 'phone in order to confirm our assumption. To our astonishment, the young lady typist informed us from the library that every letter on the notice-board was in its allotted position and none was missing. We then descended the four flights separating the laboratory from the library in order to investigate. We found every letter in its place on the notice-board and asked to see the remaining stock, if any. It appears that six specimens of each letter were supplied with the set sold with the notice-board, which had arrived only the previous, day. Upon checking the unused letters, we found that one was missing—the letter L. Only three persons in existence knew where the unused letters were kept. One of these was out, and the other two—the typist and a youth employed in the library— were actually in the room (the library), when the letter appeared in the laboratory. The unused letters were in the box secured by two fasteners, and kept in a closed cupboard. It was proved absolutely that no one in the Laboratory suite had entered the library for days—the Countess and Eleonore have never been in to this day—and the notice- board and sets of letters had not been in the building twenty-four hours. The Countess was not in the building at the time. Mr. Palmer in his report[1] stated that he saw the letter drop from the ceiling, falling upon my shoulder, and then to the ground. I distinctly saw the letter strike the girl's head and then fall upon the floor. Not being under stringent test conditions, we are not hailing the L incident as a phenomenon. On the other hand, there is not the slightest evidence that anyone was cheating; nor have we yet discovered how it was possible for a person to abstract the letter from the fastened box and closed cupboard in view of the fact that three persons only knew where the letters were kept. None of these was connected with the Laboratory. It has been suggested that because the letter is magnetic it might have had some affinity for the girl, but I think this theory is fantastic. The fact remains, though, that these magnetic letters played a major rôle in the mani- festations which occurred during the girl's visit. But how the L found its way from the library to the laboratory—a distance of forty-eight feet—is still a mystery.

Tuesday, October 5. I was not at the Laboratory during the morning of this day, but arrived at about 1.45 p.m. I made my way to the Labora- tory suite on the top floor and found that my secretary had not returned from lunch and Eleonore had not yet arrived. I unlocked the various rooms comprising the suite, opened the doors, and sat down in the office to do some writing. At 2.15 Eleonore appeared and I rose to greet her. She took off her hat, etc. and placed them in the room where coats were kept. The door, leading to séance-room, was locked. Eleonore picked up her clockwork cat and—because there was more room for it to run without meeting obstacles—went into the passage to play with her toy. She did *not* enter the séance room. As I had risen from my chair, I thought I would prepare the séance-room in readiness for the after- noon observational period. Dr. R. J. Tillyard (who had recently re- turned from the Continent) had a number (thirteen) of Danish, French and other coins, of low values, which he had marked and had placed about the room. It was these coins that I went to check and place in their prescribed positions. Four of the coins I placed on the ultra-violet ray cabinet, spaced evenly, five inches apart. The one on the extreme right was a Danish copper 1-øre piece. On the lintel of the door leading to cloak-room, I placed four more coins, about six inches apart. The third coin from the left was a brass 1-franc piece. I placed other coins in various positions or checked those that were already there. I then returned to my writing in the office. During this checking of the coins Eleonore was playing with her cat in the passage, the whole length of which I could see through the open office door. At exactly 2.30 I heard a coin drop in the séance-room. I looked at Eleonore, who also looked up at the same time. She said '*Dracu!*' I rose from my seat, and with Eleonore (who waited for me) entered the séance-room. I at once looked at the coins which I had so recently checked and arranged, and found that the 1-øre piece from the right of row on ultra-violet cabinet, was missing. The others on the lintel of the door had not been touched. After about two minutes Eleonore found the coin not far from the curtained 'cabinet' across corner of room near window. As a matter of fact, we saw the coin simultaneously. While she was stooping down to pick up the Danish 1-øre piece, and I was watching her, the French franc—which two minutes previously I had seen firmly in position on the wide lintel of the door, fell from its place and was discovered to right of gramophone cabinet. It must have rolled—at least, that would be the normal explanation—but I did not hear it roll; I heard merely the sound of the coin (weight, twenty-seven grains) falling. No other person was on the Laboratory floor—no one was nearer than the ground floor, four stories below.

The fall of the franc was a true Poltergeist phenomenon. It would have remained on that lintel (6 feet, 10¾ inches from the ground, and 3 feet wide) for a thousand years without falling. Nothing but an earthquake would have shifted it unless it was removed normally or—as I am convinced was the case—paranormally. The diameter of coin was 23 mm., the depth of lintel was 24 mm., and all coins were purposely placed hard up against the wall so that if they *did* fall there would be no ambiguity about the matter. I am as convinced of the reality of this particular phenomenon as I am of the fact that I am breathing. At one moment the coin was securely resting on the lintel, and two minutes later it was flicked to the right of the gramophone (a distance of 5 feet 9 inches), with no one nearer to it than thirteen feet. Here we have a characteristic example of a so-called Poltergeist displacement or telekinetic movement witnessed under ideal conditions. True, it was only a small and light article that was displaced; but the conditions under which the displacement occurred make it an exceptionally brilliant phenomenon. But, unlike some psychic phenomena which can be induced more or less at will, Poltergeist manifestations are of such a sporadic and spontaneous nature that their repetition at a given time and place becomes impossible. The fall of the franc was the first telekinetic phenomenon of Eleonore's witnessed at the Laboratory, concerning which I was absolutely satisfied. The falling of the coin off a ledge may be a simple movement, but for this movement to take place automatically by mechanical means would require fairly elaborate apparatus which could not be rendered invisible.

I could fill many pages with accounts of the phenomena we witnessed, under scientific conditions, during Eleonore's stay in London.[1] Her visit caused the greatest interest among scientists and others who attended many of the observational periods, and those whom I invited included: Dr. R. J. Tillyard, F.R.S., Mr. W. R. Bousfield, F.R.S., Mr. Edward Heron-Allen, F.R.S., Professor William McDougall, F.R.S., Professor Hans Thirring (who travelled specially from Vienna in order to see our experiments), the Hon. Everard Feilding, Professor A. O. Rankine, F.R.S., Dr. Theo. B. Hyslop, late chief of Bethlehem Hospital, the London mental asylum, and many more.

If the 'Poltergeist' phenomena were interesting, her stigmata were equally puzzling, and they deserve a chapter to themselves. Eleonore had an *idée fixe* that *Dracu*—the Rumanian Devil—used to bite and otherwise maltreat her—an obsession that we tried to eradicate, without success. The painful weals, teethmarks and scarifyings that she experienced were more than a match for our logic.

[1] For a full account, with illustrations and plans, see *Proceedings of the Nat. Lab. of Psy. Research*, Vol. I, Part 1, London, Jan. 1927.

CHAPTER XXIII

Poltergeists that Bite

I have not yet been able to make up my mind which of the two classes of Eleonore's phenomena, the telekinetic or stigmatic, were the more convincing.

The stigmatic marks and abrasions which spontaneously appeared on various portions of Eleonore's body were, as I have remarked, the most interesting of the phenomena said to occur with this medium. I saw several of them during the periods I kept the girl under observation. The marks were of several varieties, including teeth-marks, long scratches, oval, annular, elliptical, and other marks of varying shapes. The teeth-marks, it must be admitted, were similar to those made by Eleonore's own teeth; and tests carried out proved that if Eleonore bit her own arm, identical impressions to those alleged to be abnormal were found, except that the number of teeth indentations varied. But no one saw Eleonore play tricks of this description, although she was kept under observation for days by different investigators. Teeth-marks were never found on any part of her body not accessible to the medium's mouth; they invariably appeared on her arms or hands. This applied also to the scratches and other markings which appeared on her chest, arms, wrists and hands. But she was never caught making these marks, some of which must have been exceedingly painful. The marks were always sore afterwards. And pins and needles in her proximity would suddenly appear in her flesh.

A peculiarity about the markings—both abnormal and normal—was the rapidity with which the resultant weals arose, and the whiteness and the thickness of the ridges forming the weal. This I have witnessed over and over again. Eleonore would perhaps be playing with a ball when suddenly she would give a sharp cry of pain and immediately come over to us and allow us to roll up her sleeve or uncover her chest, when the progress of the phenomenon could be witnessed. The teeth-marks were at first visible as red indentations on a white ground—the white surround gradually becoming red at the same time as the indentations became white, rising in a thick ridge above the level of the flesh. The ridge became quite white in the course of a few minutes, and rapidly disappeared. Indentations and teeth-marks made in the fleshy part of Eleonore's hand in a normal manner acted in exactly the same way. Scratches and other marks of alleged abnormal origin produced thick white weals in the course of a few minutes, afterwards rapidly disappearing.

During my investigation of the girl in Vienna, in May 1926, and later in London, as related in the last chapter, these stigmatic markings occurred very frequently. At Vienna during the first few minutes of my preliminary observational period, Eleonore gave a short, sharp cry of pain and Countess Wassilko at once pulled up the left sleeve of the child's bodice, and on the fleshy part of the forearm, some distance above the wrist, were the deep indentations of teeth-marks, six above and five below, forming together an elliptical figure. If the reader will bite the fleshy part of his own arm, he will get an exact representation of what we saw. The length of the ellipse was 40 mm., the width 20 mm. If the marks were produced by an actual mouth, the width of the ellipse would depend obviously on how much flesh was gripped by the teeth. Though the markings *could* have been made by the girl herself, I did not see any suspicous move on the part of Eleonore. In London we proved that at least some of the stigmata could not have been produced normally.

Well, during the first stigmatic phenomenon I watched the indentations on her arm gradually 'fill up', turn red, then white, and finally rise above the surface of the flesh in the form of weals. I examined the sleeve of her bodice for marks of saliva, because if the girl had bitten her own arm, she must have done it through her sleeve. But there was no sign of moisture. The weals became gradually less distinct. Eleonore was convinced that '*Dracu*', her 'devil', had *bitten* her.

Later during the same afternoon, Eleonore gave another cry of pain, and upon examination we again found another set of teeth-marks on the girl's arm, quite near the previous bite. Four indentations formed the upper portion of the ellipse, and five the lower. The bite was the same size as the previous one. The girl was standing by my side during the appearance of the weals, and there was no suspicious movement on her part.

About ten minutes later, Eleonore gave another cry of pain and pointed to her chest. The Countess at once untied the ribbon that fastened her frock and pulled down her camisole. Between her breasts, and extending a little on to her left breast, were seven scratches in two series of four and three, in the form of a criss-cross. The scratches averaged between six and seven inches in length. As we watched them they gradually turned red, then white, and in a minute or so became hard, white weals. It might have been possible for the girl to have made the scratches herself, especially as she had just left the room for a moment. But her cry of pain was so real, and the condition of the abrasions appeared so fresh, that the theory of self-infliction becomes less tenable. Also, the girl could hardly have had time to undo her frock, make the scratches, and adjust her clothing again. That the scratches had appeared only at the moment of the girl's cry was quite evident from the rapid way they changed before our eyes into the usual hard, white weals.

Eleonore did her best to propitiate '*Dracu*' by leaving tit-bits of food about the room for him: pieces of cake, an extra large nut, or some other dainty. The girl declared that these peace-offerings prevented the 'devil' from injuring her still more. It appeared that '*Dracu*' was particularly fond of chocolates, and she often put one on the bookcase for him. This she did during my presence, with interesting results. She had hardly placed the sweetmeat when she gave another cry of pain, and upon examination of her left arm it was found that an annular marking about the size and shape of a chocolate, 20 mm. in diameter, was deeply indented in the fleshy portion, superimposed on some of the earlier teethmarks that were still faintly visible. The circular indentation developed with the usual characteristics into a round, white weal.[1]

That the stigmata were associated with some mental process, was proved by the fact that, after every phenomenon, telekinetic or stigmatic, the girl's pulse-rate increased. Her normal rate was 75 beats to the minute. Immediately after a phenomenon it rose to 95 beats. But there was no other indication of the girl's reaction except an occasional slight trembling. She appeared perfectly normal after each bite or scratch.

During my stay in Vienna, I saw scores of these stigmatic markings. All were spontaneous and there were many variations of size and design. One mark was in the form of a pair of nutcrackers. I could not help wondering if '*Dracu*', whether a real entity or a subconscious creation of Eleonore's, would survive the journey to London and the cold light of scientific investigation. As the reader knows, the telekinetic phenomena we witnessed at my laboratory were good. The stigmata were not only good, but even more convincing than those I had witnessed in Vienna, as they occurred under much better conditions of control.

I was not in London during Eleonore's first day at the laboratory, but my secretary recorded some stigmatic markings under control conditions that absolutely precluded self-infliction. A representative of the *Morning Post* was also present a day or two later and in his report that appeared on the next publishing day[2] he said:

'An example of the stigmatic manifestation occurred yesterday morning in my presence. Soon after I entered the room a mark was noticed rapidly growing on the girl's arm. As I watched it it grew into a number of cruel-looking weals which might have been inflicted by a whip or a thin cane. I am satisfied that neither the girl nor anyone else could have inflicted any such blow. Within a few minutes the marks had disappeared. Some minutes later, while I was helping Eleonore to wind up a clockwork cat, of which she is inordinately fond, I myself saw similar weals beginning to appear on her other arm and at the back of her neck.

---

[1] In the *Blätter aus Prevorst*, Vol. V, pp. 171 ff., is an account of a Poltergeist in the house of Prof. Schupart, whose wife was 'bitten, pinched, and knocked down' by the entity.

[2] *Morning Post*, October 4, 1926.

Nobody but myself was near her at the time and both her own hands were fully occupied with the toy.'

On the following day there was another observational period and one of our members, Captain Neil Gow, and the representative of the *Daily News*, Mr. E. Clephan Palmer, were present. Captain Gow reported:

3.20 p.m. Eleonore cried out. Showed marks on back of left hand like teeth-marks which afterwards developed into deep weals. I got Eleonore to bite her right hand and noted the kind of marks caused by this bite, but could trace no similarity between this and the first alleged stigmata.

3.25. Eleonore gave a soft cry and pointed to her right wrist. She undid the sleeve of her blouse and rolled it up. I saw some freshly made red marks like scratches. There were several of these, about five inches long. After a few minutes they rose up into heavy white weals.

4.12. Eleonore was just raising a cup of tea to her lips, but suddenly gave a cry and put the cup down hastily; there was a mark on her right hand similar to those caused by a bite. Both rows of teeth were indicated.

4.15. Eleonore again raising cup of tea to her lips when she gave a cry. There immediately appeared three long weals extending from the centre of her forehead right down the right cheek. Each was about ten inches long. Eleonore gave every sign of pain. I can state that for several minutes her hands had not been near her head or face.

Mr. Palmer's report[1] on the same phenomena states:

'It may be only coincidence but, at any rate, it happened yesterday that these phenomena came thick and fast only when I turned up with another offering in the form of a toy. We were having tea in the laboratory and Eleonore was in the act of raising her cup to her lips when she suddenly gave a little cry of pain, put down her cup and rolled up her sleeve. On her forearm I then saw what appeared to be the marks of teeth indented deeply in the flesh, as if she or someone else had fiercely bitten her arm. The marks turned from red to white and finally took the form of white raised weals. They gradually faded, but were still noticeable after an hour or so.

'While Eleonore was sitting in her chair under full observation similar markings appeared every few minutes. Once she jumped in her chair and pointed to the side of her face as if she had felt an acute pain there. On immediately examining her face I found two long parallel marks, like superficial scratches, extending from the top of her forehead down to her chin. As I watched they developed into prominent raised white weals and were quite a nasty disfigurement. For about twenty minutes the markings continued to appear more or less severely in various places. The whole time the girl appeared very uncomfortable and resentful of what she considers the attentions of '*Dracu*' or the Devil. Although I

[1] *Daily News*, October 5, 1926.

kept a close eye on her I failed to detect any self-infliction of the marks. The laboratory was brilliantly lit and I was at liberty to go as near Eleonore as I liked.'

The next day a group of our members met at the laboratory in order to keep Eleonore under observation. They included Captain H. W. Seton-Karr, the big-game hunter; Colonel W. W. Hardwick, Mr. Robert Blair, and others. The markings appeared spontaneously and quickly, covering the girl's face and forehead, arms and wrist. Mr. Clephan Palmer was also present and his report duly appeared :[1]

'Eleonore was sitting at the table tying up in its box the toy I had given her the day before, when she suddenly winced violently as if in acute pain. On looking at her face we found long scratches which gradually developed into white weals. A few minutes later, when she was standing near the window in a corner of the laboratory to be photographed, she winced again, and pointed to her arm. What looked like teeth-marks, including two that seemed like attempts at the letters 'B' and 'O', also appeared. *Within fifteen minutes Eleonore looked indeed as if she had been tatooed all over her face and arms.* All the keen observers present agreed that there was no sign of trickery. Captain Seton-Karr and Mr. Robert Blair, entirely independent inquirers, both insisted that they had Eleonore under the closest observation, and were satisfied that she did not cause the marks by her own physical action. It must be remembered that these stigmatic phenomena occurred in full daylight. There is no question, as in some other psychic investigations, of any difficulty of observation owing to darkness or a dim red light.'

Colonel W. W. Hardwick, in his report on the same phenomena, said:

'At 5.40, after tea, Eleonore was tying up a box, when she gave a gasp and moved her right hand towards her left wrist—distinct teeth-marks appeared on her wrist, then scores like scratches appeared on her right forearm, cheeks and forehead. Shortly after, a series of marks like some form of letters appeared on her left forearm, all rising to distinct white inflammatory swellings within three or four minutes, fading slowly. The girl was under close observation, and could not have produced these herself by any normal means.'[2]

Captain Seton-Karr wrote me under date October 18, 1926:

'I was present on October 5 when the so-called "stigmatic" markings appeared on the face, arms, and forehead of Eleonore Zugun under conditions which absolutely precluded the possibility of Eleonore producing them by scratching or other normal means. The marks were photographed in my presence.

(*Signed*) 'H. W. SETON-KARR.'

[1] *Daily News*, October 6, 1926.
[2] In the Phelps Poltergeist case (1851–52) one of the girls concerned was pinched paranormally.

EXPERIMENTS IN HYPNOSIS

Thursday, October 7. Eleonore was kept under strict observation from 10.30 in the morning. At 2.45 a long weal, extending from left ear to mouth, slowly developed. I at once photographed the girl. Later in the afternoon the following members of the Council of the National Laboratory of Psychical Research and others assembled to keep the girl under observation: Dr. R. J. Tillyard, F.R.S., Dr. R. Fielding-Ould, Dr. A. L. Urquhart, Colonel W. W. Hardwick, Mr. W. R. Bousfield, K.C., F.R.S., and myself. Among the visitors were Professor William McDougall, F.R.S., of Harvard University, and Dr. Theo. B. Hyslop, late Chief of Bethlehem Hospital, the London mental asylum. Dr. Hyslop examined the girl and scratched her forearm on one of the spots on which the stigmata often appear. The resultant weal was indistinguishable from those arising spontaneously. Soon after, at 4.46, two weals appeared simultaneously on her right arm, and later two small ones on the left cheek.

In Vienna Countess Wassilko frequently hypnotised the girl, and suggested to her that certain marks—usually letters—should appear on various parts of the arms. These experiments were often successful. It was decided among the medical members of our Council that this afternoon, the events of which I am relating, would be propitious for some similar experiments. Eleonore was accordingly placed on the special settee designed for the purpose, and the Countess then endeavoured to put her into a hypnotic sleep. It is doubtful if the girl went under complete control; I think the presence of so many strangers somewhat excited her. While she was under this partial control the Countess suggested that the letter 'G' should appear on her right forearm ten minutes after she 'awoke'. Some faint marks appeared after a few minutes, but it required some imagination to construe them into the suggested letter.

After the Countess's experiment Professor McDougall stated that he would like to try his skill in hypnotising the girl—who thoroughly entered into the spirit of the experiment. So Eleonore was once more placed on the settee, and for about fifteen minutes Professor McDougall exercised his skill in putting the child to sleep. Eleonore became very drowsy, but did not completely succumb to the Professor's efforts to put her into the trance state. He 'suggested' that five minutes after she became normal the letter 'B' should appear on her arm, but no signs of a letter were visible at the prescribed period. Professor McDougall stated that Eleonore was a very difficult subject and that it would require a considerable number of experiments to make her quickly react to his influence. These experiments in post-hypnosis were interesting, but not very successful.

Various theories have been formulated to account for Eleonore's spontaneous stigmata. Though many saints and ecstatics have been subject to stigmata, I believe that Eleonore is the only *medium* who has produced such phenomena. There can be little doubt that the infliction is a psychological one, and must not be confused with urticaria, a disease of the skin characterised by evanescent rounded elevations resembling weals raised by a whip, attended by intense itching when the skin is knocked or rubbed. Eleonore's stigmata did not itch. And in urticarial subjects, the weals do not appear spontaneously, as in the case of Eleonore's markings. There is a curious belief that those who suffer from urticaria have a layer of skin too few!

As for the psychological theory, Mr. G. E. Browne, the scientist and student of psychic phenomena, wrote me during Eleonore's visit, and his remarks deserve some attention. He said:

'All physical phenomena, if caused by, worked through, or bound up with a human being as medium, have a psychological foundation, or perhaps it is better to say a *nexus*. This is admitted by all writers. Now in Poltergeist cases (with few exceptions) and in *all* stigmatisation cases, there is hysteria at the base: not advanced or pathological hysteria, but a decided thinning of the crust or division between the thinking mind and the underlying dreaming mind. (Supraliminal and subliminal or hypnotic stratum.) "All mediumship", said Janet,[1] "is dislocation." Students of the mental side have been struck by the repeated emergence of an habitual control showing the intelligence of a child—usually a girl, undeveloped, whimsical, tricky, full of mischief and energy; in large measure uncontrollable and reckless of consequences. . . . Saints dream God and His wounds, and the dream mind in ecstasy (self-induced hypnosis) produces the wounds. Another type of secondary adopts the child's conception of a devil, and uses it to spite the primary by marking its face with scratches, and its arms with bites. Naturally there is no biting on the back or face; *it can't imagine it*, but you suggest it under hypnosis and it is most probable that it would be done. It bites when it is particularly displeased with its primary, waiting until in a moment of distraction it can get command of the body and its functioning (vascular). It bites *when it is bored*. I will engage that when Eleonore Zugun is kept amused there is no biting, no scratching; for then the secondary is also amused, which it loves most of all. Similarly, when the secondary enjoys the play of the primary, *especially motion of any kind*, ballplaying, running about, motion games—then you may look for objects being thrown about and perhaps even more elaborate telekinesis.'

Mr. Browne (who did not see Eleonore during her visit) was quite correct in his hypothesis that the telekinetic phenomena occurred more frequently when the girl was in motion; also, that the 'stigmata' appeared usually when the girl was quiescent. My own experiences with the girl fully confirm this theory.

What had happened to Eleonore was this: during her early childhood,

[1] The famous French psychologist.—H.P.

270

when the Poltergeist phenomena became first apparent, the simple peasants of Talpa threatened her so often with '*Dracu*', and what he would do to her, that her subconscious mind had become obsessed with the idea of whippings, bitings, etc., which would be inflicted upon her by '*Dracu*'. We tried to eliminate the '*Dracu*' complex, without success. What apparently happened was that the stigmata were the outward and visible signs of influences that radiated from the higher nervous centres as reflex responses to external stimuli. What these stimuli were we never discovered. We did not have the girl long enough to make the necessary

'Eleonore's subconscious mind had become obsessed with 'Dracu'.'

experiments. But the stigmata—and all her phenomena—ceased very abruptly, as the reader will learn in the next chapter.

But we did have the girl with us long enough to prove scientifically that (*a*) the stigmata were genuine; (*b*) they were spontaneous; (*c*) they were not self-inflicted. The Press representatives also proved these things for themselves. In a leading article headed 'The Poltergeist' in the *Daily News* (for October 12, 1926) the writer said:

'If there is one thing about the Poltergeist girl that is beyond dispute it is the fact that she is responsible in some way for uncanny manifestations. Things are wafted away in her presence, she is bitten by unseen teeth, her face becomes scarred and disfigured, stilettos fly across her room. The suggestion that she is possessed of evil spirits is unsatisfactory, and certainly unscientific. The temptation to believe that these phenomena are produced by trickery is obvious. Yet it must be remembered that these 'stigmata' have appeared not in a darkened room before the credulous, but in a laboratory of psychical research in South Kensington, before men expert in tracing every form of conscious deception or complex hysteria. The genuine character both of the markings on her flesh and the movements of the articles in her room have survived the most searching tests. . . . Altogether the eccentricities of the Poltergeist girl have provided one of the most bewildering problems, both psychical and psychological, of this generation.'

Another leader writer said,[1] in discussing Eleonore's telekinetic phenomena: 'The same difficulty [explaining the phenomena] occurs in the attempt to discover by what means the coins were moved in the recent experiments conducted in the National Laboratory of Psychical Research . . . Was the force employed drawn from the medium? Or was it external to her? Or was it an external force acting upon the medium? No one knows. Nor does anyone know the nature of the force we call electricity, whose utilisation in wireless telegraphy has prepared the minds of men to believe that to be possible which has hitherto been inconceivable.'

It is difficult to estimate which were the more interesting phenomena, the telekinetic or stigmatic. For centuries visionaries and ecstatics have been—as they imagine—singled out by the Almighty as worthy of bearing replicas of Christ's wounds in the form of the stigma of the crown of thorns or the nails. I believe that up to the year 1894, no fewer than 321 saints received these peculiar marks of God's favour. The first good case is that of St. Francis of Assisi; the latest, Padre Pio of Foggia, who is still living.

One of the most, if not the most, interesting cases of what I will call ecstatic stigmatisation occurring in modern times is that of Louise Lateau (1850–83) a Belgian peasant, who, like Eleonore, attained notoriety (1868) on account of her presenting the appearance at periodic intervals of stigmata, or marks on the skin similar to those on the body of our Lord—a condition known to physiologists as 'stigmatic neuropathy'. Periodic bleeding of the stigmata every Friday was a feature of Louise's case, which is worth studying.[2] The case was verified by the Belgian Academy of Medicine.

An interesting case was also reported[3] by Fr. Herbert Thurston, S.J.

The purely pathological cases of stigmatization which undoubtedly are due to a form of hysteria are as interesting as those recorded above.

[1] *Morning Post*, October 20, 1926.

[2] See Dr. Warlomont's *Rapport médical sur la Stigmatisée*, 1875; E. Lefébure's *Louise Lateau—A Medical Study* (trans.); *Macmillan's Magazine*, Vol. XXIII, 1871, pp. 488 ff; *Dublin Review*, 1871, p. 170.

[3] *Proceedings*, *S.P.R.*, Vol. XXXII, 1922.

Well-known cases include the production of cruciform marks by suggestion,[1] and the case of 'Ilma S.'[2] (1888) in which blisters, red patches, burns, etc., were produced by suggestion. Then we have the experiments of Dr. Pierre Janet who produced red marks by means of imaginary mustard plasters.[3] Experiments have shown that in some subjects red marks could be produced by suggesting that drops of water were burning sealing wax. Dr. J. Rybolkin produced blisters on a subject by 'burning' at an unlighted stove[4] and many other cases have been recorded where the potent power of suggestion on suitable subjects has been responsible for hemorrhage, bleeding stigmata, etc. Most large hospitals have investigated cases of alleged stigmatisation. Within the limits of this chapter I have been unable to do more than touch the fringe of this fascinating subject.

[1] Three cases. Dr. Biggs of Lima. *Journal, S.P.R.*, Vol. III, page 100.
[2] Dr. R. von Krafft-Ebing, *An Experimental Study in Hypnosis*, London, 1889.
[3] See l'*Automatisme Psychologique*, Paris, 1889, p. 166.
[4] *Revue de l'Hypnotisme*, Paris, June, 1890.

CHAPTER XXIV

Dr. Tillyard's Poltergeist

Before I dismiss Eleonore Zugun from these pages, I must relate an incident so startling and dramatic that it deserves a chapter to itself.

In my account of 'Poltergeist Mediums' I have told how a metallic and magnetic letter 'L' disappeared from a closed and fastened box on the ground floor of our laboratory premises, traversed four flights of stairs and, apparently, fell from the ceiling of the top floor on to Eleonore's head as she was playing with a fire-spitting mechanical cat. This was on October 1, 1926.

On October 11, I requested the staff responsible for looking after these letters to check their stock again, report to me and then lock the remainder up. This was done, after it had been discovered that the letters 'C' and 'W' were missing. A search was made for them, without success. The 'W' has never been seen since, but the 'C' returned in an amazing manner. These magnetic letters played a major rôle during Eleonore's visit.

The evidence for this story was supplied solely by Dr. R. J. Tillyard, though some of the minor details could be confirmed by Dr. Julian Huxley. Dr. Tillyard, now dead,[1] was a distinguished scientist. He was a Fellow of the Royal Society and chief entomologist to the Australian Government.

Eleonore and the Countess were returning home on Sunday, October 24, 1926, according to our agreement. I said goodbye to them on the Thursday, October 21, and did not see them again. I was not in London on the Friday, October 22. But what happened on that day was related to me by Dr. Tillyard, whom I saw during the following week. He, too, was due to leave England in a few days. Here, then, is an account of the doctor's adventures as he told them to me.

On Friday morning, October 22, Dr. Tillyard searched his coat pocket, where he *always* kept his penknife, which was contained in a leather case with a snap fastener. In the afternoon he again brought out his knife, still in its case. About 8.45 p.m. on the same day he once more brought out his knife to cut the pages of a book and to his amazement *found the metallic magnetic letter 'C' tightly threaded on the metal rim of his knife-case and firmly sealing it*! Dr. Tillyard fully recorded this extraordinary incident and drew a sketch (reproduced) of the metal letter and knife-case exactly as he found it.

[1] Dr. Tillyard was killed on Jan. 13, 1937. The manner of his death was exactly foretold on July 7, 1928, by Mlle Jeanne Laplace, and published at the time. See my *Search for Truth*, London, 1942, pp. 156–57.

Dr. Tillyard visited the Laboratory on the Friday for a few minutes only. He saw Eleonore and the Countess for a minute or so, and said goodbye to them. Neither came nearer to him than arm's length; yet to get the 'C' on or off the case was a somewhat difficult and fiddling job. No one else was in the Laboratory except my secretary, and Dr. Tillyard informed me that he saw no one and spoke to no one in the building. I am not going to attempt to offer any hypothesis as to how the letter became firmly attached to his knife. As a student of deceptive methods I can see no way in which Dr. Tillyard could have been tricked.

I asked Dr. Tillyard to write out a complete report of the 'C' incident, and I will reproduce it in his own words:

OCCURRENCES OF FRIDAY, OCTOBER 22, 1926

Having a very busy day, I had no intention of going to the Laboratory at all. Mr. Price was away, and I had not heard of any arrangements for a séance, though I understood that Professors Thirring and Rankine had arranged for a private séance. Eleonore's engagement was due to end the following day.

While going to the Underground train in the morning, I felt in my left overcoat pocket for some coppers for my fare. I pulled out what I thought was sixpence, and was just going to present it to the booking office when I noticed that it was a bronze 50-centime French piece. Thinking Eleonore might have put it there somehow, I decided to examine it carefully. Having found some other coppers and got my fare, I settled down in the train and examined the coin, which I discovered was not one of my thirteen marked ones. I therefore placed it carefully away in the left pocket of my coat where I always keep my knife and scissors, and I distinctly remember feeling carefully in the pocket to see if there were any other coins in it and extracting an odd halfpenny, which I transferred to my greatcoat pocket for use on the railway. I also quite clearly felt my knife and scissors, and if anything else had been in the pocket, I am sure I should have noticed it.

I had arranged to lunch with Professor Julian Huxley. We met at King's College at 1 p.m. and went to the Common Room for luncheon. After lunch we returned to his rooms, where we met Dr. Church, and had a long talk. This man left later, and talk turned to psychic matters. Huxley asked me to demonstrate to him the method of tying thumbs by which I had secured Harold Evans, the physical medium, in a séance held in June last. I consented, and Huxley went to look for some white cotton for which I had asked him. He returned and stated that he could not find any cotton, and asked whether a piece of thin string would do. I said it would, but that it was too long and must be cut (it was too strong to break). I then felt in my left-hand coat pocket for my knife and scissors. These I produced in my left hand, the scissors in a cloth case,

275

the knife in a leather case. While I momentarily debated as to whether I should cut the string with knife or scissors, Huxley had got his own knife out, and we agreed to cut the string together with his knife. I replaced my knife and scissors both in my left hand pocket, and held the string while he cut it in the place indicated by me. I then showed him how I tied the thumb-knots and left special lengths hanging on each side, so as to catch Evans, and he thanked me. At 2.45 p.m. I took my leave, but, just before I went, Huxley presented me with an autographed copy of his book, *Essays of a Biologist*, for which I thanked him and then walked down the stairs.

That afternoon I went to the Natural History Museum and later attended a meeting of the Association of Economic Biologists at the Botany School of the Imperial College of Science. Having lost my way, I arrived late, but stayed for afternoon tea and a talk with Dr. Pethebridge and Dr. Imms of Rothamsted.

Leaving shortly after five, I took farewell of my Rothamsted friends and began to think what I should do next. I had arranged to go down to my wife's people at Rochester for the week-end, but had told them I should catch the 8.20 train from Victoria Station. As I had about three hours still to fill in, it suddenly occurred to me that I had not said goodbye to the Countess and Eleonore, so I decided to walk to the Laboratory to do so. Arriving somewhat warm after a brisk walk, I went to the men's room on the third floor and took my greatcoat off and washed my hands. I then walked upstairs into the Laboratory, where I saw Countess Wassilko sitting at the table writing in a small book of accounts. I stood and talked to her for about two minutes, passing compliments on the success of her visit and finally saying goodbye and shaking hands. I then asked where Eleonore was, and was told that she was probably in the next room. As I thought I heard her playing in the baffle-chamber,[1] I went to the door of it, but she disappeared quickly and ran round to the outside of the door of the Laboratory, where she stood smiling at me with a diabolo set in one hand and holding out the other to me. I took her hand and said goodbye, then went out and downstairs, put on my overcoat and walked to the Underground Station at South Kensington. From there I travelled to Charing Cross, picked up my baggage at the cloak-room, returned by the Underground to Victoria, walked up to the restaurant there, and sat down to a quiet dinner at a table all by myself. About 8 p.m. I got up and paid my bill, took a ticket for Rochester and found a seat in the train. Before it started (8.20 p.m.) one other man came in and sat, immersed in his newspaper, opposite me. I had an evening paper, which occupied me about as far as Bromley. Then I took out Huxley's book from my greatcoat pocket and began to read it. By the time we reached Swanley, I had read eight pages and was then inter-

---

[1] A narrow chamber separating the laboratory and séance room, which trapped the light when a person passed from one room to the other.—H. P.

ested enough to be considerably annoyed when I found that the next few pages had not been cut. So I opened my greatcoat, put my hand down into the left pocket of my coat, and felt for my knife to cut the pages with. Then a curious feeling came over me. The knife did not feel like my knife at all. I drew it out and found firmly attached to the metal half-ring of the leather case enclosing it a white metallic 'C' which effectively closed the case. I realised at once that it was the 'C' which had been lost eleven days before from the notice board of the ground floor of 16, Queensberry Place, and the loss of which had been generally attributed to '*Dracu*'.

(*Signed*)   R. J. TILLYARD.

So Eleonore left London with a great flourish of trumpets, psychically speaking, and with the two great mysteries unsolved. We never dis-

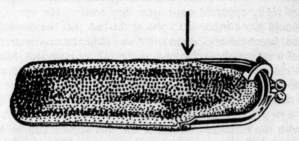

The metallic letter 'C' firmly locked on knife-case. The arrow denotes only place where the latter could have become threaded on fastener. (From sketch by Dr. Tillyard.) (See text).

covered the secret of either her Poltergeist or stigmatic phenomena. She was surprisingly successful during her visit, considering she was in a strange country surrounded by people speaking a strange language. If her benefactress had not accompanied her, it is doubtful if we should have had any success with her. It often happens that when these young people are separated from friends and relatives, a psychological change comes over them, and phenomena cease.

Eleonore left the Press a legacy in the shape of the word 'Poltergeist'. Until her visit I never saw the term used in a British newspaper. After her visit the word became common. During her stay with us, all the dailies were full of the 'Poltergeist Girl' and her doings. Our experiments familiarised the public with the name, now common enough in newspapers and other lay journals.

I have still to record the strangest phenomenon connected with Eleonore. A few months after she left my laboratory, the menses appeared and, almost overnight, the girl became perfectly normal. No more stigmata, or falling coins, or flying stilettos were witnessed. She also 'grew up' mentally very rapidly, and in addition there was a marked physical development.

It has been my experience with many young mediums that the subtle change that takes place at puberty is closely linked with their 'powers'— a psycho-physiological connection that is beginning to be recognised by those medical men who take an interest in these things.[1] In a girl medium the catamenial period seems to be the dividing line between 'phenomena' and 'no phenomena'. The psychic powers of Miss Stella C. did not manifest themselves until she had first menstruated; and it is probably correct to state (although I have no precise information on the subject) that with 'Teddie' Fowler, the girl upon whom the 'Mill on the Eden' phenomena centred, the advent of menstruation coincided with the cessation of the manifestations. The Schneider boys' phenomena were not really apparent until after they reached the age of puberty. And I could give further examples of the fact that the development of the sexual functions appears in some way either to *stop* mediumship, or to reveal what latent psychic powers the subject possesses. Most of the famous mediums, male and female, did not become prominent until adolescence was fairly well advanced.

I am sure that the reader will like to know what became of Eleonore, who is now a young woman of thirty. Well, during the years that she spent with the Countess Wassilko, she was apprenticed by her benefactress to a Vienna firm of ladies' hairdressers. Here she did well and gained a diploma. A few years before the present war, Eleonore sent me her trade card, and from it I learnt that she had a flourishing business of her own in Czernowitz, Rumania (her native land). From her advertisement I gathered that she was happily and lucratively engaged in catering in every way, from *ondulaire* to *cosmetica*, for 'woman's crowning glory' —and '*Dracu*' was no more!

[1] For an interesting monograph on the psychological change that takes place at puberty, see *Printemps Sexuels. L'Épopée au Fauborg*, by Alfred Machard, Paris, 1928. (With ten coloured drawings by Jean Auscher.) For further studies of pubescency and adolescency, see *Schoolgirl*, by Carmen Barnes, London, 1930; *A Young Girl's Diary* (Prefaced with a letter by Sigmund Freud), London, [1919]; *Magia Sexualis*, by P. B. Randolph, Paris, 1931; *La Vie Mentale de l'Adolescent et ses Anomalies*, by Auguste Lemaitre, Saint-Blaise, 1910, and *Fifteen. A Diary of the Teens*, by a Boy, London, n.d.

CHAPTER XXV

Borley Rectory: A Century of Poltergeists

There can be few people interested in ghosts or psychical research who have not heard of Borley Rectory, 'the most haunted house in England'—or anywhere else, come to that.

The Borley Rectory disturbances have become classic for two reasons: it is probably the best-documented and best-authenticated case in the annals of psychical research; and the haunting has persisted, to our certain knowledge, for nearly a century, and phenomena are occurring there to this day.

I do not propose to give a detailed account of what has happened at Borley during the past hundred years, as the full story has already been told in my book[1] on the subject, and there is in course of preparation a second book which will bring the case up to date, and will offer at least one solution to the mystery. And the more recent evidence is even more remarkable—if that were possible—than the first-hand testimony of one hundred witnesses, already published.

But first a word about the place itself. Borley Rectory was—before it was gutted by fire in 1939—a large, rambling, uncomfortable and inconvenient house, built in 1863 by the Rev. Henry Bull, a typical 'squarson',[2] who was incumbent of the parish. This red brick monstrosity was enlarged in 1875, the new wing converting the existing structure into a rectangular building, containing thirty-five rooms, almost completely enclosing a bricked courtyard. This very large house was needed for Mr. Bull's very large family.

The Rev. Henry Bull was succeeded by his son, the Rev. Harry Bull, and the two of them successively held the living (in the gift of the family) for sixty-five years. The Bulls were succeeded by the Rev. G. Eric Smith, who was inducted in 1928. He stayed a few months only. The Rectory was then empty for four months. Then came a relative of the Bulls, the Rev. L. A. Foyster, who arrived in October, 1930, and relinquished the benefice in October, 1935. It was then decided by Queen Anne's Bounty, or by the Bishop, or both, that on account of the amazing occurrences recorded there—and the consequent publicity—the house was not suitable as a Rectory and it was sold. It was offered to me for £500, with three acres of land. It was bought in 1938 by Captain W. H. Gregson, the present owner,[3] who renamed it Borley Priory. As I have stated, the

---

[1] *The Most Haunted House in England: Ten Years' Investigation of Borley Rectory,* London, 1940.

[2] A landed proprietor in holy orders.

[3] Since the above was written, the Rectory has again changed hands.

place was severely damaged by fire in February, 1939—and storms have further reduced the fabric. Today it is a rather unpicturesque ruin. After Mr. Foyster resigned the living, it was combined (1936) with that of Lyston, a nearby parish, and the Rev. A. C. Henning became Rector of Lyston-cum-Borley. And that is the situation today. Mr. Henning lives in his own snug rectory at Lyston. Both Lyston and Borley are near Sudbury and Long Melford, Suffolk, though Borley Rectory is just within the Essex border.

The phenomena witnessed—or experienced—at Borley are of many types. They comprise 'materialisations' (a 'nun', 'Harry Bull'; headless man, or men; a 'figure in grey', and a 'girl in white'; 'shadowy forms'; visions of horses, a strange insect, and a coach). The auditory phenomena include a woman's voice, whisperings, sounds of galloping horses, dog padding round the room, scratchings, incessant bell-ringing, footsteps and similar sounds; raps, taps, and knockings; displaced or projected objects; 'clicks' and 'cracks', the noise of doors closing; knocks, bumps, thuds, jumping and stamping; a 'dragging' noise; wailing sounds; rustling or 'scrabbling' noises; metallic sounds; a noise like rushing water; crashing, as of falling crockery, and the smashing of windows; impression of furniture being moved; and music—'like church music'.

Other phenomena seen were the amazing 'wall-writings'; pathetic messages asking for help, a requiem mass, prayers, etc., scribbled on walls, and other marks. Sometimes these appeared spontaneously when a room was under control. Pieces of paper, on which were written similar appeals for help, also 'appeared'. Then there were the spontaneous locking and unlocking of doors—once under what amounted to test conditions. There were strange lights seen in the windows of the Rectory; spontaneous falling of keys from locks; several outbreaks of fire; appearances, disappearances, and reappearances of various objects; luminous phenomena; matter-through-matter—apparently fourth-dimension 'miracles'; smoke where there was no fire; odours—pleasant and unpleasant; sensations of coldness; tactual phenomena (touchings); unidentifiable footprints in the snow, etc. Then there were the strange reactions to phenomena by various animals, and so on.

The phenomena I have listed above were experienced, not only by villagers and the unlettered, but by persons of culture and education: scientists, and medical men, university students, consulting engineers, members of the British Broadcasting Corporation, army officers and R.A.F. pilots, etc. And not by one or two people—but by *a hundred observers*, most of whom sent in written reports of their experiences. Every incumbent who has lived at Borley has recorded the most amazing incidents, and some of them have been forced to leave the Rectory.

I do not propose to detail how and under what conditions all the above phenomena were witnessed. This I have done in my book, already alluded to. But what I am going to do is to describe the principal Polter-

Borley Rectory before the Fire.

geist phenomena seen and heard in this Poltergeist-infested rectory, and in most instances the evidence is first-hand and documentary. Some of it has not been previously published. I will try to record the evidence in chronological sequence.

As I have stated, the present Rectory was built in 1863 by the Rev. Henry Bull. But in the cellars we came across the foundations and footings of a very much earlier building composed of old-fashioned two-inch bricks. This building was probably another rectory on the same site. There is also a persistent tradition that a monastery once occupied the site many years ago. But we have no concrete evidence for this.

The first documentary evidence we received for Poltergeist activity at Borley came from Mrs. E. Byford, of Parsonage Farm, Newport, Essex, who wrote me to the effect that she was a nursemaid at the Rectory in 1886. She says (June 11, 1929):

'Much of my youth was spent in Borley and district and it was common talk that the Rectory was haunted. Many people declared that they had seen figures walking at the bottom of the garden. I once worked at the Rectory forty-three years ago, as under-nursemaid, but I only stayed there a month as the place was so weird. When I had been there a fortnight, something awakened me in the dead of night. Someone was walking down the passage towards the door of my room, and the sound they made suggested that they were wearing slippers.'

The other servants tried to laugh her out of it but she was 'convinced that somebody or something in slippers had been along that corridor, and finally became so nervous that I left.'

Miss Ethel Bull, one of the surviving daughters of the Rev. Henry Bull, confirms Mrs. Byford's experiences. She told me that when she was a young girl, there occurred the same phenomena. Every night, about 10.30, steps could be heard passing her bedroom door and upon the landing outside her room, and always stopping outside one of the night nurseries. When the sounds of the footsteps ceased, three taps—and three taps only—were always heard. These footsteps and taps were heard at least a hundred times.

About this period there was an outbreak of paranormal bell-ringing. On one occasion Miss Ethel Bull was in the house, when all the bells— of which there were about twenty—suddenly started pealing simultaneously. Immediate investigation failed to solve the mystery. This phenomenon was followed by the sound of rushing water. No explanation. A sister who was sleeping in one of the smaller bedrooms was awakened by something slapping her face. No explanation. For a long period, quite regularly every night and just before she retired to rest, a series of sharp raps was heard on her bedroom door. Later, many crashes were heard in the house. Raps and footsteps have been heard in the Rectory by every person who has ever resided in the place for any length of time.

Independent confirmation of the Misses Bull's experiences reached me after my book was published. Mr. P. Shaw Jeffrey, M.A., writing from Lenox Hotel, Gardens, Cape Town, on January 10, 1942, said:

'I have just been reading your book about Borley Rectory. I am very interested because Harry Bull and I were born in the same year. We went to Oxford together, I at Queen's, he at Exeter College, and in the long vacations I used to go and stay with him at Borley. I was there in 1885 and 1886. I had lots of small adventures at the Rectory. Stones falling about, my boots found on the top of the wardrobe, etc., and I saw the "nun" several times, and often heard the coach go clattering by. But the big adventure that would have been worth your while recording was one time when I missed a big French dictionary [1] which I had been regularly using for some days. Nobody could find it, but one night I was awakened by a big bump on the floor and after I had lit my candle, there was the dictionary, with its back a good deal knocked about, sprawling on the floor. My bedroom door was *locked*.

'Another much more startling adventure was in August, 1886, and this happened at the Rev. Felix Bull's neighbouring rectory. (Felix was a brother of Henry Bull.) I can't remember the name. [2] But it had a watch tower in the garden built by some former incumbent who had a crazy idea that if he built it tall enough, he could see the sea. Felix Bull was having trouble with a Poltergeist and he came to lunch and told us about it.

'Next day Harry Bull and I borrowed the family coach and drove over to Felix's. He was out, but the cook said, "Well, Master Harry, if there's any foolishness going on, it's all along of our new housemaid—that's what *I* say!" "Where is she?" asked Harry. "Up in the best bedroom making the beds." "Right you are, we'll go up." So up we went. The room was large and long with three windows along one side. We stood by the door. The maid was at the far end of the room, making the beds. Close to *us* was the fireplace. Harry Bull said, "Well, Mary, cook says you can show us a few tricks—what about it?"

'The maid said nothing, but a tooth-glass came flying across from the washing stand behind the maid's back and circled gracefully around, hitting the jamb of the door just above my head. Just afterwards, the fender and fire-irons and grate moved right out across the room with a clatter. The maid never spoke a word, and neither did we. We bolted! Later on, this maid went to London and became a medium.

'I saw very little of Harry Bull after I came down from Oxford as I was living abroad. But about 1920 he came over to Colchester (I was then Head Master of Colchester Royal Grammar School) to ask me if I could recommend him a *locum* as he wanted to take a holiday. But by that time parsons were beginning to fight shy of Borley Rectory, and I failed.'

---

[1] See Mr. C. J. P. Cave's 'dictionary' phenomenon, p. 346.—H. P.

[2] Pentlow, five miles N.W. of Sudbury.—H.P.

In an article in the *Cape Times*, which was sent to me, Mr. Jeffrey elaborated the information he gave me in his letter. As regards the 'coach', he said: 'The ghostly coach-and-four I heard sweep down the much too narrow lane beside the Rectory so often that I used to sleep through the noise, and a variety of disconcerting incidents happened to me.' He adds that the Rev. Henry Bull had seventeen children, all at home during the vacations. No wonder he wanted a large house!

The Bull family became so used to the various 'manifestations' that they did not trouble to keep any account of them. Consequently, at the early period of which I am writing, from 1863 onwards, we have no detailed diary of the incessant bell-ringing, stone-throwing, shuffling footsteps, phantasms, face-slapping and other phenomena that occurred there *for years*. If the Bull children were witnesses of these strange events, so was the father, the Rev. Henry Bull. He used to stand outside the gates of the Rectory, and actually wait for the *sounds* of the 'coach-and-four' to pass the house. The rumbling of the coach and the galloping of the horses he heard literally hundreds of times—and so did other members of the family, some of whom, fortunately, are still with us to supply the evidence. And the independent testimony of observers like Mrs. Byford and Mr. Jeffrey is valuable corroboration of the Bull family's own accounts.

When Henry Bull died a new phenomenon was heard over and over again. This took the form of sounds as if someone was entering the back door. The door could be heard opening and then closing, but investigation always proved that no one was there. This particular phenomenon occurred usually when most of the members of the family were at church and Mrs. Bull, the invalid mother, and a daughter were alone in the house.

When the Rev. Harry Bull succeeded his father in the incumbency and lived at the Rectory, he, too, experienced all the old phenomena: phantasms, the rumbling coach-and-pair—which he *saw*—and all the other Poltergeist manifestations. This evidence was confirmed by Mr. J. Harley, of Nottingham Place, W.1, who wrote to us in 1929. He says: 'In 1922 I resided for some weeks at the Rectory with the Rev. Bull, and I distinctly recall him assuring me that on many occasions he had had personal communications with spirits.' He also told Mr. Harley that if he was discontented after death, and was able to do so, he would 'return' and cause some violent physical reaction, such as smashing of glass or other noisy demonstration. As a matter of fact, the ghost of Harry Bull was seen on several occasions by the wife of a subsequent rector, the Rev. L. A. Foyster. As we shall see later, it was during Mr. Foyster's incumbency that the most remarkable—and certainly the most spectacular—Poltergeist phenomena occurred. Did Harry Bull fulfil his threat to Mr. Harley, and 'return' in this violent manner?

Before I give an account of my own experiences at the Rectory I must

283

hark back a little and relate the strange adventures of Edward Cooper, a groom-gardener in the employ of the Bull family for many years. Mr. Cooper is one of the 'good old sort', a sturdy, honest, intelligent, forth-right man of the yeoman type, with no nonsense about him.

Mr. Cooper now lives at Great Cornard, near Sudbury. He joined the staff of the Rectory in 1916, when the Misses Bull were in residence there. He and his wife occupied the four rooms over the stables (a de-tached building) now euphemistically known as 'the cottage'. I will pass over his astonishing vision of the phantom coach-and-pair, brilliantly lit up and glittering in the moonlight, that silently raced across the church meadows, through trees, walls and hedges, and finally disappeared in the farmyard below him. I will not detail this story, or that of how he and his wife frequently saw the 'nun', as this volume is concerned solely with Poltergeist phenomena.

Well, for more than three years during his occupation of the cottage, the Coopers, when in bed, were disturbed on most nights by the sounds of pattering that appeared to come from the adjoining living-room. It was just as if a large dog or small child had jumped from a height and was padding round the room. Naturally, at first they were some-what concerned at what these noises could be, and more than once lit the candle and explored the contiguous rooms, without success. Finally, they got used to the *pad-pad-pad*, which usually began soon after they got into bed, between 10 and 11 o'clock, and thought nothing of it.

One night, about three years after the 'padding' sounds were first heard, and soon after the Coopers had retired to rest, the 'dog' pheno-menon was again experienced. They heard the soft but heavy *pad-pad-pad* in the next room, when suddenly there was a terrific crash as if all the china on the kitchen dresser had fallen to the floor simultaneously. Mr. Cooper leapt out of bed and lit a candle, quite expecting to find part of his home demolished. To his astonishment, not a thing in the cottage was displaced, and no damage was done. From that night onwards they were never again disturbed. The 'dog' had gone for ever.

After the death of Harry Bull, the Rectory was empty for some months. If, as Mr. Jeffrey told me in his letter, parsons fought shy of the place in 1920, they were still more shy in 1928. In that year, twelve men refused the living. However, an incumbent was found at last and the Rev. G. Eric Smith took up his duties there on October 2, 1928.

On June 11, 1929, the News Editor of the *Daily Mirror* rang me up to say that one of his staff, Mr. V. C. Wall, was at the Rectory and was witnessing the most extraordinary happenings. Things were flying about, strange lights appeared at windows, etc. He asked me whether I would investigate. I said I would. I had never heard of Borley, but the story sounded so convincing that I immediately telephoned a telegram to the effect that the Rector was to expect my secretary and me the next morning. We arrived in time for lunch. I little thought that the case would engage my attention for the next fifteen years.

Over the meal, I heard all about the phenomena and something of the history of the Rectory. Mr. Smith and his wife had an exciting time before I was called in. In addition to the usual things flying about, one summer afternoon, when the Rector was alone in the house, he left his bedroom and upon going to the landing heard loud whisperings over his head. As he stopped to listen, the sounds ceased instantly. He later heard these whisperings many times. On one occasion, at dusk, when he was crossing the same landing, a woman's voice, half moan and half appeal, said loudly, 'Don't, Carlos, don't!' dying away in a sort of muttering. Other phenomena experienced at the Rectory were bell-ringing, slow and deliberate footsteps in rooms and passages, strange lights seen in rooms and the smashing of crockery. And a skull, in perfect condition, was found in the library cupboard. It was buried in the churchyard.

After lunch my secretary and I made a minute examination of the Rectory and grounds. We scrutinised every brick and board of the house, from cellars to attics, and made plans of the place. We tested the walls for cavities, hiding-places and secret passages. But the building was architecturally normal. We sealed all the windows and exits from the house, except the one we were using. We looked in ovens and coppers, moved furniture, took down pictures and took up carpets. Everything was normal. We traced each bell wire from the bell itself to its anchorage in the attics. Some of these wires had been cut in order to stop the incessant ringing. It didn't! We descended to the cellars, dark and damp, and the frogs, toads, newts and lizards scurried away from the glare of our electric torches. We discovered what appeared to be a filled-in well in the cellar. This was covered with boards. Then I interviewed the young maidservant and the gardener—the only staff employed.

After tea, and after another thorough search of every nook and cranny in the place, Mr. Wall (who was paying a further visit to the house) and I arranged that we should take up our vigil in the garden in a position that commanded a view of the Nun's Walk (favourite haunt of the 'nun') and the window of the unused room in which Mr. Wall and others had seen the 'strange light' the previous evening.

We saw neither nun nor light, though we waited until it was almost dark. Then we thought we would go indoors and again examine the house where the Smiths and my secretary were on guard. The maidservant had gone home. Just as we were about to enter the French windows that opened out of the study on to the glass-covered verandah that abutted the lawn, there was a terrific crash as a half-brick hurtled through one of the thick panes of glass above our heads. We were splashed with splinters. We picked up the missile (that must have been propelled from behind us), but it was just an ordinary half-brick.

Our friends had heard the smash and feared for our safety. We found

285

that nothing untoward had happened in the house during our vigil in the garden, and we decided to make still another examination of the premises. In spite of our previous searches, we thought it conceivable that someone *might* have entered the house in some way. So we again examined the place from top to bottom, but all my seals were intact, and we found nothing.

On my numerous journeys up and down the house I had noticed in the Blue Room (notorious 'focus' of manifestations) a pair of very nice red glass candlesticks. Wall and I had seen them on this—my third—latest examination. Just as we had completed our scrutiny, and were descending the main staircase that led to the hall, another crash was heard and one of those nice red candlesticks hurtled past our heads (we saw it plainly), hit the iron stove in the hall, and disintegrated into a thousand fragments. It had been hurled down the well of the stairs. Wall and I raced upstairs again, but found no one, and nothing that could have caused the flight of the candlestick. All this took place in the full light of a powerful duplex paraffin lamp that our friends, who were waiting below for us, had placed on the hall table. In quick succession, and in full light, the following articles came tumbling down the stairs: first of all some common seashore pebbles, then a piece of slate, then some more pebbles.

Later in the evening several bells rang of their own volition. The wires could be seen moving, and even the pulls in some of the rooms were swinging when we entered them. After supper a new phenomenon occurred: As we all stood in the hall, the keys in the doors of the library and drawing-room, that opened on to the hall, *shot out simultaneously* at right angles to the doors, and fell to the floor. I at once examined them, and the locks, and doors, but there was nothing to suggest a normal explanation. I was told that this key-dropping phenomenon was common. And during the incumbency of the next rector, every key in the house vanished!

During the evening two of the Misses Bull came to see me—and the phenomena. At about 1 a.m. it was suggested that we should hold a séance. There was no medium of course, but we all adjourned to the Blue Room, closed the doors, and formed a 'circle' by sitting on beds and chairs. The room was furnished in the usual way. A heavy mahogany-backed mirror stood on the dressing table by one window, and there was a washstand with jug, etc., near the door at the far end of the room. In order to open the proceedings, I said—addressing the four walls of the room—'If any entity is present here tonight, will it please make itself known?' I might have added 'in the usual manner', but I didn't. I repeated my request three times, when suddenly a faint, but distinct tapping came from the back of the mirror I have mentioned. We placed our chairs round the dressing table, thus re-forming the 'circle'. The duplex lamp fully illuminated the room.

I will not relate what took place at this séance, but it lasted three hours, during which period the mirror was tapped incessantly—and with intelligence. We asked questions of the 'entity' and by the traditional three taps for 'yes', one tap for 'no' and two for 'doubtful', we *did* receive some sort of information. The 'entity' alleged that it was the Rev. Harry Bull, and it was upon this gentleman that the 'conversation' centred. I am not a spiritualist, but I can affirm that the taps were absolutely genuine, and the 'communicator' may have been what it claimed to be.

I must relate one further incident: a true Poltergeist phenomenon witnessed under ideal control conditions. If I had witnessed only this one manifestation, I should have been convinced of the paranormality of the Borley disturbances. I will let Mr. Wall describe[1] the incident:

'Finally came the most astonishing event of the night. A cake of soap on the washstand was lifted and thrown heavily on to a china jug standing on the floor with such force that the soap was deeply marked. All of us were at the other side of the room when this happened.'

This was a perfect paranormal phenomenon, and if I had witnessed no other phenomenon in my life, it would have convinced me of the existence of Poltergeists. No one was nearer to the washstand than about 12 feet (the Blue Room was nearly 16 feet square); the room was well illuminated and the soap was a new cake. Of course I at once examined everything—with the usual result.

I slept in the Blue Room that night, or rather morning, and my only fear was that the other nice red candlestick might do me an injury. So for safety I put it under my pillow. I was not disturbed.

It can be imagined that the Smiths did not 'stick it' long! My first visit was on June 12, 1929, and a month later (July 14) the Smiths moved out— after spending £200 in doing the place up, etc. They took rooms in Long Melford, a mile or so away, and the Rector visited his parish by car every day. The following April they left the district and went to live at Sheringham, Norfolk.

During the few months that the Rector was living at Long Melford, Mrs. Smith occasionally visited the house in order to see that everything was all right. It wasn't! She kindly reported her visits to me and it was clear that the Poltergeists were still active. Though every window and door was either locked or barred, or both, on one occasion she found that the small bedside table in the Blue Room 'had been hurled over from in front of the fireplace to the washstand in the corner'. A fortnight later it was discovered that windows had been unlatched from the inside and one of them opened. Then, on another visit, it was found that 'half a fireplace has been deposited on the main staircase', although every door and window was locked and bolted just as Mrs. Smith had left them. On March 14, 1930, Mrs. Smith wrote: 'Funny things are con-

---

[1] *Daily Mirror*, June 14, 1929. For Mr. Wall's personal experiences during this period, see the *Daily Mirror* for June 10, 1929, and following issues.

tinually happening at the Rectory, and lumps of stone are on the main stairs from whence we do not know. The window still "lights up" at night,' though the Rectory was then unoccupied. On March 18, 1930, the Rector's wife wrote: 'It is queer to see what lumps of stone and broken glass are about the place while, recently, on entering the Rectory just at about full moon, we heard the most horrible sounds in the house.'

During the period that the Smiths were at Long Melford, my friends and I visited the unoccupied Rectory two or three times. We first obtained the keys from the Rector. One evening a party of us was present when incessant bell-ringing occurred. This was accompanied by the throwing of small pebbles, a shower of several keys, a small gilt medallion or pendant of Roman Catholic[1] origin, and a medal issued in 1799 after the French Revolution. No one knows the origin of these objects or where they came from. They just tumbled down the stairs.

After the Smiths left Borley, the Rectory was again empty for some months. However, a relative of the Bulls, the Rev. L. A. Foyster, and his young wife, accepted the living and the new Rector was inducted in October, 1930. Mr. Foyster had recently returned from Canada and knew a little of the 'trouble' at the Rectory. He was soon to learn more!

On the very first day (October 16, 1930) of their residence at the Rectory, a pathetic voice was heard calling 'Marianne' (Mrs. Foyster's christian name) and the phantasm of Harry Bull, in a grey dressing-gown, was seen on the stairs.

Mr. Foyster is a methodical man and he took notes of the occurrences as they happened. His notes developed into a diary, and the diary into a volume of 184 typed quarto pages—roughly 50,000 words; or, say, half the size of this book. And his diary records *many hundreds* of phenomena. The diary covers a period of only fifteen months, because the Rector became tired of recording the phenomena: there were so many of them. It says something for his pluck that he remained at the Rectory for five years.

Here, then, are a few incidents from Mr. Foyster's diary, reproduced verbatim:

October 16, 1930. Jugs and other utensils disappearing and coming back. Peculiar smells—especially one most nearly resembling lavender—noticeable particularly in our bedroom. Bells rung. A bracelet detached from wrist-watch while Marianne is in room only a few feet away, and no one else in the house, besides Adelaide, who was in her own room. Bracelet was taken and has never been seen since. Lavender bag, which no one has ever seen before, discovered on mantelpiece of Marianne's sewing-room. Lavender bag disappears and again appears in my pocket: discovered when putting on coat one morning.

February 1931. Books found on window-sill of w.c. As soon as one is

[1] In another Poltergeist case, that of the haunted castle at Calvados, Normandy, in 1875, a shower of Roman Catholic medals fell on the owner's wife.

taken away, it is replaced by another. (These books had been left by the Bulls and were stowed away on shelf in housemaid's pantry.) Last of these had a torn cover, which was thrown on floor.

February 25. A big return of crockery (that had previously unaccountably disappeared). Marianne asks for a tea-pot: this is also returned. At my suggestion, Marianne asks for return of bracelet, but in very uncomplimentary language.

February 26. Books found under our bed in the morning. A consignment of hymn books, unknown before, discovered on the rack over the kitchen range in the afternoon. In the evening Marianne is given a terrific blow in the eye—a cut under it; black eye next day—by an invisible assailant on the landing outside bedroom. She was carrying a candle.

February 27. Shortly after we had retired and light extinguished, first a cotton-reel and then a hammer-head with broken handle attached were thrown across our bed. Lamp lit and throwing discontinued.

February 28. I write a letter on the subject (of the hauntings). Directly afterwards (the room had been empty for only a few minutes in between) two pins discovered with their points sticking upwards. One was on seat of arm-chair; the other on chair I had been sitting on. About an hour or so later an erection, composed of an old lamp and saucepan (neither of them seen before) was found outside my door.[1] Later, the handle of a floor-polisher is put across the passage I have traversed on my way to supper. Still later a tin of bath salts placed just inside bathroom door trips up Marianne.

March 5. Two articles thrown after lights were put out in our bedroom. Then, after an interval, I was aroused by a hairbrush on my head.

March 6. The knob off a door thrown with some force from just behind her, at Marianne as she comes along bathroom passage.

March 7. Marianne thrown at in the afternoon. In the evening, I attempt to exorcise spirits. Stone hits me on shoulder. Books thrown out of shelves in Marianne's sewing-room. Pictures in hall and on staircase are taken down and laid on ground. Things thrown in bedroom. (This night, window was first opened a few inches at bottom; then at top. The veranda roof outside would make it very difficult for things to be thrown from outside *into* bedroom.)

March 10. A little pile of five stones found behind Marianne's pillow when she woke in the morning. More objects carried into the house. A stone through a pane of glass in staircase window. It was thrown from *inside* while Marianne, Adelaide and myself were standing by hall stove. I think that on this night a small tin travelling trunk (not seen before) suddenly noticed in kitchen while we are sitting at supper there. This stayed in the house for some time, but eventually disappeared. China

[1] This 'erection' is a little reminiscent of the clothes tableaux witnessed in the Phelps case (1850–51).—H.P.

powder-box and wedding-ring discovered in bathroom. It (the ring) disappeared during the following morning.[1] Marianne stumbles over brick placed outside bathroom door. Next morning two stones found behind my pillow.

March 11. Two Anglican priests go thoroughly over the house with Marianne and myself, using incense, holy water, and prayers. A 'presence' of some sort is felt, but no active demonstration. Later a stone is thrown at a boy from the cottage. I was out most of the remaining part of the day. After my return, a stone was thrown at me. Then, as we three were standing round the hall stove, another stone fell only a few inches from my head.

March 12. Clean linen was taken out of the kitchen cupboard, and trailed over the floor.

March 13. Marianne hit on the head, and hurt, by a piece of metal thrown down back stairs. A piece of brick dropped on to supper table, close to my plate, but without breaking or touching any crockery.

March 15. As I am typing out a diary of events in the house, first my collar (which I had taken off for comfort) is thrown at me. Then a stick and a piece of coke were thrown across the room.

March 16. Marianne in the early morning of this day finds kitchen table upside down, and the contents of a store cupboard partly inside, and partly scattered broadcast. In the evening, bedroom window which had been left open was discovered closed the wrong way round.

March 23. Marianne, while carrying a tray in one hand and a lamp in the other, up the front stairs, has the inside of an iron thrown at her from a few feet ahead of her. It breaks the lamp chimney.

March 24. Small articles thrown at Marianne while she is sweeping, etc., outside bedroom. 'Harry Bull' seen again by Marianne at night about this time; and, probably, by cottage tenant through stair window.

March 28. Marianne sees a monstrosity (seen by her and others on other occasions) near kitchen door. It touches her shoulder with iron-like touch.

March 29. Palm Sunday was still.

April 11. Saturday in Easter week. A small demonstration. With this one exception, there was absolute quiet during Holy Week and Easter week.

April. Milk jug is mysteriously found empty. I request a clean one and made a rude remark about 'drinking after ghosts'. While we are sitting at tea in broad daylight with doors and windows closed, missiles are thrown at me. At night, I count up 12 or 13 times I was thrown at, between approximately 6 p.m. and 11 p.m. in different parts of the house.

May. A bad half-hour in the kitchen one evening ended by my going upstairs to get creosote with which we fumigate the house. On my way

---

[1] This ring, or one like it, suddenly appeared in the Blue Room on the last day of my tenancy of the Rectory. (See p. 296)—H.P.

'*Marianne sees a monstrosity near kitchen door.*'

291

up a lump of dried mortar hit me in the neck. On the way down a metal spanner passed through my hair. After fumigation, the trouble stops at once. Pepper, however, dropped on us in bed. Some had previously been thrown in Marianne's face in the kitchen. Next evening, Marianne does some fumigating, but is rather lenient with creosote. Bells ring; stone thrown at her, and jam-jar crashes against the kitchen door as she is returning. I go round with the creosote and trouble ceases. On the next day (Monday) I collect six articles thrown in the late afternoon and evening to show Sir George and Lady Whitehouse (who arrived about 9 p.m.), to see if anything was doing. While they are here, skirting board of unused bedroom (not entered by anyone on that day as far as we knew) discovered to be on fire. Some throwing after it had been put out. We accept their invitation and stay a few days with Whitehouse. One evening, when up at Borley, Marianne sees paper in air; it at once falls to the ground. It is discovered to have some hardly decipherable writing on it. Next day when we come up, it had disappeared. Other pieces of paper with 'Marianne' written in a childish hand, were found about the house from time to time.[1]

June 6. Worst outbreak begins with a stone being thrown.

June 7. Stones thrown in the evening. A chair in spare room (in which Marianne was lying in bed, very unwell) twice thrown over. Strange noises heard on landing during the night : bangs, taps on door, etc.

June 8. Monday. Proceedings start soon after 10 a.m. These include a variety of things. Books, stones, clothes, suit-case, and a basket full of soiled linen were thrown over balustrade from landing to stairs and hall. The soiled linen basket was thrown twice. Marianne hears turmoil going on in what was usually our bedroom. She gets up from sick bed to see. Noise at once stops, but room found to be in confusion. Bed moved, furniture overturned. Doctor calls and witnesses some throwing. Richard Whitehouse visits house and also witnesses some throwing. Marianne turned out of bed three times during the day, but each time when alone in the room. Lady Whitehouse, coming up in the evening, hears more throwing. Matters are so bad that she and Sir George insist on our going down to their house for a time. During the rest of the month of June, house is empty at night except for a few nights when I could get someone else to sleep in the house as well. On one of these evenings, when a friend was there, I heard a noise just before retiring. I went to his room to see if it came from there. I found him asleep, and an empty paint pot (which he knew nothing about) had been placed close up against the door inside.

August (or perhaps September). Study attacked. Writing desk thrown on its face; chairs overturned; books pushed out of the shelves; room in confusion.

---

[1] Compare this phenomenon with the written messages received in the Battersea case (p. 238).—H.P.

September. We are locked out of our room one night. Adelaide was locked *into* hers. (All doors unlocked with help of relic of Curé d'Ars.)

On the kitchen being left empty for a few minutes, a saucepan full of potatoes, left on the stove, was found to be empty. Witnessed by Marianne and a maid. (N.B. We had no resident maid in the house from the time we arrived till September 1931.) About this time different things were moved about in the house (or disappeared altogether) to a great extent. Amongst them was a big pile of typewritten sheets, and a portable typewriter. Though money was removed, we cannot be certain that it was ever taken.

October. I am awakened one morning by having a bedroom water jug dropped on my head. I left it on the floor, and a little time afterwards it is dropped on Marianne's head.

January 1932. One night, both doors of our room were found locked. One door was locked from the inside.[1] The other door, communicating with dressing-room, had a chest of drawers pushed right up against it from the inside. This showed the impossibility, therefore, of the locking having been done by a human agent. Once more we sought admission by means of prayer. But door was still found locked. We went to the Chapel and while we were there, a terrific noise started up in the hall, which we found was due to the cat having its claw caught in the rat-trap. When we returned to the Chapel, we found a key lying on the corner of the altar. This turned out to be the key belonging to the door between our bedroom and dressing-room.

*   *   *

The above few extracts from Mr. Foyster's voluminous notes convey a little of what they experienced at the Rectory. The names of Lady Whitehouse (a friend who lived near Sudbury) and her nephew, Dom Richard Whitehouse, O.S.B., are mentioned in the diary. Lady Whitehouse sent me an independent report relating her experiences. On one occasion when visiting the Rectory, she found the contents of the cupboard strewn all over the place. Then a whole row of bells began ringing simultaneously. And an outbreak of fire occurred in a locked room: She helped to put it out—just in time, as a strip of skirting board was glowing red. As she was assisting, 'a flint about the size of a hen's egg' was flung at her. The window was closed, and the missile must have entered through the door. Then more flints fell. Then all the bells started ringing again. She then 'burnt a lot of lavender on a kitchen shovel' in order to fumigate the house, and the Poltergeists quietened down a little. However, things looked so dangerous that she insisted on the Foysters and their little adopted girl Adelaide (aged 3 years) leaving the Rectory, and she took them all back in her car to her residence, Arthur Hall, Sudbury.

[1] Mr. Foyster, in order to enter the room, applied to the door a relic of the Curé d'Ars. It was at once 'magically' unlocked.—H.P.

Lady Whitehouse was at the Rectory one day during the following summer. Mrs. Foyster was ill in bed. She placed her gloves and parasol *on the bed*. She turned her back, Mrs. Foyster gave a scream, and her gloves and parasol had been transported across the room on to the *dressing table*! She fetched Mrs. Foyster a cup of tea. As she entered the bedroom, 'a small glass bottle seemed to start from the middle of the room, and fell at my feet.' After that, Lady Whitehouse remarks, 'Things were very active and horrible'. It was on this day, as recorded by her husband, that Mrs. Foyster was thrown out of bed *three times*.

If Lady Whitehouse's experiences were remarkable, they were nothing to those recorded by her nephew, Dom Richard Whitehouse, O.S.B. He spent many hours at the Rectory and had known all the incumbents there since he was a child. He, too, sent me a long independent report of his experiences which are recorded in full in my first book[1] on the Rectory. On one occasion he found a bed completely overturned when the Foysters were away and the house locked and unoccupied. He records outbreaks of fires, and the mysterious locking and unlocking of doors. He also had an extraordinary experience when one of the famous 'wall messages' spontaneously appeared in his presence. Bell-ringing was a common phenomenon and several times 'the large bell in the yard used to ring out. There was no rope attached to it and it was high up in an angle of the yard.'[2] 'More than once', said Dom Richard Whitehouse, 'I have stood in the kitchen passage and watched the bells moving to and fro, the only people in the house often standing alongside of me, witnessing the same performance. The wires of some of these old-fashioned pull bells had been cut.'

By far the most amazing incident recorded during Dom Richard's investigation occurred on Friday, November 13, 1931. He, Mrs. Foyster, and a maid named Katie were seated in the kitchen having supper. Mr. Foyster was in London. I will quote verbatim from his report:

'Mrs. Foyster was sitting in a small easy chair in one corner of the kitchen. The windows and both doors were closed. Without warning of any kind, there was a sudden crash underneath her chair, a wine bottle bursting into fragments on the stone floor beneath her. A quarter of an hour or so later, precisely the same thing happened to me as I was drawing up a small chair to sit down to my supper. Katie was kept busy sweeping up the broken glass and looking quite mystified, having been in the house only a week or so. Shortly after this, all three of us witnessed another extraordinary incident. We were standing in a row with our backs to the fire, talking and looking out towards the window. Suddenly, before our very eyes, a wine bottle poised itself in mid-air within a foot

---

[1] *Op. cit.*

[2] I am particularly interested in this bell as Capt. Gregson gave it to me as a souvenir after the Rectory fire. It hangs in my garden in Sussex and I am still waiting for it to ring paranormally!—H.P.

or so of the kitchen ceiling. It remained there for a second or two and then fell with a crash on the floor before us. I repeat, that all three of us witnessed this incident.'

As I have remarked, the Foysters occupied the house for five years. When they left (October 1935), the ecclesiastical authorities decided that never again should a rector of Borley live in the place. They decided to sell, and it was offered to me 'for a song'. But I lived 150 miles away from Borley and felt I could not look after the building. But I decided to rent it, and this I did for one year, my tenancy beginning on May 19, 1937.

My idea was to form a panel of critical and educated observers who knew nothing about Borley and little about psychical research. To this end I inserted an advertisement in *The Times*[1] and from the shoals of offers I received, I selected about forty men: doctors, scientists, army officers, university men and so on—all from the cultured classes, and all intelligent. No mention of Borley appeared in my advertisement. I wanted some independent and fresh minds to be brought to bear on the hauntings and I was determined to eliminate everyone—including myself—who had had anything to do with Borley in the past. All of my new observers were strangers to me and to one another, except one or two B.B.C. men who came in later. I rarely visited Borley during my tenancy, but just directed the whole affair from my offices in Berkeley Street, W.1.

My 'official' observers who, of course, paid their own expenses, were under certain obligations. They had to furnish reports to me, whether good or bad. They were pledged not to convey any information about what happened at the Rectory to anyone but myself. This was to prevent garbled and sensational stories getting into the Press. And there were certain other minor regulations all designed for one object—the scientific and independent investigation of what has now been proved to be the most convincing and best-documented case of haunting—especially Poltergeist haunting—in the annals of psychical research.

I cannot possibly do more in this chapter than mention a few of the most remarkable paranormal happenings that occurred during my observers' vigil that lasted, night and day, for twelve months. All their reports have been published in my book,[2] to which I must refer the reader. But I will relate some of the outstanding phenomena, witnessed and recorded under scientific conditions:

On June 1, 1937, a strange coat, a woman's, mildewed, torn and dirty, appeared in one of the cupboards. Owner never found. June 20, Mr. S. H. Glanville, one of my most active and intelligent observers, heard 'cracks' and bumps at night. Five days later Colonel F. C. Westland recorded the sudden appearance of a blue box at the Rectory. The new Rector of Borley, the Rev. A. C. Henning, and Mr. Mark Kerr-Pearse (one of our proconsuls at Geneva) held a little informal séance and

[1] For May 25, 1937.　　　　　　　　　　　　[2] *Op. cit.*

'extraordinary noises were heard coming from the kitchen'. On September 21, a 50-pound bag of coal, carefully controlled and under test conditions, moved laterally 18 inches of its own volition.

One of the most striking phenomena was when Kerr-Pearse was having his supper in the living-room that had been prepared for my observers. He was alone in the locked and sealed house. The key of the door was on the *inside*, in full view of Kerr-Pearse as he was eating. Suddenly there was a click. He looked up and found that he was locked in—though the key was on his side of the door. Whatever locked him in must have been in the room with him.

I could fill pages with accounts of the thuds, thumps, 'draggings', strange odours, lights (a university student saw a luminous patch on the Blue Room ceiling; it hovered a little and then disappeared) and especially the strange wall-markings that were recorded by my observers. Then there were the phantasms, etc., that I am not dealing with in this volume. All were seen.

Mr. Henning, Mr. Glanville, and their friends experimented with the Planchette, with interesting results. By its means they 'discovered' the name of the 'nun' that haunts the Rectory, together with some details of how she was murdered. The 'communicator' said its name was 'Mary Lairre'. Another 'communicator', 'Sunex Amures', said it would burn down the Rectory. Asked where the fire would start it said, 'Over the hall'. A few months later the Rectory *was* gutted by fire,[1] the first part to be burnt being 'over the hall'.

On May 9, 1938, I gave up the tenancy of the Rectory. My experiment had been brilliantly successful. Nearly every type of phenomenon experienced at Borley was repeated, *under scientific conditions*, and recorded by disinterested and dispassionate witnesses. On the last day of my occupation, when Mr. Geoffrey H. Motion (a friend of mine) and I were clearing up, an apparently new (though made in 1864) 22-carat gold wedding-ring suddenly 'appeared' in the Blue Room—at midnight! We had entered that room several times during the afternoon and evening, and hád *searched* the floor for any paranormal marks or objects. And yet on our last visit to the room, the first thing that Motion and I saw simultaneously as we passed through the doorway, was the glint of the gold on the floor. We never found its owner. Very curiously, a gold wedding-ring suddenly 'appeared' in the bathroom at the Rectory a few years previously, and just as suddenly disappeared, as the Rector recorded in his diary. The same ring might have figured in both incidents.

Captain W. H. Gregson bought the Rectory at the end of 1938, and he experienced all the old phenomena with the addition of some new ones. For example, he lost, in succession, two valuable spaniel puppies. Both acted—and reacted—in the same way. In his report, Captain Greg-

---

[1] Epworth Parsonage, home of the Wesleys, was also destroyed by fire, *before* the Poltergeist disturbances there.

Remains of Borley Rectory, August, 1943.

son says that he heard footsteps in the courtyard and went to investigate. His dog was at his heels. Suddenly 'my dog stopped dead, and positively went mad. He shrieked and tore away, still shrieking'. The next dog he had behaved in exactly the same way and neither has been seen since. Other phenomena recorded by Captain Gregson included the usual movement of objects, footsteps, etc., and strange footmarks in the snow (Christmas, 1938) that neither he nor anyone could identify. They were neither human nor made by any animal that could be identified.

On October 27, 1938, Miss Ethel Bull wrote to us and said that 'a clergyman friend of ours who was staying in the neighbourhood a few weeks ago, walked up to the Rectory one evening and prowled around outside. He heard an awful noise coming from the house as though a lot of furniture was being thrown about. Nobody was in the house (which was then unoccupied). He felt a bit scared and took himself off.'

A few months after Captain Gregson bought the Rectory, it caught alight. While he was sorting out books in the hall a paraffin lamp fell over—and that was the end of the Rectory. But certainly not the end of the phenomena. During the height of the fire a local policeman testified that he saw 'a woman in grey and a man wearing a bowler hat' in front of Captain Gregson as he walked about the courtyard. This was at 2 o'clock in the morning. Of course, no such persons were present. Then two of the local residents informed me later that they had seen 'figures moving amongst the flames near the Blue Room window'. Still a few weeks later, Miss Rosemary Williams of Borley Lodge, and Mr. C. G. Browne of Pound Hall, Long Melford, informed me that they had recently visited the Rectory ruins by moonlight, and had seen a young woman dressed in pale blue or white suddenly appear at the Blue Room window. 'She remained for several seconds and then turned towards the wall and, as it seemed, walked through it.' As there were neither walls nor floor for the figure to stand on, it could not have been a human being.

In addition to the above testimony, I have received many reports to the effect that phenomena are still occurring. As a few of the lower rooms are habitable, investigators visit the place, with interesting results. And people who were *not* investigators have also experienced startling phenomena there. I get reports almost weekly from various quarters. I will select a few of them.

On August 7, 1943, I wrote an article for *Everybody's Weekly* on the Borley phenomena. Amongst the many scores of letters about the article that were received by the editor or me, was a long one from Mr. Gilbert Hayes, the well-known film comedian. It was sent to the editor. The letter was really a report on some extraordinary experiences that befell the writer and his wife in September, 1939—after the Rectory had been burnt. Mr. Hayes had seen an advertisement in *Dalton's Weekly* to the effect that a large piece of ground in Essex, suitable for tea gardens, was to be let. The name of the place was not mentioned, and he had never heard of Borley, until he wrote in answer to the advertisement. Even then the name conveyed nothing to him. He and his wife travelled to Sudbury and then hired a car to take them to the Rectory. He was a little ahead of his wife and before examining the 'cottage', he thought he would thoroughly examine the grounds as to their suitability for tea gardens. So he walked on and on, and as he could hear his wife's footsteps behind him all the time, made a running commentary about the trees, the paths, the summerhouse, etc. He went right round the grounds, along the Nun's Walk, to the greenhouse. The footsteps were close behind him all the time. At the greenhouse he turned to face his wife, and was astounded to find that no one was there. He hurried back to the house and found that his wife had been exploring the rooms in the cottage, and had never been near him in the garden. And there was no one else about. So whose footsteps were they?

His wife had a similar experience. She climbed the stairs to the rooms over the stables and, hearing footsteps on the landing, thought that Mr. Hayes had followed her up. When she investigated, she found that no one was in the cottage or on the landing; and, as we know, her husband was exploring the garden. Then *she* went to look at the garden, leaving her husband to examine the cottage.

A few minutes after he entered one of the rooms he noticed on the wall near a shelf a sort of pocket, or hold-all, containing, as he found, a bundle of old bills that were rammed in tightly. Out of sheer curiosity, he examined the bills and as some of them amused him, he called out the items to—as he thought—his wife, whom he heard on the landing outside the room. He thought she had returned from the garden and had climbed the stairs to the rooms. As he received no reply or comment to his jokes about the bills, he carefully rammed all the bills back into the pocket on the wall and went to the door of the room to see why his wife did not answer him. There was no one on the landing! Puzzled, he turned round and was about to re-enter the room. He says: 'I stood in the doorway and gazed around. The bills that I had a few seconds before placed securely in the hold-all, *were laid on the shelf*.' There were other phenomena, too. It was not until they got back to Sudbury station and mentioned their adventures to a postman, that they learned the Rectory was 'haunted'.

Another strange experience befell Mr. H. F. Russell, a distinguished engineer who lives at Chelmsford. Having read my book, and his R.A.F. sons (one a Wing Commander and the other a Squadron Leader) happening to be home on leave, they all decided to take the car and have a look at the Rectory. This was on November 12, 1941. Mr. Russell shall relate his adventure himself:

'We left the car on the opposite side of the road and my two boys at once entered the house and had a good look round. I followed some twenty yards behind them when I was suddenly seized (so I imagine) and despite my attempts to keep vertical, was dashed to the ground. I felt an unseen, unknown power trying to throw me down, in which it succeeded, and I landed in a pool of mud which necessitated the sending of some clothes to the cleaners.'[1]

About this time I had a report to the effect that the military authorities tried to use the building for billeting purposes, but 'were so annoyed by Poltergeists that they had to seek quieter quarters'. An officer who spent the night in the place by himself got no rest on account of incessant bell-ringing.

A Cambridge scientist, Mr. Andrew J. B. Robertson, of St. John's College, who holds an honours degree in chemistry, and some friends and fellow-scientists, have sent me at least twenty reports on visits to Borley where, with scientific instruments, they recorded some most interesting phenomena. These include thermal variations, footsteps, raps, etc. All their reports will be published in my next Borley book.

Mention of the footsteps that dogged Mr. Hayes and his wife reminds me that Mr. Arthur S. Medcraft, of Goodmayes, Ilford, wrote me that in July, 1943 he decided to visit the Rectory. As it was a nice morning, he thought he would walk the three miles from Sudbury to Borley: 'At about 12.15 p.m., on getting within two hundred yards of the Rectory, I became aware of footsteps following me and, on turning, saw nothing but the empty road, the footsteps ceasing at once.' Then the footsteps became slower than his, though previously they had kept in step. It was a perfectly still day. While eating his lunch on the lawn, Mr. Medcraft heard a door slam heavily in the Rectory, and then a noise like a click. There was no one in the Rectory.

Among the many investigators who have visited the Rectory since my book was published are Lieut. G. B. Nawrocki (who is a doctor of medicine), Colonel J. Wroblewski, and some Polish fellow-officers. They spent two nights there, on June 28 and July 28, 1943, respectively. In their reports they record some interesting phenomena: Door-slamming; stone-throwing; a black shadow moving slowly along the Nun's Walk; 'scratchings'; a half-brick that apparently fell from the ceiling on to their heads; many 'whisperings' from the kitchen passage and so on. A shadow of a man that appeared to be silhouetted on the wall remained without moving for 10–20 seconds 'and then vanished very slowly'.

Before I leave Borley I must relate one very curious incident that happened, not in the Rectory, but in London. As I have stated more than once, I have concerned myself with Poltergeists only and have barely mentioned the 'nun', the other phantasms seen, and the many types of phenomena (such as odours, sweet music, etc.) recorded by many observers. The 'nun' is, of course, the centre of interest in the Borley story.

[1] Glanvill (*Saducismus Triumphatus*, 1681, Part II, p. 243), relates a similar incident.

299

There is a great deal of evidence for the nun—evidence going back for seventy years. But who *was* the nun? I will be quite honest—I have never had the time to find out. But it has occurred to at least one person that she was probably a member of the famous Waldegrave family who owned Borley for hundreds of years, and whose ornate marble memorial takes up a good deal of room in Borley Church.

When my book was published in 1940, Canon W. J. Phythian-Adams, D.D., D.S.O. (Canon of Carlisle and Chaplain to the King), read it through twice and sent me a most convincing and logical analysis of the evidence. He came to the conclusion that the nun was the 'Marie Lairre' of the Planchette writings, or at least a young French nun who had been inveigled to England on some pretext (perhaps by a false lover) and then murdered at Borley. He based his conclusions on the evidence recorded in the book, a new interpretation of the wall-writings,[1] etc.

Canon Phythian-Adams, in his report, believed that the remains of the nun would be found in the filled-in well in the cellar of the Rectory. So on August 17 and 18, 1943, the Rev. A. C. Henning, some friends, a labourer and myself cleared out the well, and dug up the cellar floor under which we found the parietal and temporal portion of a human skull, and a left mandible with five teeth *in situ*, that experts tell us belonged to a young woman 'under thirty'. We also found other objects of interest, all pointing to the fact that a nun had been buried there. But this is not the place to tell the story.

On September 13 following I took the skull, jawbone and other objects to the well-known art photographers, Messrs. A. C. Cooper, Ltd. to be photographed. While Mr. A. C. Cooper (the Governing Director of the company) and I were examining the skull, and each of us had hold of it, it slipped out of our hands, fell to the wooden floor of his studio, and broke into four almost equal pieces. I was very annoyed, though we managed to stick it together again. Mr. Cooper remarked that never, during the twenty-five years he had been in business there, had an accident occurred to anything of value entrusted to him. I said I would call for the photographs on the next morning.

When I went next day to collect the prints of the skull, etc., together with my 'exhibits', Mr. Cooper had a curious story to tell me. During the few hours that he had the skull and other objects in his possession, the following things happened: Two valuable oil paintings (one worth a thousand guineas) fell off their respective easels in his studio, when he was in the room, but not near them. Such a thing had never happened before during his business career. On the same afternoon he spoilt two batches of plates because he omitted to put the 'stop' in the lens of the camera—a thing he had never done before. And a clock on the wall, that had not gone for ten years, and could not be made to go, ticked for

---

[1] In the Phelps case (1850–51) scribbled messages appeared spontaneously on the walls.

twenty minutes of its own volition![1] Mr. Cooper, who knows little about psychical research, told me that he was very glad to get rid of my property!

But his troubles had hardly begun. On Wednesday, February 23, 1944, I took into his studio two pamphlets concerning Poltergeists. I wanted the title-pages photographed for reproduction in this book. Fortunately, I called for my pamphlets later in the day, arranging to collect the prints on the following morning. On this night of February 23–24 the studio was destroyed by enemy action. I am not claiming a relation between Poltergeists and Mr. Cooper's misfortunes—I am merely stating facts.

Just as I was concluding this chapter, the Rev. Father John Wright, of the handsome Roman Catholic Church of S. Philip Neri, Arundel, wrote to say that a Requiem Mass for the soul of the Borley nun was being said[2] on the following morning (Saturday, October 30, 1943). *Requiescat in pace!*[3]

As we are in the Borley district, I will relate the story of the Scrap-faggot[4] Green Poltergeist that so disturbed the good people of Great Leighs, Essex—a village six miles north-east of Chelmsford and not far from Borley.

On October 6, 1944, the *Sunday Pictorial* rang me up and told me that their representative was at Great Leighs, where the most extraordinary things were happening all over the village. He reported the following incidents: The tenor bell in the church tower tolled in the early hours of the morning, and the bell ropes played reversed chimes on Sundays; the church clock struck midnight at 2.30 a.m., and lost an hour each day; a farmer's haystacks had been found pushed over in the night; corn stooks were found in adjoining meadows; cows in calf gave birth prematurely; the hens stopped laying; chickens—which no one had lost—were found drowned in water-butts; others had escaped from locked fowl-houses; sheep strayed through unbroken hedges; three geese, belonging to Mr. Arthur J. Sykes, landlord of the St. Anne's Castle Inn (said to be the oldest in England: it dates from 1170), disappeared from his garden, though there was no break in the enclosure; a builder complained that a pile of scaffold-poles had been scattered about his yard, like matchsticks; a dozen paint pots, many brushes and other paraphernalia, neatly stacked over night, had been found by a

---

[1] In the Worksop Poltergeist case (*Proc., S.P.R.*, Vol. XII, pp. 45–58) in 1883, a clock that had not struck for eighteen months, suddenly chimed. It then leapt over a bed and fell to the floor.

[2] As the wall-writings (see p. 280) directed us to do.

[3] Since the above was written, I was lecturing at Oxford University where I was told that, some time previously, a Mass had been said for the 'nun' in one of the Oxford Roman Catholic churches.

[4] Probably a corruption of the Suffolk word 'scratch-fagot', an opprobrious term for an old hag or witch.

decorator under the beds in a cottage where his men had been working, and so on. Nearly every person in the village had some story to relate, of strange happenings or displacement of objects.

With a friend I spent a day at Great Leighs on October 11, 1944, and we interviewed several of the victims, all of whom confirmed the reports I had received. A few hours before our arrival, thirty sheep and two horses had been found dead in a field. It was said they had been poisoned. During the same night, chickens in a yard and rabbits in hutches had mysteriously changed places, though the fasteners were undisturbed. Mr. William Reynolds, the licensee of the Dog and Gun Inn, showed me a large boulder, weighing some 200 pounds, that had been deposited outside his front door—just where one was likely to fall over it. I examined the stone carefully. It was of irregular shape, much worn, with no signs of moss or moisture on it. No one had lost such a stone, and its origin has not been traced.

Perhaps what interested me most was a certain bedroom in the St. Anne's Castle Inn, which cannot be slept in—peacefully. Mr. Sykes asked me what I thought of it. I told him that the contents of the room appeared to have been shaken out of a pepper-pot. He said : 'It is always like this. Nothing will "stay put". Over and over again we have straightened up the place, only to find next morning that everything was higgledy-piggledy. We now use it as a lumber room, but boxes and furniture are scattered about night after night. No other part of the house is affected.' It was from this inn that the B.B.C. broadcast (April 15, 1939) a 'haunted house' programme.

The villagers declare that their misfortunes dated from the day when American bulldozers widened the road at Scrapfaggot Green, the centre of the village, thus displacing a two-ton stone that marked the remains of a seventeenth-century witch who had been buried (with a stake through her chest) at the crossroads there. They asked me what they had better do about it. I told them that if they believed the witch to be responsible for their troubles, the logical thing to do was to restore her tombstone to its original site. This they did, ceremonially, at midnight on October 11–12, placing the stone east and west in the traditional manner. The phenomena ceased. The result of my visit was that I came to the conclusion that the Scrapfaggot Green manifestations were partly genuine, partly the work of a practical joker, and partly due to mass-hysteria.

By courtesy of the Sunday Pictorial

Great Leighs, Essex, the scene of the Scrapfaggot Green Poltergeist disturbances. The Church of St. Mary the Virgin, seen in the picture, was the focus of many alleged phenomena. Photographed on October 6, 1944, during the manifestations.

CHAPTER XXVI

Poltergeist-Infested Rectories

A whole library of books could be written on haunted rectories, apparitions in churches, tales of phantom funerals, churchyards where the grass will not grow, bewitched coffins, corpse candles, bells that toll of their own volition, skeletons' dance of death, congregations that can be seen through—literally—and so on.

It is a curious fact that the clergy appear to be more frequent percipients or witnesses of psychic phenomena than men of any other calling. I will not attempt to explain this; I state merely what has come within my own experience. The *Journals* and *Proceedings* of the various psychic societies are full of accounts of ghosts seen by parsons, in church and out. It is a fact that in psychical research many of the best cases of haunting and Poltergeists have been recorded by parsons. I will give one or two examples, taken from recent records. The classical cases of 'Poltergeist rectories' in England are, of course, those of Epworth and Borley, included in this volume.

One of the most extraordinary rectory hauntings ever brought to my notice was that of Hamstall Ridware, four and a half miles north-east of Rugeley, East Staffordshire, in the Diocese of Lichfield. The rectory is old and large, and the River Blythe runs through the village.

It was in August, 1938, that the rector, the Rev. G. S. Hewins, B.A., told me of the curious happenings that had been experienced at the rectory. I will relate the story in his own words:

'In March, 1934, we took up residence at Hamstall Ridware Rectory, of which I enclose a photograph. It is a house of happy atmosphere, and is a true home. In September, 1934, a young nephew came to stay with us. He had a bilious attack, and my wife left his bedroom door open, and also ours, in case he should be bad in the night.

'About 4 a.m. the next day, she heard someone in bedroom slippers slithering along the landing. Thinking the boy was bad she sat up in bed, and waited as the footsteps approached the bedroom door. As she described to me later, she said that the air became icy as the footsteps came up to her bed. She lay down and shut her eyes, not daring to open them. Her first thought was that she was up against something which she had never experienced before, and she held a small cross which she had, believing nothing evil would touch her. She felt the mysterious presence bend over her, and over me. After seconds that seemed hours, there was distinctly a deep sigh, and gradually the thing melted away.

303

'Her own belief is that it is some small man in trouble, but that he went out happier than when he came in. She slept afterwards like a child until morning, when she told me what she had experienced. I slept through it, and knew nothing of the visitation. She was nervous all the week.

'Later, she ceased thinking of it until the next year, when she insisted on moving into a bedroom in a wing of the house of later date, but over a century old. One night in September, 1935, she was awakened by three tremendous raps and heard the sound of the footsteps. She woke me up and told me. She was trembling.

'The following year, we were on holiday in September, and so escaped anything.

'Last September, 1937, we went back into our usual bedroom, thinking the date was past, when I myself heard three loud thumps on the bedroom door at 6.30 a.m. This was on September 12. This time my wife did not hear it. I felt it very strange and unaccountable. Now that September again approaches, we feel nervous as to what will occur, and we are writing to you to see if you can suggest any explanation of the strange phenomenon. We know of no local event of the past which occurred in September, and which would be likely to account for it. It seems to concern this one bedroom in the central block of the house, a portion of the building which is about 200 years old. The church is a twelfth-century foundation and is of much historical interest.

'We have recently moved from the Rectory garden back into the churchyard, an old pedestal of a cross, which had been taken out when a new War Memorial cross was placed there. We wonder whether this will have any effect. We give you the foregoing facts as we believe they will be of interest to you.'

In some further correspondence I learned that the first visitation, in 1934, occurred on September 10. I arranged to visit Hamstall Ridware Rectory for the September, 1938, 'visitation', but at the end of August found that I should be unable to get away. However, I arranged for a competent observer to take my place. The day agreed upon was Saturday, September 10.

My disappointment can be imagined when I had a telegram on the Saturday from my friend saying that, owing to illness, the visit could not be made. It was then impossible for me to make other arrangements, and so I missed the 1938 visitation. However, the manifestations did not occur until September 17. In a letter dated September 21, Mr. Hewins says:

'At 12.30 a.m. on the 17th instant, my wife suddenly woke up and heard *two* loud raps. She thinks the first must have awakened her. She woke me up and said "It has come".'

It will be seen that the 1938 visitation was just a week later than that of 1934. In his letter, Mr. Hewins said that they had experienced no

Hamstall Ridware Rectory, Staffordshire, where a Poltergeist manifested itself regularly every September. See the Rev. G. S. Hewins' remarkable story, pages 303–6.

further phenomena during 1938. I had intended visiting his rectory in 1939, and had made all the arrangements when the war came. I have not yet heard whether anything occurred.

It is difficult to account for the Hamstall Ridware manifestations without a long inquiry, such as I made into the Borley haunting. But Mr. Hewins makes some suggestions in a letter dated September 8, 1938. He says:

'In my letters I have forgotten to mention to you another possibility, and that is that the disturbances have some connection with the Pre-Reformation chalice and paten belonging to this parish, and which are now on loan to the Victoria and Albert Museum. This chalice and paten were, I believe, originally given by an ancestor of Lord Leigh, who is Lord of the Manor, but buried in troublous times in a field on Hamstall Hall Farm. About 1823, they were accidentally discovered by some workmen in the course of digging a drain. Then they were taken to Stoneleigh Abbey, the seat of Lord Leigh, where they remained a number of years. They were then brought back to the parish, kept at the Rectory, and used on certain occasions. In view of their great value, however, and the fact that there was no really safe repository for them in the parish, the Rector decided some years ago, with the approval of the Diocesan Authorities, to place them in the Victoria and Albert Museum, where they would be easily accessible to students. There has been a certain amount of discussion regarding them since I have been here, but no decision was reached, and they still remain at the Museum on loan. I give you these facts as they may provide some possible clue to the manifestations'.

I am afraid that the history of the church treasures does not help us very much with our inquiry into the Hamstall Ridware manifestations, but the facts are interesting. What is also interesting is another curious experience Mr. Hewins related to me. The incident occurred in the autumn of 1937. The rector says: 'We were undressing at bedtime [in the "haunted" bedroom], and I had forgotten something, so I took the candle for a few minutes, leaving my wife in the dark. When I returned, I found her nervous and white, and she told me that as she lifted her petticoat over her head, it "burst into flames", and fell to the floor, with the appearance of a shower of sparks. I picked the petticoat up, and it felt limp. Have you heard of a similar experience?'

As a matter of fact, I had not—at least in that form. As Mr. Hewins suggests, the flames might have been caused by electricity generated by the friction when Mrs. Hewins pulled the garment over her other clothes. A similar effect, as is well known, can be produced by briskly rubbing a cat's back in the dark in a dry room. This is caused by static electricity, but I should be astonished to hear that a petticoat—whatever material it is composed of—could be set on fire by the simple act of pulling it over one's head.

The recurrence at repeated and definite intervals of the other phenomena at Hamstall Ridware Rectory is more interesting. In my *Fifty Years of Psychical Research*[1] I have postulated a theory concerning the periodicity of phenomena. It is that a room, place, or building becomes saturated with a person's ego, personality, or intelligence which—sometimes slowly and sometimes quickly—increases or 'accumulates' exactly like a storage battery. If the emanations (personality or intelligence) are strong, then the 'battery' takes little time to fill: perhaps a few hours or days. If the emanations are weak, then the 'battery' will take longer to fill—roughly twelve months in the case of the Hamstall Ridware phenomena. I have elaborated this theory in my book, which should be consulted. But it is quite possible that Mr. or Mrs. Hewins somehow form a focal point for the manifestations, which would not occur with anyone else living in the Rectory.

Another of my correspondents, the Rev. D. L. Booth, of S. Michael's Vicarage, Sutton Ings, Hull, in a letter dated November 24, 1942, related his experiences with Poltergeists. He had been reading my autobiography, *Search for Truth* (London, 1942), and this is what he says:

'One or two references in your book struck me as being somewhat similar experiences to those of my own, my wife and a friend.

'Before settling down here at home, I was for seven years a "Bush parson" in North West Australia, and on two occasions, in two different "rectories", I suddenly awoke in the night; felt the air become icy and lay very rigid as I felt a mysterious presence bend over me. There was a deep sigh,[2] and the thing melted away. It was something black in the form of a man, each time.

'The first time it happened was at Greenough Rectory—an old and lonely stone building in a desolate part of the rugged coastline, a house alleged to be haunted by a former rector, who had murdered his wife in that particular room.

'The second time it happened in a more modern building—the wooden (bungalow) rectory at Northampton, some fifty miles away farther north on the same coast. These happenings occurred in 1930–31.

'In connection with the other experience mentioned in your book, on page 281, my friend, the Rev. S. C. Kell, then vicar of Watton Priory, near Driffield, Yorks, told me of an experience he had at the Vicarage there, where on more than one occasion he and his wife had been awakened in the "small hours" by repeated and distinct thumps on their bedroom door; and of the old-fashioned "swinging" door-bells in the kitchen ringing of their own accord, sometimes in daylight, and at other times in the night. The house is modern, though built on or near the site of the old Watton Priory, in a very eerie neighbourhood. A twelfth-

[1] Longmans, London, 1939, pp. 299–302.
[2] Compare Mrs. Hewins's experience, above.

century church and remains of the old Abbey are situated not far away from the vicarage.'

I asked Mr. Booth whether he could get me particulars and a first-hand account of the Watton Abbey Poltergeist. He was good enough to do so, and sent me Mr. Kell's own story of the disturbances in Watton Vicarage. The Rev. S. C. Kell is now Vicar of Hempnall, Norfolk, and was Vicar of Watton from 1935–38. This is his answer to Mr. Booth's request for information:

'What, I wonder, is your interest in Poltergeists?—not that I suggest it is a new one, for I recollect that you showed vivid attention when P. of Watton Priory unfolded some of the queer "goings on" there!

'Some of the things that occurred at the Abbey were strange and P. and the little lady who was compiling material for a book on the Watton excavations, both said that they saw things.

'The Watton Vicarage "noise" was to us quite inexplicable, for the domestic bells would ring out of their own volition now and again and my wife and I would be opening front and back doors to see who might be there, but of course no one was there. The bells were altogether in a line near the kitchen ceiling, and I thought the explanation might be that a rat might have run along the lot. But, to be candid, we were fortunate in not having rats as far as I remember.

'If there was some ordinary explanation of the bells, there *could not be any ordinary one about the bedroom door bangings.*

'When the wind was strong and high the house would shake, together with the windows and doors, but *on three Sunday nights* there was no strong wind, and *about the same time on those three Sunday nights*—as we were dropping off to sleep, there were *thunderous bangs* on the bedroom door where we were sleeping.

'On the first occasion I got up to see what it was about, *forgetting that we had no guests or maid in the house*. There was nothing to be *seen*.

'The next Sunday night *at exactly the same time* the banging started again. This time I got up because I didn't want to appear a coward to myself, so opened the door and called out loudly; but nothing was to be seen.

'The same thing happened on the third Sunday night. This time, I admit, I did not open the door. I was annoyed as I was so tired, so shouted out rudely—"Oh, shut up!"

'There was no explanation of the door-banging, but bangs they were and not knocks.

'Nothing happened to us and life continued as before; perhaps the bells did a peal again off and on, but that was all.'

In his original letter to me the Rev. D. L. Booth mentions another case of Poltergeist-haunting at Patrington Rectory, East Yorks. Again, at my request, he obtained evidence of the haunting, and the Rector, the Rev. P. R. Frost, M.A., sent the following information:

'An aunt who was sleeping in a bedroom upstairs was hurled out of bed.'

The Rectory,
Patrington,
Janry. 11*th*, 1943.   *East Yorks.*

'Dear Booth,

'The information I gave you (1935 or 1936?), I received from the daughter of the late Canon Maddock. She would be a young girl at the time. According to her statements, "One night, the heavy furniture in the dining room was hurled about in disorder by supernatural agency. Another night, an aunt who was sleeping in a bedroom upstairs was hurled out of bed[1] on to the landing!

'Canon Maddock was succeeded by Durell, and on the morning of Durell's first night at the Rectory, he came down to Winestead (a neighbouring village), where the girl was staying, and said to her, "Why didn't you tell me that Patrington Rectory was haunted?" Evidently he had himself had some strange experiences during the night. Nothing remarkable has happened here since, so far as I am aware.

(Signed) 'P. R. FROST.'

Mr. Booth once slept in the room at Patrington Rectory occupied by the aunt mentioned in Mr. Frost's letter. He had been preaching at the Harvest Thanksgiving service at the church and stayed overnight at the Rectory in the spare bedroom, 'from which guests in times past had been ejected on to the landing by strange powers. I had been asleep, but suddenly awoke to hear "something" pattering about the room.' When Mr. Booth switched on the light, the pattering ceased. When he switched it off again, the sounds recommenced. No explanation. Mr. Booth was fortunate in not being pitched out of bed.

Another case brought to my notice at about this period was mentioned in a letter that I received from the Rev. N. C. Murray, The Vicarage, Ainstable, Carlisle. Under date December 11, 1942, he wrote: 'My wife and I experienced some Poltergeist effects at a house in Ellerthwaite Road, Windermere, where I was once curate. Also, when my father was curate-in-charge of Bungalow Town, Shoreham, I remember being repeatedly called by my nickname, though there was nobody else in the old house, in the Lower Road, which was our home'.

I have received many scores of letters from the clergy, giving first-hand experiences of hauntings and Poltergeists, and of phenomena that seem quite inexplicable by any physical laws known to us. For example, the Rev. F. Daly Briscoe, of Radley Vicarage, Berkshire, in a letter dated April 30, 1939, says:

'I should like permission to say that in this old Parsonage House, built about 1380, "ghosts" (i.e. disembodied spirits of men) have definitely appeared since I have held this benefice, and before that time. I am told that the late Bishop Gore, who at one time held this living, had

[1] Compare Mrs. Foyster's experiences at Borley.—H.P.

309

himself seen these spirits about the house, and there is evidence that others had been conscious of their presence. At one time the house was a Priory and I personally have seen monks about the place—i.e. definite spirits of men separated from this physical state of our earthly life. In a former house in which I lived, one room was undoubtedly "haunted"—but I dislike the use of this word—and it was not possible to remain in that room for any length of time. But this is quite another phenomenon, and it would serve no useful purpose to go into that matter here. But the appearing of disembodied "spirits" is by no means a rare occurrence, and I think there is more than sufficient evidence, for their existence, apart from any Theological dogma laid down by the authority of the Church of God.'

In my reply to the above letter, I asked if it would be possible to witness the manifestations said to occur at Radley Vicarage, and whether Mr. Briscoe had had any further experiences of a like nature. In his reply (May 3, 1939) my correspondent said:

'In a Rectory quite near to Oxford there were some strange happenings when a former butler who had departed this life used to make himself very objectionable in blowing out the candles, putting out the lamps, and banging the doors. I believe I am right in saying that Father Fitzgerald, of the Mirfield Community, was called in and the "ghost" was, after his visiting the place, finally set at rest.

'I do not know how it would be quite possible to witness any manifestation of the monks who appear in this place; for one might remain here for a considerable length of time without anyone "appearing".'

My next case of a haunted rectory is taken from Major Moor's *Bealings Bells*,[1] published in 1841. I have chosen this one—out of many—because it is strangely reminiscent of Borley.

Major Moor had heard of the extraordinary happenings at Sydersterne Parsonage, near Fakenham, Norfolk, and wrote to the rector, the Rev. John Stewart, to know whether the manifestations recorded there included that of 'bell-ringing'. This is the rector's reply:

'You have indeed sent your letter to the House of Mystery. In the broad lands of England you cannot, perhaps, find such another. But I regret to add that I can afford you no assistance in the "bell" line. Our noises in this parsonage are of a *graver* character; smart successions of tappings, groanings, cryings, sobbings, disgusting scratchings, heavy trampings, and thundering knocks have distressed us, here, for a period of nearly *nine years* during my occupancy of this Cure. They *still* continue, to the annoyance of my family, the alarm of my servants, and the occasional flight of some of them. And I am enabled, clearly, to trace their existence in this Parsonage, to a period of sixty years past. I have little doubt either that, were not all the residents anterior to that

[1] pp. 93–5.

time (in fact, of a former generation), now passed away, I could be able to carry my successful scrutiny *on and on*!

'In 1833 and 1834, we kept almost open house to enable respectable people who were personally known by, or introduced to, us to satisfy their curiosity. But, our kindness was abused, our motives misinterpreted, and even our characters maligned. We, therefore, closed our doors—and they remain hermetically sealed!

'In 1834, I had prepared my "diary" for publication. My work was purchased by Mr. Rodd of Newport Street, London. But as the "end" had *not* arrived, I postponed my intention from day to day and year to year—in hope of such consummation. But the "noises" occasionally recur, and my "diary" occasionally progresses until it has, now, assumed rather a formidable appearance.'

The variety and type of phenomena, their persistence, the 'flight of the servants', the 'open house' for investigators, and the keeping of a daily log of the manifestations, were exactly paralleled at Borley. Even psychic history repeats itself! Where the record of Sydersterne differs from that of Borley is that apparently there was no bell-ringing in the former rectory. But the paranormal ringing of bells is a very distinctive —and a very common—feature of Poltergeist activity; the most famous case of all is that of the two months' incessant ringing which occurred in a house at Great Bealings, Suffolk, not very far from Borley. This case is so important that, as the reader is aware, I have devoted a chapter to it.

Sir Ernest Bennett, M.P., in his collection[1] of ghost stories, cites a few rectory or churchyard Poltergeists. The first related to the minister of S., a small hamlet in the south of Scotland.

July 23rd, 1889.[2]

'It affords me much pleasure, in answer to your letter of the 20th, which I only received today, to give you an account of my experiences in connection with the music in D. woods, which does not seem due to any ordinary source.

'I have heard it, I think, four times, and always at the same place, viz. on the public road, which runs along the south bank of the Tweed, and which passes at the distance of three-quarters of a mile the old churchyard of D. The churchyard, from which the music always seems to come, is south of the road, and at a much higher elevation, and the intervening ground is densely covered with wood. The first two or three times I heard the sound it was very faint, but sufficiently distinct to enable me to follow the swellings and cadences. I do not know why, but on those occasions I never for a moment thought it was real music. Neither did I think it anything very unusual, though the tones seemed more ethereal than any I had heard before. I am exceedingly fond of

---

[1] *Apparitions and Haunted Houses*, London, 1939 (Case 10).

[2] This case was originally published many years ago.

music, and in my walks, frequently sing without sound (if I may use such an expression) tunes, pieces, and "songs without words". As there was on every occasion a breeze swaying the branches, I thought that, in my imagination, produced the result, though it did seem strange that I never heard anything similar in other woods.

'Years passed, and I had forgotten all about the matter, when I heard it again, and I will not soon forget the last performance.

'Last year I was walking up to X. to drive with Mr. and Mrs. M. to a tennis match. When I reached the usual spot, there burst upon my ear, from the direction of the churchyard, what seemed to be the splendid roll of a full brass and reed band. It did not recall the former occasions, and I never for a moment doubted its reality. My first thought was that Sir Y.X. had lent his park for a Sunday-school treat, and my second was that the band was far too good, and the music of far too high a class for such a purpose. I walked on, enjoying it thoroughly, never dreaming that I was not listening to good ordinary music, till it suddenly struck me that the sound, though now faint, ought to have been inaudible, as there was now between me and the churchyard the big, broad shoulder of S. (a hill). I began to remember the other—infinitely less distinct—performances I had heard, and though not superstitious enough to believe that there was anything which could not be explained on natural grounds, I felt that the explanation was beyond my power of discovery or conjecture. Of course, I intended immediately telling my friends at X., but my attention must have been called to something else, as I did not do so. We drove away, and after some time, we all, except Mrs. M., got out to walk up a very steep hill. Walking at the side of the carriage I told the most minute circumstances of my strange experience. Mrs. M. seemed to take it very seriously, but Mr. M. ridiculed the whole affair as a freak of the imagination.

'I tell you these little incidental circumstances to show you how indelibly the events of the day are engraven upon my memory.

'I had not, at that time, heard that the sounds had been listened to by any other person, but it is now well known that they have often been heard by Sir Y.Z. and once by Lady Z.

'In the last case the music resembled that of a choir, unaccompanied by instruments. In my case there was nothing resembling vocal music.

(*Signed*) 'J. L. B.'

This case was corroborated by other witnesses. Both Lady Z. and her husband, Sir Y. Z., heard the chanting and they testify as follows;

'On the hot, still afternoon of July 12th, 1888, I was sitting resting with some old ladies at our pretty little cemetery chapel, within the grounds of our house in Scotland, far away from all thoroughfare or roads. Whilst I was talking I stopped suddenly and exclaimed, "Listen! what is that singing?" It was the most beautiful singing I had ever heard, just a wave of cathedral chanting, a great many voices, which only lasted a few seconds. The lady said she heard nothing, and thinking she might be deaf, I said nothing. I quite thought it *might* be haymakers at work, and yet I turned my head round, for the singing was so close by. It dawned upon me, "The Scotch need not say they cannot sing." There were several others sitting with us, but they heard nothing (which astonished me). I said nothing more till the evening, when I casually said to my husband, "What was that singing where we were sitting this p.m.?" thinking he would reply, "Oh, it was the men at work"; but, to my astonishment, he replied, "I have often heard that before, and it is *chanting* I hear." (Mark, I had not said I had heard several voices, only singing, which was very remarkable.) And then, and not till then, I saw that the voices could not have been human, and certainly I had not imagined it. I had never heard such heavenly (that is the only adjective I can use) music before, and would not have missed it for anything. I was in no wise in a sentimental or fanciful state of mind when I heard the music, but only talking of the common subjects of the day. This is my written statement, and accurately true.

(*Signed*) 'A. Z.'

From Sir Y. Z.
'When alone at the cemetery I have occasionally heard, from within the chapel, sounds as of chanting.

(*Signed*) 'Y. Z.'

A more modern case[1] is that recorded by the Rev. F. G. Shepherd, Rector of Ludlow. There had been circumstantial and well-authenticated accounts of an apparition of a woman who was seen to haunt the churchyard of the parish church of St. Lawrence, Ludlow. So Sir Ernest Bennett wrote to the rector, who replied as follows:

The Rectory,
Ludlow,
23rd July, 1937.

'In reply to your letter of yesterday's date I have to say that I have never seen anything in the nature of an apparition round our churchyard.
'My experience is confined to this house. We came here in 1930 and soon afterwards heard noises at various times during the night, such as someone passing along the upstair passages of this house. The noises may be described as shuffling feet rather than footsteps. This continued at irregular intervals until two years ago—it has been heard say two or three nights in succession and then not again for a month or two. However, about two years ago at 10.45 to 11 p.m., I saw an apparition coming down our front stairs. It was a woman; she came down slowly but did

[1] *Op. cit.* (Case 78.)

not seem to notice me. I was standing in the hall. She was tall and slim with grey hair and wearing a light blue-grey dressing-gown; she passed into our drawing-room, which was in darkness. I followed her and without switching on the light closed the door behind me. I saw her pass into the drawing room and was then four or five yards behind her, but when I reached the room she had vanished. My object in closing the door was to have the experience of being in a room with a "ghost" but she made no re-appearance.

'I am afraid this isolated experience is of no value to you.

'We have heard no further noises in this house until last week, when the shuffling was heard again. These noises are not loud, but just audible.'

Another old case was recorded by John Timbs, who relates[1] how 'a sort of rumbling, as of wagons, was heard for upwards of an hour at Bulwick Rectory, North Northamptonshire'. This was on July 16, 1850. On the 19th, 'a black rain fell'. But whether there was any connection between the two phenomena, I cannot say.

In the *Cambrian Daily Leader*[2] for July 7, 1887, is an account of a Poltergeist 'transportation' said to have occurred in the home of the Rev. David Phillips, of Swansea. In addition to the usual phenomena associated with Poltergeists, a woman of Mr. Phillips's household was 'transported over a wall, and towards a brook, where she arrived in a "semi-conscious condition".' Mr. Phillips and his son, a Cambridge undergraduate, asserted that this 'transportation' had occurred.

A curious case was reported in *The Times* (September 6, 1919) by the Rev. H. P. Bryan, of Askerwell Rectory, Dorchester. In his employ was a young maid and the usual Poltergeist disturbances (which included the fall of immense pieces of rock from the ceiling) occurred. She was discharged. At her next 'place', the house caught fire.

The next case does not relate to an English rectory, but it concerns an English Bishop, so I will include it. In his biography[3] of Bishop Weston of Zanzibar, Dr. H. Maynard Smith, Canon of Gloucester, tells of Poltergeist phenomena near the mission station, at Weti, East Africa. Clods of earth, of unknown origin, were bombarding a house in which lived a man and his wife. Some of the clods fell *inside* the house. The bishop investigated, and he, too, was struck by a clod. Inside the house, he saw a mass of mud appear on the ceiling. The door was open, but this point on the ceiling was in such a position that could *not* be hit by anyone throwing anything from outside. There was no open window. The bishop exorcised the 'spirit' and the mud-throwing stopped. Then the woman became ill.

Another rectory Poltergeist was that said to have infested Binbrook Rectory, Lincolnshire. There were the usual disturbances.

[1] *Year Book of Facts*, London, 1851, p. 270.
[2] Published at Swansea. (Cited by Charles Fort.)
[3] *Frank, Bishop of Zanzibar*, London, 1926.

In 1913, Poltergeist phenomena occurred at Weston Vicarage, Yorkshire, the home of the Rev. Charles Tweedale. No explanation.[1]

In the same year, at Asfordby Rectory, near Melton Mowbray, Leicestershire, were experienced many Poltergeist phenomena. Loud noises, rappings, tugging of bed-clothes by invisible entities, etc. Witnessed by the Rev. F. A. Gage Hall, and others. Never explained.[2]

Barnack Rectory, near Stamford, Northamptonshire (the birthplace of Henry Kingsley, 1830–76) was once troubled by a Poltergeist when Charles Kingsley (1819–75) was living there as a youth. There were the usual disturbances, including the displacement and rolling of barrels in the cellar, strange noises, etc. Some account of the phenomena is given by Charles Kingsley's widow in the *Life*[3] of her husband that she wrote. In the Deanery at Exeter there was also a 'ghost', according to the *Daily Mail*.[4]

Leadenham Rectory, near Caythorpe, Lincolnshire, has—or had—a Poltergeist. Miss Monica Shorten, daughter of the Rector, the Rev. W. G. Shorten, M.A., has told me some interesting things about both the Rectory and the *Geist*. Dr. John Dee (1527–1608), the mathematician and magician, once held the living, though I am afraid he was seldom in residence. Anyway, there is a carved stone inscription over the back door, recording the fact that he was once the incumbent. It is dated 1568—a period when Dee was much on the Continent.

It is not surprising that, with the Dee connection, Leadenham Rectory should be haunted—or 'infested'. The story is that the ghost of a certain Canon Mallet makes a thumping noise when he places his—detached—head heavily on the table, before commencing his wanderings. The Canon, by the way, was executed at Chelmsford for high treason because he opposed Henry VIII at the time of the dissolution of the monasteries. So much for the legend. But it is a fact that the 'thumps' are heard; and thuds and crashes were numerous, Miss Shorten tells me, when she was a child.

Like the Rev. John Stewart (cited above), I could go 'on and on' giving examples of Poltergeist-infested rectories. But there is a sameness in the phenomena—a proof, I think, of their genuineness. And I do not want to weary the reader.

I could give details of many cases of Poltergeist infestations at rectories in other lands, were I to enlarge the scope of this monograph. The classical cases are those known as the 'Phelps case'[5] (1850–51), and the 'Cideville case' (1850–51). In the former disturbance, that occurred in the house of the Rev. Eliakim Phelps, of Stratford, Conn., there were

[1] See *Yorkshire Observer*, April 2 and 7, 1913.
[2] See C. G. Harper's *Haunted Houses*, London, 1927 (3rd Ed). pp.148–9.
[3] *Charles Kingsley, his Letters and Memories of his Life*, London, 1877.
[4] For December 24, 1904.
[5] See *Historic Poltergeists* by Hereward Carrington, New York, pp. 8–12.

the usual 'little girls', that apparently formed a *nexus* with the extra-ordinary happenings that occurred. I have referred to these in my chapter, 'What Poltergeists Do'.

The Cideville[1] (Seine Inférieure) disturbances took place in the house of the parish priest, who charged a local shepherd named Thorel with being a 'wizard'. The case is remarkable for the fact that Thorel brought an action for slander against the curé. The case was heard in court and the shepherd was non-suited. By implication, the phenomena were accepted as genuine.

What is the link between the clergy, their habitations, young girls, and Poltergeists? Mr. Howard Spring noted this connection and com-mented upon it (*Country Life*, December 18, 1942). He mentions the rectories of Epworth and Borley; the Shropshire manor-house (where the canon resided); the Corpus Christi Poltergeist, etc. He says: 'It is strange to me how often Poltergeists appear in an ecclesiastical context. ... Mr. Price writes that the presence of a young girl in the house appears often to be the exciting cause of the strange phenomena; and I have wondered whether in these ecclesiastical precincts the poor "flesh" has been tortured overmuch, leaving frustration to inhabit dark places.'

A phenomenon sometimes associated with rectories is that of the paranormal displacement of coffins in nearby vaults. In the crypt of Borley Church, about 1880, some of the coffins were found to have been paranormally moved from their prescribed positions. At Staunton, in Suffolk, something similar happened. A number of leaden coffins were displaced three times, about the year 1760.[2] An exceptionally well-authenticated account of paranormal coffin-moving is that of Gretford (or Greatford), near Stamford, Lincolnshire. Mr. F. A. Paley, a Cam-bridge graduate and son of the Rector of Gretford, tells the whole story in *Notes and Queries*.[3] Though the vault in the church was always properly sealed, it was found that on three occasions, when the vault was opened, all the leaden coffins had been thrown higgledy-piggledy all over the place. One coffin, says Mr. Paley, took six men, with difficulty, to carry it.

The classical case of Poltergeist coffin-displacement is, of course, that of the 'haunted vault' of Christ Church at Barbados—a case authenti-cated and documented up to the hilt, and testified to by many dis-tinguished witnesses, including Lord Combermere, Governor of the Island. The vault (100 feet above sea level, and dug out of the living rock to the extent of two feet, belonging to the Chase family), is twelve feet long by about seven feet wide, and contained six coffins, all of which, with one exception, were of lead. The vault, made of stone, was

[1] See *Footfalls on the Boundary of Another World*, by R. D. Owen, London, 1875.
[2] See the *London Magazine* for 1760, and *European Magazine*, Sept., 1815.
[3] Third Series, Vol. XII, Nov. 9, 1867, p. 371.

Entrance to the Chase Vault, Christ Church, Barbados, the scene of Lord Combermere's experiment in 1819–20. The vault, with arched roof, is mostly above ground, but is sunk 2 feet into the live rock. Steps lead into the interior, in which, though hermetically sealed, heavy leaden coffins were repeatedly displaced. The internal dimensions are 12 feet long by 7 feet wide. The Chase Arms are visible on the carved tablet above the entrance. (Photo taken by Dr. E. J. Dingwall. October 2. 1936.)

sealed with a huge slab of blue Devonshire marble, which required four men to move, cemented into the opening. The vault had a stone floor. Apparently, there was no disturbance until a suicide was buried there. Five times in eight years, the coffins were found in confusion, thrown all over the place, and sometimes on end. This occurred in the case of the heaviest coffin, which enclosed the remains of a very big man. The coffins were found disturbed on the following dates: August 9, 1812; September 15, 1816; November 17, 1816; July 7, 1819; and April 18, 1820. After the July, 1819 disturbance, Lord Combermere decided to make a test. The coffins were restored to their proper positions, a plan made of them, and fine white sand sprinkled all over the floor of the vault. Then the heavy slab of marble was cemented by masons into the aperture, and Lord Combermere and others impressed their official and personal seals into the soft cement. The closing and sealing of the vault took place in the presence of several distinguished witnesses, including the Rector of Christ Church. The vault was hermetically sealed.

On April 18, 1820, a noise was heard coming from the interior of the vault. Lord Combermere and the other original witnesses were at once informed and it was decided to open the vault immediately. Thousands of people gathered for the opening. All seals and cementing were found intact and undisturbed, and 'not a blade of grass round the vault had been touched'. When the slab was at last removed, after much difficulty, the six coffins were found to have been moved from their proper positions and thrown all over the vault. The heaviest one (that required the strength of seven or eight men to handle), was standing on its head, and the smallest had been hurled across the vault, making a dent in the wall. The fine sand bore no imprints or other markings, but was perfectly smooth and even, exactly as it was when the vault was sealed. There was no trace of water or of anything that could have moved the coffins normally. A full report was drawn up and accurate diagrams (reproduced) of the displaced coffins were made. All the coffins were then removed from the vault and buried in separate graves.

Several copies of the official report were made and circulated, and a tract was published in Barbados giving the complete history of the hauntings. I have been unable to find the name of this tract, but it was republished in England under the title of *Death-Deeds* (Skeet, London, 1860) by, Andrew Lang says, a Mrs. D. N. Cusson. A kinsman of Mr. Lang possessed one of the manuscript copies of the original report. Actually, the pamphlet was signed 'K.R.', i.e. K. Redding, afterwards Mrs. Cusson.

Mr. Lang told the whole story of the Barbados hauntings[1] at a meet-

[1] For original sources, see *Transatlantic Sketches*, by Sir J. E. Alexander, London, 1833, Vol. I, p. 161; *History of Barbados*, by Sir R. H. Schomburgk, London, 1848, pp. 220–21; and *Memoirs and Correspondence of Field-Marshal Viscount Combermere*, by Mary, Viscountess Combermere and Capt. W. W. Knollys, London, 1866, Vol. I, pp. 385–393. A very full detailed account. But perhaps the best account of all,

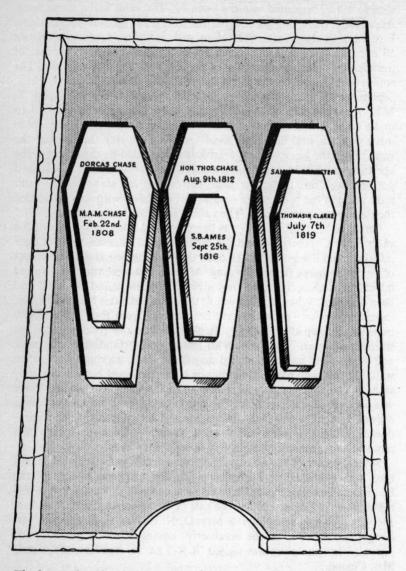

The haunted vault at Christ Church, Barbados. Position of coffins before the vault was sealed by Lord Combermere, July 7th, 1819.

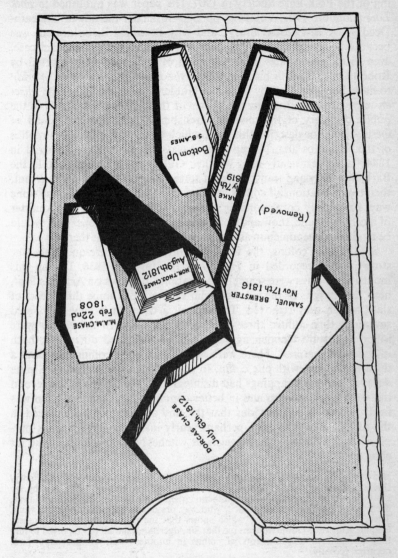

The haunted vault at Christ Church, Barbados. Position of coffins when vault was opened by Lord Combermere on April 18, 1820. The heaviest coffin (that of the Hon. Thos. Chase) was found standing on its head. The coffin of the child, S. B. Ames, had been flung across the vault, denting the wall, and was found bottom upwards.

ing of the Folk Lore Society in 1907. His paper was published in *Folk Lore* (London, 1907, Vol. xviii, pp. 376–90) under the title of ' "Death-Deeds"—A Bi-Located Story', and why he called it 'bi-located' was because he made the curious discovery that an *exactly* parallel case, even to the exact dates of the openings of the vaults, was reported by Robert Dale Owen in his *Footfalls on the Boundary of Another World*,[1] to have been recorded by Baron de Guldenstubbé—this time the *mise-en-scène* is the vault under the chapel of the Buxhoewden family in the public cemetery of the town of Arensburg in the Russian island of Oesel. I will not describe this case, which to the last detail, is a replica of the Barbados affair, except that it was alleged to have occurred in 1844. Lang pertinently asks whether Guldenstubbé merely retold the Barbados story and transplanted it to the Baltic. He thinks not. *If* not, then two collections of coffins were paranormally displaced in the same way, on exactly corresponding dates (though separated by a quarter of a century), and thousands of miles apart—a coincidence that would be as great a phenomenon as the movement of the coffins themselves!

Speaking of coffins, the most extraordinary, picturesque, and true story[2] is that recorded in *The Times* for July 20, 1836. During this month some boys were searching for rabbits' burrows on Arthur's Seat, near Edinburgh. In the side of a cliff they noticed some thin sheets of slate, which they removed. They found a cave. In it they discovered seventeen tiny coffins, three or four inches long. In the coffins were found miniature wooden figures. They were dressed differently, both in style and material. There were two tiers of eight coffins each, and a third tier begun, with one coffin. In the first tier, the coffins were quite decayed and the wrappings had disintegrated. The coffins in the second tier were more modern and in better condition, and the top coffin was fairly recent. It was obvious that the tiny coffins[3] had been placed in the tiny cave at intervals—perhaps yearly intervals. But for what purpose? And by whom? Poltergeists or witches? The reader can take his choice.

and one easily available, is the story printed in Sir Algernon Aspinall's *The Pocket Guide to the West Indies* (London, 1927, pp. 99–105; first edition, 1907). It is by the Hon. Forster M. Alleyne, from an authentic manuscript by the Hon. Nathan Lucas, Member of the Legislative Council, who was present at the opening of the vault. There are illustrations, one of which shows that the roof of the vault is arched. Comdr. Rupert T. Gould informs me that Sir Algernon Aspinall has reported to him that unexplained displacements of coffins in another vault at Barbados have occurred recently.

[1] London, 1861, p. 186.

[2] Cited by Charles Fort.

[3] Both coffins and figures are pictured in the *Proceedings* of the Society of Antiquaries of Scotland, Vol. XII, p. 460.

CHAPTER XXVII

Poltergeist Incendiaries

Poltergeists are fire-raisers. They burn houses, barns, ricks, and furniture. They cause the spontaneous combustion of clothing and other inflammable material, even in closed drawers and boxes. They burn people, too; at least, there are many cases on record where persons have been seriously burnt, or burned to death, when no normal explanation was forthcoming. A curious feature of some of these cases is that only the victims themselves were destroyed, no sign of burning or damage by fire being apparent in their vicinity.

Poltergeists cause explosions, or make explosive noises, detonations, bangs like pistol-shots or even cannon fire. It was at Ballechin House, it will be remembered, that Father Hayden reported noises 'like the continuous explosion of petards'. These sounds are not usually accompanied by either fire or smoke. At Willington Mill, shots, as from a pistol, were heard.

As for fires in houses, their name is legion, and a volume could be written on this particular facet of Poltergeist incendiarism. At the Scotch 'Poltergeist Manor', seventeen fires broke out spontaneously during the course of a few days, 'to the amazement of the police'. To the still greater amazement of the present writer, as I have already recorded, an insurance company paid out £400 compensation—and, by implication, admitted the existence of Poltergeists.

At Borley Rectory, an undergraduate, Mr. S. G. Welles, saw a luminosity floating near the Blue Room ceiling, and Dom Richard Whitehouse, O.S.B., reported several spontaneous outbreaks of fires. His aunt, Lady Whitehouse, helped to put out a fire that broke out in a locked room: 'the skirting board was glowing red'. Strange lights were seen in the Rectory, and on March 27, 1938, 'Sunex Amures', a Planchette entity, threatened to burn the place and promised that the fire would start 'over the hall'. On February 27–28, 1939, the Rectory *was* burnt down, and the fire started 'over the hall'. It is a curious fact that both of the two famous 'Poltergeist rectories' in this country should have been destroyed by fire: Epworth in February, 1709, and Borley in February, 1939. It was at Borley, too, that clouds of smoke were seen rising from the lawn. Investigation by two witnesses revealed that there was *no* fire.

At the Shropshire manor house, home of the 'stumbling Poltergeist', glowing embers from the dying fire were thrown all over the room after the residents had retired to rest; at Battersea, red-hot cinders (origin

321

unknown) were hurled at the occupants. At the 'Mill on the Eden' a
piece of flaming paper was found in a lumber room, and I could go on
multiplying these examples indefinitely.

Some of the most convincing and amazing 'Poltergeist fires' were those
that occurred in the household of Andrew Mackie of Ringcroft, Galloway, Scotland, in 1695. As the reader is aware, the case is well-authenticated. First, a quantity of peat was found on fire, and the smoke nearly
suffocated the family. Several times the house was set on fire, and a
'sheep house' was entirely consumed by the flames. On April 29, 1695,
'being Monday, it continued setting fire to the house so frequently, that
Andrew Mackie being weary with quenching it, he put out all the fire
about the house, and poured water on the hearth; yet it set the House
on fire again several times, tho there was no fire to be had within a
quarter of a mile of the House'.[1]

I am convinced that some affinity exists between 'Poltergeist mediums'
and Poltergeists proper—or improper. Stella C. and Frau Maria Silbert
were famous physical mediums and both produced 'sparks' and 'lights'
—some percussive and some lambent—feeble detonations, and 'fire-
works'. These induced phenomena were witnessed at séances and were
therefore expected and under control. The famous medium, D. D.
Home, produced lights on many occasions. So did the mediums
Stainton Moses, William Eglinton, Franek Kluski, and Jean Guzik.
Some of the phenomena were probably fraudulent.

One of the most convincing of these 'luminous mediums' was Anna
Monaro, of Pirano. She puzzled Italian scientists by emitting a glow of
light from her chest as she slept. After an intensive investigation in
hospital by Professors Fabio Vitali, G. C. Trabacchi, and Sante de
Sanctis, they declared the phenomena genuine. Professor Vitali kindly
sent me their printed report.[2]

I will now give some well-attested cases of supposed Poltergeist
incendiarism. In 1878, the *Glasgow News*[3] reported a case of fire-raising
in the farmhouse of John Shattock, who lived near Bridgwater.

Included amongst the fires was a hayrick which blazed as a policeman
was passing. As a young girl named Ann Kidner (aged twelve), belonging to the house, was near it at the time, he suspected her. He visited
the farmhouse, where he heard loud raps, and saw dishes and loaves of
bread wandering about the kitchen. All the policeman could think of
was to arrest the girl. She was taken before the magistrates, who released her because of lack of evidence.

Another court case centred upon a young girl named Elizabeth
Barnes, aged ten. She was accused by John Wright, a linendraper, living
in Foley Place, Marylebone, of having repeatedly and 'by some extra-

---

[1] *A New Confutation of Sadducism . . . op. cit.*
[2] *Sul Fenomeno di Pirano*, Roma, 1934.
[3] For May 20, 1878.

ordinary means' set fire to the clothing of Wright's mother, who was burned so severely that she was not expected to live. The girl was a servant in the Wright household. On January 5, 1820, a mysterious fire had broken out in Wright's house. On the 7th, Mrs. Wright and the girl were sitting by the hearth in the kitchen. Suddenly the woman found her clothes on fire. On January 12, they caught alight again. On the 13th, Wright heard screams from the kitchen and again found his mother in flames. The girl was not then present. Mrs. Wright's daughter then arrived at the house in order to 'guard her'. Again, 'by some unknown means', the old lady caught fire. 'She was so dreadfully burned that she was put to bed'. When she had dropped off to sleep, her son and daughter left the room, but hastened back upon hearing their mother's screams. Mrs. Wright was blazing, though Elizabeth was not then near her. The girl was ordered out of the house—and the conflagrations ceased. There was not the slightest evidence that Elizabeth Barnes was normally responsible for the fires, and Mrs. Wright herself declared it was impossible that the girl could have set her clothes alight. But she was hailed before a magistrate, who thought that Elizabeth was guilty. However, he adjourned the case until Mrs. Wright recovered sufficiently for her to give evidence.[1]

At Binbrook Farm, near Great Grimsby, there were mystery fires and typical Poltergeist disturbances in December and January, 1905. There are several contemporary accounts of the case. Things were thrown about the rooms, objects burst into flames, and the young maidservant—the eternal 'young girl'!—was burned, or was attacked by something that was burning. A school teacher of Binbrook, writing to the *Liverpool Echo* (January 25, 1905), stated that a blanket had been found burning in a room in which there was no fireplace. At the same time, chickens were being killed in the farmyard. They all had their throats torn.

In the *Louth and North Lincolnshire News* for January 28, 1905, is a report of the disturbances. Objects unaccountably fell from shelves, and things were transported: 'A story that greatly dismays the unsophisticated is that of the servant girl, who, while sweeping the floor, was badly burned on the back. This is how the farmer relates it: "Our servant girl, whom we had taken from the workhouse, and who had neither kin nor friend in the world that she knows of, was sweeping the kitchen. There was a very small fire in the grate: there was a guard there, so that no one can come within two feet or more of the fire, and she was at the other end of the room, and had not been near. I suddenly came into the kitchen, and there she was, sweeping away, while the back of her dress was afire. She looked around as I shouted, and, seeing the flames, rushed through the door. She tripped, and I smothered the fire out with wet sacks. But she was terribly burned, and she is at the

[1] See *Annual Register*, London, 1820, p. 13. (Cited by Charles Fort).

Louth Hospital, now, in terrible pain." This last sentence is very true. Yesterday our representative called at the hospital, and was informed that the girl was burnt extensively on the back, and lies in a critical condition. She adheres to the belief that she was in the middle of the room when her clothes ignited. Out of 250 fowls, Mr. White, the farmer, says that he has only 24 left. They have all been killed in the same weird way. The skin around the neck, from the head to the breast, has been pulled off, and the windpipe drawn from its place and snapped. The fowl house has been watched night and day, and, whenever examined, four or five birds would be found dead.'

Charles Fort, in recording[1] this case, points out that Binbrook Farm is at Market Rasen, and it was at Market Rasen, on January 16, 1905, that a fire occurred in a fowl-house and destroyed fifty-seven chickens. This affair was recorded in the *Louth and North Lincolnshire News* for January 21, exactly a week before the case of the burning maidservant. It was never discovered how the fowl-house caught alight.

Another curious coincidence—if it were coincidence—is that a man named Ashton Clodd, aged 75, died in Louth Hospital through burns caused by falling into the fire, a few days after the farm fires. The maid-servant from Binbrook Farm and Clodd were in the hospital at the same time. At the inquest on Clodd, a witness testified: 'If there was a fire in the fireplace, it was very little'.[2]

I was an ear-witness, and partly an eye-witness, of a remarkable curtain-burning drama when I was a youth. We were then living at Brockley and on my rambles I used frequently to pass through a thoroughfare named Shardeloes Road. In it was a house known locally as the 'house with the yellow curtains'. It received its name on account of the fact that at all the windows visible from the road were hung long, lace curtains dyed an *écru* colour—rather a bright, but dirty yellow. Another peculiarity about the house was that its flight of front steps were, once a week, red-ochred. It was the residence of a Captain Petersen (a retired Norwegian merchant navy man), his wife, and the—inevitable—'young girl' as a servant. Altogether, a delicious *mise-en-scène* for Poltergeistic pranks. Probably some peripatetic entity objected to the horrible curtains, as I did!

I had been playing in the local recreation grounds known as the Hilly Fields and on my way home I passed through Shardeloes Road. As I turned the corner, I saw the familiar house with a most unfamiliar crowd outside. Hurrying, I soon joined the assemblage and saw that every window was minus its curtains and that the Venetian blind belonging to one of the lower (drawing-room) windows was ablaze. The inmates had opened all the windows, and were throwing buckets of water over the burning blind. There was no other sign of damage.

[1] *Books of Charles Fort*, New York, 1941. pp. 662–65.
[2] *Lloyd's Weekly News*, February 5, 1905.

It was not until a few days later that I heard the true story. I knew a number of people who lived in the road, and they told me what had happened.

It appears that at about 5.30 on the afternoon in question, every curtain in the house blazed up in quick succession—first one side of the window, then the other. It was as if a train of gunpowder had been laid in all the rooms, up the stairs, across the landing, etc., with trails leading to the various windows, and then ignited. I believe there were nine pairs of curtains burnt that afternoon—all in the space of as many minutes. The Fire Brigade had been called, but the engines had left when I arrived on the scene. A strange feature of the burning was the fact that, apart from the loss of the curtains and the scorching of the wooden cornice-poles on which they were hung, little damage was done. The burning Venetian blind that I saw had, I was informed, ignited after most of the firemen had left. Though I have no recollection of being told about them, I suspect that the usual 'disturbances' accompanied the burnings.

Though I had, some months previously, investigated my first 'haunted house',[1] I did not then realise the true significance of the blazing curtains. I believe the Fire Brigade held an inquiry, but the old sea captain and his wife were exonerated from any participation in the affair. The young maid was suspected, but no proof was forthcoming. She was dismissed.

In connection with the 'lace curtains' phobia, Fort tells of a strange affair that took place in Chicago in March, 1892. A family had been away from home and returned to find that every lace curtain in the house had been torn down and trampled on. Drawers had been ransacked—probably for more lace curtains—but nothing had been stolen. A feature of the case was that the police never discovered how the house had been entered. I wonder whether the curtains were *écru*-coloured!

Another strange tale of mystery fires is recorded[2] by Charles Fort, who took his data from the London *Times*[3] and the local Bedford papers:

On August 12, 1856, a resident of Bedford, named Moulton, was absent from home. He was on a business trip in Ireland. At home were Mrs. Moulton and the housemaid, Anne Fennimore. To fumigate the house, the girl had burned sulphur in an earthenware jar on the floor. The jar upset and the burning sulphur was spilt on the floor and set the house on fire. This fire was put out.

About an hour later, a mattress was found burning in another room. But the fire from the sulphur had not extended beyond one room and this mattress was in another part of the house. Then smoke was seen coming from a chest. Later, smoke was seen coming from a closet, and

[1] See 'The Poltergeist that Stumbled', p. 213.
[2] *Wild Talents*, New York, 1932. [3] For Aug. 21, 1856.

in it linen was found burning. Other isolated fires broke out. Mr. Moulton was sent for, and he returned upon the evening of the 16th. He took off his damp clothes and threw them on the floor. Next morning these clothes were found burning. Then came a succession of about forty fires, in curtains, in closets, and in bureau drawers. Neighbours and policemen came in to help and were soon fearful for their own safety. Not only objects around them flamed, but even their handkerchiefs caught alight.

It was decided to hold a judicial investigation. There were many witnesses and some of them testified to picking up pillows and setting them down again—blazing. There was no question of arson, as neither the house nor its contents was insured. Everyone felt that there was some connection between the original sulphur fire and the scores of later ones. But that connection, if there was one, was never found, and the jury returned a verdict to the effect that the first fire was accidental, and that there was no evidence to show what caused the others.

The story attracted a good deal of attention in the Press and started a long correspondence in *The Times*. At the inquiry it was stated that the fires—which occurred over a period of five days—also broke out amongst chairs and sofas that had been carried into the yard. So the theory that sulphurous fumes had spread all over the house, etc. had to be abandoned. Anyway, someone pointed out in *The Times* that sulphurous fumes are oxides and are not inflammable. The mystery was never solved.[1]

A case that has correspondences with the Bedford affair, concerned another young English girl, though she happened to be in Canada. In the *St. Louis Globe-Democrat*[2] was an account of how there had been extraordinary occurrences in the home of Robert Dawson, a farmer, at Thorah, near Toronto, Canada. In his household were his wife and an adopted daughter, an English girl named Jennie Bramwell, aged fourteen. The girl had been ill. She went into a trance and exclaimed: 'Look at that!' at the same time pointing to the ceiling. It was ablaze. Shortly after the girl startled her foster parents by pointing to another fire. Next day many fires broke out. As soon as one was extinguished, another started. While Mrs. Dawson and the girl were sitting facing a wall, the wall-paper caught alight. Jennie's dress blazed, and Mrs. Dawson's hands were burned in extinguishing the fire. For a week, fires broke out, during which period a kitten caught alight. The mystery remained a mystery, but the girl was sent back to the orphanage.

From fires to explosions is but a short step, and usually a violent one. There are scores of accounts of explosions occurring in Poltergeist-

[1] In the *New York World* for August 8, 1887, is an account of Poltergeist incendiaries in the home of Reginald C. Hoyt of Woodstock, N.B. More than forty fires broke out in a few hours. Curtains, quilts, clothes, etc. were destroyed. A young girl was in the household.
[2] For Dec. 19, 1891.

infested houses. Charles Fort cites[1] many of them. Ada M. Sharpe, in her brochure, *A Disturbed House and its Relief* (Oxford, 1914), records a sort of 'psychic bombardment', with detonations, explosions, etc., that began on April 24, 1905, lasting three years. They occurred in her home at Tackley, near Woodstock, Oxfordshire. Miss Sharpe's brochure is very rare, and I was twelve months searching for it. However, her niece, Miss Florence M. Sharpe, found a copy in the village of Tackley, and kindly sent it to me. Outside of the British Museum, I do not know of another specimen.

Miss Sharpe entered into possession of the house (parts of which are three hundred years old) in June, 1900. The disturbances began nearly five years later. Every incident was recorded in a diary with the date and time of its occurrence, and many witnesses, including friends and maid-servants, testified to the phenomena. As in so many other haunted houses, there was a 'Blue Room', and the reader will not be surprised to learn that this apartment was much 'disturbed'.

The first manifestations were the sounds of strange voices and of doors being slammed. Then a terrific 'explosion' was heard: 'It sounded like a bomb; I thought it was an earthquake', records Miss Sharpe. It was heard by many people. Then came the noise of 'chains being dragged across the roof'. Candles were often extinguished and sometimes they were dimmed by shadows passing between them and the observers. Footsteps running up and down the stairs was a frequent phenomenon, and figures (including one 'like a burly farmer', and another, wrapped in a cloak, kneeling, with an 'expression of derisive contempt' on its countenance) were met with in the bedrooms or seen bending over the beds. One sleeper was shaken by the shoulders; Miss Sharpe had her head banged violently as she lay in bed, and the effect of the blow was felt for hours; a visitor complained of something 'clawing the bedclothes'; a child was tickled in bed; and bedclothes were often disturbed. There were also knockings and tappings behind the beds' heads.

One of the most curious phenomena was witnessed in a bedroom: A sleeper was awakened by hearing—and seeing—a figure go over to a bookcase, withdraw a book from a shelf, open it, and replace it in its proper position. The figure then vanished. Investigation proved that the title of the book was, most appropriately, *In Strange Company*, because the sliding of the book from the shelf had made a furrow in the dust that had accumulated on the bookcase.

In addition to the many loud bangs and 'explosions' that were heard, several witnesses saw 'starry lights' floating over beds, and flashes were seen. Occupants of beds complained of receiving 'electric shocks', 'feet cold and tingling', and heavy weights on their feet and bodies.

Other phenomena during 1905–6–7 were 'furious sounds as of a

---

[1] *Wild Talents, op. cit.*

mason using a pickaxe', that lasted for hours; a 'noise like tearing down wallpaper'; skipping, and a 'football being kicked'; 'stones being rolled'; the 'rustling and swish of a silk skirt'; 'impression of furniture dragged along on its castors; heavy weight dropped from a height, and 'boots being thrown about'; incessant tapping, and the 'dragging of a heavy weight across the floors'. One remarkable phenomenon was a sound 'like the jingling of a watch chain' that accompanied the running footsteps heard on the stairs. Mrs. Mara Mack's mother experienced an identical auditory impression.

Miss Sharpe sought relief from the disturbances, and on July 12, 1907, the Rev. L. de Clare exorcised the house with prayers, incense, and holy water. The atmosphere of the house at once changed, and everything remained quiet until January, 1908. Then Miss Sharpe heard 'a dog walking round her bed', and, later, could not close the door of her bedroom because something on the other side was pushing against it. (A similar experience befell Suky Wesley, who had the kitchen door 'violently thrust against her' when she tried to close it.) Then Miss Sharpe saw a form huddled up in bed: it vanished as she approached. Then she heard a 'tussle on the bathroom landing' and the doorhandles rattled. This sort of thing went on for some months, and Miss Sharpe decided she would have the house exorcised again.

On February 21, 1908, the Rev. J. C. Fitzgerald, of the Mirfield Community, visited 'Beth-oni' (the name of the house), and again exorcised the place with prayers, incense, and holy water. The phenomena immediately and completely stopped and (writing in 1914) Miss Sharpe tells us that there was no recurrence, and the house was never again disturbed. It is not often that Poltergeists can be exorcised so successfully.

Tragedies have occurred at 'Beth-oni'. In June, 1875, a man named Bart Chaundry, in a drunken fit, fell over the banisters and broke his neck. And Miss Sharpe, a philanthropist, used to take dying villagers into her home and nurse them to the end. Miss Florence M. Sharpe tells me that her aunt was 'an iron-willed old lady' and not given to imagining things. She carried out some tests, including the placing of threads across passages and stairways, but the entities passed through them. As at Borley Rectory, the dogs reacted to the phenomena, and were restless or cowed during the manifestations, the most remarkable of which, I think, were the terrific explosions 'as if caused by bombs'. On May 1, 1911, unaccountable fires broke out in the house of Mr. J. A. Harvey, York Road, Wandsworth. Preceding these fires, there were three explosions of unknown origin.[1] In 1892, a house in Peterborough was repeatedly shaken as if by bombs. No one and nothing was injured.[2]

---

[1] *Lloyd's Weekly News*, July 30, 1911.
[2] *Peterborough Advertiser*, Jan. 10, 1892.

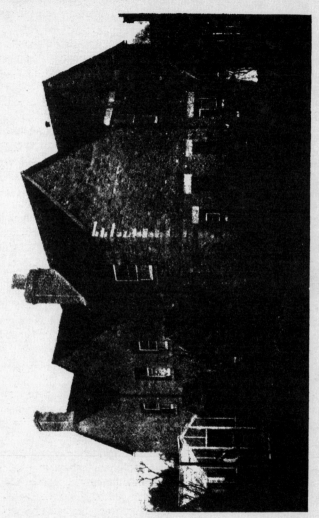

North-East view of 'Beth-oni', the 'disturbed house' at Tackley, near Oxford, photo-graphed in 1914. For Miss Ada M. Sharpe's account of the phenomena, see pages 327 8,

Colonel G. T. Plunket reported[1] an experience that occurred in his home at Wimbledon in July, 1909. He and his wife were sitting in one of their rooms when Mrs. Plunket saw a luminous thing moving towards them. It went to a chair, on the back of which it seemed to rest for a moment. Then it exploded. Colonel Plunket did not see the luminosity, but heard the explosion. It was a fine evening. Clarence Winchester, the well-known journalist, told me of a similar experience in his own home, but in his case the 'thing' that exploded disintegrated into what looked like glass fragments.

In July, 1925, a mystery explosion occurred at a house in Riverhall Street, South Lambeth.[2] A boy named Charlie Orchard, aged five, was seriously injured by something that exploded as he was about to have his breakfast. He was hurt on the face and chest and some of his fingers were blown away. He was taken to hospital in a serious condition. Neighbours who heard the explosion thought the house was on fire and summoned the Fire Brigade. The mystery was never solved.

Another 'mystery explosion' occurred at a house in Walm Lane, Cricklewood, in 1920. The *Willesden Chronicle*[3] called it 'a fire of a most mysterious character ... absolutely no cause can be assigned for the outbreak, which was followed by a terrific explosion, completely wrecking the premises'. A nearby policeman on point duty saw the house catch fire and blow up. 'Windows and doors at the back of the house were blown a distance of 60 feet'. Fortunately, the family were out of town and had turned off the gas at the main—so it was *not* a gas explosion. The Home Office and the Salvage Corps held an inquiry, but the mystery was never solved.

In the years 1921–23 there was an epidemic of strange and mysterious fires and explosions; mystery was added to mystery by the fact that, in many cases, the detonations originated in the grate—presumably in or amongst the coal. A curious feature of this particular visitation was that similar explosions and detonations were occurring all over Europe and America at the same time. Charles Fort lists[4] many of these.

In Guildford, Surrey, in 1921, a woman was killed by a violent explosion that originated in the grate and blasted the walls down.[5] The obvious conclusion to be drawn from this incident was that explosives had been mixed with the coal. But in this case, and in every other case of grate-detonations, explosives were *never* found in the coal, and *never* was there an accident or explosion amongst coal in transit during this 'epidemic'. At this period, explosions in grates were occurring in France, Switzerland, Belgium, etc.

An amazing Poltergeist case was investigated at this time. About the first of January, 1921, Mr. T. S. Frost, of Ferrestone Road, Hornsey,

[1] *English Mechanic*, Vol. 90, p. 140.   [2] See *Daily Mail*, July 23, 1925.
[3] September 30, 1920.   [4] *Wild Talents, op. cit.*
[5] *Daily News*, Sept. 16, 1921.

N.8, bought a load of coal. He had three children, Gordon, Bertie and Muriel. In the grates of his house, coal exploded. Also coal in buckets exploded. A policeman was called in, and in his report he stated that coal not only exploded in the grates, but hopped out of the fire and ran along the floors. Then a police inspector arrived on the scene. According to the local Press,[1] the inspector is said to have stated that he had picked up a piece of coal which had broken into three parts. Then it vanished out of his hands! It was alleged that burning coals leaped from the grates, and fell in showers in other rooms, passing through walls without leaving any marks where they penetrated.[2] Flatirons, coal scuttles, and other objects danced about. Ornaments fell off shelves to the floor, without breaking. A pot on a tripod began swinging when no one was near it. The phenomena occurred usually in the presence of one or other of the young boys.

This case was well-attested. One of the witnesses was the Rev. A. L. Gardiner, Vicar of St. Gabriel's, Wood Green, who is reported to have said: 'There can be no doubt of the phenomena; I have seen them myself.' Another witness was Dr. Herbert Lemerle, of Hornsey, who is alleged to have related how a clock mysteriously vanished. On May 8, 1921, a public meeting was held in Hornsey to discuss the phenomena.

There was a tragic sequel to this affair. Charles Fort,[3] who records the case, states that the girl, Muriel, was so terrified by the disturbances that she died on April 1st. The boy, Gordon, was frightened into a nervous breakdown and was taken to Lewisham Hospital.

A case, comparable with the Hornsey affair, is puzzling the Canadian police as the proofs of this book are being corrected. I am indebted to Mr. R. S. Lambert for Press reports concerning it, and I take my account from the *Toronto Globe and Mail* for April 14, 1944:

'On March 28, R. L. Swenson, Stark county superintendent of schools, called the marshal's office to report "strange happenings" at the Wild Plum school-house, twenty miles south of Richardton, which led people in the community to believe the school-house is "bewitched".

'State Fire Marshal Charles Schwartz said his investigation disclosed "a remarkable story beyond belief". The story, as pieced together by Schwartz from the sworn testimony of officials, pupils and the teacher, is: Mrs. Pauline Rebel, teacher, and her eight pupils were amazed when a pail of lignite coal near the stove began to stir restlessly without any apparent cause. Lumps of coal started popping out of the pail like Mexican jumping beans, striking the walls and bounding back. Jack Steiner, a pupil, was hit on the head and slightly injured. The coal pail tipped over and the lumps of lignite ignited. Window blinds on all nine

---

[1] *The Hornsey Journal* and *North Middlesex Chronicle* for this period.

[2] Compare these incidents with the coal phenomenena recorded by Mrs. Mara Mack, pp. 339–42.

[3] *The Books of Charles Fort*, New York, 1941, pp. 947–8.

windows started smouldering, and a dictionary began to move. A book-case caught fire. Schwartz said school officials testified that when they arrived the coal was still reacting to a mysterious force. Pieces trembled in their hands. Analysis by the state chemist failed to reveal any chemical which might have caused such action. "We plan to send the pail, the dictionary, and a sample of the coal to the F.B.I. in Washing-

'A sharp detonation and the clothes on the line shot upwards.'

ton," Schwartz said. School officials have closed the school pending an investigation.'

I cannot leave this subject of strange explosions without citing a few examples of those mysterious outdoor detonations that accompany the spontaneous disappearance of various objects. On a perfectly windless day, at Liverpool, on May 11, 1842, a row of clothes that were drying on a common suddenly shot upward into the blue and were never seen again. One report says there was a sharp detonation as the pants and pillowcases left the line to which they were pegged. High up, there was a slight southerly breeze, but the garments drifted northwards.[1]

At Cupar, Fife, on June 30, 1842, women were hanging out clothes on a common. It was a bright, clear day. Suddenly there was a sharp detonation and the clothes on the lines shot upwards. A few fell to the ground, but the others soared up and up and vanished.[2] Something similar occurred at Islip, near Thrapston, Northamptonshire, in June, 1919. There was a loud explosion and a basketful of clothes soared into the air. These particular articles came down again.[3]

It will be noted that all these sudden explosive 'levitations' of objects occurred in the summer months. Two of the incidents were recorded within a few weeks of each other. It would be interesting to know what became of the Cupar *lingerie*. 'What goes up must come down'. Or must it? It is my feeling that in the late spring of 1842, someone, somewhere, recorded a phenomenon: 'A shower of clothes from nowhere'. But there is no record of the return of the garments.

Self-combustion, spontaneous combustion, Poltergeist combustion. There are many cases on record of persons having been burnt to death—'cause unknown'. If the reader thinks I am unduly digressing from the subject of this monograph, I will retort that as we do not know what Poltergeists are, or what they can, or cannot do, we are not in a position to deny them the power of destroying people. If a Poltergeist can set fire to a house, or burn down a hayrick, or make clothes smoulder, or cause explosions—and there is much evidence for all these incendiaristic activities—then they can burn people, too.

At Blyth, Northumberland, in 1905, a woman was found lying on a sofa, burned to death. Her name was Barbara Bell, aged 77. 'The body was fearfully charred', as if it had been for a long time in the midst of intense flames. No explanation of the tragedy was ever forthcoming.[4] A few weeks earlier, in the *Daily News*,[5] was an account of the death of Mrs. Thomas Cochrane, of Rosehall, Falkirk, who was found burned to death in her bedroom. 'She was burned almost beyond recognition'. No fire in the grate and no cries for help. Nothing else was burned. She was found sitting in a chair, surrounded by pillows and cushions. The mystery was never solved.

In the same month there was an inquest on another woman, Elizabeth Clark, who died of mysterious burns in the Trinity Almshouse, Hull,

[1] See *Annals of Electricity*, Vol. VI, p. 499.

[2] *The Times*, London, July 5, 1842.

[3] *Daily Express*, June 12, 1919. What did *not* come down was a horse and barn that a tornado sucked upwards at Wisconsin on May 23, 1878. Not a trace of either horse or barn was ever seen again. (*Monthly Weather Review*, Washington, D.C., May, 1878.)

[4] *Blyth News*, February 28, 1905.   [5] For December 17, 1904.

late at night. There was no outcry, and the bed on which she was lying was not even scorched. She was found in the morning, covered with burns, though still living. She could give no account of her injuries, and died with the mystery unsolved.[1]

Charles Fort cites another case, recorded in `Science`[2], which prints a paper that was read by Dr. B. H. Hartwell, of Ayer, Mass., before the Massachusetts Medico-Legal Society. Dr. Hartwell said that on May 12, 1890, while driving through a forest near Ayer, he had been called, and going into the wood, saw, in a clearing, the crouching form of a woman. Fire, which was not from clothing, was consuming the shoulders, both sides of the abdomen, and both legs.

My next case comes from Whitley Bay, near Blyth. On the evening of March 22, 1908, a woman named Margaret Dewar ran into a neighbour's house, saying that she had found her sister burned to death. Upon investigation, the charred body of Wilhelmina Dewar was found on a bed, which was not even scorched. And it was proved at the inquest that there was not the slightest sign of fire in any part of the house. The mystery of her death was never solved.[3]

Even as I am writing these lines, I see from the *Evening Standard*[4] that there has been another 'mystery death' by a mystery fire at Plumstead. A man named 'Old Jimmy' Evans lived alone in a small house in St. John's Terrace. A neighbour visited him and entered the house. She found the passage full of smoke. She called out to Evans that he had set the house on fire. He replied that it was all right and that 'the flames were dying down.' She went for help. When she returned, the man was found burnt to death on his bed, *under* which the fire had originated. There was no cry for help, and no clue as to how the fire started. Mr. W. R. H. Heddy, the coroner, stated at the inquest that it was 'a remarkable case', and how it happened no one knew.

Still another case has recently been puzzling doctors and the police. A Mrs. Madge Knight lived with her husband, an elderly retired architect, and a sister named Mrs. Moore and her husband—the four of them occupying a house at Aldingbourne, Sussex—a few miles from my home. On the night of November 18, 1943, Mrs. Knight was awaiting the return of the Moores, who were out. They returned soon after 10 o'clock. Mr. Knight was then in bed. His wife and the Moores then had some conversation together, and the three of them retired to their respective rooms, Mrs. Knight sleeping alone in a small, spare room—which was unusual.

Between 3.30 and 4 a.m. the Moores heard Mrs. Knight screaming. They rushed to her room. 'She was in bed, and covered by the bed

---

[1] *Daily Mail*, Dec. 4, 1904; *Hull Daily Mail*, Jan. 6, 1905.
[2] Vol. X, p. 100.
[3] See the *Blyth News* (period Mar. 23 to April 10, 1908).
[4] For Nov. 29, 1943.

clothes, but her body was bare', and as she lay on her left side they 'saw the skin was peeled off her back.' But they smelt no burnt clothing or flesh. Mrs. Moore attended to her sister, who appeared to be in much pain. Early next morning, they telephoned for a doctor, who found Mrs. Knight in such agony that he could not examine her without administering morphia. 'There were extensive burns over the whole of the back.' But there was no smell of burning. Then he called in a Harley Street specialist, who told the coroner at the subsequent inquest, that when he saw the patient, her condition was definitely due to some kind of burn—probably from a liquid. On more than one occasion, he said, he asked her how it happened, but Mrs. Knight's reply was always that 'she had nothing to tell him'. On December 2, she was taken to St. Richard's Hospital, Chichester, where she died from toxæmia on December 6.

At the resumed inquest on December 20, four doctors gave evidence, and some remarkable facts emerged. They were agreed that the burns had the appearance of being caused by some corrosive fluid, but (*a*) the hands, head, hair, bedclothes and Mrs. Knight's clothes, showed no signs whatever of burning or scorching; and the police found no evidence in the house of burnt or stained floors, and no bottles that had contained acid; and (*b*) there were no fires in the house except electric ones, and these were all switched off when Mrs. Knight was discovered screaming.

The *West Sussex Gazette* for December 23, 1943 (from which my account is taken), calls the case 'one of the most baffling combinations of circumstances which a coroner could have to investigate.' The jury brought in an open verdict. The mystery was never solved. No one knew how Mrs. Knight came to be burned—not even the poor woman herself.

Apparently, some victims of Poltergeist incendiarism are not affected by the flames. In the *New York Times* for August 25, 1929, was a remarkable story of a young Negress, named Lily White, who lived in the village of Liberta, on the West Indian Island of Antigua. Lily constantly burst into flames as she was walking along the street, sitting in her home, or having her meals. In bed, the sheets blazed. All her clothes were burnt off her back over and over again, and she became dependent upon her neighbours for something to wear. The extraordinary part of the story is that *she was never burnt*, and did not feel the flames.

I could continue citing scores of further examples of fire-raising, explosions, burnings, psychic pyrotechnics, bonfires of furniture, smoking mattresses, blazing clothing, flaming hayricks, incandescent skirting-boards, lighted matches falling from ceilings, and smouldering human beings—all the alleged work of 'mischievous ghosts' or Poltergeists, which are supposed not to hurt anyone! And I could add to my list hundreds of similar cases recorded abroad. Charles Fort alone must have collected notes on thousands of such incidents.[1] But I think that my selection will give the reader a good idea of the activities of incendiary Poltergeists—real or alleged.

Nearly all the cases I have cited are documented and well-attested. But I have many notes in my case-books of Poltergeistic incidents, of an incendiary nature, that have been reported to me privately or have come within my own experience. I will conclude with a few of these stories.

In 1929, at a house in Lillington Avenue, Leamington, during the usual disturbances, a saucepan of *cold* water, containing peeled potatoes, began to boil over at midnight. There was no fire in the kitchen range, on which the saucepan was resting. The potatoes had been peeled ready for the next morning's meal. They were half-cooked when removed from the range. Another kitchen incident was the switching on, in the night, of every electrical appliance that the 'Poltergeist' could lay hands on. The occupier's wife was ill in bed and the only staff was a young nursemaid who looked after a child of three. The husband was first down in the morning and found the electric oven turned full on; the electric iron, on its side, was burning a hole in a portable ironing table; and a small electric cream-maker was going full blast. The appliances that were *not* plugged in (e.g. the vacuum cleaner, etc.) had not been interfered with. Returning to the upper portion of the house, the husband found the young girl peacefully sleeping in her room with a look of innocence on her face that disarmed all suspicion. The child was asleep in its cot. There were other disturbances in the kitchen—popular playgrounds[2] of Poltergeists—during the week. The maid was discharged. All this happened in a house in New Street, Salisbury, in 1920.

Another alleged Poltergeist case I have noted was reported from Morningside Road, Edinburgh (in 1932). The chief feature of this was the finding of pieces of flaming paper that had been dropped all over the house. A peculiarity of the case was the fact that the ignited papers had been torn from copies of the *Edinburgh and Leith Observer*, a journal that the occupier (an official connected with the Forth Bridge) did not take, and did not even read. There was the usual 'young girl' in the family. These incipient attempts at incendiarism lasted about a week.

I have several notes on cases where glowing embers, hot coals—and even fire irons—have jumped from grates and have scattered themselves

---

[1] See *The Book of the Damned* (1919); *New Lands* (1923); *Lo!* (1931); and *Wild Talents* (1932). All published in New York, and subsequently issued as an omnibus volume under the title, *The Books of Charles Fort*, New York, 1941.

[2] A striking example of kitchen phenomena recently appeared in the Delhi Press. Reporting a Poltergeist case, the *Hindustan Times* (Jan. 15, 1944) says: 'Strange happenings have been taking place in the village of Hasanpur, in Muslim homes especially, for a long time past. It is often noticed by villagers that breads in the process of being cooked over ovens fly in the air and disappear, and that earthen pots containing milk also fly with their contents and are dropped empty and undamaged. Fire accidents are also sometimes noticed, but the moment people rush to extinguish them, they find that there is no fire.'

over living-rooms and kitchens. I believe the burning of a house in Worcestershire was attributed to this cause. Speaking of burning, one curious case I heard of concerned a house in Bute Street, Cardiff. There had been the usual typical disturbances (pans falling off shelves, jugs of milk being spilt, etc.), but in addition two witnesses testified that they had seen a lambent, *blue* flame in one of the living-rooms. It was about five feet from the ground, and was moving slowly from point to point, 'licking' the furniture, curtains, etc. The two witnesses, who had darkened the room in an endeavour to 'catch' the Poltergeist, were fearful of the place catching fire and switched on the light. The flame disappeared. Later, they tried to recapture the experience, without success. In another Poltergeist-infested house I heard of, blazing petroleum dripped from the ceiling of one of the rooms, though there was not a drop of paraffin in the building. In still another house, I was told that one entire wall of a room was ablaze with bluish, lambent flames as if it had been drenched with methylated spirit and then ignited. The flames did not even scorch the wall and nothing was burnt. These lambent flames are rather reminiscent of the slow-moving luminous patch that Mr. S. G. Welles saw on the ceiling of the Blue Room at Borley Rectory. The reader will remember that many fires occurred at the Rectory, which finally went up in smoke.

CHAPTER XXVIII

My Friends' Poltergeists

On an average, I receive every week between twenty and thirty letters from people who are complete strangers to me. The subjects dealt with in these letters cover the whole field of psychical research, with its many facets, but the greater number of my correspondents are good enough to relate to me their psychic experiences—or experiments. When a stamped envelope is enclosed, I endeavour to answer their many queries. This sometimes leads to an exchange of letters, and even an occasional friendship.

Through some of my 'letter friends' I have become acquainted with many good cases of paranormal happenings—especially Poltergeist happenings. I now propose to detail a few of the more recent ones, which, because they are recent, are valuable additions to this monograph; the more so as, with one exception, they are all here published for the first time. I have included some other recent cases from my friends in my account of Poltergeist-infested rectories.

One of the most interesting Poltergeist cases comes from Mrs. Mara Mack, of 38, Causewayside, Fen Causeway, Cambridge, who, on July 18, 1943, sent me the details of a Poltergeist visitation that began in her home when she was a child; a visitation that persisted and apparently still persists, though the house is no longer in her family's occupation. Mrs. Mack has sent me the full name and address of the house, which is situated in one of our most beautiful and remote counties, famous for its landscapes and seascapes, an ideal spot for artists—and Poltergeists. Mrs. Mack also sent me an excellent coloured plan of the principal rooms concerned. She would make a good investigator!

I will not reveal the location of Mrs. Mack's old home, as I have not the permission of the present occupiers to do so. In her letter, Mrs. Mack also mentions another house 'some thirty miles or so from the one under discussion, which used to be owned by friends of ours. *It* was haunted, too, one of the manifestations being most unpleasant: sharp slapping of the would-be sleeper's face, etc. This is apparently still going on—or was a few years ago. So much so, in fact, that that particular bedroom can no longer be slept in.' Here, then, in her own words, is the story of Mrs. Mack's Poltergeist home:

The main part of the house is a little over one hundred years old; but attached to it is a small, low building—very much older—containing two large kitchens (though one of these we called the scullery), two bedrooms, and a store-room. The rest of the house, downstairs, consisted of a dining-room and a drawing-room, a hall, a study, and large cellars.

Upstairs, were two large bedrooms on right of landing (one of these having an approach to the old part of the house), then a third room known as the Blue Room,[1] and a linen cupboard which terminated that part of the landing. From there a passage led to, and ended in, a room known as the schoolroom, and to a bedroom next door. The windows of the Blue Room, the room next to it, and those of the schoolroom all commanded beautiful views over cliffs and bay.

My first memory of any phenomena is hearing sounds like heavy goods being shifted and moved about in the schoolroom after we children were all in bed, and the grown-ups downstairs. We used to compare the disturbances with those noises that would be made by people packing up in a hurry.[2] Sometimes the sounds would be much lighter, and just as though the schoolroom ruler was moving about on the table. The room next door was the focal point of many strange happenings. When the windows were closed and fastened, and the curtains drawn, a large calendar hanging on a cupboard, would start to swing violently to and fro. And a rattlesnake skin (complete with rattle), sent home by one of the family from California, would swing in the same way, making an eerie sound. I well remember one of my sisters having a fright (conditions in the house were then somewhat primitive) when the utensil she wished to use rolled itself away and went under the bed!

My mother (a practical and unusually intelligent woman), whilst sitting in the schoolroom, used to hear what she described as 'dreadful sounds' coming from the next room. And one spring day (the sounds seemed always more prevalent in the spring) she said it was just as though a dead body was being thrown on to the floor—with other indescribable sounds. She could stand no more of it, and went into the room. And, to use her own words, she said, 'I told them to shut up their damned row!' And the noises instantly ceased!

Some years later, I had a strange experience in that room. My mother was worn out with nursing my father (he was in bed, very ill with pneumonia, down the passage next to the Blue Room) and I persuaded her to lie down in this particular room, and I would read her to sleep. We were expecting the doctor, but as he was a personal friend, we knew he would just walk in and go straight to father's room. I had just succeeded in getting my mother to sleep, when I heard a man walk down the passage towards our door, which was shut. I thought it must be the doctor and wondered why he had come to the wrong room. Then there were three loud, sharp knocks on the door. I opened it instantly, intending to warn the person (I should here remark that there was no one in the house except a very orthodox old maiden aunt, sitting with

[1] It is curious that so many haunted houses contain 'Blue Rooms'. The reader will call to mind those of Borley, Ballechin, Willington Mill, Tackley, etc.

[2] Compare this phenomenon with a similar one recorded by Mr. Procter in the Willington Mill case (page 188).

my father, my mother and myself) against waking my mother. But there was no one there, and the next room (the schoolroom) was empty. And the passage was so long that nobody could possibly have got away without my seeing them. Well, that identical experience occurred a second time, in exactly the same way, about twenty minutes later. And then a *third* time. On this last occasion the steps and the knocks were so vigorous that they woke my mother. And as we looked at the door, we both saw the handle turn and the door opened for a moment—wide enough for anyone to look in. And then it was closed and firmly latched, and the steps receded down the passage. The doctor never came at all that afternoon; also, my father recovered!

My mother used to sit and sew upstairs, when the house was empty. And she often told me that she used to hear a man run up the stairs, as though he were taking two steps at a time. And, she informed me, she could even hear his watch-chain jingle as he sped up the stairs.

When my people first went to the house, they used to hear a baby crying down in the cellars. This disturbed them very much, but that particular phenomenon did not last long. A figure (a woman in a dark dress) was occasionally seen in the kitchen. And the bells (old-fashioned wire-pulled ones) hanging in the hall would ring quite strongly. (This may, of course, have been due to atmospheric effects on the wires. It didn't seem so, but it may have been.)[1]

I remember one evening while I was with my father in the study, and we were discussing a journey he was going to take the following day. He pointed to a Gladstone bag in the corner of the room and said, 'I think I shall only take that bag'—whereupon, the bag suddenly jumped up in the air and turned a complete somersault!

The sound as if a quantity of gravel had been flung against the windows of the Blue Room, was heard at rare intervals.

In the kitchen was a very large and heavy old dresser. So heavy, in fact, that it was never even moved away from the wall. It was there when my parents bought the house. On it were kept large well-dishes, plates, etc. Imagine the consternation it caused when, one day, it suddenly started to tilt forward, shedding the china as it went!

During one autumn, there was a regular orgy of coal-throwing. I quote from notes made at the time (those who were present are designated by their initials):

November 27th.

'Present in the kitchen, two maids, M. H., and F. S. Alleged sounds of knocking in series of three, repeated at intervals, and always in threes;[2] but at irregular intervals during the evening.

---

[1] This is an old theory, but I would go a long way to witness the ringing of a row of bells by 'atmospheric effects'.—H.P.

[2] It is strange how fond Poltergeists are of giving *triple* blows or knocks. At Willington Mill, Epworth, etc., the knocks were usually three in quick succession.—H.P.

'While washing up between 7 and 8 p.m., coal was violently pitched into kitchen, apparently from above the back stairs, at three distinct intervals, the third time striking M. H. Each time sounding loud as if from a gun (*sic*). On examination, it appeared to be anthracite. No human agency apparent.

'*November* 28.—Present in kitchen at 7.40 p.m., M.H. and F. S. Coal was thrown with loud report on floor near lift under window. L. H. informed at time and found the above witnesses very agitated. Cross-examined and made light of it. He himself picked up the coal.

'*November* 29.—Present in kitchen K. F. (old and very trusted outside worker) and the two maids. K. F. having made fun of the alleged occurrences, was startled by hearing loud reports and coal was thrown violently with great noise on floor in same place as before. M. H. at closed range pouring water on teapot and F. S. at same, pouring water in jug for tea. K. F. standing near and certain that no human agency could have thrown said coal. The rest of the family were all in Dining-Room, except N. N. in her own room and L. H. in study: the latter was called out and saw the fright of the three, and himself picked up the coal, as last night he cross-examined severely but could not shake evidence, K. F. being very firm.

'*November* 29. (*Later*).—Present: Two maids and Mrs. L. H. in the kitchen at 7.5 p.m. Mrs. L. H. was at closed range, cooking, both maids attending her and making remarks about the occurrence. When, suddenly, a loud report, and with seeming violence, coal was shot over floor and stairs. All much frightened. L. H. came out and picked up coal—the larger pieces distinctly warm. But there was *no* possibility of its having proceeded from the fire. And neither maid had moved from her position when L. H. arrived and cross-examined them. All remaining household were in schoolroom, save L. H. himself, who was in his study typewriting. Mrs. L. H. had made excuse to cook so as to be company for the terrified girls, and their shouts caused L. H. to come into the kitchen.

'*November* 30.—At 7.10 a.m. F. S. (housemaid) reported to Mr. and Mrs. L. H. that at 7 a.m., while she was at the cupboard (near passage door) in kitchen getting cups and saucers for early tea, and M. H. was just beyond the door leading into hall, coal was thrown as before, with loud report. It fell in about the same place as before, and no one had touched it. On the arrival of L. H. at 7.48 a.m., he was told by both maids that more coal had been thrown at 7.35 a.m., when both were leaving by the same doorway to go upstairs to finish doing schoolroom, etc. This coal was also left until L. H. had made plan of kitchen and scullery. The letters 'A' denote position of the coal first thrown and the letters 'B', the coal thrown later. There are many points where fragments were found, but the plan serves to make clear the general *locus in quo*.

'The girls appeared less nervous to-day, it being in partial daylight

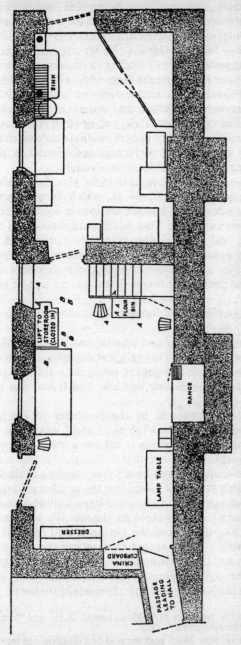

Plan of the kitchens of Mrs. Mara Mack's old home, where so many Poltergeist phenomena occurred. (See text.)

341

may be the reason. The peculiarity being that *both* were not *in* the kitchen on either occasion today and that the rest of the household were in bed or only just rising from it.

'*November* 30.—3.30 p.m. Mrs. L. H. reported to L. H. that while she was standing inside doorway leading to scullery, she saw a piece of coal strike with great force near the hinge of flour-bin—making a dent—one of the maids having just cleaned with wet cloth the lid of bin from the coal dust previously collected, and was sweeping up chips of coal from the floor. The other maid, F. S., was at lamp table dusting knives and it was *impossible* that she or either *could* have thrown it. It is worthy of remark that several pieces were previously found in places most unlikely to form a receptacle under normal conditions.

'*December* 1.—L. H. called to kitchen by Mrs. L. H. who reported this to him: At about 4.50 p.m., M. H.[1] and F. S. were both standing at large table by side-door in kitchen, the former lighting the lamp, and the latter washing her silver. They both heard a sound in the scullery as if something had fallen. Upon examination it proved to be coal broken in many pieces in granite sink at farther end of the scullery—there being neither coal therein normally, nor were any members of the family in that part of the house. There was no sign of coal, save in the sink.'

I am enclosing a plan [reproduced] made at the time; also some of the coal.[2]

For a long time after we all got married and left home, there seemed a cessation of activities, until the very last day of our possession of the house. I was clearing up and getting ready for a three days' sale. My father was dead and my mother had left. And I, too, was leaving that day.

An architect had been sent by the purchaser to examine certain things and he was round about the place and I was in the kitchen. A relative of the new owner came in to ask me if she could speak to the architect a moment. I told her that I thought he was on the lawn, viewing a buttress, etc. She and I were then standing in the hall and we both heard a man's firm steps walk down the upstairs passage. Then the schoolroom door opened and the same steps walked across the room and halted at the window overlooking the sea. We both exclaimed together, 'No, he's upstairs,' and she ran up to find him, returning in a few moments with a white, scared face, to say that she had made a thorough search and there was no one there. At that moment we looked from the hall through the dining-room window and saw the architect coming towards the house from the farther side of the lawn!

---

[1] The initials 'M.H.' represent Mrs. Mack herself, 'L.H.' and 'Mrs. L.H.' being her father and mother respectively.—H.P.

[2] In a further letter, Mrs. Mack said the coal had disintegrated into powder, and that it was hardly worth sending. I agreed.—H.P.

It is interesting to note that the new owner kept the house a very short while. She complained that 'everything went wrong' after she bought it. When the next owner had been in residence a few years I met her for a few moments and she asked me if I could tell her whether the house had been built on consecrated ground. I asked her why, and she said, 'Oh, everything has been *dreadful* for me since I have lived in this house'. And there certainly has been a series of tragic events in her family since their residence. Perhaps we got it one way, and they another. Who knows?

*   *   *   *

In a postscript, Mrs. Mack said that in addition to the phenomena listed in her report, there was the 'losing of things and the finding of them again in queer places'—exactly as at Borley. Also, doors opened and closed of their own volition and 'dreadful smells that we always hopefully attributed to rats in the wall, but which used to suddenly flit from room to room.'

I am sure the reader will appreciate, as I do, the skill and clarity with which Mrs. Mack has presented her story. It is a truly typical Poltergeist case. There was a 'nest' of children and adolescents in the house, many of them young girls, who doubtless served the Poltergeist as a *point d'appui* or *nidus*. When the girls married and departed from the scene, so did the Poltergeist. When Mrs. Mack had occasion to return to the house, so did the Poltergeist. It is true that, apparently, phenomena afterwards occurred; but they were of a different order. It will be noted that the manifestations ceased when the girls were married. In the case of Olive W., the Poltergeist did not become active *until* she was married, as the reader will presently learn. A feature of Mrs. Mack's account is the curious behaviour of the coal, and the reader can compare these phenomena with similar incidents mentioned in the chapter, 'Poltergeist Incendiaries.'

Miss Ethel Wilkinson, of 40, Holland Park, London, W.11, also sends me (September 15, 1944) a vivid account of how their household was disturbed by Poltergeists when she was a child—an infestation that lasted for seventeen years; in fact, during the whole period of their residence in the house, a Queen Anne mansion at Walton-on-Thames. The phenomena persisted from 1894 to 1911.

The Wilkinson family consisted of eight persons: The father and mother, five young girls, and a small brother. The three youngest girls were aged twelve, ten, and seven years respectively. Every member of the family had many experiences, and here are some of them as listed in Miss Wilkinson's convincing first-hand account:

'A table in an upper bedroom moved from the wall to the centre of the room. In the same apartment occurred incessant hammering, thumping, and banging, but sounds stopped immediately if one approached the room. More frequent in the autumn. In an empty bedroom opposite was kept an incubator. On one oecasion it was moved, the lamp extinguished, and all the eggs were hard-boiled. Footsteps had been heard in the room, but investigation proved that no one was there.

'Very frequently, and in daylight, the girls' skirts were pulled and their faces slapped. [As at Borley, etc.] In the schoolroom a heavy dining-room table was turned a half-circle, all books and inkpots being upset. Certain doors could not be opened, though unlocked. After an interval, they would open easily. On one occasion, three notes were struck on a locked piano. Heard by several people.

'Other phenomena were the faint sound of bagpipes heard in a bedroom by two people. Very hea˙y breathing in the same room awakened both occupants who discussed the unusual noise as it continued. A very loud voice awakened two of the girls who were sleeping in this room.

'The shadows of swaying branches, illuminated by a red light, was a frequent wall-phenomenon, accompanied by the sound of a door opening. On investigation, the door was always found closed and locked. In this room two of the children slept. They were not frightened, but were frequently awakened by the occurrences and the movements of ornaments on the mantelpiece. Sounds of lively conversation on the landings, etc. were frequent. [As at Borley, Hinton Ampner, the mill on the Eden, etc.] Investigation always proved that no one was there.

'When Mrs. X. (the owner of the house) died, a merry peal of bells was rung at the Church during the funeral. Her sons called on us and said we had probably thought it strange that such a peal was rung. No human hand had pulled the ropes. Previous to that, two of us, sleeping in the same room, had been awakened in the middle of the night by a merry peal on the same bells. We leant out of the window and listened, thinking perhaps it was the anniversary of a Boer War victory. Next day, one of the bell-ringers assured us that they had never rung the bells at night. But from the owner's son we discovered that his mother was taken ill at the very hour on that night when we heard the bells.

'Servants in our employ often told us of the things they had heard in the night. The phenomena were similar to those we experienced. On one occasion only was a figure seen. This was at midday, when two people on the staircase saw a figure emerge from a room, cross the landing, and disappear into the nursery. They quickly followed, but the nursery was empty. On another occasion a loud and distinct voice said "Oh, yes!" And there was the sound of someone loudly spitting in the bathroom when one of us was having a bath—with, of course, the door locked. In some of the old rooms, one never felt that one was alone, when in fact one was quite alone. The house had been built on to, but in the newer rooms nothing unusual ever happened.

'After we left the house in 1911, a woman who did sewing for us was engaged as caretaker. She had two children and she told us that in the

Photograph of Miss Ethel Wilkinson's old Poltergeist home at Walton-on-Thames, Surrey, taken during the manifestations which lasted from 1894 to 1911. The house belonged to the North family, and in 1894 was occupied for three months by Prince Louis of Battenberg. It was during this period, and in this house, that the Cesarevich, afterwards the ill-fated Nicholas II, Emperor of Russia, became engaged to Princess Alix of Hesse, daughter of Princess Alice and grand-daughter of Queen Victoria.

room where they slept, they were constantly awakened by the blind being drawn up.'

Miss Wilkinson's remarkable story (which has correspondences with Mrs. Mara Mack's account of her Poltergeist home) supports the theory that Poltergeists are associated with places as well as people. And there are some unusual features in this case: The swaying shadows on the wall and the pealing bells are new to me. The mansion (I have full particulars of the place) is probably still haunted: The resident entities are now quiescent, and only require the necessary stimulus—in the shape of a young child or adolescent—for them to become active again.

Another Poltergeist case brought to my notice by a correspondent is that of Timberbottom Farm, Bradshaw, near Bolton, Lancs. It has many correspondences with that of the Shropshire manor 'stumbling Poltergeist' that I have included in this volume.

The case of Timberbottom Farm first attracted my attention in 1929, when accounts of the affair appeared in the Press. This Timberbottom ghost stumps up and down the stairs just as the Shropshire one did, and I read that it often 'stumbled' and knocked things over. The clatter of fire-irons was heard at night, but in the morning nothing appeared out of place. There were loud knockings in the passages, and shufflings would be heard behind closed doors, and on one occasion a woman said she felt 'something' pass her, and go up the stairs. The legend connected with the farm is almost identical with that connected with the Shropshire manor. It is said that a man once murdered a woman at the farm. The reader will remember that the tradition attached to the Shropshire haunting relates how a demented uncle killed his young niece. One cannot help wondering whether men who murder helpless females are doomed to become stumbling Poltergeists when they 'pass over.'

The owner of the property on which Timberbottom Farm is situated happened to read my book on the haunting of Borley Rectory and wrote to me. He is Colonel Henry M. Hardcastle, of Bradshaw Hall, Bolton. In some correspondence that passed between us during November, 1940, the Colonel told me some interesting things about the farm, which has been in the possession of his family for generations.

The Poltergeist, I was informed, has infested the farm for the last 150 years. In addition to the manifestations I have recorded above, the Poltergeist has a knack of opening and closing a certain chest of drawers in a room above the kitchen, in which many tapping sounds occur. Sometimes the cat will follow the taps round the room. The 'visitations' of the *Geist* are at long intervals: once nine, and at another time, eleven years.

Colonel Hardcastle related to me a remarkable story of two skulls— one male and one female—that used to be at the farm. Many years ago, during one of the periodic disturbances, his grandfather suggested, as a possible way of stopping the trouble, that the skulls should be buried in the churchyard. This was done, whereupon the most violent manifestations broke out all over the house. The Colonel's grandfather could only make a further suggestion that they should be dug up again. This was done and he put them on the family Bible, where they have remained ever since. The woman's skull, about six inches across, he had mounted in silver and placed on a stand.

About nine years ago, Colonel Hardcastle accidentally damaged the mounting and took it, and the skull, to a Manchester silversmith to be repaired.

That very day, the most violent disturbances occurred at the farm. These continued incessantly until the skull was restored to its place alongside its male companion on the family Bible. Then all was quiet again for nine years, when a recrudescence of the trouble occurred in the autumn of 1940. The Colonel has asked me to investigate the case, and perhaps see what a medium can do. I have promised to help when the present War is over as Timberbottom Farm has great possibilities in the way of experimentation. For example, we might induce phenomena by again removing the silver-mounted skull. The connection between the Timberbottom skull and the phenomena may be similar to the connection between the Borley skull and the incidents that occurred in Mr. A. C. Cooper's studio—if there *was* any connection in the latter case.

Mr. C. J. P. Cave, M.A. J.P., F.S.A., the meteorologist, writing from Stoner Hill, Petersfield, Hants, sends me particulars of a remarkable Poltergeist infestation. In referring to Borley Rectory, he says (October 14, 1941): 'It interests me in all sorts of ways, but very largely because I lived from 1880 to 1888, from the age of 9 to 17, in a haunted house in this neighbourhood. Of course it was nothing like Borley Rectory, but it had a long history—about 80 years. The principal phenomena were noises, knocks at the doors, loud bangs, described as though a heavy dictionary had been dropped on the stairs; noises as though someone was moving the furniture about in a room overhead, when there was none there; and the occasional opening of a door. Very occasionally, a tall, dark figure was seen, and I myself saw it once. The phenomena have, I believe, completely ceased.' The dropping of the 'dictionary' is reminiscent of Mr. P. Shaw Jeffrey's adventure at Borley Rectory.

Mrs. Violet L. Salmon, of Tewkesbury Park, Tewkesbury, Gloucestershire, recently sent me a most interesting account of the Poltergeist disturbances that have occurred in her residence which, incidentally, is her birthplace and ancestral home. In her letter of January, 1943, she says: 'The variety of strange occurrences cover a period in my life of roughly forty years. Before that I have no information from anyone as to similar occurrences, but that does not mean that there were none. When I was seven years old, I was standing one winter night at the top of a flight of stairs when I heard very heavy footsteps coming up immediately behind me. My pet cat was with me and showed fear. I was terrified and ran at once to my bedroom after glancing back to see who was there. There was no one. A few years later, when my parents and some people staying in the house were at dinner, a terrific crash was heard. It appeared to come from the hall. Everyone, including the domestic staff, rushed to the hall, but nothing was broken and nothing had moved. The next day my father sent for workmen to examine chimneys, cellars and roof. Nothing was found that could throw any light on the occurrence. A similar crash happened at nearly the same hour many years later. Again, nothing was found that could in any way explain it. Heavy footsteps have been heard at intervals by myself, my husband, and by friends staying in the house. I have also heard voices where no one can be seen, late at night, and these have also been heard by male friends of my husband.

'My grandmother, when in an upstairs room, saw the door open a little way, a hand come round the door,[1] almost immediately withdraw, and the door close. No one was there and she was filled with such terror that she left the house the next day. A cousin in the same room heard loud raps on the wall above her bed. My husband in this room heard footsteps come past the door, but he found no one there. One still summer afternoon, I was with a housemaid in an adjoining room when the door unlatched, slowly opened, remained open for a moment, and as slowly shut again.[2] We were afraid and ran away by another door. A friend sleeping in another room saw two female figures dressed in full flounced dresses, and with long ringlets. They were sitting together on a window-seat and almost immediately vanished. This was in 1936. Footsteps and rustling dresses have been heard by yet another friend who has been so terrified that she would never sleep alone here. I have seen a spaniel, in daylight, fix its eyes on a certain corner of the room, put all its hackles up, and retreat, growling. Another spaniel which slept on a landing spent the whole of one night growling and snarling at something we could not see.

'Once in the garden I heard an organ playing. It was in the summer and I can only describe it as incredibly beautiful.[3] It seemed to be high up. My husband had the following experience: He was in bed, wide awake, when he suddenly felt a heavy weight pressing him down, all over his body. He tried to move, was unable to do so, and was also unable to speak or cry out. He was quite well at the time.

'In the same room I saw a light burning for a fortnight. It was like a candle flame and only moved once, from side to side, and after closing

[1] This identical phenomenon was witnessed by a Borley observer.—H.P.
[2] Compare this experience with that of Mrs. Mack and her mother.—H.P.
[3] Compare this with the 'heavenly music' heard by Sir Y. and Lady Z. ('Poltergeist-Infested Rectories'.)—H. P.

all shutters and curtains to exclude the possibility of light from outside causing this phenomenon, there was no difference. My mother was sitting in her bedroom one afternoon and felt a heavy blow struck on the back of her chair when no one was in the room with her.'

Mrs. Salmon gave me some interesting details of the house in which she was born and in which she has spent all her life. The Battle of Tewkesbury (1471) was fought on the ground surrounding the house and there has always been a house or villa on the site since Roman times. Roman coins are frequently dug up on the estate. My correspondent says that she has 'always been conscious of a peculiar atmosphere about the house, and so often I feel I am not alone, when humanly speaking I am by myself.'

Mrs. Salmon and her husband (Colonel H. M. B. Salmon, D.S.O.) have kindly invited me to make an investigation there, as the phenomena still persist—spasmodically—and the 'footsteps' have been heard quite recently.

As Mrs. Salmon pointed out in a further letter, there have been many young girls and adolescents connected with Tewkesbury Park during the whole of her psychic experiences—that is, all her life; so in this respect the case has been running true to type.

Another correspondent, Mrs. Susie J. Brand, of St. Feock, Cornwall, wrote me on January 5, 1943, and gave me an interesting account of the Poltergeist that sometimes 'visits' her house. The usual 'young girl' *nexus* appears to be missing in this case. She says:

'Before I had been here many days, I noticed queer sounds, but thought "in a fresh house there will be fresh noises". Every night came a pad, pad, pad noise like a two-footed dog or child in soft slippers jumping off the 3-feet high cupboard[1] in my bedroom. It went along the hearthrug and there made clattering and rustling noises under the window. It got so disturbing that I said "Please do let me get to sleep; I am old and not very well." This has been successful. Now sometimes there are sharp, snappy noises as if an electric switch was being operated. And generally during the day, odd noises sound, over by the window, sometimes overhead, like when the coalman folds the first empty sack and it falls *smack* on the brick floor. And now something quite different: One evening, as I was about to pick up a glass of hot milk from a tray by my bedside, it spilled. Next morning, a cup of tea tipped over as I was about to pick it up. Both the milk and the tea tipped over before I ever touched them!'

In a further letter (February 3, 1943), Mrs. Brand says: 'Since writing to you last, the screw from the top of an accumulator has been moved across my room. But I will not enlarge on this, as you must be bored stiff with Poltergeists!' I assured my correspondent that Poltergeists do not bore me in the least; in fact, news of these 'creatures' is always

[1] Mr. Cooper experienced the same phenomenon at Borley. (See p. 284.)

most welcome. Mrs. Brand was the victim of typical Poltergeist pranks.

Mrs. Brand mentions things being moved across her room. A striking case of the paranormal displacement of small articles was related to me a few weeks ago at the Reform Club, where I was lunching with Mr. A. F. Hardiman, R.A., the distinguished sculptor, whose Earl Haig Memorial Statue is well known. In Mr. Hardiman's large lock-up studio is a heavy steel turn-table used for revolving massive models. On this turn-table Mr. Hardiman kept a cheap American metal clock. One morning, when he let himself in the studio, the clock was on the floor. Hardiman thought that it must have 'ticked itself off', as these metal clocks will sometimes do, owing to vibration. The next morning the clock was on the floor again. So Hardiman poured a pool of hot wax on to the turn-table, and pressed the feet of the clock into it—thinking that, when set, the wax would stop the clock from 'creeping'. But it did nothing of the sort: on the third morning the clock was reposing on the floor. A few days later, as the sculptor unlocked the door of his studio, and advanced into the room, *the clock leapt into the air*, and crashed to the floor—broken. Mr. Hardiman was several yards from it when this happened. There was no explanation.

What is the affinity between Poltergeists and clocks? It will be remembered that in Mr. Cooper's studio, during his photographing of the Borley exhibits, a wall clock, that had not gone for years, ticked for twenty minutes. And in the Worksop case, a clock that had not functioned for eighteen months, suddenly began chiming and then 'leapt over a bed and fell to the floor'. I have now received the account of another clock that leapt over a bed. In my story of the Borley Poltergeists, I mentioned that one of our investigators was Mr. Sidney H. Glanville, a consulting engineer who, with his son, Mr. Roger H. Glanville (now an R.A.F. officer), recorded many of the phenomena witnessed at the Rectory. It was during this period that Roger was, one morning, lying in bed in their home at Streatham. Near him, on a bedside table, was an American alarm clock of the usual type. This duly 'went off' at the prescribed hour and thoroughly roused him. He was perfectly wide-awake, and was pondering whether he should get up, when the clock suddenly rose in the air, leapt across the bed, and fell to the floor. Roger, too, leapt out of bed, but the mystery was never solved.

Mrs. D. Brierley, of Park House West, Park Place, Cheltenham, had a fascinating (to me!) Poltergeist in her home at Worcester (why do so many strange things happen in Worcestershire?)[1] and on February 15,

[1] One of the strangest phenomena was surely that which occurred in Worcester, England on May 28, 1881. On that day many tons of periwinkles, small crabs, and hermit crabs were found deposited in the streets of Worcester after a violent thunderstorm. They were quite fresh and the fall was confined to the Cromer Gardens Road area and the contiguous fields and gardens. In the *Worcester Evening Post* for June

1943, she wrote and told me about it. She said: 'In many ways, your record of Borley Rectory coincided with my experiences in a haunted house at Worcester, where I lived for eighteen months during the last war. Put briefly, here are a few facts about the Worcester house: Distinct footsteps up garden path; a "load" put down in porch; shuffling noises. No one to be seen. (This happened almost *every day*.) Footsteps at night, coming upstairs, walking across landing, walking round and round a certain bedroom. Bangs on furniture in this room. (Almost *every night*.) Sound of silk dresses—crinolines, I imagined from the rhythmic, rather lovely sound. (Heard many times on top landing.) Figure of a man. (Seen by two different persons.) Bed shaken violently from underneath. (Many times.) Nightlight blown out. (Once.) Fingers run round rim of water-filled glass at bedside. (Two or three times.) Sound of hand feeling along wall over bed. (Two or three times.) My hand touched as I lay in bed. (Once.) Medicine bottles taken up and put down again on washstand. (Many times. Unluckily, I never thought of "ringing" them!)[1] Heavy mahogany lid of bath let down on me. (Once —and quite often enough!) This lid was hooked back on the wall with very large and strong metal hooks. Lights, two varieties: (*a*) sort of luminous balloons floating near ceiling; and (*b*) cone-shaped fountains, leaping up from, say, a foot almost to ceiling. These were very beautiful. My nerves suddenly went after eighteen months of being really interested in it all—and I fled! I am told the house is still there, and "often to let".'

Mrs. Brierley must have had an exciting time! The 'lights' are very interesting, and I have recorded several examples of similar phenomena in this volume.

Worcestershire furnishes another most interesting and important case, particulars of which have been sent to me by Dr. W. G. Shakespeare of West Malvern. I had previously heard of the disturbances from a friend of mine, who investigated and was impressed by the evidence.

Miss Clancy, of 'Clanmere', Malvern, engaged a young woman as cook and—well, I cannot do better than quote the verbatim report (dated September 29, 1944) which was sent by Dr. Shakespeare, who himself witnessed some of the phenomena. The manifestations occurred in 1942:

'Since the arrival of a new cook, the staff complained that objects were beginning to "fly about" in the kitchen. Persons in the rooms next to the kitchens were astonished to hear loud bangs and thumps caused

9, 1881, it was stated that ten sacks of periwinkles were picked up and sold in the local markets. A man named Maund collected in his own garden as many winkles as would fill two sacks. As Worcester is many miles from the sea, where did the winkles come from? (Extract from my letter to *The Times*, July 1, 1939.)

[1] A reference to the fact that in our Borley experiments, we used to ring objects with circles drawn with chalk, as a control, to tell us whether they had moved paranormally.

'*A cone-shaped fountain of light . . . . leaping up to ceiling.*'

351

by heavy bodies hurtling down the corridor outside. Miss Clancy was sceptical until one morning she saw a heavy wireless set leave a shelf and fly across the room, settling on the floor on the other side. She also saw a pudding cooking in a "Pyrex" dish leave the oven and alight on the table. A bag of new-laid eggs jumped off a table and crashed on the floor. One of the staff, who is quite honest and a reliable witness, saw a huge bucket of coal rise in the air and apparently pursue the cook across the kitchen, eventually emptying its contents over her shoulders before falling to the ground.

'I have always been sceptical of such stories and believed that there was probably some trickery involved. But one morning when in the kitchen with Miss Clancy, I was surprised to see a cullender leave a hook in the pantry and fly into the kitchen, dropping on the floor near my feet. I carefully examined the hook and the utensil, but found no spring or wires, etc. I should say that Miss Clancy and some of the staff are Irish and devout Catholics. A priest was summoned to bless the kitchen and he sprinkled it with Holy Water. This had little effect!

'Another incident was witnessed by six people in the kitchen and they gave a signed statement to the following effect: While the cook was standing on the kitchen table on the far side of the range, a poker detached itself from a hook by the fire and flew up in a trajectory to the ceiling, missing the electric light, and falling point downwards on the table where it came to rest between some cups and saucers which it did not damage. On another occasion she was talking to one of the staff outside the kitchen in a passage. A heavy and full swill-tub rose from the scullery, flew through the open door of the kitchen into the passage and unloaded its contents over her head and shoulders. The same thing happened to her with a large strainer full of old tea-leaves, which flew down the 20-foot china room and emptied itself over her. Eventually, the cook was asked to leave on account of the phenomena which scared the staff out of their senses! And the place was getting a bad name.

'Wherever she has been in these parts, she has been asked to leave very shortly on account of these phenomena. From "Clanmere" she went to a haberdashery shop in Malvern, but owing to suitcases and boxes of socks flying about the shop, she was asked to leave. I can get witnessed account of this if necessary. Then to a large girls' school, where the same things happened in the kitchen, and then she entered the service of two old ladies whose valuable collection of china began to fly about and get smashed. I have today visited the cottage of Mr. Roberts, of "Hawthorn Villa", Hawthorn Lane, Malvern Common, where she lodged for a time until asked to leave. Mr. Roberts, a postman, tells me: "Whenever she came into the sitting-room in the evening, great lumps of burning coal used to fly out of the open grate about the room and burned the furniture." He showed me the marks of the burns in the leather arm chair.'

The importance of this case lies in the fact that the subsequent history of the 'medium' is known, and that identical disturbances followed her from place to place. I am in possession of the girl's name, but refrain from publishing it. The reader will hardly fail to notice the many correspondences between the Malvern affair and the 'astonishing transactions at Stockwell', where Ann Robinson made pandemonium in the kitchen, 172 years ago.

Another experience comes from Mr. A. S. Medcraft, an electrical engineer, of 102, Ashgrove Road, Goodmayes, Essex. He was working late one evening on a radio set. The other members of his family were in bed. During the repairs, he put a Ferranti resistance ($2\frac{1}{2}$ inches long by 1 inch wide) on a table, which was clear of other objects. The table was in front of him. He turned his back on it for a moment, without leaving the room, and when he again looked at the table, *the resistance had gone*! He says (January 10, 1944): 'This I will swear to. Of course, I moved the table to see where the object had fallen. Upon not finding it, I put the table back in its original position, when I noticed that the resistance was in the same place where I had originally put it. I am positive of this. I was very wide awake; the current I was using required that I should be. But this happening struck me as being so strange, that I must confess to feeling rather queer and I went straight to bed.'

Mrs. Enid Eve, of Rosehill, Orford, near Woodbridge, Suffolk, sent me the details of a most interesting case. A friend of hers, a Lady X., had a small son, aged four, for whom she engaged a young French *bonne*, who occupied the same room as the boy. Lady X. noticed that the child was frightened of going into the bedroom, so she decided to take the nurse's place for one night. Very soon after her son was put to bed, but was not yet asleep, he gave a terrible shriek, pointed to the foot of the bed and fainted. Later, Lady X. was awakened by having the bedclothes pulled off her bed several times, 'and all round the room lights were flashing'. This sort of thing happened throughout the night.

In the morning Sir X. consulted a scientific friend of his who at once suggested that the French *bonne* was the cause of the trouble. She was interrogated and admitted that she was the unwilling agent through whom these strange phenomena occurred. She was asked to leave the house, and advised to give up her occupation of 'nurse'. No further trouble in the house was experienced. Six months later, the little boy was asked what he saw at the foot of his bed when he gave the terrible shriek. He replied: 'A great tall thing covered with fur, with a long tail.'[1]

A friend of mine, Mr. John W. Evans, happened to pick up my *Search for Truth* in Tasmania. Mr. Evans is a scientist and married to the daughter of the English scientist, Dr. R. J. Tillyard, F.R.S.

---

[1] Adelaide, a child of about the same age, at Borley Rectory, saw a 'nasty thing' that gave her a bruise under the eye. Mrs. Foyster saw a monstrosity 'that touched her with an iron touch'.

Mr. Evans writes me (on May 2, 1943) from 27, Lipscombe Avenue, Sandy Bay, Hobart, on the subject of Poltergeists, which I have discussed in my book. He says: 'We live in an old (for this part of the world) house, about one hundred years old, and during our first few years here certainly heard strange noises, scamperings on the stairs, people moving about, the sound of light-switches being turned on,[1] etc. Nowadays we hear nothing.' I will add that Mr. Evans is an Englishman.

The Hon. Mrs. Greville-Nugent, of Preston House, Benson, Oxon., also writes of an interesting experience that she had with a Poltergeist. She says (September 14, 1943): 'I personally have suffered from Poltergeists, who have taken bank-notes *out of my hand* (no other human being being in the room!); and one Easter morning *stole all my hats*, so that I had to borrow one from my daughter, in order to go to Mass! Two mornings later, the hats suddenly reappeared, piled one on top of another, right on top of a high gilt cornice from which hang the curtains of my French bed. Eventually I got a priest to exorcise the room, and was not troubled again. It was a house at Hove, pre-war.'

The next—my penultimate—citation from recent correspondence is from Mr. Harry B. Agate (brother of the well-known writer, Mr. James Agate), 46, Ainsty Avenue, Dringhouses, York, and refers to showers of frogs, those 'unnatural' natural phenomena, beloved of Charles Fort. Mr. Agate, who wrote on August 20, 1943, told me that during the previous six years, three separate showers of frogs had descended on his garden. The frogs were alive and hopping and my correspondent asked whether I could account for the phenomenon. To date, no one has solved the problem of these strange falls of animate and inanimate objects that just tumble out of the blue. Whirlwinds and waterspouts are an easy explanation, but not the only one, because the majority of these things—which range from fish to fossils—fall on clear, fine days when there is no wind.

My last case is perhaps the most interesting amongst recent communications of this sort, as it raises a number of queries that ought to be answered. It is a sort of Poltergeist case in reverse, as the reader will note.

The report came from Mrs. W., a doctor's wife living in Sunderland who, for 'personal and professional reasons' desires to remain anonymous—obviously. However, she gives me the fullest details, with correct names and addresses, as a sign of good faith. Here is her story:

Sunderland,
February 23, 1943.

I have just been reading your book[2] with much interest, the chapter on Poltergeister especially, as it strikes a personal note. My husband is

[1] This particular sound is a very common phenomenon in Poltergeist cases.—H.P.
[2] *Search for Truth.*—H.P.

a doctor with a practice at M——, where his surgery is, though we live on this side of the river. We have one daughter, Olive, now just turned nineteen. She is our only child, and it is about her that I am writing.

Olive is, apparently, a normal girl in every way. She remained at school until she was 17½ and did well, though she could never pass examinations, though very intelligent pin every way. She was very fond of sports and excelled in several of them. She is a normal, robust, healthy girl, vivacious and with a sense of humour. And is in fact a 'good sort', in every way. She has never had a serious illness.

Soon after leaving school, Olive became engaged to a Flight-Lieutenant in the R.A.F., rather against our wishes, as we considered her too young. As it was a true love match, we gave in. They were married from here in January of last year, and went to live with her husband's people at Consett, as they will not begin home-building until after the war, and we thought she would be out of the raids there. They are very happy. I am telling you these details as it may help *you* to help us.

Olive's husband left for the Near East in March, 1942. My daughter was then *enceinte* and on the fourth of last November, gave birth to a beautiful baby girl. The labour was normal, with no complications, and the infant weighed 9½ pounds.

I will now describe our residence. We live in a rather large flat over some business premises in P—— Street, Sunderland. There is only one entrance to the flat and that is from the street. Access is gained to our rooms, which are on the first floor, by means of a flight of wooden stairs at the end of a short passage. The passage has no floor covering, but the stairs are covered with carpet, rather worn.

There is nothing unusual in the flat itself. At the top of the stairs is a hall, opening out of which are two living rooms, a bathroom-lavatory, a lobby, a small bedroom and a kitchen. A short passage leads to two larger bedrooms, one of which (at the end of the passage) is Olive's room. This room has not been disturbed since my girl left, as she occasionally visits us. Nearly all her belongings, unwanted clothes, wedding presents, school-books, library, tennis rackets, golf clubs, etc., are stored there, as she will eventually make her home in Sunderland. Only three keys to the Yale lock on the front door are in existence. The one that Olive formerly used, she has kept. I use another on a ring with other keys, and my husband possesses the third. We have had no maid since my daughter left school.

I now come to the real reason for writing to you. Towards the end of last February, I had been out shopping. The flat was fast-closed and no one could enter it without breaking the street door down. I returned about 11.45 and went up to the flat. I took off my outdoor garments in our bedroom and then went to my daughter's room to return a large kilt-pin[1] (that I had borrowed from the dressing table drawer) with

---

[1] A large safety-pin.—H.P.

which I had fastened my scarf. I had previously been in the room at about 9.45 that morning when I dusted it. And now, to my amazement, I saw the bedclothes carefully turned back cornerwise as if someone was about to step into the bed. I stared at it dumbfounded, as I had not the faintest recollection of touching the bed, the clothes of which had not been disturbed for at least ten days. The incident puzzled me all day and when my husband came home to dinner that evening, I mentioned it to him, fearing that someone was able to enter the flat without our knowledge. He was of the opinion that *I* had turned back the clothes, unconsciously, with which I agreed. There seemed no other solution.

Three days later, as I was in the kitchen putting the finishing touches to our evening meal, whilst awaiting my husband's return, I heard his key in the lock and the front door open. And not only did I hear his footsteps, but also those of Olive who had, apparently, come home with him. These sounds were very familiar to me, as my daughter used frequently, when at school, to call at her father's surgery and return home with him in the car, and they used to mount the stairs together. On this occasion I distinctly heard Olive's footsteps, and her father's, coming up the stairs.

I went into the hall to greet them, but could only see my husband. I said to him, 'Where's Olive?'. He replied that he had not seen her. But, I insisted, I heard her enter the flat with you, and heard her mount the stairs. He said, 'That is impossible, I heard nothing'.

Well, Mr. Price, I don't want to bore you, but from that day, for several months, the most extraordinary things happened, and in every case they were connected with my daughter's room or belongings. At least twenty times, while waiting for my husband's return at night, I heard the lock turn, the door open, and Olive's steps come tripping up the stairs. Very occasionally, it *was* she, but I could never tell until she either came into the dining-room, or I went into the hall to find she *wasn't* there. And these false alarms *always* occurred at the time my husband was expected home. I could *never* tell until I went into the hall to look (after hearing the door open) whether it was my husband by himself (or, more rarely, with Olive), or Olive in the flesh, or just no one! My husband *never* heard the footsteps walking behind him. But on one occasion, just as he had returned and had mounted the stairs, the lock turned again, and the door *appeared* to open. This time my husband heard it. But there were *no* footsteps.

Sometimes, when I had got used to the strange occurrences, I did not trouble to go into the hall, but just waited. On four occasions I heard my 'daughter' trip up the stairs, apparently change her shoes in the lobby, walk along the passage, go to her room, and even use the bathroom—*exactly*, action for action, that she used to do when returning from school. But on the few occasions when she really visited us alone during this disturbing period, she did not go to her room first, but always came to kiss me when she reached the top of the stairs.

Many other strange things happened during this period. The books in her room were found sometimes on her bed, sometimes on the floor. The bedclothes were frequently disarranged and the bed appeared to have been slept in. The mirror on her dressing-table was found, more than once, to have been swung on its pivots to a different angle. Sometimes the drawers were found pulled half out and the contents disarranged—but never seriously. And *never* was there anything broken and, as far as we know, was anything ever missing.

We told Olive only a very little of what was taking place. We were afraid, in her then state of health, that she would be seriously frightened. But, as a matter of fact, she was more interested than frightened. Thrice she visited us specially to see these things for herself, but *never* did an unusual incident occur while she was under our roof.

As her pregnancy advanced, the 'incidents' became more frequent, though not more violent. Especially, the bedclothes in her room would be disarranged; once twice in one day. Her underclothes (mostly her trousseau and wedding presents) were frequently found half-in and half-out of her wardrobe drawers. A curious thing about her bedroom disturbances was that we *never heard* anything going on in there. Again, this is curious, the disturbances usually took place in the day-time, often when I was out shopping, though I think on two occasions at night.

The disturbances *always* occurred in her room, and *never* in any other room, with one exception. An unframed photograph of Olive in her wedding-dress, that we had stood on the dining-room mantelpiece, was found by me (after shopping) to have been moved from its usual position and laid, face downwards, on the dining-room table.

And I now come to the strangest part of all. After the birth of her baby, the disturbances ceased completely. And that led us to certain calculations that we had not thought of before. We suddenly realised that all the 'incidents' had occurred within the period of her pregnancy, which had lasted 280 days. When I discovered that the clothes of her bed had been turned back on that first morning, it must have been within two days of her becoming pregnant. Do you think this was symbolic, or what? I ought to have mentioned that Olive has *never* experienced anything unusual herself, and nothing has happened in her temporary home at Consett.

And now I must mention what is troubling us and ask you a few questions. Will the same thing occur if Olive has another baby? Will little Enid (our grandchild) be one of those Poltergeist girls you mention in your book, when she gets older? Can anything be done to prevent such a possibility? Why did it happen? Do you know of any similar cases, and if so, what happened afterwards? Do please try and help us, as my son-in-law, no less than ourselves, is very worried over the matter

357

and we would like your advice. If our experiences are new to you, and you would like to include them in your records, you are at liberty to do so, but *please* do not publish anything that would lead people to write to us and annoy us. For professional and personal reasons we are desirous that our names should be suppressed, but I am sure you will quite understand our feelings in the matter. But *do* please try and help us.

*   *   *   *

I had to confess to Mrs. W. that her experiences were new to me. I also had to confess that I could not help her very much as we know so little about these things. If we had a dozen cases like Olive's, we might begin to formulate a theory. I told my correspondent that the synchronising of the phenomena in her flat with her daughter's pregnancy, might well be sheer coincidence. But I had to admit that certain factors in the case did point to some connection. The fact that nothing but Olive's belongings were touched; the repeated disarrangement of her bed and her underclothes, her schoolbooks, and other articles associated with the transition period from pubescence to adolescence—all these things are significant. Presuming there was a link between the paranormal happenings at the flat and Olive's rather precipitate blossoming into full womanhood, then I suggest that the sudden releasing of her pent-up sexual energies caused a violent reaction that manifested itself amongst her most intimate belongings in her old home. Undoubtedly, Olive was the 'Poltergeist girl' mentioned by Mrs. W. This faculty was latent all the time she lived under her parents' roof. But when, as I say, her sexual energies were released by marriage, and when she found herself in a strange home and in new surroundings, she subconsciously externalised these suddenly-acquired powers, and just as subconsciously projected them into her old home, that home where the physiological changes that herald womanhood had occurred. But all this is sheer surmise.

As for Mrs. W.'s query concerning the possibility of 'little Enid' becoming a 'Poltergeist girl' like her mother, I could be a little more definite. There is no record whatsoever of a girl possessing these strange powers transmitting them to her offspring. And I am certain that neither Olive, nor Olive's old home, will ever again be troubled with a 'Poltergeist'. The strain and shock to her organism caused by the recent physiological changes, will have killed whatever 'powers' she possessed.[1] I have never known of a case where the faculty has survived under such circumstances. And as for Olive's next child being 'affected', the odds against such an occurrence are astronomical. Anyway, I told Mrs. W. that she would have to await the event.

[1] As was the case with Eleonore Zugun.

CHAPTER XXIX

The Evidence for the Poltergeist

The word 'evidence' (from the Latin *evidentia, evideri*, 'to appear clearly') was defined by St. George Jackson Mivart,[1] the biologist, as 'denoting the facts presented to the mind of a person for the purpose of enabling him to decide a disputed question'. And it would be interesting to learn how much of the evidence for the existence of Poltergeists, that I have submitted to the reader of this book, has been accepted by him.

I will be frank, and admit at once that I do not accept all this evidence myself. And it is obvious that not all the cases possess the same evidential value. I am sure—and the reader is sure, too—that fraud, malobservation, exaggeration, and natural causes, could account for some of the 'miracles'. But even where trickery—conscious, unconscious, or subconscious—is a likely explanation, we are presented with a pretty psychological problem that is well worth studying. Unfortunately, a small majority of the cases have been cursorily reported (so far as the public is concerned) and incompletely investigated by untrained, credulous, and often semi-literate persons, whose testimony cannot always be relied upon. Against this must be set the fact that the evidence of even the uneducated and the credulous must be accepted, if of good enough quality, and if it will bear analysis. And it is significant that the same phenomena have occurred in the homes of rich and poor alike, and that both the cultured and untutored have told the same story. And this same story has been told by observers separated by centuries of time and thousands of miles of space. And the phenomena are always the same—or bear a family likeness to one another—though they occur in different settings. As Lang says,[2] 'It is certain that the royal, the rich, and the well-educated observers tell, in many cases, precisely the same sort of stories about Poltergeist phenomena as do the poor and the imperfectly instructed.'

It is the coincidental value of these phenomena that compel us to accept so many of them. I will give one striking example (out of many that I have collected). In my notes for 1928, I have an account of a Poltergeist that infested the cottage of a dairyman who lived at Lifton, Devonshire. The entity heralded its advent by a *shower of kidney beans*, which were flung all over the place. Twigs, complete with thorns, such as might have been cut from a hedge fell, apparently from nowhere, on

---

[1] *Nature and Thought*, London, 1882, p. 133.
[2] *Encyclo. Brit., op. cit.*, p. 16.

to tables and chairs and even upon the heads of the occupants, which included a young girl employed as a daily help. The showers of kidney beans continued for some days.

Now for the parallel case: Within a week or so of this same period (the spring of 1928) a friend of mine sent me from France a cutting from the Paris *Soir*. It was a short account of how the tent of an Arab *sheikh*, who was encamped in the desert outside the walls of Palmyra, had been pelted for days with *showers of pine-cones*, alternating with a rain of salt. The quantity of pine-cones weighed more than 20 kilogrammes (about

Typical Poltergeist phenomena.

45 pounds). Probably these were acceptable to the *sheikh*, as they form an article of diet in Syria.

I can think of other parallels, even in the cases I have cited in this monograph. For example, we have three reports of the Poltergeist making a noise like the winding up of a clock or a jack, which is also clockwork. And this is a most unusual noise. Then there is repeated stone-throwing,[1] bell-ringing, persons being pushed or pulled out of bed, floating bedclothes, unaccountable fires, things suddenly appearing and disappearing, the curious flight of projected missiles, the strange

---

[1] In January, 1849, a rain of stones showered down on a house near the Panthéon, Paris. No explanation. (Recorded by Prof. Alfred Russel Wallace in *On Miracles and Modern Spiritualism*, London, 1896, p. 284.)

animals seen (or the illusion of seeing them), the 'voices' heard in so many cases, the spontaneous movement of heavy objects, etc. The reader has probably discovered other correspondences for himself.

I have mentioned that some Poltergeist effects may be merely illusions —aural or visual. And I am reminded of a most extraordinary case that was reported in the *Times* for December 11, 1873. A couple of days previously, a Mr. and Mrs. Thomas B. Compston had been arrested in the early hours of the morning at one of the Bristol railway stations, and they were charged with disorderly conduct. They were in their nightclothes and Mr. Compston had fired a pistol.

At the subsequent court proceedings, some remarkable evidence emerged. Mr. Compston and his wife, an elderly couple, arrived from Leeds on the previous night, and booked a room at the Victoria Hotel. Some hours after midnight, 'the floor opened', and Mr. Compston was about to be dragged into the chasm, when his wife saved him. It appeared that earlier in the evening, both of them had been alarmed by hearing loud noises in their room. They complained to the landlady, who reassured them. Between 3 and 4 a.m. the sounds were heard again. Terrified, they jumped out of bed, and felt the floor give way beneath them. Strange voices were heard, and then the floor opened wide. The husband was falling into the opening, when his wife dragged him back. Still more terrified, they jumped out of the window, panic-stricken, and were later found wandering at the railway station, almost demented.

The landlady also testified. She, too, had heard the noises, but could not identify them. The police gave evidence to the effect that they had examined the Compstons' room, which appeared perfectly normal. The police thought they had been hallucinated. It was stated in court that the Compstons held good positions in Leeds, and had irreproachable characters. They were discharged, and a friend from Leeds took them home. They were still terrified. The detailed account of the case can be read in the *Bristol Daily Post* for December 10, 1873. The reader will recollect that Joseph Glanvill records the 'motion of Boards' when describing the bedroom phenomena in Mompesson's house. And in the ballad (*A Wonder of Wonders*—see Appendix A) the same incident is described: 'The Chamber floor would rise and fall, and never a board disjointed.'

I hope the reader does not expect me to sort out the 'good' and 'bad' cases I have cited. As regards the 'bad' ones, in many instances we have so few details to judge by that it would be unjust—and certainly unwise —for me to make an *ex cathedrâ* pronouncement concerning them. As for the 'good' cases, we are on safer ground.

It can hardly be denied that Mr. Mompesson's house was troubled by *something*, but I am inclined to think that the 'Drummer' may *not* have been the prime-mover in this case. I believe that the 'two little modest girls', Mompesson's daughters, were the *nexus*—unconsciously, of

361

course. The advent of the drummer, his arrest, his behaviour (and even threats), and the fact that his drum was seized and carried to Mompesson's house, *might* have given the Poltergeists an idea, as it were. These entities have intelligence. They might have thought to themselves, 'Here is the very *mise-en-scène* we were looking for—let's go ahead!' Even the sight of the drum probably 'inspired' them! It would be natural, of course, to associate the drummer with the disturbances; and the drummer, hearing about them, and thirsting for revenge, would, with an excusable vanity, boast about his 'achievements'. I think that the Mompesson case is a good one.

There can be no question at all that the Ringcroft disturbances happened in the way they were said to happen with, perhaps, some exaggeration. If the Ringcroft report had been published to-day, it would still be one of the best-authenticated accounts of a Poltergeist infestation that we possess. The fact that it was issued nearly 250 years ago seems incredible. The phenomena were attested by a number of responsible persons. Each incident of the narrative is individually vouched for by the person or persons who witnessed the occurrence. The account was written by the minister of the parish in which the occurrences took place, and the report is signed by the ministers of five neighbouring parishes; by the lairds of Colline and Milhouse, and by several other persons of repute, all of whom were *witnesses* of the phenomena. The report would do credit to a twentieth-century investigator.

Something similar can be said for the Wesley records, which were compiled serially as the phenomena occurred. The series of letters sent to young Samuel by various members of his family forms a perfect record of the events—a contemporary record that we are not entitled to question. It was by sheer good luck that these letters have been preserved. And it was due to the fame that two of the boys subsequently acquired that these letters were ever published. All the Wesley children were particularly intelligent, and so were their parents.

If I am so certain about the authenticity of the phenomena witnessed at Tedworth, Ringcroft, and Epworth, I am not absolutely convinced that the Cambridge Castle ghost did not originate in the brain of Professor Simon Ockley. He was in prison, ill, frail, disappointed, and worried to death about money matters. The strain of all these combined misfortunes would have turned the brain of many a strong man. Ockley was not a strong man, and the continued worry might well have affected him mentally. We have no evidence for this and I may be doing him an injustice.

If there is the slightest doubt concerning the Cambridge Castle disturbances, there is none whatever about the horrible affair at Hinton Ampner. Here is a clear-cut case of Poltergeist infestation, authenticated and documented at the time by distinguished and cultured persons, and persisting for years. In fact, the phenomena drove one family after another out of the house, which was finally pulled down in an attempt to get rid of the *Geist*.

The Stockwell case is a good one from the evidential standpoint. Like the Ringcroft affair, the report was published immediately after the occurrences, which were witnessed by a number of reputable people who at once appended their signatures to the protocol. The Stockwell case is of great interest, because Ann Robinson *knew* that she was the unwilling cause of all the trouble.

I consider that many of these old cases have a ring of truth in them apart from the intrinsic worth of the evidence submitted. And they are the more valuable on account of the fact that they may be the 'originals' of some modern cases, which are perhaps merely imitative—assuming that some of the modern ones are fraudulent.

Can anyone read the Willington Mill case without noting the ring of sincerity that is apparent in every line? Mr. Joseph Procter was an educated, hard-headed business man, intelligent, a well-known Quaker, and his 'diary' is the serial record of a transparently honest witness. Is it conceivable that such a man would, for twelve years, sit down and write a lot of nonsense—not for posterity, as he had no idea that it would ever be published—for his own amusement? That indeed would be as great a phenomenon as any recorded in his journal! And, as the reader knows, the Poltergeists finally drove him from his home, as the disturbances at Hinton Ampner drove Mrs. Ricketts from hers. And, as in the case of Mrs. Ricketts, Mr. Procter's story is confirmed by other—and sceptical —observers. We must accept it as being substantially true.

Could any person, unless bereft of all reason, live in his own house for fifty-four days with most of the bells incessantly ringing without stopping them—if stoppable—or without discovering *why* they were ringing, if the ringing was due to normal causes? Could a scientifically-minded and army-trained observer, and a Fellow of the Royal Society to boot, be fooled in his own house by a lot of clanging bells—if not paranormally clanged? Could any intelligent reader of this book be deceived, not for fifty-four days, but for fifty-four minutes, by his own bells ringing, if the ringer was a practical joker or one of his own household? The answer to all these queries is an emphatic and obvious 'No!' And so we must accept Major Moor's considered judgment that the bell-ringing at Bealings was a paranormal nuisance. As he was writing his letter to the *Ipswich Journal*, he says: 'At this moment comes a peal . . .' Fortunately for students of psychical phenomena, his experience can be paralleled, as at Borley and elsewhere.

The testimony for the disturbances at the 'Mill on the Eden' is, unfortunately, not first-hand, but I accept the evidence. The case itself has some unusual features, though similar phenomena can be instanced in other Poltergeist records. And as for my early experience in the Shropshire Manor, I can still 'pluck from my memory' the thump, thump,

thump of the Poltergeist (with wooden legs?) as it wended its uncertain way down—and up—the hall stairs as we lay crouching and terror-stricken, in the dark, behind the door of the morning-room. Fortunately, I was just old enough to appreciate the significance of the phenomena. If I had *not* heard those thumps, it is highly improbable that this book would ever have been written by me!

There is circumstantial evidence and there is concrete evidence. No one, viewing the wreckage at the Robinsons' house at Battersea, could doubt the evidence for Poltergeists! Broken furniture, smashed windows, shattered ornaments, cracked mirrors, and the débris of half a home strewn all over the place was concrete evidence with a vengeance, if words have any meaning. And the Robinsons, too, were driven from the abode that had sheltered them for twenty-five years.

The best of all evidence is, of course, that of one's own five senses, and I cannot do better than to advise my readers to investigate for themselves. I have included in this monograph some striking evidence supplied by my friends and correspondents. If old cases are good on account of their originality, these recent ones of my friends are invaluable because they *are* recent. The witnesses are alive and available; the incidents recorded are fresh in their memories; and the deponents can be cross-examined, if necessary.

It is because of the evidence of my own eyes and ears that I am so convinced of the existence of some *power* outside of the known laws of physics. The crashing candlestick, the jumping soap, and the simultan-eous fall of keys from their locks at Borley; the flying gas-lighter, and the travelling cherub at Battersea; the whirring noise at Minehead; the telekinetic phenomena of the Schneider boys and Eleonore Zugun, and the hundred other paranormal movements of inanimate objects that I have witnessed under conditions that absolutely precluded fraud—these are the phenomena that have convinced me. Because *I* have seen them!

And now I come to Borley—the best-evidenced, the best-witnessed, and the best-documented case of Poltergeist infestation in the annals of psychical research. In my book[1] on Borley I name about 100 witnesses who testified to having seen or experienced paranormal phenomena at Borley Rectory. My witnesses include the five incumbents, covering the period from 1863 (when the Rectory was built) to the present day; a Roman Catholic priest; the present owner of the Rectory; relatives and servants of the Rectors; medical men, scientists, B.B.C. officials, and R.A.F. officers; academic and university observers[2]; engineers, scholars

---

[1] *Op. cit.*

[2] As I am correcting the proofs of this book, Mr. A. J. B. Robertson, M.A., writes to say that since my monograph (*op. cit.*) on Borley was published, about sixty scientists, graduates, and undergraduates from Cambridge University have visited Borley on twenty-five nights, and that 'a number of curious happenings have been noted, especially of auditory events, such as reiterated noises....' During the period of their investigations, the Rectory was, of course, in ruins.

and students; a diplomatic representative; hard-headed business men, workmen, villagers, etc. etc. Is it conceivable that *all* of these shrewd witnesses, many of them highly educated, scientifically-trained, cultured and sceptical, were mistaken or hallucinated? No! Were my hundred witnesses in reality a hundred liars? No! Then we must accept their testimony.

But we have other testimony: the testimony of one of the most brilliant legal luminaries of our generation—Sir Ernest Jelf, King's Remembrancer since 1937, and Senior Master of the Supreme Court. Sir Ernest's testimony is that of an impartial judge who has studied the records of the Borley case. And I believe I am right in saying that no other case of haunting has ever received the attention of such an eminent jurist as Sir Ernest, and no pronouncement, comparable with the one he published, has ever been made concerning any other 'haunted house'.

Sir Ernest published his views in a leading article (which is really a review of my book) in the *Law Times* for August 9, 1941. The article is entitled 'A Question of Evidence', and the writer calls attention to the fact that in my monograph on Borley, I have emphasised (as I am trying to do now) that whether a place is, or is not, haunted, depends on the quality and quantity of the evidence. I challenged the reader to dispute this fact—or the evidence I there submitted. Sir Ernest takes up the challenge.

In his preliminary remarks, Sir Ernest says: 'Those of us who all our lives have spent a large part of our working hours in courts of law, seeking to ascertain what is and what is not worthy of belief, will be staggered by the appeal, which this book makes, that we shall believe things more contrary to the ordinary experience of mankind than we could ever have dreamed of before.' In my book I state that 'Readers of this monograph are now in possession of the evidence I have accumulated for the alleged haunting of Borley Rectory.' Sir Ernest says that I did not *quite* accurately state the position. He points out that my readers, as 'jury', have not *heard* the evidence—and have had no opportunity of cross-examining my witnesses (a few readers have, of course, cross-examined some of my witnesses) who 'seldom quite come up to their proofs', to use the legal phrase, when in the witness-box. 'But,' says Sir Ernest, 'let us suppose that we are asked, as counsel might be asked, whether, upon the perusal of the proofs, there is a good chance of substantiating the case which these proofs are designed to support.'

Sir Ernest then goes on to state that those 'proofs' 'do present a very strong case indeed—stronger than most of us could ever have believed possible before we had read the book. There are more than a hundred witnesses, most of them are still alive and available, including many persons of position and intellectual attainment. And many of them were called in as unprejudiced outsiders, on purpose to see whether they would by their own experience corroborate the witnesses who had gone before.'

Sir Ernest Jelf then mentions some of the phenomena we experienced: the movement of objects, the spontaneous outbreaks of fire, the thermal variations, the pleasant and unpleasant odours, etc. Sir Ernest remarks: 'These stories stand on a perfectly different level from the ordinary ghost story, inasmuch as the "Poltergeist" is a hypothesis to account for a force which can produce actual physical and chemical changes in matter, as for instance when things are thrown about, when wine is changed into ink, and when writings inexplicably appear and remain upon a wall.'

Sir Ernest continues, that after every allowance has been made for what he said about 'witnesses not coming up to their proofs', and so on, 'a very strong case has undoubtedly been put forward and we are at a loss to understand what cross-examination could possibly shake it.' Suggestion and auto-suggestion, he says, might be advanced during cross-examination as an 'explanation' of the mystery—but that would imply that the witnesses imagined the whole thing: 'But a hundred imaginers! But imaginers of position and intellectual repute! Imaginers brought from outside to come fresh to the examination as independent persons!'

Sir Ernest mentions the dogs. Captain Gregson, the owner of Borley Rectory, had two young spaniels that, successively, 'saw' something, went mad with fright, and bolted. Neither has been seen since. Sir Ernest naïvely asks if the dogs also 'imagined' the strange sights and sounds that so affected them. He concludes his valuable criticism with the pious hope that, one of these days, a case comparable with that of Borley, will become relevant to some issue in a legal trial. He says the jury would probably disagree! I sincerely hope that Sir Ernest Jelf will one day find time to pass an opinion on the present volume.

A great deal has happened at Borley since Sir Ernest Jelf's article appeared in the *Law Times*. We have the first-hand evidence of at least another fifty witnesses, some of this evidence relating to events that occurred as long ago as 1885. A number of Cambridge scientists have had interesting experiences there; a distinguished engineer was 'jumped upon' by an invisible 'something' that bore him to the ground; a gentleman and his wife, exploring the grounds with a view to renting them as tea-gardens, were followed all over the place by an audible, though invisible, entity. (The negotiations fell through!) All these incidents, and many more, will be told in detail in the new Borley book. And there will be no lack of additional first-hand evidence.

In a previous chapter I promised to cite a few cases of Poltergeist-infestation as further evidence that these entities do not confine themselves to any particular country, civilization, race, or set of conditions. A book could be written on the geography of the Poltergeist. In this monograph I have already included a few examples from foreign lands and I now propose to give some account of 'disturbances' in more or less out-of-the-way corners of the world. I will begin with the truly remarkable case of Damodar Ketkar, whom I investigated—vicariously—in 1929–1930.

The case of Damodar Ketkar was brought to my notice in a curious way. A Miss H. Kohn, B.A. (Lond.), a lecturer in languages at the Governmental Deccan College, Poona, and a member of Bombay University, wrote to the late Fr. Herbert Thurston, S.J., saying that a young Indian boy was 'phenomena-ridden'. She wanted to know if there was anyone in England who would investigate the case and, perhaps, give relief. Father Thurston gave her my name and the lady arrived in London. I was not aware of her existence until she wrote to me in October, 1929, asking for an appointment. She had an extraordinary story to tell: Damodar, then aged 10, was an orphan who had been adopted by her brother-in-law, Dr. Ketkar, whose name he took. Damodar, whose mother had committed suicide,[1] entered the Ketkar household at the age of 4. Soon after, curious things began to happen until the place became 'like Hell'. Miss Kohn kept a detailed diary of the manifestations as they occurred and her report reads like a fairy story. And yet it is one of the best-authenticated extant. It is impossible for me to give more than a very brief *résumé* of the phenomena, and the interested reader must consult the long and complete record of the case that Miss Kohn and I compiled for the *Journal*[2] of the American S.P.R. We published a photograph of Damodar, whose brother, Ramkrishna, was also 'troubled' by a Poltergeist, though in a much milder form. It is unusual for two brothers to be afflicted simultaneously in this way, but the reader will recollect that the two Schneider boys exhibited their mediumship concurrently.

Attempts had been made to 'cure' the boys (especially Damodar) and it sounds strange to us Westerners to hear of 'witch-doctors', 'medicine men' and exorcists, being brought in, in an attempt to stop the racket. But such was the case. Effigies of the supposed 'spirit' were buried; amulets were worn, and a lot of native hocus-pocus was tried out without success. It merely annoyed the *Geist*, though, curiously enough, prayers seem to have been efficacious at times.

The report that Miss Kohn and I published embraced a period of twelve months, from July 1928 to July 1929, and here are *a very few* of the strange things that happened: Food and drink disappeared and would sometimes return, dropping 'from nowhere'; household goods were flung all over the place, more violently when the boy was asleep; a wick was drawn into the reservoir of a paraffin lamp; Miss Kohn saw (which was unusual) a heavy mirror (16 × 12 inches) descend from the

---

[1] She soaked her clothes with paraffin and set fire to herself.

[2] 'An Indian Poltergeist', by Harry Price and H. Kohn, Vol. XXIV, 1930, pp. 122–130, 180–186, 221–232.

wall, balance itself on the floor, and gently lean itself against the wall—all this while the boy 'slept heavily'; furniture wandered from room to room; small coins, of unknown origin, were *seen* to materialise in the air and then fall to the floor; loud explosions were heard; a waste-paper basket 'walked' across the room; food and toys were repeatedly snatched from the boy's hands; once, a shower of bottles, containing medicaments, fell simultaneously around the boy, who became hysterical (all the bottles were smashed); objects suddenly 'appeared' in the boy's hands—'from nowhere'; fruit, left in a room overnight, was eaten and the 'skins, scraped clean, were flung back, and with teeth-marks clearly visible on them'; a doctor, attending one of the family, 'was literally bombarded with crashing objects, some of which hit him'; coins fell from the ceiling; Damodar was not only levitated, but was 'transported' on more than one occasion; articles missed would return, weeks later, 'from nowhere'; eggs were *seen*, by two witnesses, to vanish, one by one, from off the dish on which they had been placed; two pound packets of butter on a shelf were seen, by two witnesses, to change places twice in five minutes; the flight of many of the objects was *curved*, i.e. not in a straight line from point to point; articles disappeared from *closed* boxes and bags; mosquito curtains round the boy's bed had to be dispensed with, as stones and toys would appear *inside* the net, when he was tucked in for the night, and jump about—and so on and so on for about two dozen closely-printed pages.

Some people are lucky! What wouldn't I give to have a boy like Damodar in my house for six years—or even six days. What experiments could be made! What theories could be tried out! I attempted to get the boy to London, but the difficulty of finding someone to accompany him was an insuperable one. The subsequent case history of this boy is interesting. A year after Miss Kohn's visit to London, the phenomena became fewer and less violent—and then ceased. The boy had arrived at maturity. In hot climates children mature much earlier than they do in northern countries, and Damodar, in his twelfth year, must have been fully developed. The reader will remember that with Eleonore Zugun the phenomena ceased—almost overnight—when the menses appeared.

I have included the Damodar Ketkar case in this chapter as further 'evidence for the Poltergeist'. The phenomena were witnessed and recorded by educated and intelligent people over a number of years. Many other persons saw the manifestations, too. As in the case of Eleonore Zugun, phenomena occurred in *any* house where the 'medium' happened to be. And the Indian case is also remarkable for a number of reasons: objects were displaced, or *seen* to move, even when people were staring at them. This is very unusual. And here we have got away from the 'young girl' concept—which is also unusual. And the fact that many of the phenomena were witnessed by a number of persons *simultaneously* is likewise unusual. In fact, it is, from many angles, an outstanding case.

I will now describe, very briefly, a few of the more interesting examples of Poltergeists infesting jungles, annoying aborigines, and making a nuisance of themselves in the wide open spaces. One of the most remarkable of these 'native' cases was put on record by Mr. W. G. Grottendieck and the disturbance took place in the jungle at Dortrecht, Sumatra, in September, 1903. One night he was awakened by hearing something falling round his bed, outside the mosquito net. He investigated and found that the objects were black stones about half an inch long. He jumped out of bed, turned up his lamp, and plainly saw the stones falling through the roof in a *parabolic curve*. He awoke his 'boy', who was sleeping in the next room, and told him to explore the jungle outside. This he did, while Mr. Grottendieck illuminated the area with an electric lantern. No one was seen, and while he and his man were outside the building, showers of stones continued to fall *inside* the house, which Mr. Grottendieck re-entered. He then tried to catch the stones as they fell, without success. The house was then explored without result. The stones continued to fall 'right through the *kadjang*,[1] but there were no holes in the *kadjang*'. A curious feature of this good case (which should be read in the original[2]) is that the stones felt *hot*; they appeared to move slowly and, as I have stated, in a parbolic curve. They also 'hovered'. The mystery was never solved.

The Poltergeist is well known to the Red Indians, who have a word for it: *hobomokko*, an evil and noisy sprite. Lang, in his article in the *Encyclopædia Britannica*[3] mentions a case in the Hudson Bay territory, in which a young half-breed girl was the victim. Heavy objects moved 'and there were the usual rappings in tent and wigwam'. And in his essay[4] on 'Savage Spiritualism' he mentions Poltergeist phenomena among the Ojibway Indians. The movements of a heavy 'lodge' or medium's 'cabinet' are recorded, and 'voices' were heard. Quoting Tylor,[5] Lang points out that similar phenomena have been witnessed among the Dayaks, Singhalese, Siamese, and Esths.

Dennys, in his *Folk-lore of China* (1876, pp. 74–9) tells of Poltergeist phenomena in the Celestial Empire. He says that 'food placed on the table vanished mysteriously, and many of the curious phenomena attributed to ghostly interference took place', so that the householder was driven from house to house, and finally into a temple, in 1874, and all this after the death of a favourite but aggrieved monkey! 'Throwing down crockery, tramping on the floor, etc.—such pranks as have attracted attention at home, are not unknown. . . . I must confess that in

---

[1] A roof composed of large, dried, flat, overlapping leaves.
[2] *Journal* of the S.P.R., 1903, Vol. XII, pp. 260–66.
[3] *Op. cit.*, p. 16.　　　　　　　　　　[4] *Cock Lane*, pp. 45–46.
[5] *Op. cit.*

China, as elsewhere, these occurrences leave a *bonâ fide* impression of the marvellous which can neither be explained nor rejected.'[1]

I could go on multiplying these exotic cases which, I again reiterate, have a remarkable family likeness whether they come from Timbuktu or Tooting. In every land and in every age the Poltergeist has been pursuing its mischievous way. And it will continue to annoy us—or interest us, according to how we feel about it—until we find a means of controlling its activities.

Have I proved my case for the Poltergeist? I think I have. With so much evidential smoke, surely there must be a little authentic fire! If only *one* case in this volume is really proved, that settles the whole question. All we want is one good case scientifically proved. If we have proved that only one Poltergeist has paranormally displaced one object, the piling up of further evidence is not really necessary. Personally, and by the accepted laws of evidence, I am convinced that more than one case in this book has been proved up to the hilt. And let not the reader be afraid of 'believing' in Poltergeists. Many eminent scientists of the past believed in them, and many distinguished savants of today acclaim their conviction that, *on the evidence*, Poltergeists are a fact in Nature. And all this has nothing at all to do with spiritualism. And if anyone, when you mention Poltergeists, says 'Bosh!', gently remind him that believers in the 'unusual' and 'unexplained' have been exiled, imprisoned, and burnt at the stake for proclaiming truths which today nobody denies. It is not the man who *believes* in Poltergeists who is credulous: it is the man who *doesn't*!

[1] Cited by Lang.

370

CHAPTER XXX

Can We Explain the Poltergeist?

No! We know nothing whatsoever about *why* Poltergeists should infest a place, what they are, how to get rid of them, or how to attract them. There is a curious belief that opals do so. If there was any evidence for this, I would buy a sackful! We cannot explain the mechanism of Poltergeist movements, displacements, 'voices', how they transport things, or how they produce fire or water, or the many varieties and varying intensities of sounds and noises. We do not know where they obtain the energy from with which to move objects—sometimes heavy objects—or how they can hallucinate some people into believing they see or hear certain things or sounds, while other persons in the immediate vicinity see and hear nothing. And where do all the 'apports' (things that spontaneously 'appear' during an infestation) come from? Who loses them? And where do they go to when, as often happens, they disappear? If things 'appear', then they must have disappeared from *somewhere*, and someone must have lost them. Perhaps another Poltergeist victim! There have been speculations concerning all these puzzles, and I will later mention some of the more interesting. But they are theories only, ingenious as some of them are. We know *nothing* as to the causation of Poltergeist phenomena.

If we know so little about the Poltergeist *per se*, we are certain that there is some connection between Poltergeists and puberty and that the mysteries of sex enter largely into their doings. And all the available evidence points to the fact that Poltergeists prefer little girls and girl adolescents to boys—the ratio is about 95% to 5% respectively. Though we know there *is* this connection, we cannot explain it.

The fact that little girls are so mixed up in Poltergeist cases has led the uninformed to assume that these young creatures are consciously responsible for the phenomena; that the manifestations are produced fraudently and that the whole thing is hocus-pocus. Perhaps the reader thought like that too—until he read this book. It has probably never occurred to our hypothetical—and ignorant—critic that, if his 'explanation' is correct, and that *all* these Poltergeist girls trick, then they have been tricking *in exactly the same way, in every country, and in every age*. That would be a phenomenon in itself, and a very remarkable one. That girls *have* tricked is undeniable, but these cases are few compared with those in which girls have *not* tricked. And those girls who have tricked were sometimes of the abnormal type, psychoneurotics, hysteriacs, a 'borderline case', one who had received a nervous shock, or one with

371

a nervous disorder or some mental affliction. I have said that fraudulent phenomena are sometimes associated with abnormal girls; but this applies to genuine phenomena, too. And one can always tell where the genuine phenomena end and the spurious begin. As I have pointed out in another chapter, it was after a nervous shock that Esther Cox, in the Great Amherst Mystery, was sucked into the vortex of a violent Poltergeist disturbance. I shall have more to say about this later.

I reiterate that one of the most puzzling facts connected with Poltergeist infestations is why so many young girls are concerned in these cases. Assuming for a moment that every known case of Poltergeist

'Psychoneurotics, hysteriacs, and borderline cases.'

haunting was due to trickery, why should so often a 'young girl' be suspected and so seldom a 'young boy'? Are young girls more prone to cheating than young boys? Surely not!

Another remarkable fact is that it was usually a 'young girl' who was the victim (or the pretended victim) in the sixteenth and seventeenth-century witchcraft trials. It was so often a young girl who became 'possessed', or went into convulsions, or vomited crooked pins and tenpenny nails. Sometimes the witch mania spread to the girls themselves, who 'confessed' to the practice of witchcraft, riding on broomsticks, intercourse with the devil, the possession of 'familiars', etc. Podmore[1] cites the case of Antoinette Bourignon's girls' school at Lille

[1] *Modern Spiritualism*, Vol. I, p. 17.

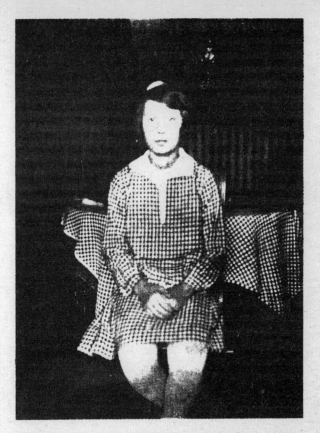

*Photograph of a young Poltergeist subject: Mar-
guerite Rozier, aged 13½ years, of Seyssel-in-Iseure,
near Lyons. In her vicinity, babies were injured and
turned over in their cradles; china was transported
from dinner-table during meals; the furniture became
volatile; semi-materializations were witnessed; knocks
and footsteps were frequent. The manifestations began in 1930, when menses appeared. Case reported by
M. René Sudre in his* A Case of Thorybism in France.
(See Bibliography.)

where, in 1639, the whole thirty-two children ultimately accused themselves of witchcraft, confessed to having dealings with the devil, and to riding through the air nightly to attend his infernal banquets. All but one of the children recanted when examined by the magistrates. The one girl who maintained her guilt to the last was imprisoned. Mlle Bourignon expressed a pious regret that for the good of her soul she had not been burnt.[1]

During the witchcraft mania in Sweden in 1669 and 1670 three hundred children in the *one village* of Moira (Mora?) confessed to the practice of witchcraft. Joseph Glanvill, whom we have so often quoted, gives a full account of the examination, confessions, trials and executions of the witches of Moira during this period. Seventy women were accused and most of these were executed. Then, says Glanvill:[2]

'Fifteen Children which likewise confessed that they were engaged in this witchery, died as the rest; six and thirty of them between nine and sixteen years of age, who had been less guilty were forced to run the gantlet; twenty more, who had no great inclination, yet had been seduced to those Hellish Enterprizes, because they were very young, were condemned to be lash'd with Rods upon their hands, for three Sundays together at the Church-door; and the aforesaid six and thirty were also deem'd to be lashed this way once a week for a whole year together. The number of the Seduced Children was about three hundred.'

Glanvill does not tell us whether all of these children were girls, but I am pretty sure they were. Anyway, he says that when the 'notoriously guilty' were executed, 'the day was bright and glorious, and the sun shining, and some thousands of people were present at the spectacle'.

I am convinced there must be something, either psychological or physiological, in a young girl's organism, that turns her into a girl-witch or Poltergeist-attractor. In this connection it is worth noting that the modern cult of spiritualism was started by two young girls, Margaret and Katie Fox, in 1848; though, as the reader knows, another young girl, Elizabeth Parsons, had produced identical phenomena in Cock Lane nearly a century earlier.

In the foregoing pages I have given several examples of the link between phenomena and pubescency. Eleonore Zugun's 'power' vanished overnight with the first appearance of the menses. Conversely, Stella C.'s manifestations were not frequent until she had matured. The same can be said about Esther Cox. On the other hand, Damodar Ketkar was troubled no more when he 'grew up'. The Schneider boys' phenomena were brilliant during and immediately after pubescency—then,

---

[1] See *Complete Works of Antoinette Bourignon*, Amsterdam, 1686, Vol. II, p. 200. In a girls' school at Derby, in 1905, forty-five girls, during a period of five days, became 'possessed', screamed, laughed, cried, and dropped to the floor unconscious. 'The girls were exceedingly weak, and had to be carried home.' A clear case of contagious hysteria. (See the *Derby Mercury* for May 15, 1905, and following issues.)

[2] *Saducismus Triumphatus*, London, 1681, Part 2, pp. 313-4.

'It was so often a young girl who became "possessed".'
374

as they approached adolescency, their powers waned. Also, with the adolescency of ailing Teddie Fowler, the 'Mill on the Eden' was troubled no more with Poltergeists.

Professor Hans Thirring, Ph.D., of Vienna University has, like myself, experimented considerably with Willi and Rudi Schneider, the famous physical mediums, and has expressed his views concerning sex and phenomena—especially in connection with these two young Austrian boys. In an article[1] he wrote for me, he refers to this subject more than once. Describing some sittings with Willi that he arranged, he says: 'During the trance, both Willi's elbows were resting on the principal controller's (Mrs. Holub's) lap and his head was lying on the same controller's left shoulder. Taking into account the possible connection between psychical phenomena and sexuality, it was not at all astonishing that the telekinetic forces were stronger when a sympathetic female was principal controller than it was when a sceptic and suspicious scientist was controlling. (As a matter of fact, we had sittings with different controllers a year later. They were successful only with a lady as principal controller.)'

Dr. Thirring returns to the subject in the same article, when discussing the best conditions for producing good phenomena. He says: 'The far more delicate metaphysical phenomena cannot be produced by the mere will of the medium. Some psychic emotion seems to be necessary—in the same way as certain sexual functions are started by emotions and imaginations. In the case of our medium the necessary emotions seem to be furnished by rhythmical music; by the touch of a woman; or by the buoyant spirit of a cheerful circle'.

On one of my visits to Vienna, I invited Professor Thirring to lecture for me in London, before the National Laboratory of Psychical Research, of which I was then Director. Dr. Thirring arrived in October, 1926, and the title of his talk was 'The Position of Science in Relation to Psychical Research'.[2] Dr. Thirring delivered his lecture at our rooms on October 19, 1926, before a large audience that included Sir Richard Gregory, F.R.S., Professor A. O. Rankine, F.R.S., Dr. R. J. Tillyard, F.R.S., Sir Horace Plunkett, and many scientists. Dr. Thirring again referred to his experiments with Willi Schneider and remarked that for good phenomena 'it seemed to be necessary for the medium to have a female very near him. The connection between sex and psychical phenomena was a well-known fact. In this instance, *no manifestation could be obtained unless a lady were near*'. In my own experiments with the Schneider boys, I have always found that the phenomena were better when women—especially young women—were present at the sittings.

[1] 'Psychical Research in Vienna', *Journal* of the Am. S.P.R., New York, 1925, Vol. XIX, pp. 693 and 705.
[2] Printed in *The British Journal of Psychical Research*, London, March–April, 1926, Vol. I, pp. 165–181.

Mention of Vienna reminds me that during one of my visits to the Austrian capital, I endeavoured to obtain sittings with a young physical medium, Frieda W. I failed, but I had a chat with her husband, who endorsed Professor Thirring's views on sex and mediumship. Herr W. told me that during the early months of their married life, Frieda's mediumship was strongly affected by their marital relations. At the height of his wife's sexual excitement, the ornaments would sometimes fall off the mantelpiece in their bedroom, or the alarm clock would start ringing. Once, he assured me, all the pots and pans in the kitchen of their flat began dancing. He also informed me that his wife never gave séances during her *Monatsfluss*, as no phenomena occurred at these periods.

The link between sex and mediumship was well known and recognised in classical times. There were young girls known as Pythias who, when 'possessed', went into a sort of trance or ecstatic condition, shivered violently, foamed at the mouth and, in their impersonation of Apollo, answered—in ambiguous hexameters—the questions put to them by the audience. Delphi and Dodona were famous for their Pythias, and lesser sanctuaries also employed them.

Plutarch, from A.D. 95 to A.D. 125, was one of the priests of the oracle and, though he has left us three essays[1] on the subject, tells us really very little about it. But we learn that the girls had to be virgins, and that loss of virginity would kill the faculty to prophesy. Plutarch mentions one priestess who, having broken the rule about chastity and who still attempted to exercise her faculty, was horror-stricken to find that her 'power' had gone. She fled, fell to the ground, and died several days later. There are many recorded cases of these young girls being violated, and this led to the employment of less-attractive virgins of fifty years or more, who were attired as maidens. At Delphi two Pythias were in constant attendance, with a third in reserve in case of the 'defilement' of either of the two regular priestesses.

If loss of virginity is said to upset the mediumistic faculty in some girls, it appears also to awaken the slumbering powers possessed by certain subjects to attract Poltergeists. A striking example is that of Olive, in the Sunderland case. And the Poltergeists appear to have departed when Mrs. Mara Mack and her sisters left the parental roof for marriage and a new sexual life. Even the *attempt* to violate Esther Cox,[2] was sufficient to set in motion those strange and terrific forces that culminated in the famous Poltergeist case known as the Great Amherst Mystery. It was on August 28, 1878, that a boy friend, Bob McNeal, drove Esther into the woods and attempted to rape her. She resisted, even at the pistol's point. She was then exactly eighteen years, five

[1] *On the E at Delphi*, *On the Pythian Responses*, and *On the Sanctuaries Where Oracles have Ceased.*

[2] Born March 28, 1860. Died at Brockton, Mass., November 8, 1912.

months old. McNeal drove the terrified girl to her home and then fled the township. Esther suffered a severe nervous shock which, coupled with the loss of Bob, of whom she was fond, effected a remarkable change in her. From this fatal night until September 3, she cried herself to sleep every evening. On September 4 (i.e. seven nights later), the phenomena began. They continued until December when Esther was ill for two weeks, and no manifestations were recorded during this period. Then they recommenced and continued until August 1, 1879.

The above facts are related in detail in Walter Hubbell's book.[1] Hubbell makes the significant statement (p. 80) that the 'power' 'was always at its greatest strength *every twenty-eight days*'—a periodicity corresponding with the menstrual flux. If only we knew more about the Poltergeist and the link with adolescency, we might glean some valuable data from the Esther Cox case. Unfortunately, the 'subjects' or victims themselves know as little about it as we do. Very rarely, as in the case of Ann Robinson of Stockwell, and the French *bonne*, adolescents *do* know that they are responsible for all the trouble.

We know it, too. One of the things that we are certain of is that there *is* a connection—psychological or physiological—between young people and the observed phenomena. The reader must also be sure of it, if he has studied the foregoing cases. All the investigators recognise this fact, and I will cite one or two views (they are *not* explanations) of writers who have devoted some time to the subject. Hereward Carrington says:[2]

'An energy seems to be radiated from the body, in such cases, which induces these phenomena, when the sexual energies are blossoming into maturity within the body. It would almost seem as though these energies, instead of taking their normal course, were somehow turned into another channel, at such times, and were externalised beyond the limits of the body—producing the manifestations in question. The spontaneous outburst of these phenomena seems to be associated with the awakening of the sex-energies at that time—which find this curious method of externalisation.' Of course, very occasionally, a Poltergeist case is remarkable for the fact that *no* young people appear to be connected with it.

Mr. Sacheverell Sitwell says:[3] 'The mysteries of puberty, that trance or dozing of the psyche before it awakes into adult life, is a favourite playground for the Poltergeist. Pregnancy,[4] it might only be natural to suppose, might produce the same sub-conscious receptivity'.

Canon W. J. Phythian-Adams, in his study of the Borley Rectory Poltergeists, says:[5] 'Whatever the explanation of them may be, it seems

[1] *The Haunted House . . . The Great Amherst Mystery, op. cit.*
[2] *The Story of Psychic Science*, London, 1930, p. 146.
[3] *Poltergeists, op. cit.*, p. 83.
[4] See the Sunderland case in this connection.—H.P.
[5] His essay will be published in the forthcoming Borley book.

certain that the energy which plays the pranks is drawn mainly if not exclusively from living persons (often young ones) who thus become its unconscious "accomplices". At Borley Mrs. Foyster was pretty obviously the most conspicuous though of course not the only unconscious "accomplice"; and the house seems to have been able to store up a reservoir of such energy, since the phenomena continued even when it was empty. . . . If we accept the view that a place can become saturated with the "mental vibrations" of a person who has lived there in a state of strong emotional tension, it is not unreasonable to suppose that they may remain on the spot as potential stimuli of Poltergeist activity.'

Dr. Phythian-Adams is of course referring to my oft-expressed opinion that a house or place can become saturated with the ego, personality, or intelligence of a person who has lived—or died—in it. And I have postulated a theory, for what it is worth, that these 'emanations' do, under certain conditions, produce phantasms or ghosts. Whether we can apply this very tentative theory to the causation of Poltergeist phenomena is another matter. Mrs. Foyster was a young woman during her residence in Borley Rectory and undoubtedly there was a very sympathetic *nexus* between her and the 'nun'—witness the wall-writings and the pathetic appeals for 'help'. But, except for a very brief period during the incumbency of the Rev. G. Eric Smith, and when I leased the place, there have always been many young girls living at the Rectory, and their 'mental vibrations' may still be clinging to their old home.

A reviewer in the *Times Literary Supplement* (October 5, 1940), in discussing the Borley manifestations, observed 'that the phenomena of the *Poltergeist* order increased and decreased in a fairly consistent ratio according to what we may assume as the potentialities of the occupants for providing "power". It could be argued, then, to take but a single instance, that during the period 1930–35, one of these occupants was an unconscious medium of the same type as Hetty Wesley in the Epworth Rectory case, which is to say that while she was innocent of any intention to produce the phenomena, her emanations (? teleplasmic) could be used by the *Poltergeister*.'

Both Dr. Phythian-Adams and *The Times* reviewer speak of the 'energy' required by the Poltergeists to produce their telekinetic phenomena at Borley. Mr. Andrew J. B. Robertson, the rising young Cambridge scientist, whom I mentioned in my chapter on Borley Rectory, has studied Poltergeist manifestations for many years and he has kindly sent me his views—the views of a physicist. Here is his essay:

THE POLTERGEIST PROBLEM: A PHYSICAL VIEW

Any discussion of the interesting scientific problems raised by the behaviour of Poltergeists must, at the present time, be speculative. This is necessitated partly by the extraordinary nature of the phenomena themselves, partly by the rather dubious nature of the evidence in many cases, especially in matters of detail, and partly by the fact that most investigations into Poltergeists have been confined to simply observing the phenomena. Few investigators have conducted experiments which might perhaps throw some further light on the problems raised, and any such investigations would be rendered very difficult by the sporadic nature of the phenomena. Nevertheless accounts of Poltergeist activity from widely varying sources show a remarkable measure of agreement, a fact tending to point to the genuineness of the happenings. On examining the various reports of Poltergeist behaviour it appears that most of the phenomena are essentially objective: this immediately raises a physical problem which one might express generally as that of the energetics or thermodynamics of Poltergeist manifestations. These objective effects seem to be of two kinds, the first being mechanical phenomena, as for example the displacement of objects, the production of ghostly footsteps and knockings, the breaking of objects, and the production of paranormal writings. The second kind of Poltergeist phenomenon can be called thermal, including such effects as the spontaneous outbreaks of fire, the heating of objects which have been displaced by the Poltergeist, the occurrence of spontaneous temperature fluctuations in the air, and possibly the appearance of paranormal luminosities.

Both the thermal and mechanical phenomena show considerable evidence of being produced by some kind of intelligence. In this and in other respects an appreciable degree of correlation is noticeable with the phenomena produced by physical mediums. According to one school of thought physical mediums merely act as the agents for definite entities or spirits entirely separate, in their normal existence, from the mind of the medium, and the view is often expressed that Poltergeists are mischievous spirits, possibly rather undeveloped, which remain confined to a particular house or locality and are able to utilise certain people, especially adolescent children, as physical mediums. On the other hand the activities of physical mediums can be interpreted without the help of the spirit hypothesis, since in many cases the apparent entities are equally explicable as being secondary personalities of the medium. In a rather similar way one might regard a haunted house (in the Poltergeist sense) either as the abode of a separate entity or spirit of some kind, or as a place where for some unknown reason certain people are able to exert some of the powers possessed by physical mediums. The connection between the occurrence of Poltergeist phenomena and the presence of certain people at the same time, and the possibility of Poltergeist phenomena taking place in the absence of any persons, are matters requiring further investigation. At the present time the evidence seems to rather favour the view that a Poltergeist is at least a partially independent entity.

In order to produce objective phenomena, such as the throwing of kitchen crockery, a Poltergeist has to exert force of some kind, and it would in fact appear that Poltergeists have access to some form of energy. The basic assumptions made here are that Poltergeist phenomena are real and not fundamentally dissimilar to ordinary physical processes involving energy changes, so that the thermodynamics of Poltergeists is a definite problem to be considered, at least for a start, in the normal scientific way. One might tentatively suggest three sources of energy as being available to a Poltergeist: First there is the adolescent child. In numerous cases it has been noticed that phenomena are produced most vigorously when the child is lying or sleeping in bed. The conditions may then be rather favourable for the removal of energy from the child by the Poltergeist; the child under these conditions approaches more closely the state of a medium when in trance. Some metabolism experiments might perhaps be carried out, although a consideration of the actual magnitude of the energy changes involved in Poltergeist phenomena shows that any correspondingly increased metabolic rate would be difficult to detect, unless the efficiency with which the Poltergeist can transform energy is very low. A second possible source of energy is from the cooling of air and perhaps other bodies. One cubic foot of air (at N.T.P.)[1] when cooled through one degree of Fahrenheit loses about fifteen foot-pounds of energy (this is the amount of work expended in lifting a fifteen-pound object through a vertical distance of one foot). The cooling of a small quantity of air therefore releases a considerable quantity of energy. Such a process, although in agreement with the first law of thermodynamics would be a violation of the second law under some conditions. It follows from the second law that a volume of air surrounded by a quantity of air at the same uniform temperature can only be cooled with respect to its immediate surroundings by means of some agency which does work and thereby transfers the heat to some other place. In actual fact the experimental evidence on temperature variations in haunted houses is scanty, but both rises and falls in temperature have been noted. It is not at all clear whether the Poltergeist can escape the restrictions of the second law, or alternatively can act in a manner similar to that of a refrigerating machine.

A third possible energy source is suggested by an examination of Poltergeist displacements themselves. In many cases it happens that the object displaced finishes on a lower horizontal level than it started from, its resultant movement being in a downward direction. An examination of some of the literature on Poltergeists suggests that movements of objects *downwards* are considerably more frequent than movements upwards. In general therefore a Poltergeist displacement is accompanied by a decrease in potential energy. At the same time it is noticed that the objects fall much more slowly than they would do

[1] Normal temperature and pressure: i.e. 0° Centigrade and 760 mm. of mercury.— H.P.

under the influence of gravity alone. Now an object when falling in the normal way loses potential energy which is converted into kinetic energy, and at any point on the path of the falling object the potential energy lost is equal to the kinetic energy gained (neglecting small order corrections). But with Poltergeist manifestations this is clearly not the case: the potential energy lost is only partially transformed into kinetic energy, and hence part of the potential energy is lost in some unknown way—perhaps to the Poltergeist. This consideration raises the general question of whether the Poltergeist can store energy. If so, and if the store of energy is situated in a localised region of space, it might perhaps be detectable with suitable instruments. One might enquire whether the 'cold spot' at Borley Rectory has some special significance in this connection, being a localised region apparently having rather curious properties at times.

The heating of objects which have been moved by a Poltergeist is of interest. This involves much larger energy changes than those involved in displacements. Thus a kilogram falling through a metre loses only about 2·3 calories of potential energy; if this quantity of energy was used in heating the kilogram its temperature would rise only by 0·023 degrees Centigrade even with a specific heat as low as one tenth. Actually, the objects have been reported to be quite hot to the hand. But in such cases an adolescent child is usually present. These thermal phenomena are of great interest and require further experimental investigation.

It must be again emphasised that the above suggestions are speculative. But the phenomena presented by Poltergeists are not readily explicable in terms of normal concepts, so that in the present state of knowledge one might hope that such speculations are not entirely valueless in that further researches may be suggested which may contribute to a further clarification of the problem.

ANDREW J. B. ROBERTSON.

*   *   *   *

Mr. Robertson notes that Poltergeist phenomena are often more vigorous when the young child or adolescent is sleeping or lying in bed—a fact I have drawn attention to in the pages of this volume, and the reader will recall how Hetty Wesley trembled in her sleep when phenomena were occurring. Perhaps energy was then being extracted from her. In many examples in this book the Poltergeist has 'attacked' sleeping children, or their beds if the children were not in them, as in the case of Olive W. of Sunderland. And Poltergeistic phenomena have been witnessed frequently where there were sick children in the house, or in the homes of dying persons (e.g. Battersea). I think Mr. Robertson is correct in stating that under such conditions, the removal of energy becomes favourable.

The cooling of the air during séances with certain subjects is now a recognised fact. With the 'Poltergeist mediums', Stella C.[1] and the Schneider boys, my very delicate transmitting thermographs repeatedly recorded a *drop* in temperature instead of a rise. Mr. Robertson has noted curious thermal changes at Borley Rectory, and so have I. Every observer who stayed in Borley Rectory was struck, as I was, with the fact that the place was consistently and unnaturally cold. Were the Poltergeistic entities at work there continuously extracting heat from the place and transforming it into energy? Perhaps. During my broadcast from the 'haunted manor' at Meopham, Kent, on March 10, 1936, my sensitive thermograph in the 'haunted cellar' showed that the temperature was quite constant during the whole of the day, by the straight line of the graph across the chart. But at 9.45 p.m., during the broadcast, the temperature suddenly rose slightly, and then fell sharply below what had been measured during the day. The kick in the graph[2] could not be accounted for in terms of normality. The 'cold spot' referred to by Mr. Robertson was a certain place on the landing at Borley Rectory, just outside the Blue Room. Several observers and others, when passing this spot, suddenly felt very cold or had shivering fits. There is good and independent evidence for these strange effects.

It is thought by some people that the energy used in Poltergeist phenomena is of an electrical nature, obtained from the atmosphere. There is no evidence for this. It occurs to me, though, that the alleged 'new current' recently discovered by Professor Felix Ehrenhaft might be an explanation. Professor Ehrenhaft, a Viennese physicist, demonstrated to the American Physical Society at Columbia University on January 16, 1944, that he had obtained experimental proof of the existence of pure magnetic current. This meant, he declared, that 'not only electric currents, but also magnetic currents flow through the universe.' He said, 'the discovery has terrific possibilities'.[3] It is possible that the Poltergeist can utilise this current in some way.

A correspondent, Mr. Percy Pigott, of Kirk Ella, Hull, has sent me his views of how the manifestations might be explained. His speculations are ingenious and novel, and I have pleasure in reproducing them:

'Is it not possible that the substance which pervades all space, inter-penetrating and enveloping our earth and our bodies, which scientists simply name ether, but do no pretend to explain, is capable of receiving and retaining pictures of our actions and the sounds which emanate from such actions and even of reproducing them when conditions are favourable, as for instance, the evening light, the temperature and the weather generally?

---

[1] See my 'Some Account of the Thermal Variations as Recorded During the Trance of Stella C.', *Journal* of the Am. S.P.R., Novr., 1927, pp. 635–41. (With many graphs.)

[2] Reproduced in my article in *The Listener*, March 18, 1936.

[3] For full account see the *Daily Telegraph*, January 17, 1944.

'In other words, this little understood substance is perhaps capable of acting as a photographic negative. This is simply what a cinema film does. It reproduces form, motion and sound. Why should not Nature also do it? May we not have a mirage of a past event as well as of a distant scene? The fact that we always associate motion with consciousness has subjected us to an error of interpretation.

'If this is so, it seems feasible that those events which have been accompanied by intense feeling and concentrated thought, such as accompany the great tragedies of life, should be more deeply impressed and therefore more clearly reproduced than those which are performed unheedingly and habitually.

'Thus I have heard of a street in London where the sound of running footsteps are sometimes heard. I am told also that the hearer gets the impression that these footsteps are being panic driven. Over this pavement a murderer once fled from the crime he had committed. Which is the more reasonable, to suppose that the murderer is constantly running again and again over this pavement, and that though his body is invisible his footsteps are audible, or to suppose that the original sound is simply being reproduced?

'Again I have heard that Ann Bullen still haunts Hampton Court and that the sound of her footsteps and the wail of her anguish as she fled from her husband, having failed to obtain the mercy she had been pleading for, are heard at certain times. Her form may have been seen, I do not know. Is it not incredible to suppose that Ann Bullen has been thus employed, at intervals at least, for four hundred years? It is not in the least incredible, in these days of gramophones and radio, to believe that the sound of her distressed wail can be, and is at times reproduced.

'Thus the coach, the galloping hoofs, the bay horses, the glittering harness, etc., at Borley, are all real in that they are an objective actuality; but the observer is mistaken if he thinks he is viewing real horses or a driver consciously directing them. The name, a spectre, a phantom literally applies. This theory would also account for the nun. I think there is generally reason to be sceptical of ghosts being conscious egos after the lapse of a number of years after passing over. It would also account for the light in the window. It could account for all the noise of footsteps, shufflings, scrabblings, tappings, thuds, etc. Is it not significant that no one ever spoke to the nun? Had they approached her for this purpose she would probably have vanished, the necessary distance, or angle, for seeing this mirage having been altered. It would then have been regarded as uncanny. Is it not significant also that no ghost of any sort was seen to account for the footsteps, thuds, etc., which were heard? Is it reasonable to suppose that spirits, or ghosts, who pass silently through solid walls, should make such a noise with their feet? I submit it is more reasonable to regard these noises as being echoes of an ancient tragedy.

'This, however, will not account for the messages on the wall, stone

383

throwing, furniture moving, bottle dropping, hair-ruffling, bell-ringing, belt-raising, etc. For these phenomena I accept your theory of Poltergeist, and of course it is possible that the Poltergeist accounted for all the noises in the house. But to give a mystery a name does not always explain it. What is a Poltergeist? You refer to "these playful little fellows."[1] For my part I cannot regard a Poltergeist as in any sense a being. In my judgment we should be more correct to regard it as a vaguely conscious, instinctual, elemental force. Such elemental force may emanate from, and in the Borley case certainly has emanated from, the distress and restlessness of some departed human being. It is fully charged with power, but power only for one sole purpose, namely, of expressing this restlessness and distress on the physical plane in the hope of receiving help from the place where its trouble originated. The vagueness of its consciousness is shown by the feeble effort either to write or compose a simple sentence or understand one. If you ask me how could a blind force throw stones or ring bells, I can only reply that neither you nor I can claim to know all the laws of nature, and that these phenomena are evidence of such a law. Because there are no visible hands it is not, therefore, necessary to postulate invisible ones. The Egyptians were supposed to be able consciously to charge objects with such a force, and there is some evidence to support this.

'The headless driver is more difficult to account for. I notice there are only two witnesses of this. I will not question the honesty of their testimony, but suggestion might account for it. They see what they believe to be a ghostly coach, ghosts are associated with tragedies and beheadings, immediately they see the driver headless. This is quite easy when viewing a mirage, which I am suggesting this was.

'Another method for accounting for this very gruesome apparition is along the following lines:

'There is little doubt that at some time there was a cruel tragedy at Borley in which a group of people were involved. Both the apparitions and the Poltergeist manifestations would have their origin in this tragedy, in which the coachman would be concerned and may have lost his head. Then he might very likely think of himself as headless after passing over. It is well known that all apparitions of the living are caused by the subject thinking of himself as with a distant friend or in a distant place, and thus projects his form to that place, and it is occasionally seen and even heard. Now I have heard, and I can well believe, that it is much easier for the so-called dead to thus project their appearances than the living. I am confident that many apparitions of those recently departed occupying their accustomed chair or walking down a certain path with their own particular gait are due to their thinking of themselves thus occupied after passing over. Perhaps the coachman thus pictured himself as headless.

[1] I, too, was being playful.—H.P.

'Finally there is in my judgment the most remarkable of all phenomena, matter passing through matter. This is not unknown at spiritualist séances. It puzzles chemists. "If it is true," I once heard a chemist say, "it overthrows all our ideas about matter." But do chemists, or anyone else, know what constitutes the solidity of matter? Another chemist, who was also an occult student, when I asked him what made a wall solid and impassable, replied, "Thought." I believe he was right. We think of things as solid and solid they are to us. But our Poltergeist friend may not have been subject to those illusions of sense to which we humans are'.

There have been other 'explanations' of Poltergeist phenomena, one of which has been called 'exteriorisation of motricity'—that is, the action of the subject's (e.g. a young girl) motor force outside the periphery of her organism. This theory is that there is a repulsive force on one side of the subject's body, and an attractive force on the other. In normal persons these two forces, it is alleged, are equal. When they are not, telekinetic movements are likely to occur in the vicinity of the subject. Obviously this theory does not cover many of the observed Poltergeist phenomena.

Another theory, postulated by Adolphe d'Assier,[1] suggests that the *noise* of crashing crockery, smashing windows, etc., when in fact nothing is broken (as in the case of Edward Cooper at Borley, who one night thought that all the china in his kitchen had been shattered) is caused by the Poltergeist hurling a sort of psychic 'double' or astral duplicate of the real objects. In other words, that inanimate things have 'ghosts'. This theory does *not* explain why the objects are broken in reality, as so often happens.

Charles Fort believed in a sort of cosmic Poltergeist, a power that permeates the Universe: that hurls lumps of distant planets, and other things to, or on, our planet. And the name he gave to these strange flights was 'teleportation': 'The crash of falling islands—the humps of piling continents—and then the cosmic humour of it all . . . or that the force that once heaped the peaks of the Rocky Mountains now slings pebbles at a couple of farmers. . . . So I'd conceive the existence of a force, and the use of it, unconsciously mostly, by human beings. It may be that, if somebody, gifted with what we think we mean by "agency", fiercely hates somebody else, he can, out of intense visualisations, direct, by teleportation, bombardment of stones upon his enemy. . . . My general expression is against the existence of Poltergeists as spirits—but that the doings are the phenomena of undeveloped magicians, mostly youngsters, who have no awareness of their powers as their own—or, in the cases of mischievous, or malicious persecutions, are more or less consciously directed influences by enemies—or that, in this aspect, "Poltergeist disturbances" are witchcraft under a new name.'[2]

[1] *Essai sur l'Humanité Postume* . . . Paris, 1883. English translation, *Posthumous Humanity: A Study of Phantoms*, London, 1887.

[2] *The Books of Charles Fort, op. cit.*, pp. 571–2, 983.

No one, I think, now believes that Poltergeists are spirits in the accepted meaning of the term. Certainly, the spiritualists do not. But in Glanvill's day Poltergeists were regarded as spirits—evil spirits—or devils. The Wesley family thought that Epworth Rectory was haunted by devils. They also thought that the disturbances presaged the early death of old Rev. Samuel Wesley, or, to their greater concern, the premature demise of young Samuel, alone in London.

Andrew Lang, in his article 'Poltergeist',[1] mentions that 'the Highlanders attribute many Poltergeist phenomena, inexplicable noises, sounds of viewless feet that pass, and so forth, to *tàradh*, an influence exerted unconsciously by unduly strong wishes on the part of a person at a distance. The phrase *falbh air fàrsaing* ("going uncontrolled") is also used.'[2] This Scotch view of Poltergeists is reminiscent of Fort's beliefs. Lang suggests the word *telethoryby*, 'a racket produced at a distance.'

There are still a few words to be said about the 'psychological' explanation, so assiduously put forward by Frank Podmore and a few other dyed-in-the-wool sceptics. They contend that these young girls and adolescents have a dual or multiple-personality, one part of which is responsible for the 'phenomena', which the other part knows nothing about. The argument is that this secondary state or 'personality' comes to the surface, 'goes *berserk*', smashes the windows, shivers the mirrors, ignites the bedding, etc.—and without a single person detecting the culprit! All this presupposes a diabolical cunning and a consummate skill on the part of the 'dissociated' victim. Although I agree that psychological abnormalities have sometimes entered into these cases,[3] they are of rare occurrence. And psychopaths and psychoneurotics exhibit certain indicia by which they can be recognised.

And there are other arguments against the acceptance of the theory as a formula. Many of the sights, sounds, and other phenomena, well-

---

[1] *Encyclo. Brit., op. cit.*, p. 16.

[2] Campbell, *Witchcraft and Second Sight in the Scottish Highlands*, 1902, pp. 144–147.

[3] A remarkable story of a 'Poltergeist' was recorded in *The Times* (Aug. 30 to Sept. 13, 1919). The disturbances occurred at the Rectory of Swanton Novers, near Melton Constable. Spontaneous outbreaks of fires; petrol, paraffin, methylated spirits, sandal-wood oil and water pouring from the ceilings; floorboards torn up and ceilings torn down, etc. The manifestations lasted for days. Finally, a passing conjurer was called in and in an hour or so had solved the 'mystery'. He set a trap and the 15-year-old maidservant fell into it. She confessed to hoaxing the family. But the story does not end there. Nevil Maskelyne, the famous illusionist, also visited the rectory and saw 'barrels of oil' pouring through the ceiling. He could not explain the mystery. Then the girl denied that she had confessed, or that she had tricked. The rector also denied (*The Times*, Sept. 13) that she had confessed. For other accounts of this case, see the *Daily Mail*, the *Daily Express*, the *Daily News*, etc., for this period, and the *Norfolk News* for Novr. 8, 1919. Two photographs of oil pouring through the ceiling were published (Sept. 3) by the *Daily Mail*. Fort (*Books of Charles Fort, op. cit.*, pp. 577–81) discusses the affair at length. The psychological aspect of the case is as important as the phenomena.

evidenced in some Poltergeist cases, could not be produced normally by man, woman, or child, if they possessed a dozen 'personalities' each. This book is full of such illustrations. And a minority of 'infestations' are not associated with 'young persons'—or in fact *any* person—at all. And to think that a 'young person' could smash half the china in the house, break the furniture, set fire to the baby, and make twenty bells ring simultaneously—and all without a single occupant in the house detecting her (whatever 'personality' she was using!) suggests that Poltergeist phenomena occur not in the private residences of sane and intelligent people looking for trickery, but in lunatic asylums!

Finally, Dr. John Layard, the psychologist, has put forward the most recent hypothesis 'that Poltergeists are not chance phenomena, but have a definite purpose, and that this purpose, like all psychological phenomena (as I believe them to be) is a curative one, having for its object the resolution of a psychological conflict.' He believes that all true Poltergeist phenomena 'are also purposeful and probably occasioned by similar conditions of unresolved tension in the psyche of those involuntarily producing them.' His paper, *Psi Phenomena and Poltergeists* (*Proc.*, S.P.R., July, 1944), should be read in full.

Well, I have come to the end of my fascinating quest of the Poltergeist and I will conclude, as I have concluded so many of my books—with the urgent demand that Official Science and official scientists should get on with *their* job of explaining these things to us. Though it is true that many scientists are completely ignorant of the serious literature of our subject, there are others who—unofficially—take a profound interest in it. Many scientists are sympathetically inclined towards us and our work. And the new science has even seeped through to a few universities in this (e.g. Oxford, Cambridge, and London) and other countries. But there still remain the die-hards, the last-ditchers and, saddest of all, those men of science who have made up their minds as to what Nature is capable, and not capable, of doing. If, for example, you broach the subject of Poltergeists to them they will murmur something about an 'outrage to common sense' and 'gross superstition'—forgetting that all scientific progress is from the 'outrageous'[1] to the commonplace, and that often the 'superstition' of to-day is the science of to-morrow.

---

[1] Charles Fort (*Wild Talents, op. cit.*) makes the 'outrageous' suggestion that the strange paranormal powers possessed by some people, which he calls 'wild talents', may one day be put to good—or bad—uses. For example, in time of war: 'A squad of Poltergeist girls—and they pick a fleet out of the sea, or out of the sky. . . . Girls at the front—and they are discussing their usual not very profound subjects. The alarm—the enemy is advancing. Command to the Poltergeist girls to concentrate—and under their chairs they stick their wads of chewing gum. A regiment bursts into flames, and the soldiers are torches. Horses snort smoke from the combustion of their entrails. Reinforcements are smashed under cliffs that are teleported from the Rocky Mountains. The snatch of Niagara Falls—it pours upon the battlefield. The little Poltergeist girls reach for their wads of chewing gum.'

APPENDIX A

A Question of Dates, and John Mompesson's First-Hand Evidence

Thanks to the 'unmethodical observations', as Andrew Lang puts it, of Dr. Joseph Glanvill, considerable confusion has arisen concerning the dates between which the Drummer of Tedworth is alleged to have caused so much commotion. Lang went to much trouble in elucidating the mystery and the result of his researches follows. I am indebted to the Society for Psychical Research for permission to republish[1] some of his remarks:

'Glanvill places the occurrences between April 1661 and January 1663. This is erroneus. The dates ought to be March 1662–April 1663. Though it is not my earliest document, I cite, from the *Mercurius Publicus* (No. 16) of April 16–23, 1663, the following sworn deposition of Mr. Mompesson:

The Information of Mr. John Mompesson of Tedworth in the County of Wilts: taken this day 15th of April 1663, upon oath: against William Drury:

Who saith that at the beginning of March last [1662] was Twelvemonth, he being at *Ludgurshal* in this County, at the Bailiff's house, and hearing a Drum beat, enquired what Drum it was. The Bailiff informed him that he was a stranger going for *Portsmouth*, having a Pass under the hands and seals of two of his Majeste's Justices of Peace for the County of Wilts for his passing to *Portsmouth*, and to be allowed and relieved in his journey; and that he had been requiring money of them, and they were collecting money for him.

He this Informant saith, that suspecting him to be a Cheat, he desired the Officer of the Town to send for him, which accordingly he did, and examining him how he dar'd go up and down in that way beating his Drum, and requiring money; he, this Informant, saith *Drury* answered I have good Authority; and produced a pretended Pass under the hands and seals as aforesaid, *Drury* positively affirming it was their hands and seals. He this Informant saith, that knowing it to be counterfeit, he charged him with it, and was sending him before a Justice of Peace: and then *Drury* begg'd, and confess'd he made it: and upon his begging he let that pass. But he this Informant further saith he took away his Drum, which *Drury* was very unwilling to part with.

He this Informant saith, he left the Drum for some time after at *Ludgurshal*; and that immediately after he had sent for the Drum to his house, a Drum began to beat in the night, *Roundheads and Cuckolds go dig, go dig* (which the said *Drury* did usually beat, and seldome any other note.) This beating of a Drum increast more and more, from room to room: at last he

[1] From their *Proceedings*, Vol. xvii, pp. 305–16, London, 1901–02, in the article, *The Poltergeist, Historically Considered*.

388

this Informant saith, he burnt the Drum that he had taken from *Drury*; and then the beating of a Drum, and some time *knocking, several great noises, scratching, troubling the Beds;* sometimes *the noise so violent, that it might be heard a mile;* and continues to this day (April 15, 1663), and more than formerly. And if they call to it, as several persons have, saying *Devil, Knocker* or *Drummer,* come tell us if the man from whom the Drum was taken be the cause of this, give three knocks, and no more; and immediately three loud knocks were given, and no more. After that, another time, Come tell us if the man from whom the Drum was taken be the cause of all this, by giving five knocks, and away; and presently five very loud knocks were given, and away, and no more heard at that time.

Drury's Examination as to this confesseth his being at *Ludgurshal* about the time named, and his beating Drum there; his false Pass, and that *Mr. Mompesson* took away from him his Drum; but denies that he hath any way practised witchcraft, or that he hath been any way the cause of that trouble.

For the Escape made by him, and the Charge given against him by *Mr. Mompesson* of witchcraft, he was sent to the County-goal at Sarum, there to remain till the next Assizes. It may be observed that this *Drury* was about four or five months since committed to Glocester-goal for felony; and *Mr. Mompesson* being informed he had several times in the gaol exprest himself pleased at the report of the troubles in his house, saying, *although the Drum be burnt the Devil is not dead: and that he had better let me and my Drum alone:* two or three days after the late Assizes holden there, resolved to go down to Glocester, forty miles from his house, to inform himself what was become of *Drury.*

The night before he took the journey, a Drum beat in his stable, where it had not been heard to beat before: and the morrow morning his Gelding being brought forth of the stable, was fain very lame; but however, he went for Glocester, and there was informed, as before related, that he (Drury) was sent away for Virginia.

Mr. Mompesson, being upon his return back from Glocester, in his way, on Munday night last, lodged at a place called Droughton in this County, within two miles of Mscut.(?) On Thursday morning he was informed that the said *Will. Drury* came to his house at Mscut, (?)[1] the Munday night, with a Drum at his back, and had beat it that night. Upon which *Mr. Mompesson* procured a warrant to search for, and apprehend him; which the same day was accordingly done, and the said *Drury* sent to goal.

It is supposed that this *Drury,* with the other prisoners, have made this escape by murthering the Bargemen.

'From this account it would appear that the quarrel between Mr. Mompesson and Drury, the Drummer, began in March, 1662. The noises and disturbances commenced in April. Drury was imprisoned on an independent charge of felony at Gloucester about December 1662: was found guilty and sentenced to transportation; escaped, and

---

[1] William Drury lived at what is now known as Uffcott, but perhaps originally Usscott, owing to the modern confusion between the ancient long 's' and its similarity to the 'f'. It is a hamlet in the parish of Broad Hinton, N. Wilts. The name Drury can still be found among the local inhabitants. There are memorials to the Glanvill family in the church of St. Peter-ad-Vincula, Broad Hinton.—H.P.

began to annoy Mr. Mompesson, who next accused him of witchcraft on April 15, 1663, at Salisbury. The ground of action was the alleged use by Drury, when in gaol at Gloucester, of expressions connecting him with the unexplained disturbances. The Grand Jury found a true bill, but Drury was acquitted on trial for lack of evidence to connect him with the affair. Mr. Mompesson, two or three neighbouring gentlemen, and the parson of the parish, gave evidence, at Salisbury, to the pheno-mena. Unluckily, we have only Mr. Mompesson's deposition: I have failed to discover the full records of the trial in MS. In the printed deposition, Mr. Mompesson does not say what he himself heard and saw; he merely complains of "knocking, great noises, scratching, troub-ling the beds", and so forth. There can be no moral doubt, perhaps, that Mr. Mompesson and his witnesses attested their personal experi-ences of these familiar phenomena. But their evidence is lost or in-accessible.[1] That Glanvill's tales about the disturbances, if not printed till 1666–1668, were current as early as 1662, and were not invented or even exaggerated between 1663 and 1666–1668, I can readily prove.

'The earliest contemporary record known to me is a ballad of the year 1662, in which the disturbance at Tedworth began. This extremely inartificial poem was hunted out by Miss Elsie Alleyne at the Bodleian Library. It is earlier, if the printed date, 1662, be correct, than the sworn deposition of Mr. Mompesson, of April 15, 1663. The ballad gives details which are not in Mr. Mompesson's printed statement, but are chronicled by Glanvill at least as early as 1668; for example, the story of the bed staff which spontaneously "went for" the clergyman while he was praying.'

Here is the broadside ballad,[2] reproduced by Lang, which was pub-lished by Gilbertson, London, in 1662. It is to be found in the Bodleian Library, Oxford, under Anthony Wood,[3] 401 (193):

A Wonder of Wonders, being a true relation of the strange and invisible beating of a Drum, at the house of John Mompesson, Esq., at Tidcomb [sic] in the County of Wiltshire, being about 8 of the clock at night and con-tinuing till 4 in the morning, several days one after another, to the great admiration of many persons of Honour, Gentlemen of quality, and many hundreds who had gone from several parts to hear this miraculous wonder, since the first tune it began to beat 'Roundheads and Cuckolds, come dig, come dig.' Also the burning of a drum that was taken from a drummer. Likewise the manner how the stools and chairs danced about the room. The drummer is sent to Glocester goal. Likewise a great conflict betwixt evil spirits and Antony, a lusty country fellow.

[1] But see Mompesson's letter, pp. 394–98.—H.P.

[2] By Abraham Miles. (See article by Dr. H. H. E. Craster, Bodley's Librarian, in the *Bodleian Quarterly Record*, Oxford, April 25, 1924, Vol. IV, No. 41.)—H.P.

[3] Wood marked his copy '*mense* February 1662' (i.e. 1662-3), the date when he acquired it.—H.P.

A Wonder of Wonders

To the tune of Bragandary

All you that fear the God on high
amend your lives and repent,
Those latter dayes show Dooms-days nigh.
Such wonders strange are lent,
of a strange wonder that you hear
At Tedcomb within fair Wiltshire,
O news, notable news,
Ye never the like did hear.

Of a drummer his use was at great Houses for to beat
He to one certain house did go and entered in at gate:
At the House of Master Mompesson
he began aloud to beat his drum
O news, notable news,
Ye never the like did hear.

Alarum, March, and Troop likewise,
he thundered at the gate,
The children frightened at the noise,
Forwarned he was to beat:
But he refused, and his Drum did rattle
as if he had been in some battle
O news, notable news,
Ye never the like did hear.

He said he would not be forbid,
neither by his back nor head,
And had power for what he did,
They did him Rascal call:
No Sir I am no such, quoth he,
two justices' hands in my pass be.
O news, notable news,
Ye never the like did hear.

'Twas counterfeit he[1] did understand,
and then without delay,
He gave his servants their command,
to set this fellow away,
And likewise took away his drum,
'This you'l repent the time will come,'
O news, notable news,
Ye never the like did hear.

About eight o'clock that present night
a drum beat in every room,
Which put them in amaze and fright,
not knowing how it did come:

[1] 'He' is Mompesson.—H.P.

391

The first it beat was this old jig,
'Roundheads and Cuckolds come dig, come dig '[1]
O wonders, notable wonders,
Ye never the like did hear.

From eight to four in the morn,
with a rattling thundering noise,
The echo as loud as a horn,
and frights them many wayes,
T' appease the noise I understand
they burned the drum out of hand,
O wonders, notable wonders,
Ye never the like did hear.

But still about the same time
this noise continuèd,
Yet little hurt they did sustain,
but children thrown from bed,
And then by the hair of the head
they were plucked[2] quite out of bed,
O wonders, notable wonders,
Ye never the like did hear.

From one room to another were they
tost by a hellish fiend,
As if he would them quite destroy
or make of them an end,
And then, some ease after the pain,
They'd be placed in their beds again.
O wonders, notable wonders,
Ye never the like did hear.

The gentleman did give command
to have the children away,
Unto a friend's house out of hand
them safely to convey.[3]
Whatever they did it made them wonder
a rattling drum was heard like thunder.
O wonders, notable wonders,
Ye never the like did hear.

A Minister being devout at prayer
unto the God on high,
A bed staff was thrown at him there
with bitter vehemency![2]
He said 'the Son of God appear
to destroy the works of Satan here.'

---

[1] Mentioned by Glanvill and in Mompesson's letter.—H.P.
[2] Incidents mentioned by Glanvill and Mompesson.—H.P.
[3] Incident mentioned by both Glanvill and Mompesson.—H.P.

O wonders, notable wonders,
Ye never the like did hear.

There's one they call him Anthony
That carried a sword to bed,
And the spirit at him will fly
hard to be resistèd,
If his hand out of bed he cast,
the spirit will unto it fast,[1]
O wonders, notable wonders,
Ye never the like did hear.

Both Rooms, Stables and Orchard ground
a drum was heard to beat,
And sometimes in the Chymney sound
by night make Cattle sweat,
Both chairs and stools about would gig,
and often times would dance a jig.[2]
O wonders, notable wonders,
Ye never the like did hear.

So dreadful were these motions all
by Satan sure appointed,
The Chamber floor would rise and fall[3]
and never a board disjointed:
Then they heard a blow from high
three times 'a witch, a witch' did cry,[3]
O wonders, notable wonders,
Ye never the like did hear.

* * * *

A most important document, containing first-hand and contemporary evidence for the haunting, comes to me as this monograph is passing through the press. It is a contemporary copy[4] of a letter, dated December 6 (1662), from John Mompesson to the Rev. William Creed, D.D., who was a kinsman of Mompesson, and a close friend of the Fetherstonhaugh-Frampton family, the present head of which, Mr. H. Fetherstonhaugh-Frampton, J.P., of Moreton, Dorchester, Dorset, very kindly sent me the letter, and still more kindly permits me to reproduce it. Andrew Lang remarks (p. 390) that Mompesson 'does not say what he himself heard and saw' and continues, 'There can be no moral doubt, perhaps, that Mr. Mompesson and his witnesses attested their personal experiences.' The letter I am reproducing is the missing link that Lang was looking for: Mompesson's own testimony under his own signature.

[1] Mentioned by Glanvill.—H.P.
[2] Incidents mentioned by both Glanvill and Mompesson.—H.P.
[3] Mentioned by Glanvill.—H.P.
[4] There are three known copies. See Dr. Craster's remarks at end of Appendix.

The letter, which, I believe, is here published for the first time, was written when, as Mompesson reveals, William Drury was in Gloucester Gaol for the 'stealeing of hoggs'.

The letter also confirms Glanvill's account of the haunting as published by him in *Saducismus Triumphatus* and his earlier tracts. In fact, it is almost certain that Glanvill saw the identical letter that I am now publishing.[1] In his accounts of the affair, he says: 'Thus, I have written the summ of Mr. Mompesson's disturbance, which I had partly from his own mouth . . . and partly from his own Letters'. The sequence of the incidents is identical in both Glanvill's and Mompesson's stories, and in describing several of the phenomena, Glanvill uses Mompesson's phraseology, as comparison between the two texts will reveal.

The reader will also note that many of the incidents recorded in the ballad, *A Wonder of Wonders*, are confirmed by Mompesson's letter, though the latter is dated December 6 (1662). The ballad, too, was published in 1662, at, I should imagine, about the same time as Mompesson wrote the letter. Drury was in Gloucester Gaol in December, 1662—a fact recorded in the title of the ballad which, therefore, could not have been issued before the 'Drummer' went to prison.

It will be noted that Mompesson threatens to prosecute Drury when he comes out of prison. The reader is aware that he carried out his threat on April 15, 1663 (more than four months after he wrote the letter), when he made the sworn deposition at Salisbury, accusing Drury of boasting that he was the cause of all the trouble.

From Mompesson's letter we learn that though Drury was a tailor by trade, he much preferred a mountebank's life, exhibiting 'Hocas pocas, feates of activity, dancing through hoops, and such like devices'. We also learn that Mompesson's mother lived with him.

It is revealed in the letter that Mompesson was contemplating vacating his house on account of the disturbances, but there is no evidence that he actually did so. What worried him most, apparently, was the 'sulphureous smell' that sometimes accompanied the Poltergeist's activities. It is amusing to note that the phenomena-hunters were nearly as troublesome as the 'ghost'. 'Twas ever thus!

Here, then, is

JOHN MOMPESSON'S FIRST-HAND EVIDENCE
[To the Rev. William Creed, D.D.]

[*Tedworth*],
December 6th [1662].

Reverend Dr,

I cannot but take myself to be very highly obleiged to you, in that you are pleased to be soe respectfull of me in this business; my wife and

---

[1] Glanvill, in his account (see p. 57) says: 'The same particulars he writ also to Dr. Creed.'

selfe were both much troubled, as soon as you were gone, that we had utterly forgotten to acquaint you with it. I shall now give you a true narrative of it and as briefly, as ye nature of it will permitt me.

In ye middle of March last being at a neighbouring Towne called Ludgarshall, and at ye Bayliffs house, I heard a drum beat, and enquired ye occasion of it, the Bayliff told me they had been troubled with a drummer whoe had been wth ye Consstable to demand money by vertue of a pass wch he produced, but the Bayliffe thought was counterfeit, soe I sent for the Constable to bring him from an Alehouse where he was, to ye Bayliffs house to me, wch accordingly was done: I then demanded of him, by what authority he demanded money of ye Kings Subjects, and how he durst menace them for not giveing him money; he told me he had good authority, and produced his pass and a warrant under Sr William Cawleys hand and seale, and Coll. Ayliffes of Greetenham, persons I both knew well, and was acquainted with their hand writeing: I presently saw it was forg'd; I commanded him to put off his drum, and told him I would seize that by my authority, and charged ye Constable to carry him to ye next Justice of peace to be proceeded against. The fellow then confest he had gotten it to be made, and beg'd of me for his drum; I told him, if I might understand from Coll. Ayliffe, whose drummer he pretended to be, that he had been formerly an honest man, he should have his drum again; but whereas he pretended to have been a souldier for ye King etc., I could give no credit to a man taken in forgery; soe I left ye Drum at ye Bayliffes, and the drummer in ye Constables hands, whoe upon much entreaty let him goe: About ye middle of April the Drum was by ye Bayliffe sent over to my house, I was then prepareing for a London Journey: Upon ye fourth day of May, when I came home again from London; my wife told me, that my house had been like to have been broken upp, and they had been much affrighted in ye night with theeves; I rejoyced with her at ye deliverance, and after I had been at home 3 nights, it was come again: Soe I rose and took some Pistolls in my hand, and went upp and down ye house, and heard a strange noise and hollow sound but could not see anything.

I must confess I did at first doubt it to be what it proved to be, because I was confident noe theeves would adventure themselves in that manner, soe then it came oftener, five nights, and absent three, (and in such course that we cou'd guess when it would come) and thump very hard, all in ye outside of my house, and constantly came when we were going to sleep, whether early or late; and soe for a month it continued in ye outside of my house; and then, it came into the room where ye drum lay, being my mothers chamber, where he was thrown under a board; for my children did use to knock and play with it, and shee delighting their company caused it to be put there: There it would be foure or five nights in seaven, and make very great hollow sounds, that the windows would shake and ye beds, and come constantly within half an hour after wee were in bed, and stay almost two houres, and when it came, wee could hear a perfect howleing in ye aire over ye house, and when it went away, many times the drum beat, the same point of war that is usually beaten when guards breake upp, as truely and sweetly, as ever drummer beat in this world, and so continued in that room for 2 moneths, I laying there all ye time to observe it, and though I could take noe rest at ye forepart of ye night, yet after two houres time (except it were now and then) it was all very quiet. We often tried what prayer would doe, and sometimes it would move to a litle way, and sometimes it would not: After this it began to go into other rooms over it, and keep the same noise still, though with some addition; Sometimes it would imitate the happering[1] of peas upon boards, the shoeing of horses, the Sawyers and many other: but, God be praised, my wife drawing neare her time of Childbed, it came a little that night she was in travaile, and forbore ye house for 3 weeks, untill she had her strength againe: and this was indeed a great mercy: Wee then hoped wee had been free; but it returned with mighty violence and applyed itself wholly to my youngest children, whose bedsteads it would beat, when there has been many of strangers, as well as ourselves present in ye room, that wee did at every blow expect they would have fallen in peices, and we held our hands upon those bedsteads all ye while and could feel no blows, but feel them shake extreamely, and for an hour together play the tune called, 'Roundheads and Cuckolds go digg, go digg,' and never misse one stroke, as sweetly and skilfully as any drummer in ye world can beat, and then the Tattoe and also severall other points of warr; then it will run under ye bedsteads and scratch as if it had Iron Talons, and heave upp ye Children in ye bedd, and follow them from roome to roome, and come to none else but them. There being but one Cockloft[2] in the house where it was never observed to have been above stairs, I put those children in there and put them in bed whilst it was faire day-light, and it came before they were covered in their beds. The 5th of November in ye morning it kept a mighty noise, and one of my men observeing in ye room where the children lay, that there was two boards stood edgelong and did seem to move, he said to it, 'give me that board,' ye board came within a yard of him; he said again, 'nay let me have it in my hand'; It came home to his very foot, he shuf'd it back again to him, and soe from one to another at least twenty times; but I forbadd such familiarity; and that morning, it left in that roome a sulphureous smell wch was very offensive, but stayed not long. I must confess I never doubted whether I should be able to stand my ground till that time; but I thank God, we have had no more of those noisome smells. At night Mr. Cragg our Minister and many of my neighbours came to me; we went to prayer by our childrens

---

[1] A West Country term for 'pattering' or 'crackling'.—H.P.
[2] i.e. attic.—H.P.

bedside where it was very loud; It went at that time of prayer into the Cock-loft, and when we came away, it returned, and in our presence and sight, the chaires did walk about, the childrens shoes were tost over our heads, and every loose thing thrown about ye room: A bed-staff was thrown at Mr. Cragg and hitt him on ye legg, but soe softly that a lock of wool could not fall more softly. I perceiving it persecuted these little children soe much, lodg'd them at a neighbours, and took my eldest daughter, about tenne years old, into my chamber where it had not been in a moneth: As soon as she was in bed, that was there too, and has continued there about 3 weeks, and still beats ye drum; and let us knock any time, it will hearken and knock the same presently, and play any tune of ye drum that wee bid it. I was forced the other night to bring my youngest children home, the house where they lay being full of strangers, and wee could not remember that it had ever been in our parlour, where wee dine and supp; and therefore laid in some beds about the ground and lodg'd our children there, but ye drum came, and they were pulled by their night-geer and their haire; each of them had a pluck and so away: I must I doubt, remove them againe, for I see the Divell hath most malice where there is most innocence. I have often after prayer followed it, and conjured it in ye name of God to appeare to me, and declare ye reason of its troubling this place soe, but could never see any appearance, neither any of my people.

S^r, you may imagine y^t I have reason enough to suspect this drummer by what hath been already said, and indeed, I had prosecuted him 'ere this, but that I was prevented, for he lyes now in Glocester Gaole for stealeing of hoggs: When I enquired into his conversation, I found he had been in ye Parliament-Army foure years, and when he came home, he wrought a little time at his trade, being a Tayler, but continued not long at worke, but went upp and down ye Countrey to show Hocas pocas, feates of activity, dancing through hoops and such like devices but as soon as he comes home, I shall visit him; for I am informed y^t he spake words, w^ch, if proved it may goe hard wth him. Here has been many Spectators, as well Divines as others, persons of Judgment, whoe all conclude it to be witchcraft, and ye truth is, It does so many antick things impossible to relate, that there is no great question, I think, to be made of it; yet I know we live in an uncharitable and censorious age, and many I suppose may be ready enough (and have been as I have been told) to judge, y^t this comes upon me for some enormous sinne or other; for my own part, I am farr enough from justifieing myself; I know I have deserved far greater punishments at ye hands of God, than these have yet been: but had my conscience accused me of any such particular crying sinne, I should scarcely have endured this; for sure myne own guilt would have driven me fast enough from it; and men were best take heed how they censure others in these or ye like cases, lest they prove themselves not soe good as they should be, whilst they take others to be worse than they are: and sure ye rule of Gods Providence is noe more revealed to these censurers than to others.

Besides; if they do but look upon Gods mercyes to us in it (wch I beseech him, give me grace never to forget), it may allay that severity of Judgement in them; for when they see ye Divell roaring and raging and ready every night about our beds to devoure us, and noe damage come to us, they must needs conclude y^t we are defended by ye almighty hand of God, and truly here have been many whoe have not seemed less to admire ye courage of this family than the strangeness of ye thing, and indeed had we not been strengthened by ye grace and power of God, wee must have sunk under it; for many passages have been very terrible, but ye same God that hath hitherto defended us, I doubt not will continue his goodness to us; and upon that confidence doe resolve to keep my house as long as I can take any competent rest, and those smells doe not return, unless I may understand from you, that you take it to be my duty to leave my house for a time, as some have perswaded me; wherefore if you please to send your opinion in that particular, or what else you conceive may be fit for me to doe in ye case, I shall wth thankfulness receive it. I have acquainted my worthy friend ye President of Magdalens, that I have given you this account (wth is very rude and much short of w^t hath been here acted) and I humbly desire you to let him see it, from whom as well as from yourselfe either seperatim or conjunctim, it would be great satisfaction to me, to receive what rules or directions you shall vouchsafe me; and I shall be carefull to follow: And soe wth my hearty thanks to your selfe, and my owne and my wifes service to my Cousen your wife I take me leave and rest.

Y^r faithful kinsman and real Servt,

JO. MOMPESSON.

I have often thought y^t if any learned man had made those observations that I have done he might have discovered much of ye nature of these Spiritts.

It has taken our Servants upp in their beds, bed and all, and lifted them upp a great height, and layed them down softly againe, and lyes often on their feet wth a great weight: Sometimes ye Candles will not burn in ye room where it is; and though it come never soe loud and on a sudden, yet noe dogg will barke. It has been often soe loud, that it has been heard upp into ye feilds, and has wakened my neighbours in ye Town. I have not been without strangers to hear it these many nights, wch have troubled me halfe as badd as ye Spirit. Now it comes a little seeming afarr off, at eight of ye clock in night, and layes still all night till about five in the morneing, and then it will drum us upp; but it often changes its course, and has not mist one night this seaven weeks.

*   *   *   *

I submitted my copy of the above letter, with an account of its origin, to Dr. H. H. E. Craster, M.A., Bodley's Librarian. In an article that he wrote for the *Bodleian Quarterly Record* in 1924 (Vol. iv., No. 41, p. 100), he mentions that Anthony Wood (1632–95), the famous antiquary whose priceless collection of ballads, etc. are in the Bodleian Library, 'made a copy of Mr. Mompesson's letter' which he (Mompesson) had sent to a certain doctor in Oxford University. It occurred to me that Wood's transcript and the one in Mr. Fetherstonhaugh-Frampton's possession might have been copied from the same original —apparently not now known to be in existence.

Dr. Craster kindly replied (June 28, 1944) as follows: 'You are doubtless right in thinking that John Mompesson's letter of 6 December, 1662, has never been published, though the material facts have been given, frequently verbatim, in Glanvill's *Saducismus Triumphatus* (1681), which you quote, as well as in Glanvill's earlier work, *A Blow at Modern Sadducism* (1668). The letter was addressed to the Rev. Dr. William Creed, Regius Professor of Divinity at Oxford; and the letter contained in Wood 467 is a copy of it, in Anthony Wood's hand. There is yet another copy, in the hand of William Fulman, the antiquarian Fellow of Corpus, in MS. Corpus Christi College, 318, foll. 161–162. I return you your typescript of Mr. Fetherstonhaugh-Frampton's copy, having marked on it in pencil the few passages in which the Wood and Fulman copies give different readings.[1]

'When I published my note in the *Bodleian Quarterly Record* in 1924, I drew attention to Wood's transcript, but not to the Corpus MS., the importance of which lies in the fact that it contains copies by William Fulman, not merely of John Mompesson's letter to Dr. Creed of 6 December, 1662, but of two later letters, which he (Mompesson) wrote to Dr. Creed on 26 December, 1662, and 4 January, 1662–3 respectively, as well as of a letter to John Mompesson from his kinsman, Sir Thomas Mompesson, dated 11 December, 1662; of a short note written from Tidworth on 6 January, 1662–3, to Francis Parry of Corpus Christi College by Parry's uncle, William Maton (who is named in John Mompesson's letter of 8 August, 1674, printed at the end of the Preface to *Saducismus Triumphatus*); and of a journal[2] kept by John Mompesson, 10–22 January, 1662–3. The gist of Mompesson's letters and journal is incorporated in Glanvill's narrative.'

So it is obvious that there is plenty of Mompesson's first-hand evidence available, and one cannot help feeling surprised that Andrew Lang failed to find it, when he was so assiduously looking for it.

[1] The differences are very slight.—H.P.
[2] I have reproduced some extracts from this journal in Plate opposite p. 52.—H.P.

APPENDIX B

BIBLIOGRAPHY

Poltergeists in Print

In the following select bibliography will be found full records of all the classic Poltergeist cases, together with a carefully-chosen cross-section of the most entertaining, interesting, puzzling, and remarkable 'infestations'. Most of these works have been acquired specially for use in the preparation of this monograph; all have been studied, and many are cited in the text. For further examples of modern Poltergeist hauntings, the *Journals* and *Proceedings* of the various psychical societies, British and foreign, should be consulted. Newspapers and the periodical Press frequently print accounts of what have come to be known as 'Poltergeist disturbances'.

Addison (Joseph), The Drummer, or the Haunted House. London, 1716. [Play based on the 'Drummer of Tedworth'.]

Arago (François). [Case of Angélique Cottin.] [In the *Journal des Débats*, Paris, February, 1846.]

Aspinall (Sir Algernon E.). The Pocket Guide to the West Indies, London, 1927, pp. 99–105. [Account of the 'haunted vault' at Barbados.]

Authentic, Candid, and Circumstantial Narrative, An, of the Astonishing Transactions at Stockwell. London, 1772.

Barrett (Sir William F.), Poltergeists Old and New. [Part of *Proceedings* of the S.P.R., Vol. XXV, London, 1911.]

——, [The Derrygonnelly case.] [Part of *The Dublin University Magazine* for December, 1877.]

Berthelen (K. A.), Die Klopf und Spukgeister zu Oderwitz und Herwigsdorf-bei-Zittau. Zittau, 1864.

Bovet (Richard), Pandaemonium, or the Devil's Cloyster. Being a further blow to Modern Sadducism.... [London, 1684].

Bozzano (Ernesto), Dei Fenomeni d'Infestazione. Roma, 1919.

Burton (Jean), The Heyday of a Wizard. New York, 1944. [A biography of D. D. Home, describing many paranormal displacements. An edition, with Foreword by Harry Price, will shortly be published in England.]

Carrington (Hereward), Historic Poltergeists. [*Bulletin* I, International Institute for Psychical Research. London (1935).]

——, The Phelps Case, 1850–1. [Part of *Historic Poltergeists*.]

400

Census of Poltergeists. [Part of *The Times Literary Supplement*, London, February 29, 1936.]

Chapman (Clive), The Blue Room. [Re the phenomena of the 'Poltergeist girl,' Pearl Judd.] Dunedin, 1927.

Christo (Homen) *and* **Rachilde (Madame),** Le Parc du Mystère. Paris, 1923. [Poltergeist phenomena in Portugal.]

Churchill (Charles), The Ghost [of Cock Lane]. London, 1763. [Poem.]

Clanny (W. Reid), A Faithful Record of the Miraculous Case of Mary Jobson. Monkwearmouth, 1841.

Cock-Lane Ghost, The, Being an Authentic Account of that Extraordinary Affair. London [*c.* 1800].

Colton (Caleb), Sampford Ghost. Tiverton [1810].

——, Stubborn Facts against Vague Assertions. Being an Appendix . . . [to *Sampford Ghost*]. Tiverton [1810].

Combermere (Mary, Viscountess) *and* **Knollys (W. W.),** Memoirs of Viscount Combermere. London, 1866. [Re the Barbados vault disturbances. In Vol. I, pp. 385–93.]

C[raster] (H. H. E.), The Drummer of Tedworth. Oxford, April 25, 1924. [Part of *The Bodleian Quarterly Record*, First Quarter, 1924.] [An informative article by Bodley's Librarian.]

Crowe (Mrs. Catherine), The Night-Side of Nature. London, 1848.

[Curé d'Ars, Re the phenomena of the]. [Part of *The Hibbert Journal*, London, January, 1927.]

Davis (H. P.), Expose of the Newburyport Eccentricities . . . the Murdered Boy of the Charles Street Schoolhouse. Newburyport, Mass. [1873].

Doster (Allie M.), The Surrency Ghost. [Part of the *Journal* of the Am. S.P.R., New York, February, 1931.]

Durbin (Henry), A Narrative of Some Extraordinary Things that Happened to Mr. Richard Giles's Children. . . . Bristol, 1800.

Evennett (H. O.), An Ancient Cambridge Poltergeist. [Part of *The British Journal of Psychical Research*, London, March-April, 1929.]

Flammarion (Camille), Haunted Houses. London, 1924. [The Calvados Castle case, etc.]

Fodor (Nandor), The Saragossa Ghost. [Part of *Bulletin* I, International Inst. for Psychical Research. London (1935).]

Footsteps of Spirits. A Collection of upwards of seventy well-authenticated stories of dreams, impressions, sounds. . . . London and New York [1859].

Fort (Charles), The Books of Charles Fort. New York, 1941. [Accounts of many Poltergeist and allied phenomena.]

Gerstmann (F. B.), Vorstellung des Gespenstes und Polter-Geistes welches in der Stadt Dortmundt und zwar in dessen Vatters Hause. Dortmund, 1714.

Glanvill (Joseph), A Blow at Modern Sadducism.... The Relation of the Fam'd Disturbance by the Drummer.... London, 1668.

——, Philosophical Considerations Concerning the Existence of Sorcerers and Sorcery. [Re the Drummer of Tedworth.] London, 1666.

——, Saducismus Triumphatus ... [Part II]. London, 1681.

[Goldsmith (Oliver)], The Mystery Revealed.... Respecting the Supposed Cock Lane Ghost. London, 1742. [*Recte* 1762.]

Goodrich-Freer (Miss A.) *and* **Bute (John, Marquess of)**, The Alleged Haunting of B[allechin] House. London, 1899.

Harper (Charles G.), Haunted Houses. London, 1907.

Heaton (James), The Extraordinary Affliction, and Gracious Relief of a Little Boy.... Plymouth, 1822.

History of Jenny Spinner, The, The Ghost of Knebworth House. (Written by Herself.) London, 1800. [A reprint of this tract appeared in *A History of Knebworth House and its Owners*, Letchworth, 1915.]

History of the Mysterious House, The, and Alarming Appearances at the Corner of Stamford Street, Blackfriars Road.... London [*c.* 1820].

Hives (Frank), Ju-Ju and Justice in Nigeria. [See Chapter V, 'A Haunted Rest-House'.] London, 1930.

Hubbell (Walter), The Haunted House.... The Great Amherst Mystery. Saint John, N.B., 1879. [Re Esther Cox.]

Illig (Johann), Der Spuk von Gross-Erlach. Leipzig, 1916.

[Jervis (Mrs. Wm. Henley, *Edited by*)], A Hampshire Ghost Story. [Parts of *The Gentleman's Magazine*, London, November and December, 1872.] [Re the Hinton Ampner Poltergeist.]

Joller (—), Darstellung selbsterlebter mystischer Erscheinungen. Zürich, 1863.

Kiesewetter (Carl), Geschichte des Neueren Occultismus. Leipzig [1891].

Lang (Andrew), Cock Lane and Common Sense. London, 1894.

——, 'Death-Deeds'—A Bi-Located Story. [Re the Barbados vault disturbances.] [Part of *Folk Lore*, London, Vol. XVIII, pp. 376–90.]

——, Hauntings. [Article in the *Encyclopædia Britannica*, Cambridge, 1910, Vol. XIII, pp. 67–8.]

——, Poltergeist. [Article in the *Encyclopædia Britannica*, Cambridge, 1911, Vol. XXII, pp. 14–17.]

——, The Book of Dreams and Ghosts. London, 1897.

——, The Making of Religion. London, 1898.

——, The Poltergeist, Historically Considered. [Part of *Proc.*, S.P.R., London, 1901–2, Vol. XVII, pp. 305–26.]

Lavater (Lewes [Ludwig]), De Spectris. Geneva, 1570.

——, Of Ghostes and Spirites Walking by Nyght, and of Strange Noyses, Crackes, and Sundry Forewarnynges ... London, 1572. [English translation of *De Spectris*.]

Layard (John), PSI Phenomena and Poltergeists. [Part of *Proc.*, S.P.R., London, July, 1944.] [A suggested explanation.]

Lytton (Bulwer), The Haunted and the Haunters. [Part of *Blackwood's Magazine*, Edinburgh, August, 1859.]

Marvellous Magnetism. Inanimate Things Imbued with Movement by a Wonderful Invisible Power. [Part of the *Pictorial Magazine*, London, for April 19, 1902.] [The experiments of Szenitzi Baslovnáyá, of Buda-Pesth.]

Memoirs of Thomas Harrington with a short account of the lights which appeared in his house at Glandore. Cork, 1840.

Mercurius Publicus. London, No. 16, April 16-23, 1663, [Early mention of the Drummer of Tedworth.]

[Miles (Abraham)]. A Wonder of Wonders. London, 1662. [Broadside ballad, with the first known account of the 'Drummer of Tedworth'.]

Middleton (Jessie A.), The Grey Ghost Book. [Berkeley Square Poltergeist, etc.] London, 1912.

Monnin (Alfred), Le Curé d'Ars. Paris, 1861.

——, Life of the Curé d'Ars. London [1862].

Montalembert (Adrien de). [Account of the disturbances at the nunnery of St. Pierre de Lyon.] Paris, 1528.

Moor (Edward), Bealings Bells. An Account of the Mysterious Ringing of Bells, at Great Bealings, Suffolk, in 1834. Woodbridge, 1841.

Müller (Egbert), Enthüllung des Spukes von Resau. Berlin, 1889.

Night in a Haunted House, A: A Tale of Facts. London [1859].

No Rest in the Mansion. New York, July 12, 1942. [Part of the *American Weekly*, describing, with photographs, the Scotch 'Poltergeist Manor' detailed in this volume.]

One Night in the Haunted House of Whittlebury Forest. Northampton, 1932.

On the Trail of a Ghost. [Re the Ballechin House Poltergeist.] [In *The Times*, London, June 8-24, 1897.]

Owen (Robert Dale), Footfalls on the Boundary of Another World. London, 1861.

Podmore (Frank), On Poltergeists. [Chap. II, Vol. I, *Modern Spiritualism*. London, 1902.]

——, Poltergeists. [Part of *Proc.*, S.P.R., London, Vol. XII, 1896-7.]

——, Studies in Psychical Research. London, 1897.

——, The Naturalisation of the Supernatural. New York and London, 1908.

Poor Little Loros and his Playful Poltergeist. New York, Dec. 15, 1940. [Part of the *American Weekly*, describing, with photographs, Poltergeist phenomena at Trumann, Arkansas.]

Price (Harry), A Report on the Phenomena Witnessed through Eleonore Zugun. [Vol. I, Part 1, *Proc.*, Nat. Lab. Psy. Research, London, Jan., 1927.]

Price (Harry), Poltergeist Over England. London, 1945.
——, The Most Haunted House in England. Ten Years' Investigation of Borley Rectory. London, 1940.
——, *and* **Kohn** (Miss **H.**), An Indian Poltergeist. [Parts of the *Journal* of the Am. S.P.R., New York, 1930. Vol. XXIV, pp. 122–30, 180–86, 221–32.] [Re Damodar Ketkar.]
Priestly (Joseph), Original Letters by the Rev. John Wesley and his Friends. Birmingham, 1791. [Epworth phenomena, pp. 118–166.]
Prince (W. F.), A Critical Study of the 'Great Amherst Mystery'. [Re Esther Cox.] [Part of *Proc.*, Am. S.P.R., New York, 1919, Vol. XIII, pp. 89–130.]
——, [The Antigonish case, Nova Scotia.] [Part of the *Journal* of the Am. S.P.R., New York, Vol. XVI, August, 1922, pp. 422–41.]
Procter (Edmund), [The Willington Mill disturbances.] [Part of the *Journal* of the S.P.R., London, 1891–2, Vol. V, pp. 331–52.]
Puls (—), Spuk-Geschichten. Der Spuk von Resau u. a. Berlin [1889?].
[Pye (John)], A True and Perfect Account of a strange and dreadful apparition which lately infested and sunk a ship bound for New-Castle, called the Hope-well of London. And of the strange deliverance of John Pye, Master, and nine men more; who were all examined and sworn to the truth of the following relation before Justice Wood of London. London, 1672.
Raines (T. Hart), The Dale Tower, Georgia, U.S.A. Case. [Part of the *Occult Review*, London, for May, 1911.]
R[edding] (K.), [*i.e.* **Cussons** (Mrs. **D. H.**)], Death-Deeds: An Extraordinary Incident Connected with Barbadoes. [Re haunted vault.] London, 1860.
Rochester Knockings! Discovery and Explanation of the Source of the Phenomena. Buffalo and New York, 1851.
Sampford Ghost!!! A full account of the Conspiracy at Sampford Peverell, near Tiverton; containing the Particulars of the pretended Visitations of the Monster ... Taunton [1810?].
Saragossa Ghost, The. [In *The Times*, London, from November 24 to December 5, 1934.]
Schrenck-Notzing (Freiherr Albert von), Der Spuk in der Augustenstrasse zu München. Leipzig, 1928.
—— Der Spuk in Hapfgarten. [Part of *Le Compte Rendu Officiel du Premier Congrès International des Recherches Psychiques*. Copenhagen, 1922.]
——, Der Spuk in Ylöjärvi (Finnland). Leipzig, 1922.
——, Der Spuk von Neureid in Oberbayern. Leipzig, 1926.
Sharpe (Miss Ada M.), A Disturbed House and its Relief; a narrative of certain circumstances at 'Beth-oni', Tackley, Oxon.,1905–1908. Oxford, March, 1914.
Sitwell (Sacheverell), Poltergeists. London, 1940.

Spuk von Resau, Der. Berlin, 1889. [Third Edition.]
Strange, True, and Dreadful Relation, A, of the Devils Appearing to Thomas Cox. First, in the habit of a Gentleman . . . and then in the shape of a Bear, which afterwards vanish'd away in a flash of Fire. London, 1684.
Sudre (René). A Case of Thorybism in France. [Part of *Journal*, Am. S.P.R., New York, January, 1931.]
Tanchou (Doctor), Enquête sur l'Authenticité des Phénomènes Électriques d'Angélique Cottin. Paris, 1846.
Tankerville (Leonora, Countess of**),** The Ghosts of Chillingham. Wooler, Northumberland, 1925.
Telfair (Alexander), A New Confutation of Sadducism. A True Narrative of the wonderful Expressions and Actions of a Spirit which infested the House of Andrew Mackie of Ringcroft. . . . London, 1696.
That Mischievous Ghost of Bible Hill. New York, May 31, 1942. [Part of the *American Weekly*, describing, with photographs, a Poltergeist case at Truro, Nova Scotia.]
Thurston (Herbert), A City of London Poltergeist. [Part of *The Month*, London, June, 1932.]
——, An Indian Poltergeist. [Parts of *The Month*, London, Sept. and Octr., 1929.]
——, A Poltergeist in a Hugenot Household. [Part of *Studies*, Dublin, June, 1928.]
——, Poltergeists. [Part of *Studies*, Dublin, March, 1928.]
——, Ghostly Visitants that Bite. [Part of *The Month*, London, August, 1928.]
——, Ghosts that Tease. [Part of *The Month*, London, Sept., 1928.]
Thyraeus (Petrus), Loca Infesta. Cologne, 1598.
True Narrative, A, of the Sufferings and Relief of a Young Girl. Paisley, 1698. [Re Christian Shaw.]
Tyburn-Ghost, The; or Strange Downfall of the Gallows. . . . London, 1678.
Wassilko-Serecki (Zoë, Countess**),** Der Spuk von Talpa. Munich, 1926. [Re Eleonore Zugun.]
Wesley (John), An Account of the Disturbances in my Father's House. [Parts of *The Arminian Magazine*, London, Octr., Novr., and Decr., 1784.]
Wright (Dudley), The Epworth Phenomena. London, 1917. [Re the Wesley Poltergeist.]

Index

The titles of books, articles, periodicals, Acts, plays, poems, manuscripts, lectures, and society publications are printed in italics. Appendix B is *not* indexed.

406

407

Index

Index

Index